Contents at a Glance

Continues on following page

Contents at a Glance

Continued from previous page

Sams Teach Yourself

Microsoft®

Office 2007

Greg Perry

SAMS   800 East 96th Street, Indianapolis, Indiana, 46240 USA

Sams Teach Yourself Microsoft® Office 2007 All in One

International Standard Book Number: 0-672-32901-8

Library of Congress Catalog Card Number: 2005938304

Printed in the United States of America

First Printing: November 2006

09   08   07   4   3

Trademarks

Warning and Disclaimer

Bulk Sales

Sams Publishing offers excellent discounts on this book when ordered in quantity for bulk purchases or special sales. For more information, please contact

U.S. Corporate and Government Sales
1-800-382-3419
corpsales@pearsontechgroup.com

For sales outside of the U.S., please contact

International Sales
international@pearsoned.com

Associate Publisher
Greg Wiegand

Acquisitions Editor
Loretta Yates

Development Editor
Kevin Howard

Managing Editor
Gina Kanouse

Project Editor
Christy Hackerd

Copy Editor
Cheri Clark

Senior Indexer
Cheryl Lenser

Proofreader
Karen A. Gill

Technical Editor
Dallas Releford

Publishing Coordinator
Sharry Lee Gregory

Designer
Gary Adair

Page Layout
Interactive Composition Corporation

Dedication

Dr. Tom and Krista Pickard are more than dear friends. They are like family to Jayne and me, even though we've only known them a few short years. One runs across people such as the Pickard family rarely; we're so blessed it happened to us. Tom and Krista, we love you both.

Acknowledgments

Loretta Yates deserves special thanks for putting up with me throughout this book's writing. She was always there when I needed something. As an editor, she is top-notch, making sure everything is in, all the t's are crossed, and the i's are dotted. Loretta, I hope we have many projects together in the future!

Speaking of being there: Kevin Howard, this book's development editor, was outstanding! This is the first time we've worked together on a book. I must say, the book went smoothly from start to finish, and I think much of that was due to Kevin. He was always on top of things and responded quickly when I asked, and I sure appreciate him.

Dallas Releford had to work through all the glitches, technical problems, and outright errors that I wrote into this book's first draft. Any problems that might be left are all mine. Dallas, I'm always thrilled when I learn you're my book's technical editor. I know that caring eyes are reviewing every word, while at the same time you give me lots of freedom to say what I want to say.

Christy Hackerd kept the files moving smoothly through the book's production. Christy always responded to my emails quickly, she made the normally horrid author review process much easier for me, and I appreciate her. Christy, you can be my books' project editor from now on.

Perhaps the hardest working editor was Cheri Clark given how quickly I had to turn in writing. I had far less time to proofread my manuscript before turning in each chapter, and I'm afraid that Cheri was the one who paid the price. I feel it's my job to make the editors work less, not more, but in this case I did the opposite. Kudos for Cheri for making my sentences readable. In addition, the other staff and editors on this project made this book better than it otherwise could be.

Finally, I want to express massive thanks to readers who keep coming back to my titles. Teaching you how to do something is nothing but a pleasure for me.

I love hearing from you, so feel free to write. Depending on my workload, I always do my best to answer. Travel and deadlines sometimes push email down to a low priority, but when I can respond, I do. You can contact me at Office07@BidMentor.com. (The BidMentor.com comes from my eBay domain; I teach others how to be successful on eBay.) Of course, in today's world, some valid emails get filtered out due to high-octane spam filters that filter improperly; nevertheless, in general my email system is highly reliable, and I should get what you send.

—Greg Perry

We Want to Hear from You!

As the reader of this book, *you* are our most important critic and commentator. We value your opinion and want to know what we're doing right, what we could do better, what areas you'd like to see us publish in, and any other words of wisdom you're willing to pass our way.

As an associate publisher for Sams Publishing, I welcome your comments. You can email or write me directly to let me know what you did or didn't like about this book—as well as what we can do to make our books better.

Please note that I cannot help you with technical problems related to the topic of this book. We do have a User Services group, however, where I will forward specific technical questions related to the book.

When you write, please be sure to include this book's title and author as well as your name, email address, and phone number. I will carefully review your comments and share them with the author and editors who worked on the book.

Email: feedback@samspublishing.com

Mail: Greg Wiegand
            Associate Publisher
            Sams Publishing
            800 East 96th Street
            Indianapolis, IN 46240 USA

Reader Services

Visit our website and register this book at www.samspublishing.com/register for convenient access to any updates, downloads, or errata that might be available for this book.

Introduction

Microsoft Corporation's Office products have an installed base of more than 25 million licensed users. More than 90% of the Fortune 500 companies use Microsoft Office. Microsoft completely redesigned the Office interface when it produced Office 2007. Microsoft's goal was to make the Office 2007 interface easier than ever to use, as well as more integrated among other applications and the Internet.

By redesigning the interface, Microsoft in effect did away with menus and toolbars and replaced the interface with an ever-changing ribbon across the top of the Office product screens. To many Office old-timers, the ribbon was a bold move—Microsoft did away with the interface we've been using for what seems like forever. At first, the ribbon might frustrate you. You'll find yourself wondering, "Where's that option I need?" If you look up at the ribbon, you'll probably find it! The ribbon changes depending on what you're doing at the time. If you need a feature that you used to have to hunt through menus to locate, you'll probably find it on the ribbon. Office pros are happily finding that after a session or two with Office 2007, they wonder how they ever worked efficiently with the clunky menus and toolbars that used to be there.

Brand-new Office users may not ever know how well they have it with the new interface. The ribbon makes it far simpler to master Office than the menu system did. In addition, the graphical features of Office 2007, especially when used with a Windows Vista–compatible computer with Aero graphics capabilities, make learning Office 2007 a pleasure—and a quick pleasure at that.

You probably are anxious to get started with Office 2007. Take just a few preliminary moments to acquaint yourself with the design of this book, as described in the next few sections.

Who Should Read This Book?

This book is for both beginning and advanced Office 2007 users. Readers rarely believe that lofty claim, for good reason, but the design of this book and the nature of Office 2007 make it possible for this book to address that wide of an audience. The reason is simple: The book you hold in your hands approaches Office 2007 the way that most users approach Office 2007 in that a task needs to be done and this book shows you how to do it. All major and most minor Office 2007 features are not taught from a theoretical viewpoint; you don't read paragraph after paragraph of background before learning how something works. Instead, you *see* how something works in a step-by-step lesson. For example, if you want to create an Excel graph, you'll jump to the task in this book that walks you through the creation of an Excel graph. Why bother with a background of color palettes when you need a simple pie chart?

Readers unfamiliar with Windows–based environments will find plenty of introductory help here that brings them quickly up to speed. This book shows you how to do work in Office 2007, as well as how to manage many of the Internet-based Office 2007 elements that you need in order to use Office 2007 in today's online, connected world. If you are new to the Internet, this book helps you get started and shows you how to combine the Internet with Office 2007 to gain synergy from both.

Quite simply, this book talks *to* newcomers without talking *down to* them.

This book also brings those who presently use a Microsoft Office product up to speed with Office 2007. You face a mighty dramatic interface change, as the preceding section explained. With the fundamental Office understanding you already have, you will appreciate the new features and added power of Office 2007, and you'll learn how to maximize your use of the Office 2007 ribbon to get your work done quickly and easily.

What This Book Does for You

Although this book is not a complicated reference book, you'll learn almost every aspect of Office 2007 from a task-based, typical user's point of view. Office 2007 includes many advanced technical details that most users never need, and this book does not waste your time with those. You want to get up to speed with Office 2007 *now*, and this book helps you fulfill that goal.

Those of you who are tired of the mass of quick-fix computer titles cluttering today's shelves will find a welcome reprieve here. This book presents both the background and descriptions that a new Office 2007 user needs without burdening you with a lot of theory. This book is practical and provides a plethora of step-by-step task walk-throughs that you can follow when you need a feature that a task demonstrates while ignoring the tasks you don't need at the time.

This is truly a hands-on book for any Office 2007 user, from novice to pro. These tasks guide you through all the common Office 2007 actions you need to perform to make Office 2007 work for you.

Conventions Used in This Book

Given that this book is task-based, almost everything shown to you is performed in a step-by-step task. When you read a task, you'll learn about other tasks that you should understand first. For example, before learning how to add text to a PowerPoint slide, you need to know how to insert a slide into a new PowerPoint presentation. The cross-reference for that preliminary task is right there for you to review.

Other tasks form a basis or a foundation for subsequent tasks in the book. For example, when you follow the task that shows you how to format Excel cells, the task also lists other tasks that might be beneficial to you after you complete the cell-formatting task.

These cross-references among the tasks form web page–like links to the other tasks so that you're sure to get a rounded walk-through of whatever you want to do. Most hands-on tasks include a "Before You Begin" and "See Also" cross-reference section like this one:

✔ BEFORE YOU BEGIN	→ SEE ALSO
54 Enter Data into a Worksheet	**75** Set Up Page Formatting
	77 Conditionally Format Data
	78 About Excel Styles, Themes, and Templates

In addition to the step-by-step tasks, you'll find several "About" tasks. These tasks give you necessary background when that background is required to do something else. For example, before learning how to apply a theme to an Excel worksheet, you need to understand how styles, themes, and templates go together to help reduce your work time and increase your productivity. Therefore, the "About Excel Styles, Themes, and Templates" task (task number 78) provides the background necessary—and no more—for you to then tackle the tasks that show you how to apply a style, theme, or template to your work.

As you follow the tasks, you'll run across several Tips such as this one:

▶ TIP

If you want to freeze only the top row, you don't need to select it first. You only need to select **Freeze Top Row** from the **Freeze Panes** drop down list. The same is also true if you want to free the leftmost column; you would select **Freeze First Column.**

These Tips give you added insight into the task you're currently learning about and show you ways to improve on something you're doing.

Several Notes are included as well to explain a task in more detail, such as this one:

▶ NOTE

Whatever format you can apply to a cell you can also apply to a range or to your entire worksheet. Select what you want to format and then select the formatting command.

It seems to be the nature of computer software to litter our language with terms that are generally unfamiliar to newcomers, and sometimes to advanced users too. When a new term is introduced, the New Term margin note will explain the term to you like this:

▶ NEW TERM

AutoFit—The capability of Excel to adjust a column's width to accommodate the widest data value in that column.

Your Job Now

With that introduction, it's time that you began learning what Office 2007 has in store for you. Turn the page and begin learning Microsoft's exciting redesigned product.

PART I

Introducing Microsoft Office 2007

IN THIS PART:

1

Start Here

Set your sights high, because Microsoft Office 2007 helps you work more efficiently and more effectively than ever before. Office offers an integrated set of tools that includes a word processor, a spreadsheet, a presentation program, a note-taking application, a contact management system, and more. Microsoft made long strides toward producing an Office product that is both a pleasure to use and as simple as possible. Its simplicity lacks nothing in power, however, because Microsoft Office is the hands-down most powerful, best integrated, and most widely used set of applications in use today.

Given that Office has such a large, installed base, the best place to start is with a quick overview of its most important new features. Two features obviously stand out, and those are the best place to begin your Office 2007 survey. If you're brand new to Office, don't fret! Before this chapter ends, you'll get a broad overview of each of the major Office 2007 features. After you have this bird's-eye view, you'll be ready to tackle the tasks covered in the rest of the book that make Office 2007 do the work you need done.

Redesigned Interface

Microsoft completely redesigned Office 2007's interface. You'll interact with the Office programs like never before. Although each version of Office has brought about some user interface changes, Office 2007 takes those changes to an extreme.

▶ **NOTE**

How extreme are the user interface changes in Microsoft Office 2007? You can perform every task without selecting from one menu or using one toolbar button! If you've used Office in the past, that statement is going to sound far too bold to be accurate. Yet it's true.

Although Microsoft changed, tweaked, and updated hundreds of Office's elements, the most significant and most obvious changes to users of previous editions will be these:

- The ribbon

- The Live Preview

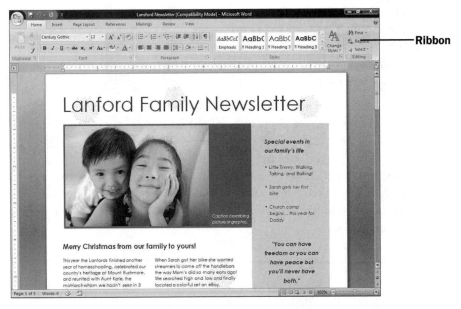

The ribbon that sits atop most Office 2007 screens is your new command center to control any and all features you need to control while using Office.

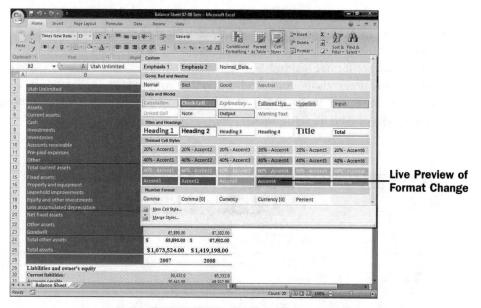

Live Preview of
Format Change

Office 2007's Live Preview feature means that you can see dramatic format changes before you actually apply those changes to your documents.

Office 2007 certainly provides far more new features than the ribbon and Live Preview, but those two features are the most visual and the most obvious differences over all the previous versions of Office. It's worth a little time to preview both features here at the beginning of the book. In a way, the ribbon and the Live Preview features are the most important to understand because everything else you do depends on your understanding them.

The Ribbon Offers What You Need When You Need It

Sure, the toolbars are gone, but the ribbon at first appears little more than a wider toolbar with buttons. It is in a way, but the ribbon is more than just a toolbar. When you work in an Office 2007 application, the ribbon displays tools you need at the time. For example, when you're creating an Excel worksheet, Excel's **Home** ribbon appears. The **Home** ribbon performs common commands such as formatting, cutting, copying, pasting, sorting, finding, replacing, and other common commands that you often use when working on a worksheet.

▶ **NOTE**

Neither Outlook 2007 nor OneNote 2007 uses a ribbon. The traditional menus and toolbars appear atop those programs as before.

If you insert a chart into a worksheet, the Excel ribbon immediately changes to the **Chart Tools Design** ribbon (see **82** **Add a Chart to a Worksheet**). Excel understands that when you insert or select a chart, you're not going to be entering a formula or format text inside a cell. Instead, when a chart is newly placed or when you select a chart, you're indicating that you want to do something to that chart. The **Chart Tools Design** ribbon appears and provides chart-formatting and editing tools you need for working with a chart.

Chart Tools Design Ribbon

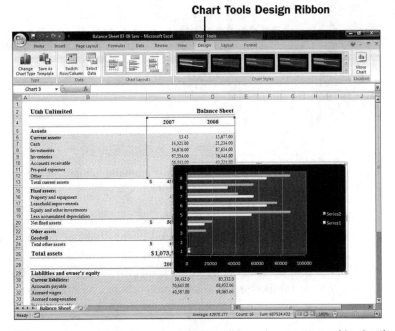

When you're working with a chart, Excel's ribbon changes to provide charting tools you might need.

The moment you stop working on the chart and click inside a cell, Excel's ribbon changes back to the **Home** ribbon, where the most common cell-editing buttons reside. Before Office 2007, you would have to select from a menu to locate chart-editing commands. No more searching; the commands appear when you need them and go away when you don't.

The Difficulty of Switching to the Ribbon

Be warned: The interface change, especially due to the ribbon, takes some time to get used to if you've used Office in the past. When you first upgrade to Office 2007, you will find yourself wanting to do something, such as use the AutoText feature, and without the familiar menus to guide you, it can be a tad difficult to locate the ribbon button that helps you accomplish what you want to do.

▶ **NOTE**

In defense of the ribbon, traditional Office menus were not always intuitive. Using the **Language** menu to get to hyphenation and thesaurus tools wasn't obvious. The ribbon will be foreign, and you will miss the menus at first, but you should grow accustomed to the ribbon far faster than you mastered the menu selections that previous Office versions offered.

You have an advantage over most new Office 2007 users in that you have this text in your hands. The task-based, step-by-step approach is the number-one way to transition to your new Office interface. By the time you've completed a handful of tasks, you'll understand the ribbon, and you will probably appreciate it more than you currently think is possible. That seems to be the usual progression others find, according to publications and *blogs* related to Office 2007.

▶ **NEW TERM**

Blog—Short for *web log*, a collection of notes by one or more website collaborators, typically arranged in order of postings with the most recent posting at the top and most visual place. Blogs are often used for spreading ideas, dialoguing with others of similar interests, and journalizing personal and public events.

▶ **TIP**

Double-click any ribbon tab, such as Home or View, and the ribbon hides itself leaving only the tabs showing.

One Menu and Toolbar Are Still There

Office 2007 does offer one universal menu and a universal toolbar that Word, Excel, and PowerPoint give you access to:

- The **Quick Access** toolbar
- The **Office** menu

The **Quick Access** toolbar is a small four-button toolbar that sits at the very top of your Word, Excel, and PowerPoint screens. The buttons enable you to do the following:

- Save your document
- Undo a command
- Repeat your most recent edit or command
- Print your document

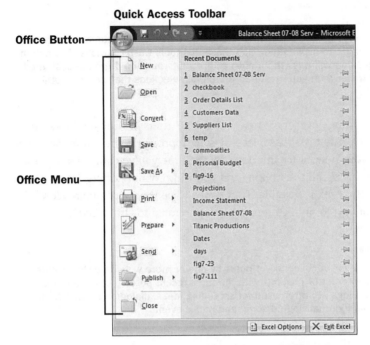

*The **Quick Access** toolbar and the **Office** menu are always available in Word, Excel, and PowerPoint.*

The **Office** menu appears when you click the **Office** button in the upper-left corner of your application. You'll find commands that formerly resided on the traditional **File** menu in these applications, namely, New, Open, Save, Save As, Print, Send, and Close. In addition to those commands, two new commands, **Finish** and **Publish**, appear on the **Office** menu. **Finish** enables you to apply protective and security elements to your document in case you want to save the document as a read-only file so that others can read but not change any data. The **Publish** command prepares your document for distribution to a wide audience such as you might do if you work in a group setting and need to distribute your document to others in the group.

► **TIP**

Because most of the **Office** menu commands used to reside on the **File** menu, you can click the **Office** button to display the **Office** menu, but you also can press Alt+F to display the **Office** menu. In previous Office versions, Alt+F displayed the **File** menu.

It's unknown why Microsoft didn't put these file-related commands on the ribbon. Perhaps these commands would have required their own ribbon, a **File** ribbon, and the Office 2007 software engineers thought another ribbon would clutter the screen more than necessary. Whatever the reason, keep in mind that the **Office** menu and the **Quick Access** toolbar are there when you need them. The tasks throughout this book alert you when you should use the **Office** menu and the **Quick Access** toolbar to perform needed operations.

Live Preview—See Format Changes Before You Make Them

Certainly the most visually stunning change to Office 2007 is the Live Preview mode. Throughout much of the Office applications, when you select text, click to select a chart or graph, or want to adjust a presentation's title, you can see what any format change to the selected item will look like before you actually apply it.

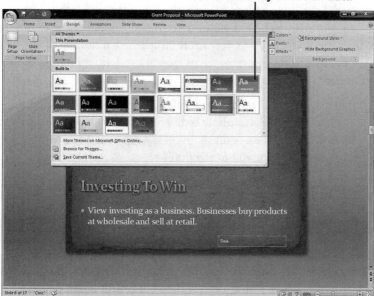

Point to Se Any Effect on Data

Point to any design and PowerPoint temporarily changes the slide to that design.

Suppose that you create a presentation and right before you give it, you begin to feel that the presentation might be too informal for the audience. You expected a more casual audience, and in came the suits. You can quickly modify the design of your entire presentation, and you could do the same with previous versions of PowerPoint. The advantage with PowerPoint 2007 is that you don't have to apply each format, one at a time, to see what that format actually looks like.

Just open the presentation, click the **Design** ribbon, and move your mouse over the various themes that appear in the **Themes** group. If you click the down arrow to the right of the **Themes** group, PowerPoint opens a larger selection of themes from which you can choose. Each theme adds a different flair to your entire presentation. As you point to each of the available themes, the slide that appears under the theme selection changes to show what that theme will look like on that slide. Point to a different theme, and the slide changes to reflect it.

▶ **TIP**

Themes are a new formatting element to Office 2007. See **16** About Styles, Themes, and Templates.

The Live Preview changes don't have to be dramatic to be effective. If you simply select text and begin to select a new font size, Office 2007's Live Preview mode changes your selected text to the font sizes you choose as you scroll through them. By doing so, you can see how the font-size change will affect the rest of the text and formatting on your page. As you scroll through each number, the Live Preview changes the text to that number's font size. Stop where it looks best and click; your text remains at its new font size.

Previously, you had to apply a format change, view the change, then undo the change, and go back to the menus to apply a different format. Now you can run through all the formatting selections quickly in one sweep, watching as they're applied to decide which is best for you at the time.

A Brief Overview of the Office 2007 Applications

In spite of the huge base of Microsoft Office installations, Office, or some programs within Office, is still new to some people. With the introduction of the ribbon, it's hoped that those who have not yet tried Office will begin to use it. Without confusing menus and toolbars that aren't always on the screen when one needs them, the ribbon's interface is a good place to jump into the Office waters if you haven't yet done so.

▶ **TIP**

Microsoft provides a comprehensive website to support its huge base of Office users. Not only do you get the expected support and some tips and advice, but the Office website also provides you with regular updates and add-in features that enable you to do more with Office. The website is http://office.microsoft.com.

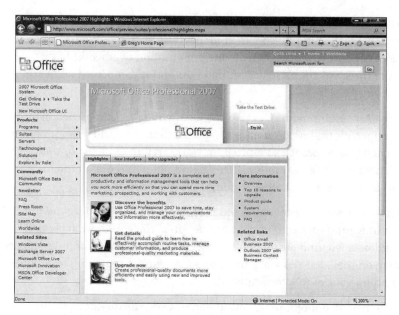

The Microsoft Office website offers updates, advice, and add-ons to help you make the most of Office.

What Exactly Is Microsoft Office?

Microsoft Office 2007 contains the most needed applications—a word processor, a spreadsheet program, a presentation program, an email and contact management program, a note-taking program—and more inside a single system. Office is designed so that its programs work well together, and although you might not need every program in Office, you can easily share information between any Office programs that you do want to use. Program collections such as Office are often called program *suites*.

▶ NEW TERM

Suite—An application that contains multiple programs, each of which performs a separate function. These programs generally work well together, with each one easily reading the other programs' data.

The following is a quick overview of the primary Office programs:

- **Word**—A word processor with which you can create notes, memos, letters, school papers, business documents, books, newsletters, and even web pages.

- **Excel**—An electronic spreadsheet program with which you can create graphs and worksheets for financial and other numeric data. After you enter your financial data, you can analyze it for forecasts, generate numerous what-if scenarios, and publish worksheets on the Web.

- **PowerPoint**—A presentation graphics program with which you can create presentations for seminars, schools, churches, web pages, and business meetings. Not only can PowerPoint create the presentation overheads, but it also can create the speaker's presentation notes and print compacted audience handouts.

- **Outlook**—An email program, appointment calendar, meeting scheduler, contact manager, alarm-based reminder, to-do list manager, and notes program. This kitchen-sink approach to a program works well in Outlook; as data moves across your life in emails and tasks and notes and appointments, you'll be able to keep track of everything.

- **OneNote**—A powerful note-taking program for desktops, laptops, and tablet PCs that integrates any kind of data in the notes. You can draw, type, and insert audio, video, and graphics into your notes and place all those elements anywhere on the page you want them to go. Advanced searching techniques make finding your data later simple.

In addition to these five major programs, different Office installations include several other programs, such as the **Access** database that helps you manage, report, and update huge quantities of data. The **Publisher** program includes desktop publishing capabilities to enable you to produce newsletters, fliers, menus, invitations, certificates, and even simple web pages easily.

The Office programs share many common features. This means that after you learn one Office program, it's easier to master the next one due to the similar interface.

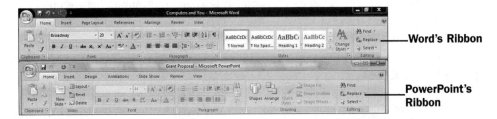

Word's Ribbon

PowerPoint's Ribbon

The Office programs share common features to make it easier to learn each program.

In addition to working with familiar interfaces in the Office products, you can insert data that you create in one program into another program within the Office suite. If you create a financial table with Excel, for instance, you can put the table in a Word document that you send to your board of directors and embed the table in a PowerPoint presentation to stockholders. After you learn how to use any program in the Office suite, you will be far more comfortable using all the others because of the common interface.

Different Office 2007 Packages Are Available

Several versions of Office are available, each with a different intended audience and each with a unique collection of programs. These are the Office 2007 suites available:

- **Office Basic 2007**—For home and small-business users. Includes Word, Excel, and Outlook.

- **Office Home and Student 2007**—Aimed at home and student users. Includes Word, Excel, PowerPoint, and OneNote.

- **Office Standard 2007**—Considered the most common programs sought in the Office suite, the Office Standard 2007 includes Word, Excel, PowerPoint, and Outlook.

- **Office Small Business 2007**—Supplies the tools that a small business might benefit most from. Includes Word, Excel, PowerPoint, Outlook, and Publisher. Outlook is enhanced with new contact-management capabilities useful for customer follow-up and sales leads with the Business Contact Manager add-in program.

- **Office Professional 2007**—Considered to be the suite most favored by medium-to-larger organizations as well as computing-intensive small businesses, the Office Professional 2007 suite includes Word, Excel, PowerPoint, Outlook, Access, and Publisher. Outlook includes the Business Contact Manager extension.

- **Office Professional Plus 2007**—Includes all of Office Professional 2007 as well as InfoPath and Communicator, allowing for the handling of forms and communication across a group of collaborators as might be required for large team projects.

- **Office Enterprise 2007**—Considered the top suite with everything, it includes Word, Excel, PowerPoint, Outlook, OneNote, Access, Publisher, InfoPath, Communicator, and Groove (another group-collaboration communications system to access Communicator and InfoPath).

Microsoft Office 2007 Is Versatile

The Office products are general-purpose, meaning that you can customize applications to suit your needs. You can use Excel as your household budgeting program, for example, and also as your corporation's interactive balance-sheet system.

You can integrate Office into your networked system. This way, Office provides useful features whether you are networked to an *intranet*, to the Internet, or to both. You can share Office information with others across the network. Office fits well within the online world by integrating Internet access throughout the Office suite.

▶ NEW TERM

Intranet—A computer-to-computer communications system that uses Internet-like techniques to communicate within a company. One department might publish a web page on the company's computer server that other departments use their web browser to view and interact with. The data isn't available outside the corporate network, however, as the same data on an Internet web page would be.

Introducing Word

When you need to write any text-based document, look no further than Word. Word is a word processor that supports many features, including the following:

- Automatic corrections for common mistakes as you type using special automatic-correcting tools that watch the way you work and adapt to your needs

- Templates and styles that make quick work of your document's formatting

- Advanced page-layout and formatting capabilities

- Numbering, bulleting, bordering, and shading tools

- Integrated grammar and spelling tools to help ensure your document's accuracy

- Newsletter-style multiple columns, headers, footers, and endnotes in your publications

- Graphical tools that enable you to emphasize headers, draw lines and shapes around your text, and work with imported art files in your documents

The next figure shows a Word editing session. Even though Word is a word processor, you can see from the figure that it supports advanced formatting, layout, and graphics capabilities so that you can produce professional documents, newsletters, invitations, and just about any publication that combines words and pictures.

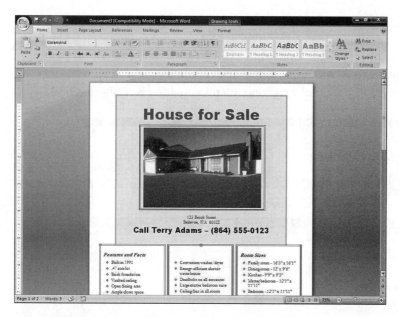

Word easily handles text, graphics, and advanced formatted layout of any document you want to create.

Introducing Excel

Excel's primary goal is to help you organize and manage financial information such as income statements, balance sheets, and forecasts. Typically such data is organized into a worksheet, sometimes called a spreadsheet. Excel is an electronic spreadsheet program that supports many features, including the following:

- Automatic cell formatting; the Live Preview feature makes formatting even quicker than ever before

- Automatic worksheet computations that enable you to generate a worksheet that automatically calculates when you make a change to a portion of the worksheet

- Built-in functions, such as financial formulas, that automate common tasks

- Automatic row and column completion of value ranges, with automatic completion of ranges of data

- Formatting tools that let you turn worksheets into professionally produced reports

- Powerful data sorting, searching, filtering, and analyzing tools that enable you to turn data into an organized collection of meaningful information

- Powerful charts and graphs that can analyze your numbers and turn them into simple trends

The following figure shows an Excel editing session. The user is entering balance sheet information for a company's projected assets and liabilities. If you have worked with other worksheet programs, you might be surprised at how fancy Excel can get. Excel's automatic formatting capabilities and the new themes available in Excel 2007 make creating attention-getting worksheets simple.

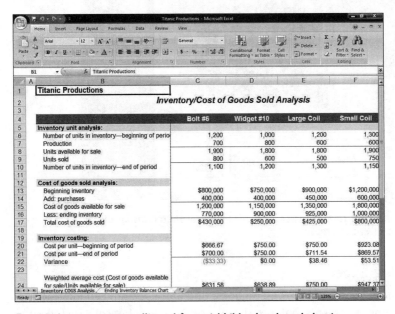

Excel helps you create, edit, and format highly visual worksheets.

Introducing PowerPoint

Have you ever presented a talk and longed for a better approach to messy over-head slides? Have you seen the pros wow their audiences with eye-catching, pro-fessional computerized presentations? With PowerPoint 2007, there is simply no reason why you shouldn't be wowing your audiences as well. Professional presen-tations are now within your reach.

PowerPoint supports many features, including the following:

- The use of extensive templates and themes to generate great-looking presen-tations with little effort

- Sample designs that provide you with fill-in-the-blank presentations

- Screen display modes that imitate how you'll eventually project your slides on a larger screen

- Complete color and font control of your presentation slides

- A collection of art files, icons, and sounds that you can embed to make your presentations more attention-getting

- Numerous transitions and fades between presentation slides to keep your audience's attention

- The capability to save presentations as web pages that you can then present on the Internet

The next figure shows a PowerPoint editing session. The user is getting ready for a presentation and has only a few minutes to prepare color slides for the meeting. With PowerPoint, a few minutes are more than enough time!

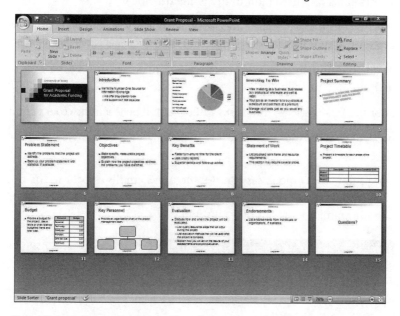

PowerPoint helps you create, edit, and format professional presentations.

▶ NOTE

Perhaps you're beginning to see that the nicest advantage to the Office 2007 programs is that they enable you to focus on your data and *not* on your data's look. Creating great-looking documents, worksheets, and presentations is the easy part, so don't worry about that. You worry about the important content, the message you want to convey. Leave the formatting to Office 2007.

Introducing Outlook

Microsoft Outlook 2007 is perhaps the Office program that does the most varied tasks. Outlook lets you manage the details of your life. Not only is Outlook a truly interactive contact, mail, planning, and scheduling program, but it's also fun to use.

Outlook helps you do many things with your contact data, including these:

- Send, receive, and manage email from multiple email accounts

- Customize your email's backgrounds and automatic signatures that give your emails the look and function you need

- Manage all your personal and business contacts; you can keep track of multiple email addresses, phone numbers, mailing addresses, and notes, and even keep a photographic image with the contact so that you'll always remember faces

- Schedule meetings and use email to invite the attendees

- Color-code appointments, emails, and tasks by category so that you can more easily organize your data and spot important data that needs your attention

- Manage all your appointments, and receive reminders when it's time to act on something in your calendar

- Track prioritized to-do lists so that tasks will never fall between the cracks again

- Write notes to yourself that act as yellow sticky notes when you view them in Outlook

The next figure shows an Outlook session. All the user's emails appear in the center column showing the recipient and the subject. You click one of these email headers to see the email's details in the right pane.

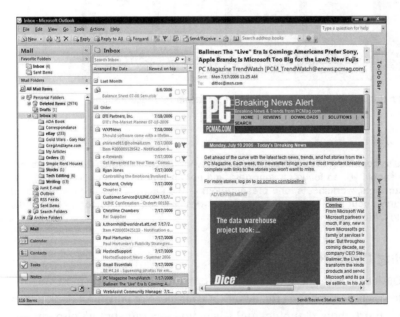

Manage your email from multiple accounts with Outlook.

To give you a preview of how Outlook's calendar feature works, the next figure shows a three-day view of a calendar that's filled with appointments and reminders. Under your calendar resides your Tasks area. Outlook tasks are things to do that don't have specific start and stop times as appointments and meetings have. As you finish tasks, you cross them off your list by letting Outlook know they're complete. Outlook draws a line through them but keeps track of them for reference.

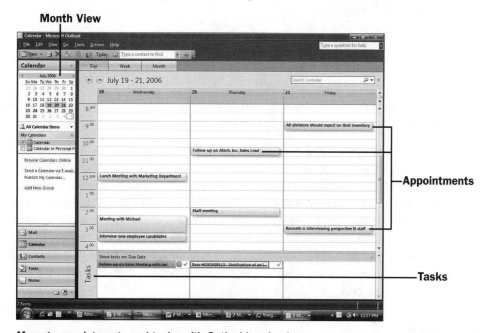

Manage appointments and tasks with Outlook's calendar.

▶ **TIP**

Outlook provides many ways to view your data. You can view a week at a time or a month at a time, or if today's appointments are numerous, you can view just a single day's calendar. When you set reminders for certain items, Outlook pops up a message and alerts you with an audible reminder as those things come due.

Introducing OneNote

Although Outlook can manage notes for you, Outlook's notes are more limited to small reminders that you might otherwise jot down on a yellow sticky note. To *really* keep track of notes, you should use OneNote 2007.

In spite of its name, OneNote 2007 is more than a note-taking program. OneNote is unique in that it manages just about any kind of data you want to manage, including the following:

- Text

- Graphics

- Handwriting (as would be needed for tablet PCs)

- Scanned data

- Audio clips

- Video clips

- Other Office 2007 program data files

OneNote begins with a blank page. What you put on that page and *where* you put it is up to you. The beauty of OneNote is appreciated only when one tries it.

Unlike the other Office 2007 programs introduced earlier, OneNote is more difficult to introduce in a simple features list. The best way to explain what OneNote does is to think of it as a big pad of paper waiting for you to begin doing whatever you might do with a big pad of paper. One thing you might do is take your pad of paper to a meeting and jot notes. You could take minutes of the meeting, write yourself reminders that you'll have to attend to later, perhaps doodle once in a while in the margins, circle important notes you take, underline key words, and if you're really prepared, use a colored highlighting pen to emphasize vital things you put on that pad.

▶ NOTE

You'll get a better introduction to OneNote later, as you will with the other Office programs. OneNote, however, is the newest member of the Office family of programs taught in this book and the one least familiar to most readers. A more thorough introduction here will reap rewards later when you begin to tackle OneNote's tasks.

When you take notes like that, you don't always start at the top and work your way down, as you would do generally if you used Word to make notes. The big pad of paper doesn't require put-it-in-this-order rules; instead, you're free to add what you what, where you want, and when you want it. Write a note at the bottom and then circle a note at the top. Draw an arrow to something in the center and annotate that arrow with a margin note.

OneNote offers those capabilities on your screen, but it goes *far beyond* what a pad of paper allows! OneNote not only enables you to keep track of the notes just described, but it also lets you insert live hyperlinks to websites mentioned in the meeting and even copy web pages to your note page. Grab an Excel table of sales data discussed in the meeting and insert that table in your notes. Grab a PowerPoint slide discussed in the meeting and annotate the slide with edits you must later make to the slide.

▶ **TIP**

Although it's easier to take more notes with OneNote than on a notepad, you will take *fewer* notes with OneNote because OneNote can record your meeting's audio *and* video if you have a webcam attached to your laptop or tablet PC. You do not need to take dictation—OneNote can record it and stick the audio recording inside your other notes. Those audio/video clips end up being another form of data on your OneNote page.

The next figure shows OneNote in action. Note the various forms of data shown: text, a table, graphics, handwriting, a bulleted and numbered list, and web graphics, and they all reside side-by-side on OneNote's screen.

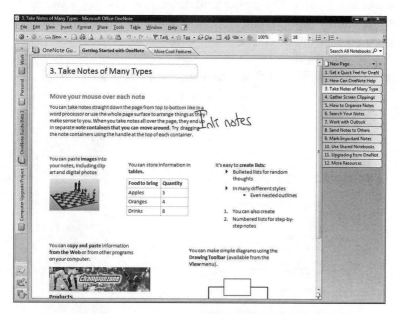

OneNote hardly cares what kind of data you add to its pages or where you put that data.

▶ **TIP**

Perhaps the biggest reason OneNote is so powerful is its capability to search through all your notes quickly. After a year or two of adding to OneNote, you may soon find yourself with *information overload*. Don't worry, when you want to locate anything you've stored, just search. OneNote even searches many of your data's graphics trying to locate text within that image that might match your search.

▶ **NEW TERM**

Information overload—A term used when too much information hides important messages within that information. A lot of data is meaningless if you cannot locate answers you need from that data. Without a way to search and organize data, that data quickly becomes too much to be useful.

After you begin to add data to OneNote, searching isn't always the best way to find what you need. For example, you might want to see all your notes on a certain project you worked on six months ago. Searching for the project name might produce a search result of nine items in your OneNote files, but many items related to that project might not include the project's name.

As you add notes to OneNote, you'll keep track of them just as you do in real life. You'll keep OneNote data in files and divide those files into named notebooks. You can further divide each notebook into sections and store as many pages of data in those sections as you need. Therefore, a project would be a good candidate for a notebook named for the project, and the sections and pages within that project's notebook would divide the project into its many elements, perhaps by job or by person working on the project.

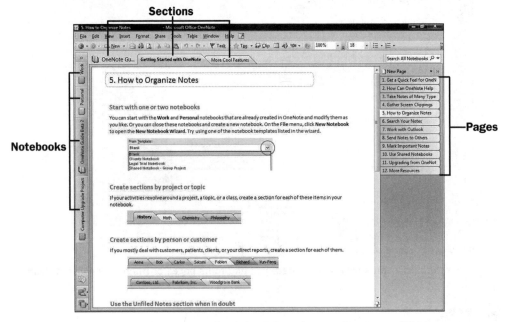

OneNote uses the concept of notebooks, sections, and pages to divide your data into meaningful chunks of information.

What Else Is New?

Now that you've read through an introduction to the five Office 2007 programs discussed in this book (or perhaps you only skimmed the text if you were already an Office Pro before Office 2007 came out), it might help you get the big picture to learn what is new with Office 2007. Not everyone has yet to upgrade, and perhaps knowing what's in store would help your decision. The ribbon and the Live Preview features are certainly the most obvious new features, but they are not alone in what distinguishes Office 2007 from older versions.

When the Microsoft people set out to improve Office, they wanted users to get more work done faster and with less effort. Although that by itself might be a lofty goal, it's been the goal of every Office since 1.0. What makes Office 2007 so unusual in that respect is that the complete redesign—such as replacing the toolbars and menus with the ribbon—is more complete and richer than that of any Office program that has come before.

The big advantage to the improved user interface is that brand-new users should be able to begin using Office more quickly. No more wading through menus, because what you need to be able to do should be on the ribbon at the top of the screen.

Office 2007 is certainly more graphical. Anyone who has used Excel's graphs and charts, for example, will see dramatic improvements in Excel 2007's graphing capabilities, including the following:

- New 3-D effects

- Shadows

- Reflection

- Glows

- Surface texture

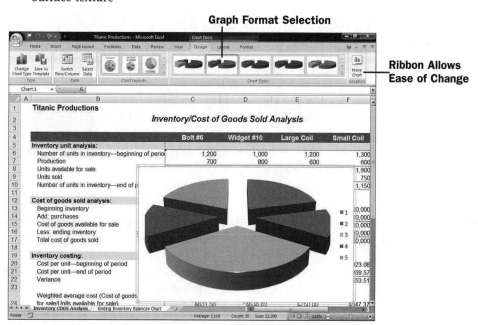

Quickly display and change your Excel 2007 graphs.

Outlook includes a new **To-Do Bar** that you can quickly show or hide to list current dates, appointments, and tasks that are the most pressing. Previous users will know that the **Outlook Today** screen did all this also, but you had to leave your email window to see your **Outlook Today** screen. Now with one mouse click, you can view your **To-Do Bar** and see what tasks are left to check off.

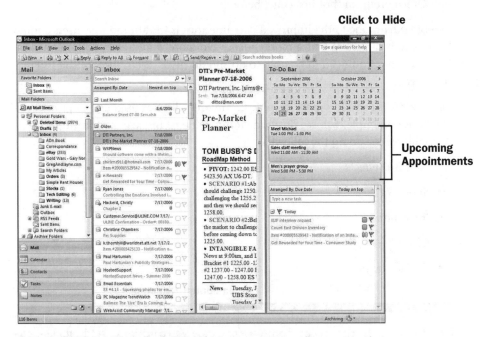

Outlook 2007 put the Outlook Today feature on your email screen so that you'll always keep tabs on what's left to do today.

Little things mean a lot in Office 2007. If you've ever tried to search for information in Outlook previously, you knew to take a long lunch break before expecting any results. Outlook 2007's search is almost instant, and Outlook begins searching the moment you start typing what you want to look for.

▶ **NOTE**

Unlike previous versions of Office, Outlook indexes your data as you work but does so unobtrusively in the background without hampering your system resources as before.

Before Office 2007, Office users would have to obtain a program to read RSS feeds from their favorite websites. Outlook 2007 can collect your RSS feeds and store them in your Inbox, where you can read them at your leisure. Outlook looks to be your central repository of data that crosses your path, so the addition of RSS feeds makes sense.

Office Works Under the Hood, Too

In addition to the user interface changes and the new features you'll enjoy, Microsoft designed Office 2007 to work better and do more internally. You'll notice the vast improvement in search speed as mentioned in the preceding section. In addition to the faster searches, Office 2007's file format is based on the XML language. The new *Microsoft Office Open XML File Format* ensures that your Office documents are smaller than before and more compatible with other programs. (See **149** **About Office's XML File Format**.)

▶ NEW TERM

Microsoft Office Open XML File Format—The new file format supported by the Office 2007 programs based on the XML data-exchange standard that should allow you to exchange your Office 2007 data with more programs and more systems.

In spite of the new Office 2007 file formats, you won't have trouble reading or writing data for Office's earlier versions. If you or co-workers need to share Office data among users from Office 97 to Office 2007, you'll be able to. When you save documents in Office 2007, you choose whether you want to use the streamlined Office Open XML File Format (the default) or save to an earlier data version such as PowerPoint XP's. Office 2007 can read and write to those previous versions with ease.

▶ NOTE

Office XP users learned quickly that this backward compatibility didn't always go as promised. When you saved under a previous format, the data wasn't always readable in earlier Office programs. You won't have that problem with your Office 2007 data.

If you work in a collaborative environment and share documents between several users, Office 2007 extends the ability to work across boundaries and share documents over a network, an intranet, or the Internet.

Get Help When You Need It

Office has been known for offering helpful advice. To take advantage of Office 2007's full help feature set, make sure that you're online when you request help. When you click the **Help** button (the circle with the question mark inside), whatever Office 2007 program you're in opens a help window with topics. After the initial help screen appears, you can browse the help by category or type a word or phrase to get specific help on that topic.

Search Box

Help
Categories

Help is always a click away. Office 2007 ensures that your help is up-to-date by downloading helpful information from the Internet every time you request help.

The **Help** window includes a **Search** box; type what you want help for, and the help engine delivers help for that topic, sometimes multiple windows' worth of help related to the keyword you entered.

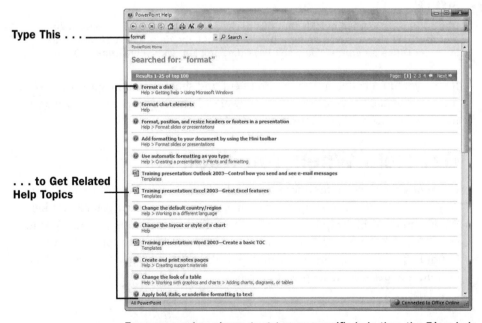

Type This . . .

. . . to Get Related
Help Topics

Type any word or phrase to get more specific help than the F1 or help button alone can provide.

Of course, the only *real* help you need is right here in your hands!

Get Ready to Begin Your Tasks

You're about to begin learning Office 2007 in the best way possible—decide what you want to do, locate the task that tells you exactly how to do it, and you're on your way! Why mess around with theory and background other than the cursory glimpse you got in this chapter? You want to get work done. Turn the page and start doing just that!

PART II

Writing with Word

IN THIS PART:

2

Learning Word's Basics

IN THIS CHAPTER:

Word is a full-featured word processor that you can use to produce notes, reports, newsletters, brochures, and just about anything that requires text. Word isn't just for text, however. With Word, you can easily create documents with graphics and charts. If you want to do something in Word, Word probably offers a way to do it.

▶ **NOTE**

Start Word by selecting **Microsoft Office Word 2007** from your Windows Start menu's **Microsoft Office** entry.

The features you'll find in Microsoft Office 2007's Word truly improve your effectiveness over previous versions. Before it gets fancy, however, helping you put text into documents is still Word's primary job. In spite of all its bells and whistles, Word is a workhorse that enables you to get your writing job done as easily as possible. This chapter gets you started if you are new to Word 2007. You'll master basic text-entering and document navigation skills that get you started.

1　Set Word Options

→ **SEE ALSO**

2 Create a New Document
3 Open an Existing Document
4 Type Text into a Document
5 Edit Text

Not everybody works the same way, so not every Word user wants to use Word the same way. By setting some of Word's many options, you will make Word conform to the way you like to do things. For example, you may want Word to hide its horizontal scrollbar at the bottom of your screen so that you have another row on your screen for text. If so, you can use Word's option to display or hide the horizontal scrollbar.

As a matter of fact, Word has an option for just about anything and everything, as you'll see in this task. The good news is that knowing about the options is less critical in Word 2007 than in previous versions because you can customize so much about your documents using the ribbon atop your screen.

1 Click the Office Button

The **Office** button gives you quick access to file-related commands that used to be available in Word's **File** menu. In addition, when you click the **Office** button, you'll have access to the **Word Options** button that opens the **Word Options** dialog box.

▶ **NOTE**

Most Windows programs have a menu with options that typically include commands such as **File**, **Edit**, and **View**. Each of those menu commands opens additional menus called *submenus*. Until you get used to the way Office 2007 products operate, you'll find yourself using the old menu-based commands. For example, when you want to open the **Word Options** window, you might find yourself using Alt+T, O to open the **Tools** menu and then selecting the **Options** command on the **Tools** menu. You'll find that Word 2007 understands you will do this and goes ahead and opens the **Word Options** dialog box for you! Over time, try to accustom yourself to working the way Word 2007 was designed to work. That is, for file-related options and the **Word Options** window, click the **Office** button to get to those options. By adapting to Word 2007's techniques, you'll more quickly adapt to all of Office 2007's products, and you'll find yourself becoming more proficient quickly.

▶ **NEW TERM**

submenu—A menu displayed by your selection of another menu option.

2 Select Word Options

Click the **Word Options** button to display the **Word Options** dialog box. From this dialog box, you change and set all the option settings within Word.

If you use Windows Vista's *Aero Glass* graphics mode, your **Word Options** dialog box window will have translucent borders that allow Word's menu and toolbars to show through. If you don't run Aero Glass, your **Word Options** dialog box window will have solid borders.

▶ **TIP**

Windows Vista dramatically changes the way you work within the Windows environment. For a helpful text that will answer your questions and teach you Vista fast, check out *Sams Teach Yourself Microsoft Windows Vista All in One* (Sams, 2007).

▶ **NEW TERM**

Aero Glass—Vista's advanced graphical features, such as the capability to display thumbnails in the taskbar and task switcher, as well as the see-through, translucent quality that enables you to see what one window is covering up.

If you're fairly new to Word, consider leaving all the options as is until you familiarize yourself with how Word works.

3 Change Popular Options

If the **Word Options** dialog box doesn't open to the **Popular** tab, click **Popular**. As the dialog box states, Microsoft considers these options to be the most popular (which will be debatable by most Word users).

1

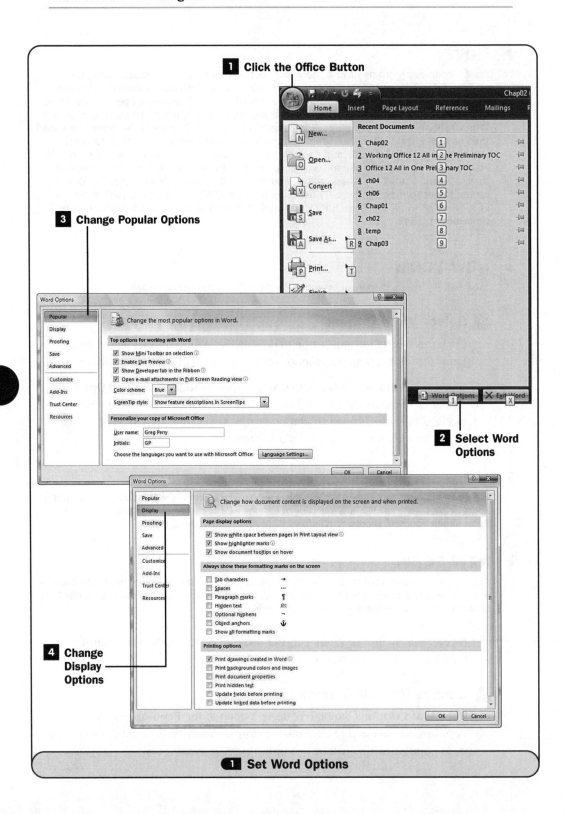

1 Click the Office Button

3 Change Popular Options

2 Select Word Options

4 Change Display Options

1 Set Word Options

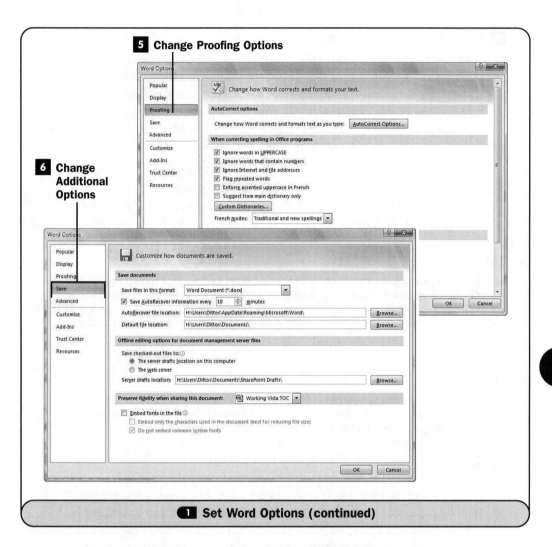

5 Change Proofing Options

6 Change Additional Options

1 Set Word Options (continued)

You can elect to use the mini toolbar (see **5** Edit Text), use the Live Preview feature (see **12** Apply Character Formatting), show the *Developer tab* on your ribbon (off by default), and open email attachments in Full Screen Reading view (see **3** Open an Existing Document). You can also change the default username and initials of Office.

▶ NEW TERM

Developer tab—An advanced section you can elect to place on your ribbon that adds programmability features to Office products.

Some Word options have a small blue letter *i* enclosed in a circle to the right of them. Rest your mouse pointer over this information request, and Word pops up a helpful description of that option.

4 Change Display Options

Click the **Display** tab to customize Word's display options. Here you adjust settings that determine how Word displays documents on your screen. You can change the display of various Word formatting characters such as spaces and line breaks. For example, if you want to see the space format character (a horizontally centered dot in place of a space) every time you press the spacebar in a document, enable the **Spaces** check box.

In the **Printing Options** section, you determine which printing options you want set. If you have a monochrome laser printer instead of a color printer, for example, you might elect to keep the option unchecked that reads **Print Background Colors and Images**.

▶ TIP

Some users prefer to see all formatting characters, such as the space format character and the end-of-paragraph mark (¶). Such characters can make some editing chores easier. For example, you'll know you pressed the spacebar seven times if you see seven space formatting characters, whereas it's far more difficult to know how many spaces appear if there are no characters to mark the spaces.

▶ NOTE

The more formatting characters you display, the more cluttered your screen will look; when you print the document that's onscreen, all the formatting characters are also printed, which can make documents look pretty confusing.

5 Change Proofing Options

Click to select the **Proofing** category to adjust Word's automatic correction tools. For example, spell-checking is turned on by default, but you might be writing a highly technical document and want to turn off the spell-checking. Normally, Word checks spelling and grammar as you type, but you might want to turn off one or both of those features. (See **8 Check a Document's Spelling and Grammar.**)

The **Proofing** category also enables you to adjust **AutoCorrect** options. Word can correct common errors as you type, such as incorrect punctuation, or flag repeated words with wavy underlines so that you'll spot them. From the **Proofing** options, you can adjust the way Word looks over your shoulder, in effect.

6 Change Additional Options

Continue viewing and changing the remaining options in the **Word Options** dialog box. Click the tab that corresponds to the option you'd like to change.

You'll find tabs for saving your work under the **Save** tab. There you can select a default file format for saving documents, which you can always override when storing any document. Another **Save** option that many find useful to change is the time interval used for how long Word waits before saving an *AutoRecover* document version. Some feel the default 10 minutes is too lengthy.

▶ NEW TERM

AutoRecover—Word's capability to save your document at various intervals as you edit the document. If your computer freezes, or your power goes out, or you experience some other problem that causes your Word session to close or requires that you reboot, Word can restore your document to one of several AutoRecover points from which you'll select when you restart Word.

The **Advanced** tab offers advanced editing options such as how Word handles hyperlinks in documents. For example, when you insert a hyperlink into a Word document such as a link to a web page, do you want a single click to send you to that page? Word doesn't default to that action, which might at first surprise you until you realize that making the link live with a single click means you'll have difficulty selecting the link's text to change its font. Most users leave the default handling for this, so such a link requires a Ctrl+click before Word leaves the document and sends you to that web page. You'll be able to use the single click to more easily highlight the link's text when you want to adjust the properties for that text.

The remaining options allow you to perform less-common option changes such as customizing the icons on Word's ribbon bar and viewing resources on the Web where you can get extra help.

When you're done specifying Word options, click the **OK** button to close the **Word Options** dialog box.

2 | **Create a New Document**

✔ **BEFORE YOU BEGIN**

1 Set Word Options

➜ **SEE ALSO**

4 Type Text into a Document
9 Print a Document
19 Use a Template

Word gives you two ways to create new documents. The first is to create a new document starting with a blank page. If you choose this approach, you must decide what text to place in the document and where you want that information to go. The blank page gives you the most freedom to create a document formatted the way you want to format it.

You can also use a *template* to open a blank, preformatted document. If you use a template, you'll be able to choose from several templates that Word provides, and you can create your own templates for use later.

▶ NEW TERM

template—A preformatted document that is without specific text but includes an outline, or skeleton, of a document you might want to create. Starting with a template of a fax cover page, for example, is far easier than starting with a blank page to create a fax cover page. The template will have a place already designated for To and From and Subject lines, as well as possible graphics. You might want to create a template for your business letterhead, too, so that the letterhead automatically appears at the top of your documents without your having to insert the letterhead each time you write a business letter. (See **19** Use a Template.)

In spite of the fact that templates provide great starting points for special documents you'll want to create, many times you'll begin with a blank document. Starting with a blank document, without preformatted logos, return addresses, and other items that often appear in templates, gives you the most flexibility in creating exactly the document you want to create.

1 Request a New Document

Click the **Office** button and select **New**. You can also use Word's previous menu structure by pressing Alt+F (simulating the **File** menu) followed by N to select the **New** option. The **New Document** window appears.

2 Determine Your New Document Type

The **New Document** window enables you to create a blank document by clicking the **Blank Document** option. Several other options appear, and most of them are related to templates you can use to create highly specific kinds of documents.

3 Scroll to See Options

Scroll down the **New Document** window to see additional templates as well as more online templates. Most of the time you'll want to create a blank document instead of going to the Office website to peruse additional material.

4 Select Blank Document

Although the **Blank Document** option toward the top of the **New Document** window might seem fairly insignificant given its appearance amid all the other template-related options in the window, most users select the **Blank Document** option when creating a new document.

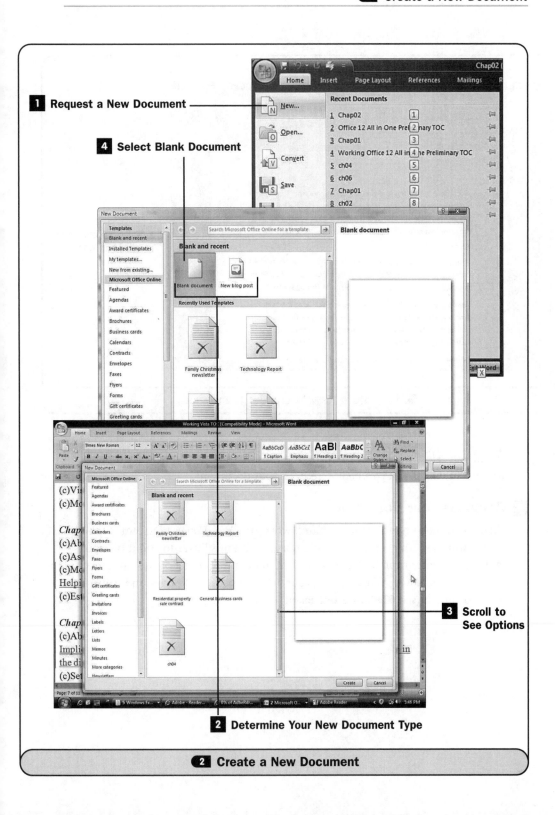

1 Request a New Document

4 Select Blank Document

3 Scroll to See Options

2 Determine Your New Document Type

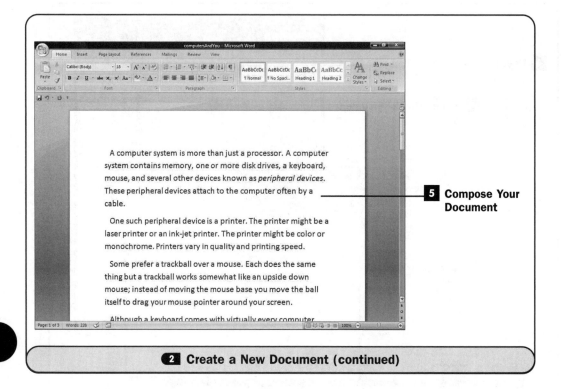

5 Compose Your Document

2 Create a New Document (continued)

When you select the **Blank Document** option, Word opens a new document window in which you can begin creating your document.

5 Compose Your Document

Create your document using the blank work area Word gives you. Start typing as you would in any word processing document. Press **Enter** to end a block of text (be it a paragraph, an item you want to be part of a list of similar items, or a signature block). You can save your work (choose **File, Save**) and print your document (see **9 Print a Document**) at any time.

---

3 | **Open an Existing Document**

✔ **BEFORE YOU BEGIN**	→ **SEE ALSO**
1 Set Word Options	**9** Print a Document
2 Create a New Document	

Opening an existing document to edit with Word is simple. You tell Word you want to open a document file and then locate the file, and Word loads the document in the editing area.

One important Word feature is its capability to open documents you create in other word processing programs. Word 2007 can open Microsoft Word documents created with earlier Word releases, as well as Microsoft Works, WordPerfect, and several other document file formats including RTF (Rich Text Format).

▶ **NOTE**

Word 2007 uses the document extension .DOCX for its documents. Word's previous file format ended with the .DOC file extension. Both types of files display when you want to locate files to open in Word.

1 **Request a Document**

Click the **Office** button and select **Open**. You can also follow previous Word versions' menu command structure and select **File**, **Open** to display the **Open** dialog box.

2 **Navigate to the Document's Location**

The document you want to open might not appear at the default location shown in the **Open** dialog box, so navigate to the folder in which the document you're looking for resides using the Windows navigation links.

▶ **TIP**

You can open documents from your computer's disk or from elsewhere in the file system. If you want to open a document located on the Web, preface the filename with http://or ftp://to open document files from those sources.

3 **Open the File**

When you locate the folder that holds the document file, select the file you want to open. Then click the **Open** button to open the selected file in Word's editing workspace.

▶ **TIP**

Feel free to open more than one file by holding down the Ctrl key while clicking multiple filenames. Word opens each document you select in its own window. Use Alt+Tab,

3

Windows+Tab (if Aero Glass is available on your computer), or Ctrl+F6 to move between your open Word documents.

After the file opens in the Word workspace, you can edit the file.

4 Return to the Most Recent Edit

When you open an existing Word document to edit or to add to, the F5 key takes you to the place inside the document where you last edited. If you worked on a lengthy document last week, for example, as soon as you open the document today, if you press F5 then Word takes you right to that page you were last editing.

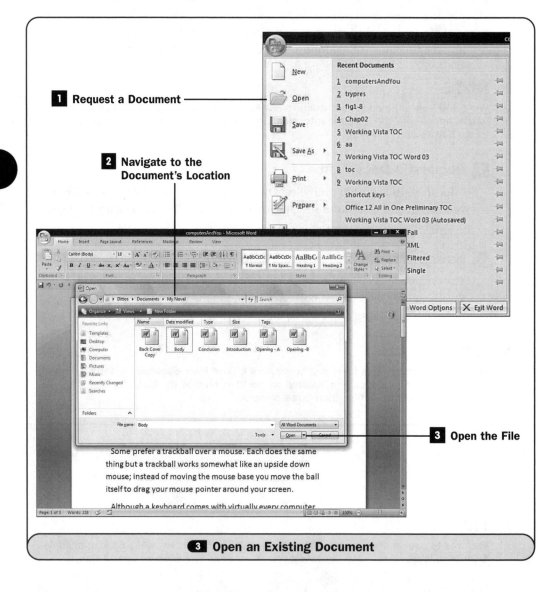

1 Request a Document

2 Navigate to the Document's Location

3 Open the File

3 Open an Existing Document

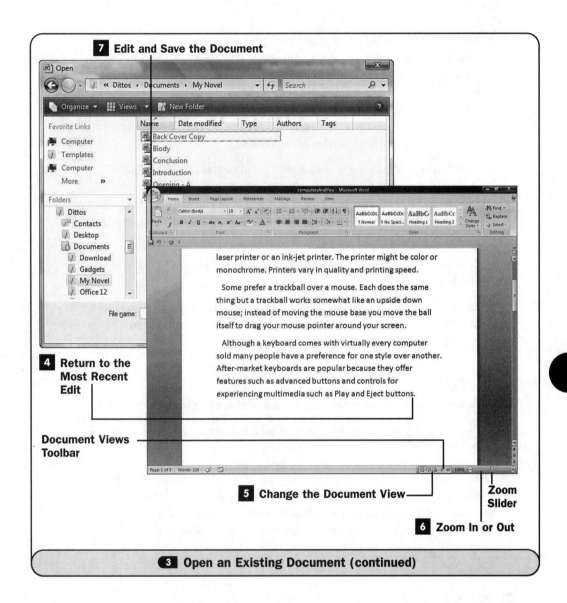

7 Edit and Save the Document

4 Return to the Most Recent Edit

Document Views Toolbar

5 Change the Document View

Zoom Slider

6 Zoom In or Out

3 Open an Existing Document (continued)

5 Change the Document View

Word offers five views of your document:

- **Print Layout**—This is the view Word users generally stay in during most of the editing session. The Print Layout view displays your document exactly as it will appear on the printed page when you print the document. By editing in the Print Layout view, you can more accurately see how those changes will affect the final printed document.

- **Full Screen Reading**—This is the cleanest view, using a highly readable font useful for reading (but not editing) Word-compatible documents on your screen. Very little space is consumed by menus and toolbars; the majority of your screen is taken up by the text itself. The pagination of the Full Screen Reading view doesn't necessarily match that of your printed documents because the Full Screen Reading view's goal is to format your document to make it as readable as possible.

- **Web Layout**—This view is useful for editing web pages inside Word. Due to Word's support for graphics and charts, and due to Word's capability to understand *HTML*, you can create and edit web pages from Word. The Web Layout view is the view best equipped to retain and respect your web page's boundaries and capabilities.

- **Outline**—The **Outline** view button enables you to manage outlines you create in Word.

- **Draft**—The Draft view hides all pagination, margins, pictures, headers, and footers from your document so that you can see and edit strictly the text inside.

▶ NEW TERM

HTML—Abbreviation for *Hypertext Markup Language;* it is a language of formatting commands that web browsers use to display web pages. Virtually all pages you view on the Internet are composed of some HTML, and most of them have nothing other than the HTML code in them.

Use the **Document Views** toolbar on your status bar to change between views. You can also select **View** from Word's menu atop the ribbon bar to produce the **Document Views** ribbon section, where you can move between these views. Word does not change your document in any way when you change the view; Word only adjusts what you see on the screen.

6 Zoom In or Out

Drag the **Zoom** slider left or right to adjust the amount of document text you see in your Word editing window. You can also click the percentage number to the left of the **Zoom** slider to select or type a specific zoom-percentage value into the **Zoom** dialog box. If your text is too small to read inside Word, adjust the **Zoom** slider to your liking.

7 Edit and Save the Document

Make changes to your document. After you have the document the way you want it for now, select **File**, **Save** (or just click the **Save** button in the **Customize Quick Access** toolbar above your document or to the right of your **Office** button to save your document's most recent edits to disk. You can also select **File**, **Save As** if you want to change the name of the edited document from the one you started with.

---

4   Type Text into a Document

✔ BEFORE YOU BEGIN	→ SEE ALSO
2 Create a New Document	**5** Edit Text
3 Open an Existing Document	**9** Print a Document

If you've ever used a word processor before, even a simple one such as WordPad found in Windows, you'll have no trouble editing text in Word. By utilizing the proper view (see **3 Open an Existing Document**), you maximize the use of your screen space so that you can better concentrate on the task at hand: producing the best document content possible.

This task walks you through a short editing session just to give you a feel for the kinds of movements and tools available to you. Many of the editing skills you acquire in one Office program, such as with Word, will apply to the other Office programs as well. For example, both Excel and Word offer the capability to apply specific editing styles and select various views. Word's ribbon across the top of your screen changes as you work depending on what you're currently doing, but you'll find that a similar ribbon acts the same across the Office programs.

1 Position the Insertion Point

Press the arrow keys to see the text cursor move around your screen. The text cursor is called the *insertion point* and moves as you press any arrow key. You can also click your mouse within the document to place the insertion point where you next want to type.

▶ **NEW TERM**

Insertion point—A vertical text cursor that shows where the next character you type will appear.

As you type text, that text appears at the insertion point. When you get to the right edge of a paragraph, Word automatically wraps your paragraph onto the next line. Do not press Enter unless you want to end a paragraph and

4

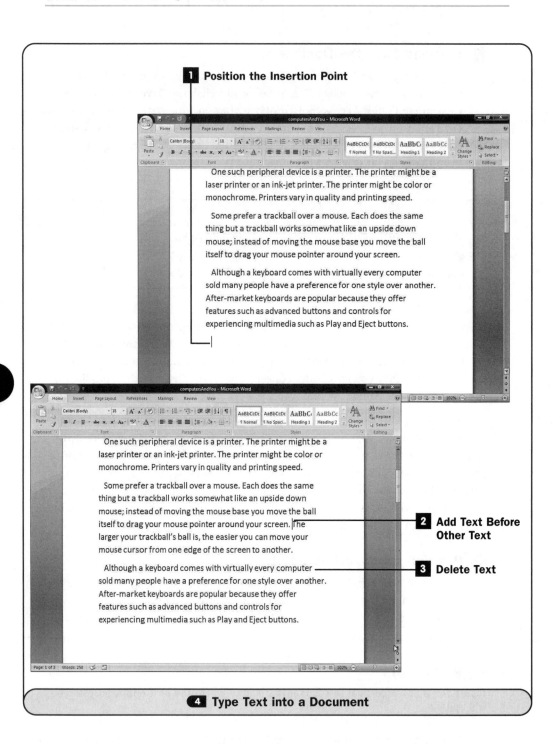

1 Position the Insertion Point

2 Add Text Before Other Text

3 Delete Text

4 Type Text into a Document

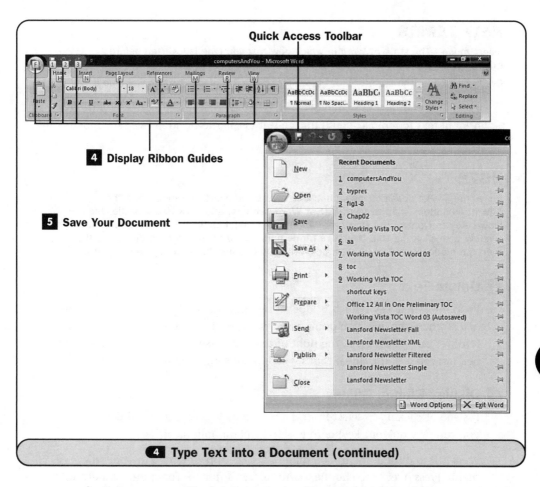

Quick Access Toolbar

4 Display Ribbon Guides

5 Save Your Document

■4 Type Text into a Document (continued)

begin a new one. Word may or may not insert a blank line between paragraphs depending on how you set up your page (see ⑭ **Set Up Page Formatting**).

If you press Shift+Enter instead of Enter, Word ends the current line and begins at the start of the line below without actually creating a new paragraph. You can easily see where paragraphs begin and end by displaying nonprinting characters (see ❺ **Edit Text**). If you press Ctrl+Enter, Word begins a new page in the document even if you had not yet filled up the previous page.

② Add Text Before Other Text

When you start typing, Word normally inserts the text you type in front of the existing text and moves the existing text over to the right. This is called *insert mode,* and it is normal behavior for most editors and word processors. If your typing replaces text on the screen, you're in *overtype mode* instead of insert mode.

▶ NEW TERMS

Insert mode—The state of Word in which new text you type is inserted before existing text.

Overtype mode—The state of Word in which new text replaces text as you type it.

Press the Insert key to switch between overtype and insert modes. If you have a lot of text to replace, you'll find that it's easier to do so in overtype mode because you'll have less text to delete.

▶ NOTE

If pressing Insert does not toggle between insert and overtype mode, open the **Advanced** options window (see **①Set Word Options**) and click to check the **Use the Insert Key to Control the Overtype Mode** option. While still on the **Advanced** option window, also click the **Use Overtype Mode** option if you want Word to default to the overtype mode instead of insert mode, until you change the mode by pressing Insert.

3 Delete Text

Press the Delete key (which is labeled Del on some keyboards) to delete characters where the insertion point appears. Every time you press Delete, Word removes one character to the right of the text cursor (including a space, number, or even a blank line if that's where the insertion point is positioned).

4 Display Ribbon Guides

Instead of clicking to select from the ribbon as you type and edit documents, you can stay on your keyboard to select ribbon options.

Press F10 to display the ribbon guides. Letters appear across the ribbon's menu. Press a letter to change to that option's ribbon. For example, normally the **Home** ribbon appears. Press F10 to display the ribbon guide letters and press S to change to the **References** ribbon. As soon as you do, all the options on the **References** ribbon will have their own letter guides so that you can stay on your keyboard without having to move and click your mouse to select an option.

▶ TIP

If you display the ribbon guide letters and decide you don't want to select a ribbon menu or option, press Esc to hide the ribbon guide letters and return to your editing session.

5 Save Your Document

After you have edited the text in the document—and periodically while you are editing—you should save your changes to the hard disk. To save the document, click the **Save** button on your **Quick Access** toolbar (or click the **Office** button and choose **Save**). Type a filename for your document and then click **Save** to save your document to your disk.

▶ **TIP**

If you want to save a document under a different name from its original name—thereby keeping both documents intact and under different names—select **Save As** instead of **Save** after clicking the Office button. Word asks you for a new filename for the current version of the document, saves it under that name, and doesn't touch the original version.

---

5   **Edit Text**

✔ BEFORE YOU BEGIN	→ SEE ALSO
1 Set Word Options	**6** Move Around a Document
2 Create a New Document	**7** Find and Replace Text
3 Open an Existing Document	**8** Check a Document's Spelling and Grammar
	12 Apply Character Formatting

Word makes it easy to edit your documents. Whether you want to edit a letter, add to your novel, or edit a report once more before sending it to clients, Word provides quick and simple tools that help you get the job done right.

If your document is long, you can navigate to the places you want to edit using your keyboard (see **6 Move Around a Document**). If you know of a key word or phrase that is close to the text you want to edit, such as a section title, you can search for that key word or phrase to jump right there (see **7 Find and Replace Text**). Word's formatting and spell-checking tools will help you ensure accuracy while making your documents look good, too. You'll find help with formatting starting in **12 Apply Character Formatting**, and you'll learn how to check your document's spelling using Word's built-in dictionary in **8 Check a Document's Spelling and Grammar**.

▶ **TIP**

Word does its best to protect you from inadvertently losing your work. Word's AutoRecover tool (see **1 Set Word Options**) helps keep your document safe if an unexpected system problem occurs. If you attempt to exit Word without saving your document, Word prompts you to specify a filename to save the document under before exiting.

1 Select Text to Work With

Select text using standard Windows selection tools (such as holding down the Shift key as you press arrow keys) to select more than one character at a time. As you select text, Word highlights the text to show exactly what you've selected.

You might want to select a large block of text for deletion or perhaps apply a special format to that selected text (see **12 Apply Character Formatting**).

▶ **TIP**

Press Ctrl+A to select your entire document. You can also make multiple selections by first making one selection and then holding down the Ctrl key while selecting additional text.

2 Display the Mini Toolbar

More often than not, when you select text, you will want to format that text in some way. When you select text by dragging your mouse over the text from the starting point to the end of the selection, the mini toolbar begins to appear. This is a floating toolbar that only dimly shows to indicate its presence, but as you move your mouse toward the mini toolbar, Word solidifies the toolbar so that you can select from it. If you ignore the mini toolbar, Word hides it as you continue working.

From the mini toolbar, you can apply character formatting, format bulleted text, and shift paragraphs right or left.

12 Apply Character Formatting explores formatting characters in more depth.

5

3 Copy and Paste Selected Text

After you've selected text, you can press Ctrl+C to copy the selection to your Windows Clipboard. The original text remains unchanged in the document. After you've copied the selection to the Clipboard, move your insertion point to another place in your document (the text you originally selected is deselected) and press Ctrl+V to paste a copy of the text in the new location.

You can keep pressing Ctrl+V to paste the text as many times as you want in your document. The normal Windows editing features work in Word, so if you instead want to move the originally selected text to a new location, press Ctrl+X (for cut) instead of Ctrl+C (for copy) to delete the text from its original location; then reposition the insertion point and press Ctrl+V to insert the text in its new location.

The ribbon bar's **Clipboard** section contains the typical **Cut**, **Copy**, and **Paste** options in case you don't want to use the keyboard shortcuts.

▶ **NOTE**

You can paste selected text into another Office program or another Windows program that accepts text. The Windows Clipboard is handy for copying and moving data between programs.

Ribbon's Clipboard Section

3 **Copy and Paste Selected Text**

Quick Access Toolbar

1 **Select Text to Work With**

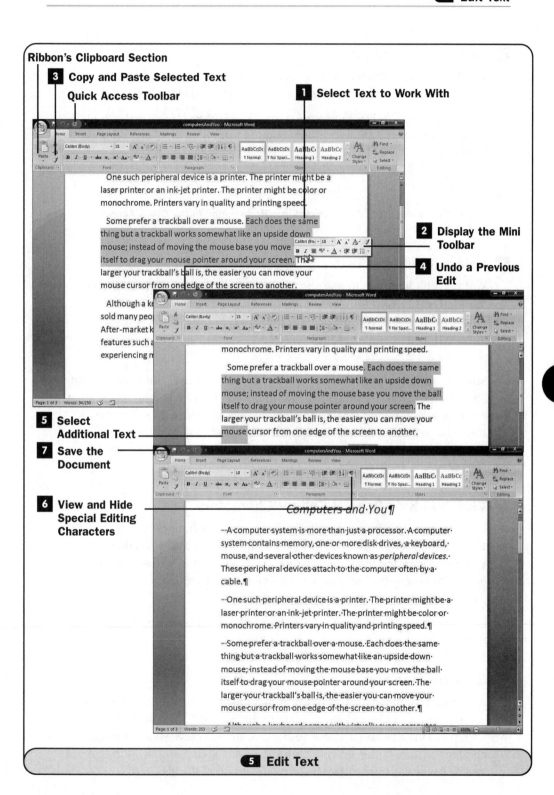

2 **Display the Mini Toolbar**

4 **Undo a Previous Edit**

5 **Select Additional Text**

7 **Save the Document**

6 **View and Hide Special Editing Characters**

4 Undo a Previous Edit

Word's Undo feature undoes your previous edit—whatever that may have been. To invoke it, press Ctrl+Z or select **Undo** from the **Quick Access** toolbar.

Therefore, if you accidentally erase a large block of text, press Ctrl+Z and Word puts the text right back. You can undo just about any edit you make in Word.

▶ TIP

You can redo an undo! Press Ctrl+Y or click the **Redo** button in the **Quick Access** toolbar to reverse the previous Undo you performed.

5 Select Additional Text

Word doesn't limit you to one selection at a time. You can select multiple blocks of text in your document. After you've highlighted to select the first block of text, hold down the Ctrl key and select another block of text. You may do this as often as needed to select all the text you want to work with as a group.

Multiple selections can be useful when you want to make similar edits to different parts of your document. For example, you may be writing about great works of literature and you realize you did not italicize each book's title. Instead of selecting and italicizing each title individually, you can select all the titles and apply italics to them in one step (see **12 Apply Character Formatting**).

6 View and Hide Special Editing Characters

Click the **Show/Hide** button (it looks like a paragraph mark [¶]) on the **Home** ribbon (or press Ctrl+*) to turn on nonprinting characters that show you where paragraph divisions, blank spaces, and other editing elements occur. These nonprinting characters normally don't print, but on the screen they help you see exactly what you're editing.

Click the **Show/Hide** button on the **Home** ribbon (or press Ctrl+*) again to turn off the display of nonprinting characters.

7 Save the Document

After you have edited the text in the document—and periodically while you are editing—you should save your changes to the hard disk. To save the document, click your **Office** button and select **Save**. You can also save your document by clicking the **Save** button on your **Quick Access** toolbar. Word saves the current version of the file, overwriting the previous version of the file.

▶ **TIP**

If you're not sure that you want the current version of the file to overwrite the existing version when you save, choose **File, Save As** instead. Word asks you for a new filename for the current version of the document, saves it under that name, and doesn't touch the original version.

6 **Move Around a Document**	
✔ **BEFORE YOU BEGIN**	→ **SEE ALSO**
2 Create a New Document	**4** Type Text into a Document
3 Open an Existing Document	**5** Edit Text

The faster you can move around a document, the faster you'll get your work done. If most documents consumed less than a screenful of real estate, the capability to move around the document wouldn't be needed. Most documents, however, require far more than a single screen of room. Being able to navigate from place to place becomes second nature quickly because it's a skill needed before you can edit seriously.

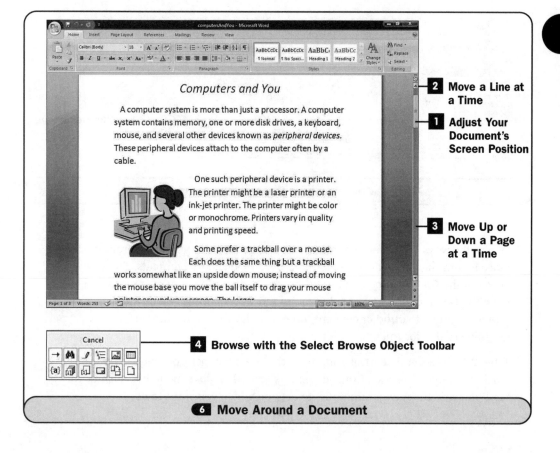

2 Move a Line at a Time

1 Adjust Your Document's Screen Position

3 Move Up or Down a Page at a Time

4 Browse with the Select Browse Object Toolbar

6 Move Around a Document

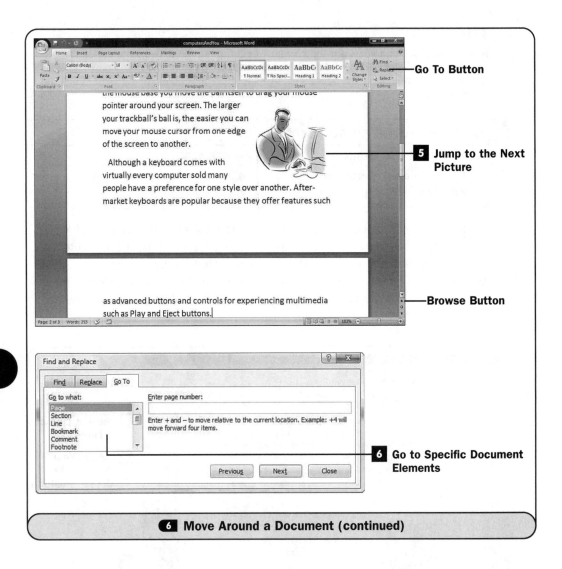

Go To Button

5 Jump to the Next Picture

Browse Button

6 Go to Specific Document Elements

6 Move Around a Document (continued)

One of the ways Word and the other Office programs help you move from place to place is with the **Go To** dialog box and a bevy of keyboard shortcuts. The true power of the **Go To** dialog box really shows when your document is many pages long; the **Go To** dialog box enables you to move from any element, such as a picture or footnote, to another element, no matter how far apart those elements might be in the document.

Table 2.1 lists several keystroke shortcuts that help you get from place to place quickly in Word. The rest of this task shows you other ways available, such as the scrollbars and the navigation pane, to get you where you want to go.

TABLE 2.1   Word Keyboard Navigation Shortcuts

Keyboard Shortcut	Description
F5	Displays the **Go To** dialog box
Shift+Enter	Moves the text cursor to the next line but does not start a new paragraph or insert a paragraph mark
Ctrl+left arrow	Moves the text cursor to the beginning of the word
Ctrl+Shift+left arrow	Moves the text cursor to the left and selects text as it moves by highlighting the text
Ctrl+right arrow	Moves the text cursor to the end of the word
Ctrl+Shift+right arrow	Moves the text cursor to the right and selects text as it moves by highlighting the text
Up arrow	Moves the text cursor up one line at a time
Down arrow	Moves the text cursor down one line at a time
Home	Goes to the beginning of the current line
End	Goes to the end of the current line
Ctrl+Home	Moves the text cursor to the beginning of the document
Ctrl+End	Moves the text cursor to the end of the document
Page Up	Moves up one screen at a time
Page Down	Moves down one screen at a time
Ctrl+Delete	Deletes text to the end of the current word
Ctrl+Backspace	Deletes text to the beginning of the current word

▶ **NOTE**

Word supports a wealth of additional keyboard shortcuts. Table 2.1 lists only the ones that are the most popular or useful for moving around a document. The other Office programs such as PowerPoint support similar keystrokes, so when you learn how to move around in Word, you also learn how to move around in PowerPoint, Excel, and the other Office products.

1 **Adjust Your Document's Screen Position**

When editing your document, drag either the vertical or the horizontal scrollbar to position a different part of your document on the screen.

▶ **NOTE**

Dragging the vertical scrollbar up and down the screen is much faster than paging through a very long document.

2 **Move a Line at a Time**

Click a scrollbar arrow to move one line up or down (or about 5 characters left or right if you click a horizontal scrollbar arrow).

3 Move Up or Down a Page at a Time

Press Page Up or Page Down to move up or down one page at a time.

4 Browse with the Select Browse Object Toolbar

Click the vertical scrollbar's **Browse** button to display the **Select Browse Object** toolbar. From the **Select Browse Object** toolbar, you can jump to the following elements in your document: field, endnote, footnote, comment, section, page, edit, heading, graphic, table. You can also quickly reach the **Find** and **Go To** dialog boxes from the **Select Browse Object** toolbar.

Here's how the **Select Browse Object** toolbar works: When you want to jump to an element in your document, such as a picture, click the vertical scrollbar's **Browse** button to display the **Select Browse Object** toolbar. Select what you want to browse to, such as a graphic (which represents pictures and clip art). When you do, the **Select Browse Object** toolbar disappears but your vertical scrollbar's function changes. The buttons right above and below the scrollbar's Browse button now become **Previous Graphic** and **Next Graphic** buttons.

▶ **NOTE**

6

Obviously, the longer and more complex your document, the more useful the **Select Browse Object** toolbar becomes. For a small document of only a few pages, you can probably locate where you want to go by pressing the Page Up and Page Down keys just as easily as selecting from the **Select Browse Object** toolbar.

5 Jump to the Next Picture

After you display the **Select Browse Object** toolbar and select **Browse by Graphic**, click your vertical scrollbar's **Previous Picture** and **Next Picture** buttons to navigate through your document picture by picture.

As you can see, after you've selected how you want to navigate, the **Select Browse Object** toolbar changes your vertical scrollbar buttons' functions to reflect what you want to move to.

▶ **TIP**

If your scrollbars are not visible, click your **Office** button, click the **Word Options** button, and click the **Advanced** tab to display the scrollbar's display options. You can display one or both of your scrollbars (see **1 Set Word Options**). You may have to scroll to the **Display** section after clicking the **Advanced** tab to see the scrollbar options.

6 Go to Specific Document Elements

Press F5 to open the **Go To** dialog box. The **Go To** dialog box mirrors most of the **Select Browse Object** toolbar's functionality but is more easily accessed from your keyboard than from your mouse clicks.

The **Go To** dialog box enables you to jump to a page, section, line, bookmark, comment, footnote, endnote, field, table, graphic, equation, object, or heading. Depending on the complexity of your document, not all of these elements will be available as a go to location.

Select the element you want to jump to, such as **Page** if you want to jump to a specific page in your document, and type a page number. Press Enter (which automatically selects the **Go To** button), and Word takes you to that page.

---

7 Find and Replace Text

✔ BEFORE YOU BEGIN

3 Open an Existing Document
5 Edit Text
6 Move Around a Document

→ SEE ALSO

12 Apply Character Formatting

Long documents make quickly locating what you need important. Perhaps you need to make changes to some text in a table, or perhaps a caption is wrong on a figure. Word provides text-locating tools that will be familiar to you if you've done similar text-locating tasks in the past.

Of course, along with finding text, you'll sometimes need to replace text you find. For example, you may have written a letter to Kim McDonald and learned that her name was Kim MacDonald before you mailed the letter. With Word's find and replace tools, you can make quick work of changing all the McDonald references to MacDonald throughout the document. Whether the document is 1 page or 100 pages, you'll be able to find and replace text such as this quickly and easily.

▶ NOTE

The **Browse Specific Objects** toolbar (see **6** Move Around a Document) is great for locating generic elements such as pictures and edits within your document, but use the Find and Replace tools, shown in this task, to locate specific text and editing marks within your document.

1 Find Text

Click the **Home** ribbon's **Find** button to display the **Find and Replace** dialog box. You can also press Ctrl+F to display the **Find and Replace** dialog box.

2 Enter Search Text

Type the text you want to find in the **Search for** text box.

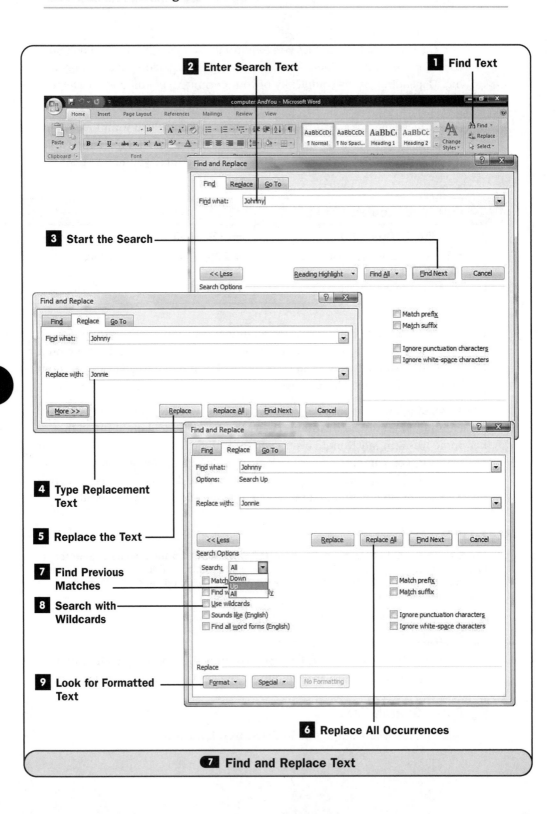

2 Enter Search Text

1 Find Text

3 Start the Search

4 Type Replacement Text

5 Replace the Text

7 Find Previous Matches

8 Search with Wildcards

9 Look for Formatted Text

6 Replace All Occurrences

7 Find and Replace Text

► **TIP**

If you've searched for the same text before, you can click the down arrow to open the **Search for** drop-down list and select the text to search for it again.

3 Start the Search

Click the **Find Next** button. Word searches from the current text cursor's position in the document to the end of the file. If Word finds the text, it highlights it. You may be able to see the highlighted text, but if not, you can move or close the **Find and Replace** dialog box to see the highlighted text. (If you had clicked the **Find All** button instead of **Find**, Word would have highlighted all occurrences of any matching text in the document.)

4 Type Replacement Text

Instead of locating text, if you want Word to replace the found text with something else, click the **Home** ribbon's **Replace** button instead of the **Find** button to display the **Find and Replace** dialog box. You'll see an entry for **Replace With** in the dialog box now.

Type the new text into the **Replace With** text box.

5 Replace the Text

Click the **Replace** button to replace the next occurrence of the found text with your replacement text.

6 Replace All Occurrences

Instead of **Replace** (or after you do a replacement), if you click the **Replace All** button, Word replaces all the matches with your replacement text throughout the document. Such a change is more global and possibly riskier because you may replace text you didn't really want replaced. By clicking **Find** before each **Replace**, you can be sure that the proper text is being replaced, but such a single-occurrence find and replace operation takes a lot of time in a long document.

7 Find Previous Matches

Click **More** and select **Up** before doing a find or replace operation if you want to find or replace from the current text cursor's position *back* to the start of the document.

8 Search with Wildcards

With **More** clicked, click the **Use Wildcards** option if you want to perform a *wildcard search*. Table 2.2 describes some of the more common search expressions you may use in Word and gives an example of each.

7

TABLE 2.2   Search Expressions That Form Advanced Wildcard Searches

Search Expression Character	How Used
?	Represents one and only one character in a search. Therefore, h?s matches *his* and *has* but not *hands*.
*	Represents zero, one, or more characters. Therefore, i*n matches *in*, *i123n*, and *ion*.
<	Represents a search term located at the beginning of a word. Therefore, <door matches *doorknob* but not *outdoor* or *indoor*.
>	Represents a search term located at the end of a word. Therefore, >door matches *outdoor* and *indoor* and *door* but not *doorknob*.
[char]	Requests that a match be made if either one of the search characters inside the brackets is found. Therefore, m[oa]p matches all occurrences of *map* and *mop*.
[charFirst-charLast]	Requests that a match be made on the ascending range of single characters inside the brackets. Therefore, [b-h]oop locates *boop* and *hoop* but not *loop*.
[!charFirst-charLast]	Requests that a match be made on anything except characters that fall in the ascending range of letters. Therefore, [!b-h]oop locates *loop* but not *hoop*. You can negate single letter searches as well; [!w]* ensures that all words are matched except those that begin with the letter *w*.
{#}	Locates a repeating string of characters. Therefore, me{2} matches *meeting* and *meet* but not *meaning* or *met*.
{#,}	Locates a certain number of characters or more. Therefore, me{1,} locates *met* and *meeting*.
@	Locates one or more of a string of characters as did the {#,} wildcard search. Therefore me@ locates *meeting* and *met*, but not *mat*.

▶ **NEW TERM**

Wildcard search—Allows you to use wildcard characters, such as *, to replace characters in a search.

9 Look for Formatted Text

If you want to search only for certain text values that are formatted in a particular way, such as all italicized *McDonalds* but not boldfaced *McDonalds*, you can do so by clicking the **Format** button to display a list of character and paragraph-formatting dialog boxes and selecting the format you want to search for.

For example, to search for the next italicized word in your document, click the **Format** button in the **Find and Replace** dialog box, select **Font**, and click to check **Italic**, and the search or replacement text you enter will find a match only if Word locates matching italicized text.

When you finish finding and replacing all the text for this search session, click the **Find and Replace** dialog box's **Cancel** button to close the dialog box and return to your document's work area.

8	**Check a Document's Spelling and Grammar**	
✔ **BEFORE YOU BEGIN**	→ **SEE ALSO**	
2 Create a New Document	**9** Print a Document	
3 Open an Existing Document		

Word can check your spelling and grammar in two ways:

- All at once, after you've composed or opened a document

- As you type, by highlighting your words with a wavy line under the incorrect ones

▶ **NOTE**

Don't rely solely on Word's spell-checking and grammar capabilities because they don't replace proper proofreading skills. As a good example, consider that Word will find absolutely no misspelled words in the following sentence: *Wee went two the fare too sea the bares.*

If Word flags a word or phrase as incorrect but everything is fine, you'll tell Word to add that word to its spelling dictionary or perhaps to ignore the word or phrase for the rest of the editing session. Word occasionally flags some proper nouns and technical terms as misspelled that are not, and sometimes believes that a sentence is only a fragment when the sentence is grammatically complete.

▶ **TIP**

In addition to spelling and grammar checks, Word can offer synonyms from its online thesaurus.

1 Request a Spelling and Grammar Check

Click the **Review** ribbon tab to display the **Proofing** options. Click **Spelling & Grammar** to check your document's spelling and grammar. F7 is the shortcut key for this.

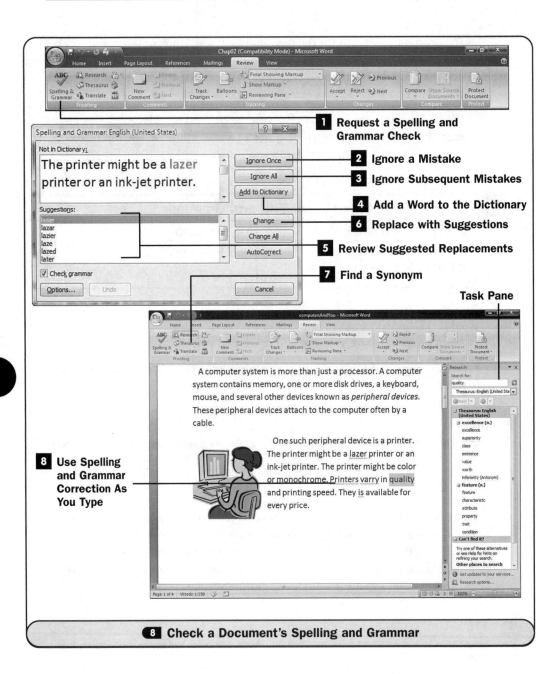

1 Request a Spelling and Grammar Check

2 Ignore a Mistake

3 Ignore Subsequent Mistakes

4 Add a Word to the Dictionary

6 Replace with Suggestions

5 Review Suggested Replacements

7 Find a Synonym

Task Pane

8 Use Spelling and Grammar Correction As You Type

8 Check a Document's Spelling and Grammar

Word begins checking your document, from beginning to end. If it finds a misspelled word, it displays the **Spelling & Grammar** dialog box and highlights the misspelled word in your document.

▶ **TIP**

If you want Word to check your document's spelling but not the grammar, click to uncheck the **Spelling & Grammar** dialog box's option labeled **Check Grammar**.

2 Ignore a Mistake

If Word finds a word that is not really misspelled, click the **Ignore Once** button. Word will ignore the word and continue checking the rest of your document. Proper nouns and abbreviations and technical terms can trigger Word's spell-checker when they are correct.

If Word finds a phrase that it believes is not grammatically correct but that you don't want corrected, click the **Ignore Once** button and Word will ignore the problem and continue checking the rest of your document. Unusual capitalization and writing styles can trigger Word's grammar checker when there is no actual problem.

3 Ignore Subsequent Mistakes

If you often type the abbreviation or other word that's found to be misspelled but really isn't, click the **Ignore All** button and Word will ignore that word in all subsequent spell-checking sessions for that document.

If you want Word to ignore a grammatical problem it might find as it checks the rest of the document, click the **Ignore Rule** button when Word locates the first instance of that grammatical problem.

4 Add a Word to the Dictionary

If Word finds a properly spelled word that it thinks isn't, such as a strange last name, you can add that word to Word's spelling dictionary by clicking the **Add to Dictionary** button. Not only will Word not flag the word as misspelled in the future, but Word will offer the word as a possible correction for subsequent words found to be misspelled that are close to that one.

5 Review Suggested Replacements

If Word finds a word that truly is misspelled, it tries to offer one or more suggestions in the **Suggestions** list box. Usually, the top word that is highlighted is the misspelled word, but you may have to scroll down to locate the proper correction depending on how many close matches Word finds in its spelling

8

dictionary. To replace the misspelled word with its correction, double-click the suggested word you want to replace it with. (You can also click once to select the suggested word and click **Change** to make the replacement. If you click **Change All**, Word locates any and all misspellings that match the current one and replaces all of them with the correction so that you don't have to make the correction manually again.)

If Word locates a grammatical error, it offers advice for correcting the problem. You can accept the suggested correction if Word offers one, or you can click the **Explain** button for further details on the problem. Word's **Explain** button offers surprising depth into whatever grammatical problem you've encountered.

6 Replace with Suggestions

If the top highlighted word is the word to replace the misspelled word with, click the **Replace** button and Word will replace the misspelled word with the selected correction. If the correction is not the top word in the **Suggestions** list box but appears farther down the list, click the correct replacement word and then click the **Replace** button to make the replacement. You can do the same with suggested grammar corrections that Word will often provide upon locating a grammatical problem.

7 Find a Synonym

If you want to see synonyms of any word, select a word and click the **Thesaurus** button to display the **Thesaurus** task pane at the right of your screen. If the task pane offers a more appropriate word than the one you originally typed, click the down arrow that appears as you point to the word in the task pane and select **Insert** to replace your document's original word with that synonym.

▶ TIP

The **Thesaurus** dialog box also appears when you press the Ctrl+F7 keyboard shortcut.

8 Use Spelling and Grammar Correction As You Type

Often you'll see wavy lines appear under words and phrases. Red indicates that you typed a misspelling (or Word thinks you did), and green indicates a possible grammar problem.

Instead of checking a document all at once, many people prefer to see these corrections appear as they type so that they can correct or ignore them then. When you right-click on a word or phrase with a wavy line, Word displays options that correspond to the ones in the **Spelling & Grammar** dialog box from which you can correct the problem. All of the options in the previous steps work when you correct as you type.

▶ **NOTE**

You can turn off Word's automatic spelling checker by changing your **Word Options** dialog box to **Check Spelling as You Type** and **Mark Grammar Errors** options. (See **1** Set Word Options.)

▶ **TIP**

If you find yourself repeating the same spelling mistake regularly, when you right-click over the word to correct it, select **AutoCorrect** and select the correct spelling from the list that appears. The next time you make that same mistake, Word corrects the word automatically without your having to intervene.

---

9 | **Print a Document**

✔ **BEFORE YOU BEGIN**	→ **SEE ALSO**
2 Create a New Document	**10** About the Rulers
3 Open an Existing Document	**14** Set Up Page Formatting
4 Type Text into a Document	

After you're done creating your document, you'll want to print it to paper. Word supports the standard printing options that most Windows programs support. If your document has color charts and you have a color printer, the charts will print just fine. Otherwise, the charts will print in shades of black and gray (and still look fine!).

Be sure to save your document before you print it. Actually, it's a good idea to save your document throughout its editing. (Quickly save your work by clicking the **Save** button on your **Quick Access** toolbar in the upper-left corner of Word.) If your printer jams or the Windows print queue messes up during the printing process (rare, but it can happen) and you haven't saved, you could lose changes you made to the document before you printed it.

1 Request a Preview of Your Printed Document

Click your **Office** button, select **Print**, and select the **Print Preview** option there. (Alt+V is the Office button's shortcut key.)

2 Review a Sample of the Printed Document

Look over the preview of the document to see whether it appears to be properly formatted.

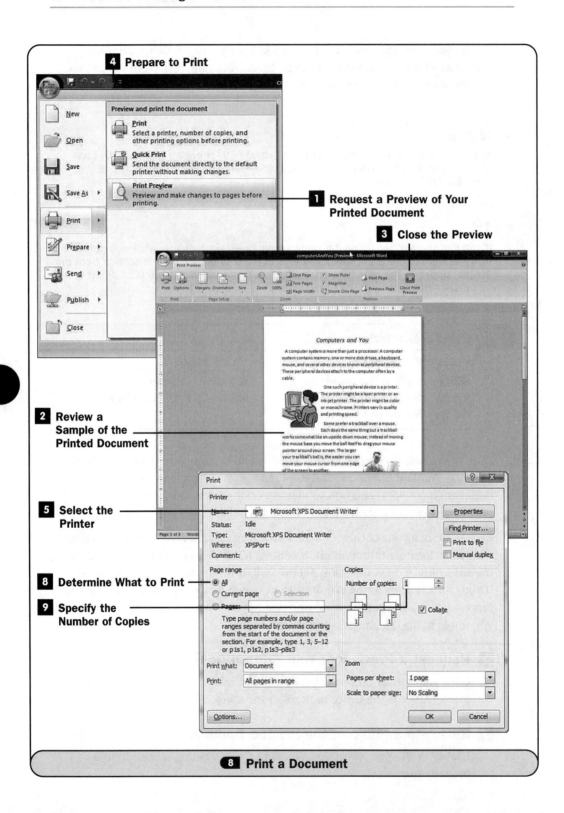

4 Prepare to Print

1 Request a Preview of Your Printed Document

3 Close the Preview

2 Review a Sample of the Printed Document

5 Select the Printer

8 Determine What to Print

9 Specify the Number of Copies

8 Print a Document

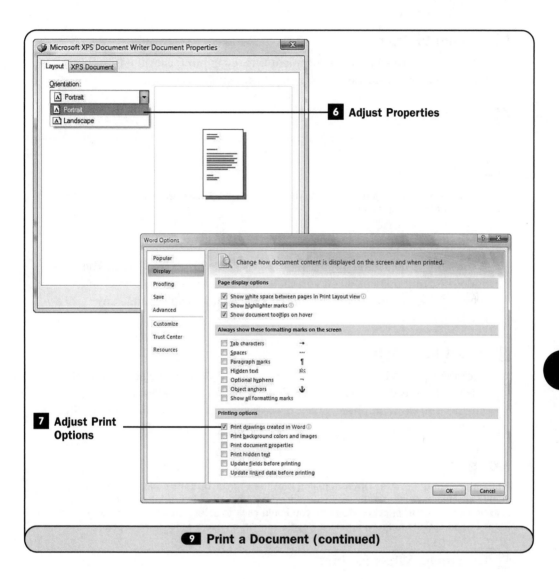

6 **Adjust Properties**

7 **Adjust Print Options**

9 Print a Document (continued)

▶ **TIP**

You can preview two pages at once by clicking the **Two Pages** button in the preview's ribbon area. You may also adjust the zoom-in factor to read more of the text or zoom out to get a bird's-eye view of the document.

8 Close the Preview

After you've previewed what your document will look like printed, click the **Close Print Preview** button (or press Esc). If you need to make further edits to your document, do so from the regular editing window that appears.

4 Prepare to Print

After you're satisfied that the document is ready to print, click the **Print** button on your **Quick Access** toolbar. The **Print** dialog box appears.

5 Select the Printer

Select the printer you want to print to from the **Name** drop-down list.

▶ TIP

If you have a fax modem, you can select your fax from the **Name** drop-down list to send your document to a fax recipient.

6 Adjust Properties

If you want to adjust any printer settings, click the **Properties** button. The dialog box that appears when you click **Properties** varies from printer to printer. Close the printer's **Properties** dialog box after you've made any needed changes.

7 Adjust Print Options

Click the **Options** button to display the **Printer Options** dialog box. From the **Printer Options** dialog box, you can adjust several print settings, such as whether you want graphics, tables, and drawings printed or omitted from the printed document.

▶ NOTE

Although called the **Printer Options** dialog box, the **Printer Options** dialog box is not printer specific but controls the way your document appears when printed. If, for instance, you want to print for a binder, you could click to select the **Left Pages** and **Right Pages** options to leave an extra middle margin on every other printed page.

8 Determine What to Print

Click to select either **All** or **Pages** to designate that you want to print the entire document or only a portion of it. If you click **Pages**, type the page number or a range of page numbers (such as "2–5" or "1–10, 15–25") that you want to print.

9 Specify the Number of Copies

Click the arrow next to the **Number of Copies** option to determine how many copies you want to print.

After you've determined how many pages and copies to print, click the **OK** button to print your document and close the **Print** dialog box.

3

Making Your Words Look Good

IN THIS CHAPTER:

Word adds flair to your documents. It can not only make your words read more accurately with its automatic correction tools, but it makes your writing look better. Word supports character, paragraph, and even complete document formatting.

When you begin learning Word, don't worry about the formatting. Just type your text before formatting it so that you get your thoughts in the document while they are still fresh. After you type your document, you can format its text. Many Word users follow this write-then-format plan throughout their entire careers.

10 | About the Rulers

✔ BEFORE YOU BEGIN	→ SEE ALSO
2 Create a New Document	**11** About Paragraph Breaks and Tabs
4 Type Text into a Document	**13** Apply Paragraph Formatting
	14 Set Up Page Formatting

10

Word has two rulers: the *horizontal ruler* and the *vertical ruler*. Both of these rulers are onscreen guides that display measurement values so that you'll know where on the page your text will appear. For example, if your Word **Options Advanced** tab's measurement **Display** option is set to **Inches** (see **1** **Set Word Options**), the **2** on your horizontal ruler means that all text beneath that ruler's **2** is exactly 2 inches from the left margin.

▶ TIP

Through the **Word Options** window, you can change your onscreen measurements to a different setting, such as from inches to centimeters.

If you don't see the rulers on your screen, click the **View Ruler** button at the top of your vertical scrollbar. If you only see a horizontal ruler across the top of your document but do not see a vertical ruler, click your **Office** button, select **Word Options**, click **Advanced**, and scroll down to the **Display** section. Click to check the **Show Vertical Ruler in Print Layout View** option.

The ruler measurements are relative to the left and right margins.

▶ NEW TERMS

Horizontal ruler—A guide you can display across the top of your document that shows the horizontal position of text and graphics on the page.

Vertical ruler—A guide you can display down the left side of your document that shows the vertical position of text and graphics on the page.

In addition to showing margins and the page width, the horizontal ruler can display these items:

- *Tab stop* (see **11** **About Paragraph Breaks and Tabs**)
- Paragraph *indent* (see **13** **Apply Paragraph Formatting**)
- Columns (see **15** **Create a Multicolumn Newsletter**)

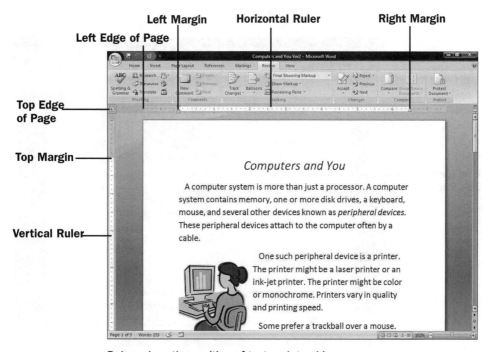

Rulers show the position of text and graphics.

▶ **NEW TERMS**

Tab stop—Controls the horizontal placement of text on a line.

Indent—The space between the left and right page margins and the current paragraph. Word supports several forms of paragraph and line indents.

If you format different paragraphs in your document differently from one another, the ruler will change to reflect those differences. In other words, if the first paragraph has two tab stops and a first-line indent, when you click any-where within that paragraph, the ruler changes to show those tab stops and the first-line indent, as shown in the following figure.

If a subsequent paragraph has a different set of indents, tab stops, and margins, the ruler will show those differences if you click within that paragraph.

The horizontal ruler is so tied to overall page and paragraph formatting that if you double-click the ruler, the **Page Setup** dialog box appears. **14 Set Up Page Formatting** explains how to use Word's Page Setup features.

10

First-Line Indent

Tab Stops

First Line Indented

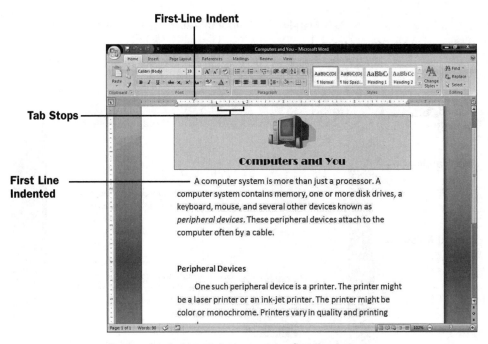

A ruler showing two tab stops and a first-line indent.

Obviously, it's important that you keep in mind that the current horizontal ruler showing at any one time is only reflecting the current paragraph's tab and mar-gin settings. A ruler can reflect each paragraph differently. Only when you select your entire document does the ruler reflect every paragraph in the document. If you have formatted some paragraphs differently from others, the ruler displays only the values (such as the first-line indent perhaps) that are universal to all the selected paragraphs.

The ruler does more than update to reflect the current paragraph's settings. You can use the ruler to change tab, indent, and margin settings without using dialog boxes. Unless pinpoint precision is required, the ruler is actually the best place to make these changes.

For example, click anywhere on the ruler and a tab stop appears at that location. You can drag that tab stop left or right to adjust its position. You can drag any tab stop left or right, even those you applied using the **Paragraph** formatting dialog box. Word supports several kinds of tabs, as you'll see in **11** **About Paragraph Breaks and Tabs**. To change the type of tab you place, first click the tab character box at the left of the ruler to change the type of tab you next place on the ruler.

Click to Change the Type of Tab Stop

Drag to Change the First-Line Indent

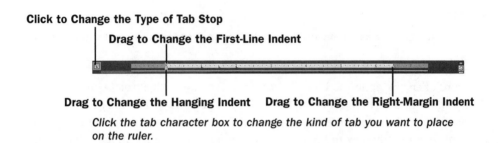

Drag to Change the Hanging Indent   Drag to Change the Right-Margin Indent

Click the tab character box to change the kind of tab you want to place on the ruler.

If you want to increase a paragraph's *left-margin indent*, click in that paragraph to display its horizontal ruler measurement. Then, drag the ruler's left-margin indent character to its new location. After you drag the ruler's left-margin indent character, the paragraph's actual left-margin indent changes to reflect the new setting. To change the *first-line indent*, drag the ruler's first-line indent character to a new location. To change the *right-margin indent*, drag the ruler's right-margin indent character to a new location. To add a *hanging indent*, drag the hanging indent character to the right.

Although the horizontal ruler is constantly linked to individual paragraphs, the page's overall left and right margins also appear on the horizontal ruler. The margins are set off of the gray areas on either end of the ruler. You can change the left or right margin by dragging the ruler's edge of either margin (the position between the gray and the white of the ruler's typing area) left or right.

▶ NEW TERMS

Left-margin indent—An indentation of the left edge of all lines in a paragraph. Increasing the left-margin indent moves the left edge of the paragraph closer to the document's center.

First-line indent—A right indent of the first line in a paragraph in which subsequent lines in the same paragraph align closer to the left margin.

Right-margin indent—An indentation of the right edge of all lines in a paragraph. Increasing the right-margin indent moves the right edge of the paragraph closer to the document's center.

Hanging indent—Occurs when the first line of a paragraph is flush with the left margin but all subsequent lines in that paragraph are shifted to the right.

▶ NOTE

Be careful that you always leave enough room for your printer's required margin. For example, many laser printers will not print less than one-half inch from the edge of the paper, no matter how narrow you attempt to make your margins.

▶ TIP

Click the **Quick Access** toolbar's **Undo** button to undo changes you make to the ruler.

You won't use the vertical ruler as much as the horizontal ruler, which is why Word offers the option to hide the vertical ruler. The vertical ruler can be handy for showing the top and bottom margins on a page as well as the general position on a page where certain elements appear. For example, you can tell from the vertical ruler exactly how many inches down a page a graphics image will appear when printed.

You can drag these margins to a different location, and when you're satisfied with the new margin settings, you can again hide the vertical ruler to give yourself more editing area on the screen.

---

11 | **About Paragraph Breaks and Tabs**

✔ **BEFORE YOU BEGIN**

1 Set Word Options
4 Type Text into a Document
10 About the Rulers

→ **SEE ALSO**

13 Apply Paragraph Formatting

Understanding exactly how Word treats paragraphs is the first step in understanding Word's formatting capabilities. Knowing exactly where a paragraph begins and ends is not always obvious. For example, in the next figure, it appears that the document has three paragraphs.

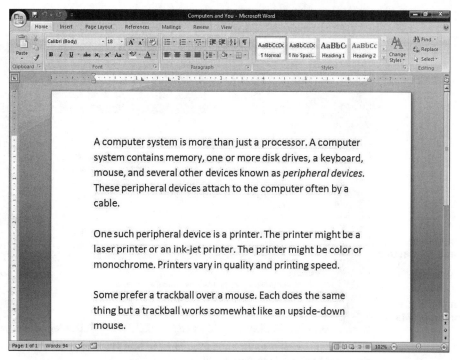

Seeing isn't always believing—how many paragraphs are in this document?

▶ **NOTE**

Word's nonprinting characters enable you to see the hidden elements that Word uses to determine where certain formatting should begin and end (see **4 Type Text into a Document**).

If you glance at the screen or print the document, three paragraphs certainly appear to be there. As far as your readers are concerned, the document does contain three paragraphs. Nevertheless, as far as Word is concerned, this particular document contains only a single paragraph! Clicking the **Nonprinting Characters** button on this particular document shows nonprinting characters, which reveal that this document contains only a single paragraph, as the following figure shows.

Show/Hide Nonprinting Characters

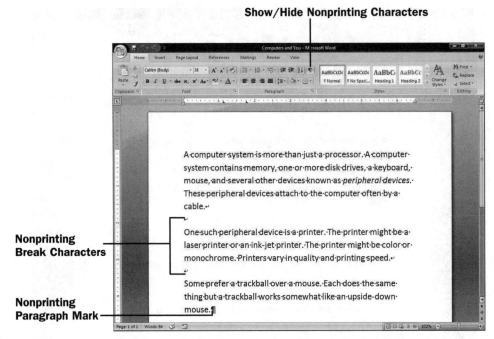

Nonprinting Break Characters

Nonprinting Paragraph Mark

11

Only one paragraph mark appears, meaning that Word views the entire document as one long paragraph.

You can press Shift+Enter to insert a soft return (as opposed to a hard return that occurs when you press Enter), end one line, and start another without actually initiating a new paragraph. A newline nonprinting character appears when you turn on nonprinting characters to indicate that a paragraph break has not occurred but only an early line break. Without the nonprinting characters appearing, it looks as though the document will have multiple paragraphs.

▶ **TIP**

You'll run across reasons for keeping multiple groups of text broken with newline characters instead of paragraph marks, although you'll certainly press Enter at the end of most paragraphs to generate a normal paragraph break. One advantage of keeping an entire **section** in one long paragraph is if that you make a paragraph adjustment to the text later, your change applies to all the text and you won't have to apply the change multiple times over multiple paragraphs. Of course, to change the formatting of multiple paragraphs, you only need to select all the paragraphs before making the format change.

▶ **NEW TERM**

Section—A block of document text that contains its own formatting, including possible headers and footers, that will differ from surrounding text.

You'll generally never create an entire document without paragraph breaks. If you are typing a section of text that is more than one paragraph, and you want to format that section differently from the rest of the document, one way to do so is to place the text together in one paragraph. You'll press Shift+Enter to give the lines the look of multiple paragraphs, but Word will see them as being only one. Then, any paragraph formatting you apply to the text—either from the ruler (see **10 About the Rulers**) or from the **Paragraph** formatting dialog box (see **13 Apply Paragraph Formatting**)—applies to all the text in that section. You won't have to format more than one paragraph individually.

This multiparagraph trick using Shift+Enter is wonderful to remember for the times when you have a couple or more paragraphs that you may need to adjust formatting for later. If, however, you have several paragraphs to format differently from surrounding text, or even a page or more of text, you may be better off creating a new section for that text. You can then easily change the formatting of all the paragraphs in that section without affecting the surrounding text. **14 Set Up Page Formatting** discusses sections in more detail.

You'll find tab stops to be extremely useful in documents. Tab stops enable you to align values consistently across multiple lines. Also, when you use a tab stop, you don't have to press the spacebar many times to move to the right on a line. Tab stops enable you to start paragraphs with an indented first line. Word supports five kinds of tab stops, as detailed in Table 3.1.

11

TABLE 3.1 Word's Five Tab Stops

Tab Stop	Description
Left tab	Sets the start of text that continues to the right of the tab stop as you type.
Right tab	Sets the start of text that continues to the left of the tab stop as you type. In other words, as you type, the text moves left toward the left margin, against the tab stop. A right tab stop is useful for page or chapter numbers in a list because it ensures that the right edges of the numbers will align with each other.
Bar tab	Inserts a vertical bar at the tab position but does not adjust the position of any text. (Not to be confused with the invoice you get at Cheers before paying.)
Decimal tab	Ensures that a column of numbers aligns at their decimal point. After you press Tab, the insertion point jumps to that tab stop and the numeric values you then type will position themselves so that the decimal points all align vertically.
Center tab	Sets the start of text and continuously adjusts the text so that what you type remains centered on the stop's location.

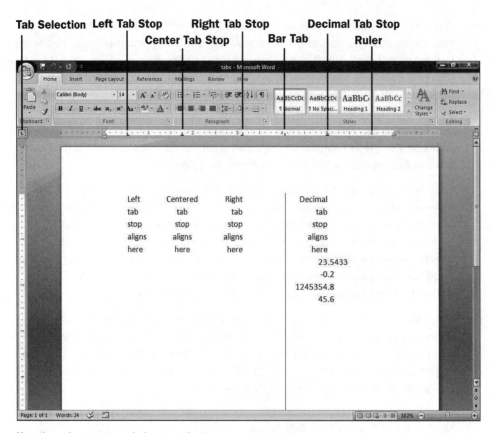

Use the ruler to set and change tab stops.

To set a tab stop, use either the ruler or the **Tab** dialog box. You can click the **Tab** selection button on the ruler to select which tab stop you want to place. Every time you click the **Tab** selection button, the symbol changes to a different kind of tab stop. When you then click anywhere on the ruler, that kind of tab appears on the ruler where you click.

To delete any tab stop, drag it down from the ruler and Word removes the tab stop from that location.

To use the **Tab** dialog box, double-click the ruler at any tab stop or select **Format**, **Paragraph** to display the **Paragraph** dialog box. Click the **Tabs** tab to display the **Tabs** page.

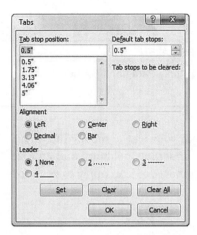

The Tabs page enables you to set tabs for the current paragraph.

Table 3.2 describes each of the options in the **Tabs** page.

TABLE 3.2   The Tabs Page Options

Option	Description
Tab stop position	Enables you to enter individual measurement values, such as 0.25", to represent one-fourth of an inch. After you type a value, click **Set** to add that value to the list of tab settings. To clear an existing tab stop, select the value and click **Clear**. Click **Clear All** to clear the entire tab stop list.
Alignment	Determines the type of tab stop (such as a left tab stop) you want to place.
Default tab stops	If you set no specific tab stops, the measurement here determines how far forward your text insertion point moves forward every time you press Tab.
Leader	Sets the leading characters you want to appear, if any, in the gap left by pressing Tab. The fill character forms a path for the eye to follow across the page within a tab stop. For example, a fill of dotted lines often connects goods to their corresponding prices in a price list.

12   **Apply Character Formatting**

✔ BEFORE YOU BEGIN	→ SEE ALSO
4 Type Text into a Document **5** Edit Text	**13** Apply Paragraph Formatting

When you want to make a point, you can format your text to modify the way it looks. Common character formatting styles are underline, boldface, and italicized text. Word offers several additional character formats you can apply to your document's text.

▶ **NOTE**

Although these are called *character* formats, you can as easily apply them to multiple characters, paragraphs, and even complete documents as to single characters. Word applies character formats to any text you select.

One of the most common character formats you can apply is to change the **typeface** (loosely called a **font** in general discussions) in your document. The typeface determines the way your characters look, whether artsy or elegant. Fonts have names, such as Courier and Times New Roman. The size of a font is measured in **points**. As a rule of thumb, a 10- or 12-point size is standard and readable for most word-processed documents.

▶ **NEW TERMS**

Typeface—A character design that determines the style of how your characters look.

Font—Loosely used as another name for typeface.

Point—Approximately 1/72 of an inch.

As you type and move the insertion point, Word displays the current font name and size on the **Object** bar, as well as showing whether the current character is boldfaced, italicized, or underlined. Word also enables you to change the color of your text.

When you're using character formatting, express but don't impress. Too many different kinds of characters make your documents look busy and distract the reader from your message.

1 **Select the Text**

When you want to format characters, select the characters first. You can select a single character, an entire word, a sentence, a paragraph, or multiple paragraphs. Whatever text you select before applying a format is the text that will take on the character formatting you apply.

When you select text with your mouse, Word displays the mini toolbar (see **5 Edit Text**). Most of the common character formats are available on the mini toolbar, which makes quick formatting changes simple and quick. Just click a button, such as the **Bold** button, and Word applies boldface to your selected text.

You can also apply a character format to text before you type it. Instead of selecting text first, pick a character format and then type the text. The text you type will have those character format attributes.

2 Choose a Format

Click the **Boldface, Italics,** or **Underline** button on the **Font** section of your **Home** ribbon to apply any of those formats. You can click two or all three to combine the character styles. Other formats appear on the ribbon's **Font** section, including strikethrough, subscript, superscript, and color.

▶ TIP

Ctrl+B, Ctrl+I, and Ctrl+U are all shortcut keys to apply boldface, italics, and underlining.

12

3 Select a Font

To change a selected text's font (or text that you're about to type), click the drop-down arrow to the right of the ribbon's **Font Name** box and drag your mouse through the font names. As you do, your selected text will change to reflect that font, showing you exactly what your selected text will look like if you stop at that font name. (This live font preview was never before available in Word until Office 2007.)

After you click to select a new font, your selected text will change to that font.

4 Change the Point Size

To choose a new point size for the selected text, click the drop-down arrow to the right of the **Point Size** list. You'll also see a live preview of the font size change if you selected text before changing the point size. When you click to select a size, your selected font will change to that size.

You can also click the **Grow Font** and **Shrink Font** buttons to the right of the **Font Size** list box to increase or decrease selected font sizes by one point each time you click the button.

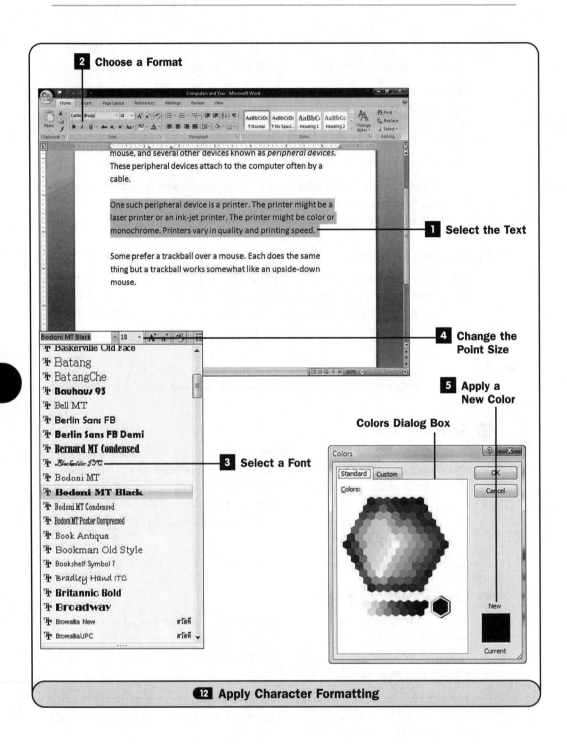

2 Choose a Format

1 Select the Text

4 Change the Point Size

5 Apply a New Color

Colors Dialog Box

3 Select a Font

12 Apply Character Formatting

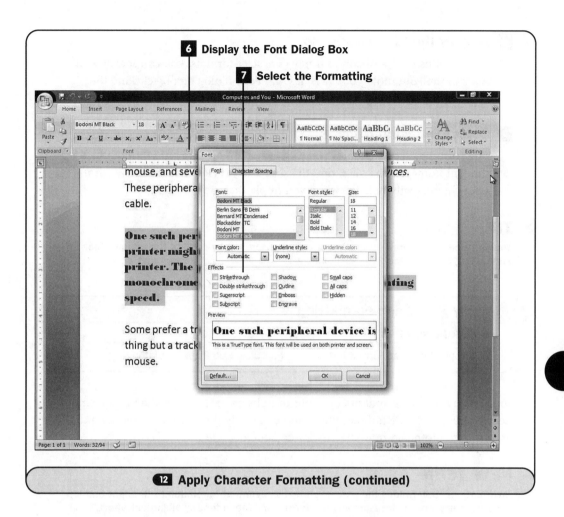

5 Apply a New Color

To change the color of selected text (or text you're about to type), click the **Font Color** button on the ribbon. A **Colors** dialog box showing a *palette* appears if you want to select a color that doesn't show on the drop-down color choice. Click a color on the palette to change your selected text to that color. You can change the background color as well by selecting from the **Text Highlight Color** tool on your ribbon's **Font** section.

▶ **NEW TERM**

Palette—A collection of colors from which you can choose.

6 Display the Font Dialog Box

Instead of using the ribbon to apply character formats, you can set such formats in the **Font** dialog box. Display the **Font** dialog box by clicking the **Font Dialog** button at the lower-right corner of your ribbon's **Font** section.

7 Select the Formatting

The **Font** dialog box enables you to select common character formats such as the font name, bold, italics, and the size. The **Preview** section shows what your changes will look like when you apply them to your text.

▶ **TIP**

You can clear all the font formatting of any selected text by clicking the ribbon's **Clear Formatting** button in the **Font** section.

---

13 Apply Paragraph Formatting

✔ BEFORE YOU BEGIN	→ SEE ALSO
12 Apply Character Formatting	**14** Set Up Page Formatting

You can change the format of entire paragraphs of text, such as the line spacing, *justification*, and indentation of text. You can apply that format to selected paragraphs or to all the paragraphs in your document.

▶ **NEW TERM**

Justification—Determines the paragraph text's alignment in relation to the right and left margins. Many word processors use the term *justification* for any alignment effect, such as right, center, and left justification.

One of the most common ways to format a paragraph is to justify it. Word supports these justification options:

- **Left justification**—Aligns (makes even) text with the left margin. Personal and business letters are often left-justified. The right margin is *ragged*.

- **Center justification**—Centers text between the left and right margins. Titles and letterheads are often centered atop a document.

- **Right justification**—Aligns text with the right margin, and the left margin's text is not ragged.

- **Full justification**—Aligns text with both the left and the right margins. Newspaper and magazine columns are usually fully justified; the text aligns with the left and right margins evenly.

▶ **NEW TERM**

Ragged—A paragraph's text ends wherever on the line it naturally ends, instead of align-
ing down a straight edge.

Word provides many additional ways to format your paragraphs, such as the
capability to put a border around them and indent the first lines.

1 Select the Text

Select the text you want to format. As **11 About Paragraph Breaks and Tabs**
explains, Word considers all text up to the next nonprinting paragraph symbol to be one paragraph. If you apply a paragraph format to any part of a
paragraph, the entire paragraph changes to reflect the new format. You can
format multiple paragraphs at once by selecting multiple paragraphs before
changing the format.

2 Change the Justification

After you've selected the text you want to format, you may change the paragraph's justification by clicking the **Align Left**, **Center**, **Align Right**, or **Justify**
button on the **Home** ribbon. As soon as you click the button, Word changes
the selected paragraph's justification to reflect the change.

13

3 Change the Indentation

If you want to indent the entire selected paragraph to the right, click the
Home ribbon's **Increase Indent** button. For each click of the **Increase Indent**
button, the paragraph shifts to the right one-half inch. After you indent using
the **Increase Indent** button, the **Decrease Indent** button appears so that you
can move the indentation back half an inch. (Of course, your **Quick Access**
toolbar's **Undo** button also undoes any indentations you make.)

▶ **TIP**

Remember that you can make more precise paragraph indentations by dragging the
ruler's **Left Indent** or **Right Indent** buttons.

4 Select a First-Line Indent

Drag the ruler's **First Line Indent** button to the right to indent only the first
line of the selected paragraphs. Adding a first-line indent ensures that your
paragraphs have their initial lines indented to the right without your having
to press Tab manually each time you begin a new paragraph.

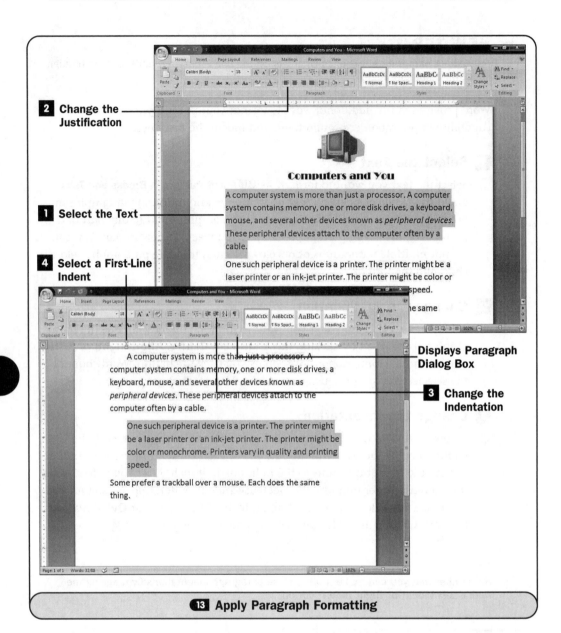

2 Change the Justification

1 Select the Text

4 Select a First-Line Indent

Displays Paragraph Dialog Box

3 Change the Indentation

13

13 Apply Paragraph Formatting

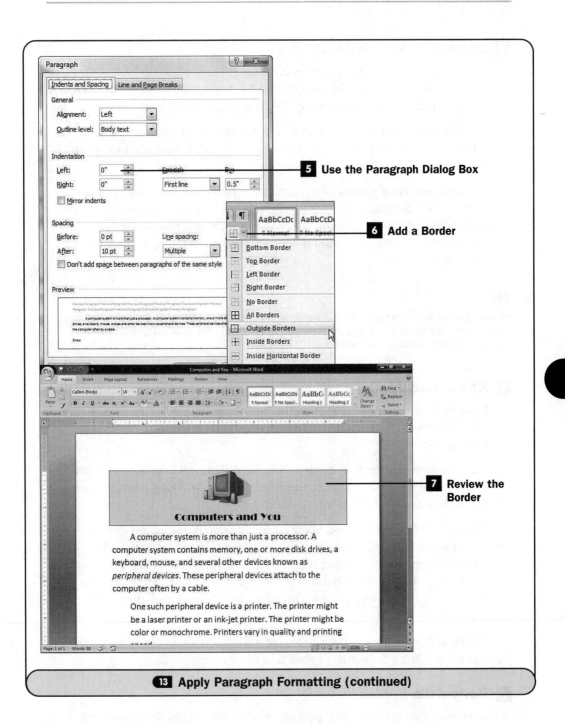

5 Use the Paragraph Dialog Box

6 Add a Border

7 Review the Border

13

5   Use the Paragraph Dialog Box

All of Word's paragraph-formatting commands are available from the **Paragraph** dialog box. Click the arrow in the lower-right corner of the ribbon's **Paragraph** section to display the **Paragraph** dialog box.

The **Paragraph** dialog box's **Indents and Spacing** page enables you to set precise indents as well as specify alignment and the amount of blank space that is to appear between your paragraphs.

The **Line and Page Breaks** page enables you to set automatic hyphenation so that Word can insert hyphens as needed to make long words wrap better at the end of a line. In addition, you can control how a page begins and ends by specifying whether you want a page break to occur in the middle of a paragraph or before.

▶ TIP

As you change values throughout the **Paragraph** dialog box, the **Preview** section displays a thumbnail image that changes to show you what effect your new paragraph format will have on the selected paragraphs.

13

6   Add a Border

Click the right arrow to the right of the **Bottom Border** button to display your border options. Click one of the options to add a border around your selected text.

Word offers several kinds of borders. You can display a border around a paragraph (useful to call attention to important text), as well as put a border on two sides or only one side of selected text.

When you select **Borders and Shading** from the drop-down list, Word displays the **Borders and Shading** dialog box from which you control all aspects of bordering, including the border's width and color. Click the **Shading** tab to add shading inside the bordered text. Your shading can be a color or a shade of gray, and you can adjust how light or dark the shading appears.

The **Page Border** tab enables you to add a border around your entire page instead of putting the border around selected text only.

7   Review the Border

After you've set up a bordered paragraph, click **OK** to close the **Paragraph** dialog box and review the bordered paragraph to ensure that you've got the right effect. Remember to reserve your use of borders, shadowing, and the other special effects for those times when you want to emphasize a title or a statement. Don't overdo the use of special formats. Your document can look too busy with too many formats, making it difficult to read.

---

14   Set Up Page Formatting

✔ **BEFORE YOU BEGIN**	→ **SEE ALSO**
5 Edit Text	**15** Create a Multicolumn Newsletter
12 Apply Character Formatting	
13 Apply Paragraph Formatting	

You will often need to make format changes to your entire document. Perhaps you want to change the margins that Word uses when you print your document. You may want to add a background color or even put a border around the document.

The **Page Layout** ribbon contains Word options that enable you to modify your document's format. Any changes you make apply to all pages in your document.

► **TIP**

If your document is divided into multiple sections, page formatting changes apply only to the current section unless you select your entire document, with Ctrl+A, before modifying the page format.

If you want to start a new section, as you might do if you want to format several pages within a document differently from surrounding pages, click to place the insertion point at the position of the new section. Click the down arrow to the right of the **Page Layout** ribbon's **Breaks** section and select from the available **Section Breaks** options. Any page formatting that you apply to the section stays in that section.

To end the current page and begin a new one, as you might do at the end of a chapter, you can use the **Page Layout** ribbon to insert a new page, but most find pressing Ctrl+Enter to be far easier.

1   Display the Page Options

Select the **Page Layout** ribbon to see your page-formatting options. From this ribbon, you can format your themes (see **16 About Styles, Themes, and Templates**), set margins, insert page and section breaks, add line numbers (useful especially in the legal industry), add background colors and watermarks (see **39 Add a Watermark**), and adjust the entire document's indentation and spacing.

14

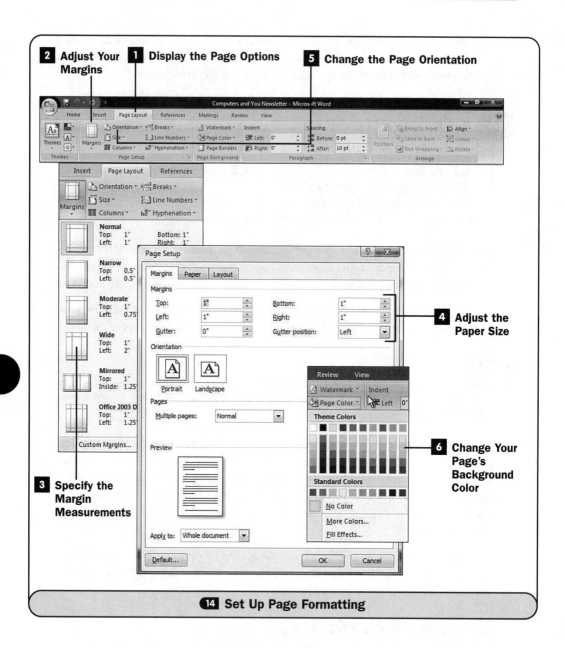

2 Adjust Your Margins

1 Display the Page Options

5 Change the Page Orientation

4 Adjust the Paper Size

6 Change Your Page's Background Color

3 Specify the Margin Measurements

14 Set Up Page Formatting

▶ **TIP**

As with character formats, don't overuse background colors. You should use a colored stationary in your printer for best effect if you want to print on a colored background.

2 Adjust Your Margins

Word's live preview feature makes changing margins a breeze. Click the down arrow under the **Page Layout** ribbon's **Margin** section and select from the several available margin settings that appear. Word offers common settings, and you'll usually find one you want to use.

3 Specify the Margin Measurements

If the ribbon's provided margin options aren't to your liking, select **Custom Margins** to display the **Page Setup** dialog box. Here, you can enter precise margin settings for each margin, as well as adjust additional page settings such as the orientation.

4 Adjust the Paper Size

When you change the type of paper you use in your printer, such as going from letter size to legal, you'll need to select the proper **Size** option, such as **Legal**, from the **Size** list. If you use a nonstandard paper size, one that is not letter, legal, or one of the other options in the **Size** list, click **More Paper Sizes** to display the **Page Setup** dialog box's **Paper** page.

▶ **TIP**

The **Size** list contains common envelope sizes for when you want to print addresses and return addresses from your printer.

5 Change the Page Orientation

You also may want to change the orientation of your printed page from *portrait* to *landscape*. Use the ribbon's **Orientation** button to select the proper orientation for your paper.

▶ **NEW TERMS**

Portrait—Printed across the narrow edge, as you might do for a letter.

Landscape—Printed across the long edge, as you might do for a wide report.

6 Change Your Page's Background Color

Click the ribbon's **Page Color** button to add a background color to your page. Although you may want to use colored paper for extensive coloring, you might want to highlight a report page that appears in your document with a light background color.

15 Create a Multicolumn Newsletter

✔ BEFORE YOU BEGIN	→ SEE ALSO
10 About the Rulers	**16** About Styles, Themes, and
13 Apply Paragraph Formatting	Templates

When you want to create newspaper-style columns—such as those that appear in newsletters and brochures—configure Word to format your text with multiple columns. You can assign multiple columns to the entire document or only to sections. By applying multiple columns to certain sections, you'll be able to span a headline across the top of two or three columns of text underneath; the headline resides in a single-column section while the news beneath resides in a multi-column section.

▶ **TIP**

Generally, you should type your document's text before breaking the document into multiple columns.

15

1 Type Your Document

Create your initial document without worrying about column placement. Type your headline and other text using Word's default styles and formats. Feel free to add graphics and borders to spruce up your headline.

▶ **TIP**

If you routinely write a newsletter or another multicolumned document, you may want to create a template that contains your headline and column layout and then apply that template to create each issue. For more, see **16** About Styles, Themes, and Templates.

2 Format Your Headline

Change your headline's format to match the style you want your newsletter to take on. Not all multicolumn documents have headlines across the top of the columns, but many do.

3 Select the Text for the Columns

Select all the text that will be converted to multiple columns. This generally begins immediately following your headline.

▶ **TIP**

Click the **Home** ribbon's **Show/Hide** button to display nonprinting characters to ensure that you don't select any part of the headline. Start selecting following the headline's final nonprinting paragraph character, which will typically be a paragraph mark.

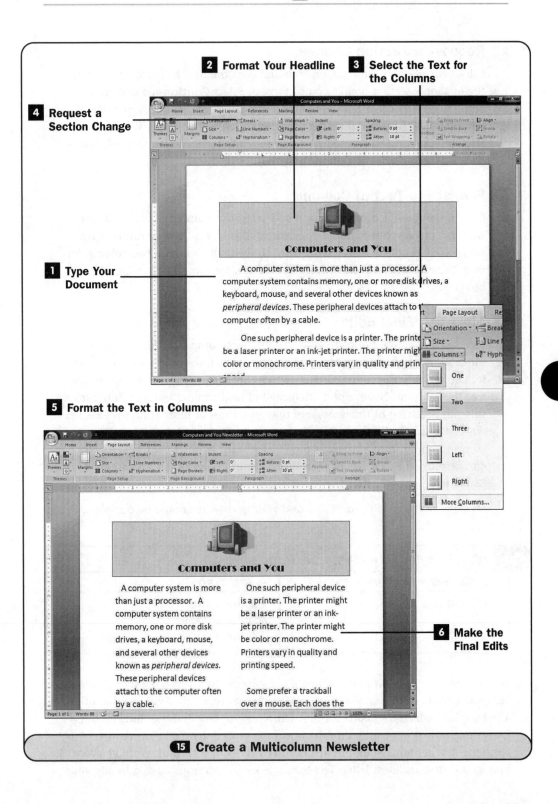

2 Format Your Headline

3 Select the Text for the Columns

4 Request a Section Change

1 Type Your Document

5 Format the Text in Columns

6 Make the Final Edits

15 Create a Multicolumn Newsletter

4 Request a Section Change

Click your ribbon's **Page Layout** tab and click the **Breaks** button to display the available section breaks you can insert. Select **Continuous** to convert your selected text to a new section and make it reside on the same page as your headline (instead of starting the section on a new page). Word adds **Section Break (Continuous)** to your nonprinting characters; this will disappear when you hide the nonprinting characters.

5 Format the Text in Columns

Click the ribbon's **Columns** button and select the number of columns you want to convert your text to. For example, if you want two columns of text under your headline, select **Two**. Word converts the text to a two-column format. Because you converted this text to a new section, the headline will not be affected.

6 Make the Final Edits

After your document appears in columns, you'll almost certainly need to make some final adjustments. For example, with three or more columns, the text becomes lumpy with too many spaces between the words if you've justified the columns. Newspapers often use full justification, but they suffer from this extra spacing at times. Most of the time, three or more columns look best when you left-justify them. Also, subheadings that you formatted before converting to multiple columns may be too large in their columns, so you can decrease the font size of such subheadings (see **12 Apply Character Formatting**).

Hide the nonprinting characters, and your newsletter should be complete.

16 About Styles, Themes, and Templates

✔ BEFORE YOU BEGIN	→ SEE ALSO
5 Edit Text	**17** Use a Style
	18 Use a Theme
	19 Use a Template

You can begin with a *template* to create a document that has a prearranged look. Templates are useful when you have a form, for example, that you need to fill in. The template will be the blank form. A template can be anything that contains formatting or text or graphics that you want to reuse later. You can create a template that contains your letterhead and then begin with that template every time you write a business letter. The template keeps you from having to add your letterhead to the top of the document every time you write a letter, as you'd have to do if you began with a blank document.

A *theme* is a document-wide set of formats that complement one another. Themes include colors, fonts, and even lines and borders when appropriate. Suppose you sell two kinds of items on eBay: MP3 players and antiques. When you write a monthly newsletter that you send to your former buyers, you might want to use a modern theme for the MP3 buyers and a more traditional theme for your antiques clients. It doesn't matter what your document says; the theme affects the overall look of your document.

You can apply a *style* to text within any document. For example, if you routinely use italicized, boldfaced text that is indented from surrounding paragraphs as you might do with a warning message that you add to documents you often write, a style enables you to apply that formatting before you type the warning or after you've completed typing it.

By using templates, themes, and styles, you reduce the amount of work you have to do to create a document.

▶ NEW TERMS

16

Template—A predefined document with styles and other formatting, such as columns and tables, that forms a model for new documents.

Themes—Preset formatting choices that include fonts, colors, margins, and possibly extra elements such as borders.

Style—A set of character and paragraph formats you can apply to text to change that text's format details.

▶ NOTE

In reality, you always use a template when you create new Word documents. Word uses a default template named `Normal.dot` unless you specify another template. The font and margin settings offered when you create a new document come from this default template. All templates have the filename extension `.dot`.

Themes are associated with entire documents. Styles are usually associated with groups of text within a document. A template is to an entire document what a style is to selected text. When creating a document that's to look like another that you often create, such as a fax letter that requires special formatting, you can elect to use a fax template you've already set up with the To:, From:, and Cover Page Note fields already placed where they belong, and you only need to fill in the details. Changing the theme of the fax document does not affect any of the words or layout of the fax document, but only the colors, fonts, and other formatting elements.

▶ **NOTE**

Given that a theme is not related in any way to your document's contents, all Office applications can share themes. If you create or standardize on a theme in Word, you can apply that theme to PowerPoint and Excel as well so that all your documents share the same overall feel. The theme is the message feeling you want to portray.

It's important to remember that a template is a model for a document. A style is often a model for smaller blocks of text, usually paragraphs. A template may contain several styles. If you want to use a style that's available to your current document or template, you can easily select that style and apply it to existing paragraphs or text you're about to type.

Word offers several preset styles you can apply to text in your document, or you can create your own. You can see the predefined styles by clicking the down arrow to the right of the **Styles** section of your **Home** ribbon.

Word supplies several predefined styles.

▶ **TIP**

Although you can use the same specific themes across Office applications, you cannot use the same styles or templates, given that the Office programs work with different kinds of documents. Nevertheless, the other Office products do support styles and templates. Learning the mechanics of Word's styles and templates prepares you to understand how to create and work with styles and templates in those other applications.

When you want to use a template, you'll click the Office button and select from one of the templates presented to you there.

---

17   **Use a Style**

✔ BEFORE YOU BEGIN	→ SEE ALSO
5 Edit Text	**18** Use a Theme
16 About Styles, Themes, and Templates	**19** Use a Template

Using a style is simple. You can apply a style to selected text to format that text with the style's character and paragraph formatting. Word comes with several styles, and you can add your own. Applying a preexisting style is far easier than formatting text repeatedly with the same formatting characteristics.

Suppose that you routinely write résumés for other people. You might develop three separate sets of character and paragraph formats that work well, respectively, for the title of a résumé and an applicant's personal information and work history. Instead of defining each of these formats every time you create a résumé, you can format a paragraph with each style and store the styles under their own names (such as **Résumé Title**, **Résumé Personal**, and **Résumé Work**). The next time you write a résumé, you need only to select a style, such as Résumé Title, before typing the title. When you then type the title, the title looks the way you want it to look without your having to designate a character or paragraph format.

You can easily apply a style to selected text by clicking to select the style you want to apply from the list of styles. Word supplies styles, and over time, you will add your own.

▶ **TIP**

You can create styles from scratch by formatting selected text to match the style you want to define and then saving that formatting as a style. In subsequent editing sessions, that new style will be included among the styles from which you can choose.

1 **Select the Text for the Style**

When you want to apply a predefined style to text, first select the text. Most of the time you'll select a paragraph to format with a style, so if nonprinting characters are showing, be sure to include the paragraph mark when you select the text if you want the style to apply to the entire paragraph. The format of the text will completely change depending on which style you apply, but the text itself will not change.

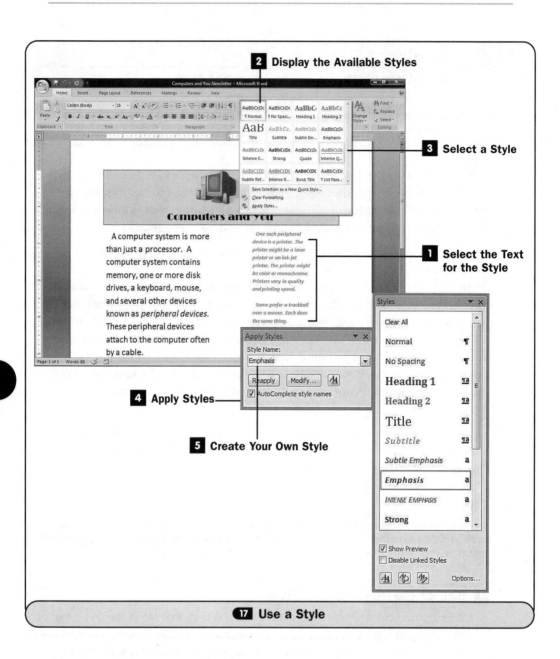

17 Use a Style

2 Display the Available Styles

Point to one of the three styles on your **Home** ribbon to see how those styles will format your selected text. As you point to each style, Word's live preview changes the selected text to reflect the current style.

Click the down arrow to the right of the three styles to display the collection of styles already defined.

3 Select a Style

Click to select the style you want to apply to your selected text. Your text changes to reflect the style's formatting characteristics.

If you want to try a different style, select another from the **Styles** section of your **Home** ribbon.

4 Apply Styles

Word names each style that it supplies, and you will do the same when you create new styles. To select a style by name, select **Apply Styles** from the list of styles that appear in the **Styles** area of your ribbon. The **Apply Styles** dialog box appears, from which you can select a style by name. When you select a style, your selected text changes to that style.

Click the **Styles** button inside the **Apply Styles** dialog box to display the styles in a list from which you can choose. Click the **Show Preview** button to see what each style looks like inside the **Styles** window.

▶ **TIP**

Ctrl+Shift+S is the shortcut keystroke for displaying the **Apply Styles** dialog box. At first, the shortcut keystroke might see awkward, but it's far simpler than selecting from the ribbon to get to the **Apply Styles** dialog box.

17

5 Create Your Own Style

You can easily create your own styles. You'll add styles to Word by example. Format text to match a style you want to create, and then tell Word to create a new style based on that formatted text.

To add a new paragraph style, for example, format and then select an entire paragraph (including its paragraph mark if nonprinting characters are showing). Display the **Apply Styles** dialog box (Ctrl+Shift+S). Type a new name in the **Apply Styles** dialog box in the text box labeled **Style Name**, and click **New**. Word adds the style to its collection. The next time you display your **Apply Styles** dialog box, your new style will appear under the name you gave it.

18   Use a Theme

✔ BEFORE YOU BEGIN	→ SEE ALSO
5 Edit Text	**19** Use a Template
16 About Styles, Themes, and Templates	
17 Use a Style	

When your document takes on the characteristics of a certain theme, the colors, format, pagination, and overall look and feel adhere to that theme's standards. Themes apply to your entire document, and you can implement the same theme across all your Office applications.

▶ **TIP**

If you design a theme that matches your company brand colors, logo style, and approved typestyles, and then you apply that theme to all your Office documents including Word documents and Excel worksheets and PowerPoint presentations, you'll help solidify your company's brand recognition for all who see any document produced by your company.

18

Microsoft provides themes with Office and also offers several themes online. In addition, you can design and save your own themes. Somewhere out there is probably a theme that's right for you. If you locate a theme that isn't quite what you want, but close, you can apply that theme, modify it to your liking, and then save the theme and reuse it afterward.

1 Apply a Built-In Theme

Open the document you want to apply a theme to. You can apply a theme to a new, blank document, but you can see the applied theme's effects far better if you apply a theme to a document you've already created.

Click to display your **Page Layout** ribbon, and then click the **Themes** button. Word displays a scrolling list of built-in, supplied themes. As you point to the various themes, your document's preview changes to reflect what each theme would look like if applied to your document.

You can click the **Search Office Online** link to see what themes Microsoft makes available over your Internet connection.

After you click to apply a specific theme, your document changes accordingly.

► **NOTE**

The more colors and standard, Word-supplied styles your document uses, the more your selected theme will show itself in your document. If you apply a theme to a document filled with straight, black-on-white text, you won't see much, if any, difference before and after applying the theme.

2 Customize Your Theme's Colors

The best way to create a customized theme is to begin with one that's close to your goal and then customize it.

Apply a theme that most closely matches your desired theme. In the **Themes** section of your **Page Layout** ribbon, select **Theme Colors**. A list of theme colors appears. Select a new theme color scheme or click **Create New Theme Colors** to create your own set. As you point to each set of possible theme colors, your document will update to reflect what that theme color will look like after you apply it.

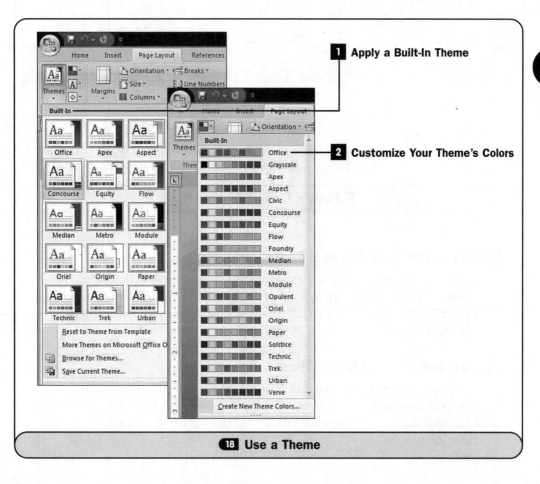

1 Apply a Built-In Theme

2 Customize Your Theme's Colors

18

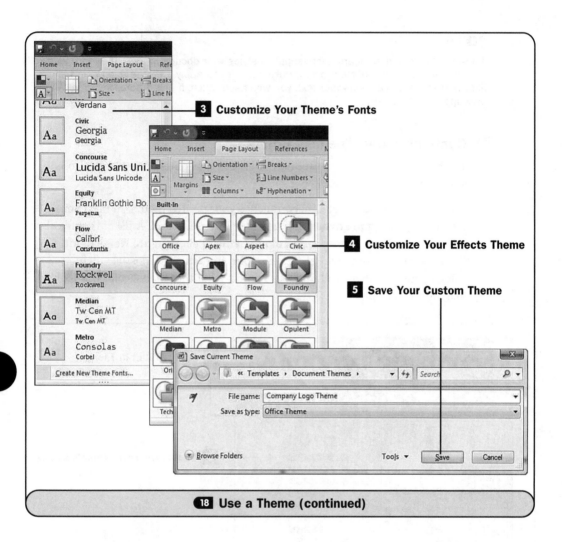

18

18 Use a Theme (continued)

3 Customize Your Theme's Fonts

To change the primary font used in your customized theme, click to select the **Theme Fonts** button to display a list of themed fonts. Again, Word's live pre-view capability shows what each font selection will do to your document as you point to each one.

4 Customize Your Effects Theme

To change your theme effects, click to select the **Theme Effects** button to display a list of themed effects you can apply to your document. (These effects are shadows and 3D effects applied to various art elements in Office documents.)

5 Save Your Custom Theme

After you specify the font, color, and theme effects you want to apply to your document, and after you look over your document to ensure that the theme's elements all work together to achieve the goals you had in mind, click the **Themes** button and then select **Save Current Theme**. Word displays a **Save** dialog box in which you can name your new theme and save it.

In subsequent sessions, when you display a list of themes, your custom theme will appear in the list.

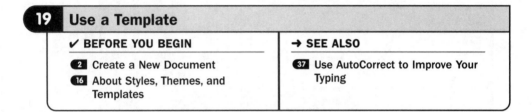

19   Use a Template

✔ BEFORE YOU BEGIN	→ SEE ALSO
2 Create a New Document **16** About Styles, Themes, and Templates	**37** Use AutoCorrect to Improve Your Typing

19

Templates almost make you think you're cheating when you want to create great-looking documents because they are so simple and they do so much. Just a couple of mouse clicks puts ready-made, preformatted documents at your fingertips. You still must supply the details because a template is only an outline (also called a skeleton or model) of a document, but by using a template, you hardly need to apply any formatting or design considerations to the documents you create.

Starting with a completely blank document might be a good idea for simple, text-only letters, and you'll certainly do a lot of that. But for all else, start with a template if one exists that you want to use. If you find yourself creating rather complexly formatted documents routinely, you'll create your own templates, so you must generate all the formatting and document layout just the first time.

Templates contain formatting for complete documents. All the Microsoft Office programs support templates. If you create a new document without specifying a template, Word uses the **Default** template style to create the empty document and to set up initial font, margin, and other formatting-related details.

1 Request a Template

Click your **Office** button and select **New**. (You can also press Alt+F, N.) Word displays the **New Document** window.

In the window's left pane is a scrollable list of template categories that contain several templates in each category. When you select a template category such as **Business Cards**, Microsoft looks online (and on your computer if any

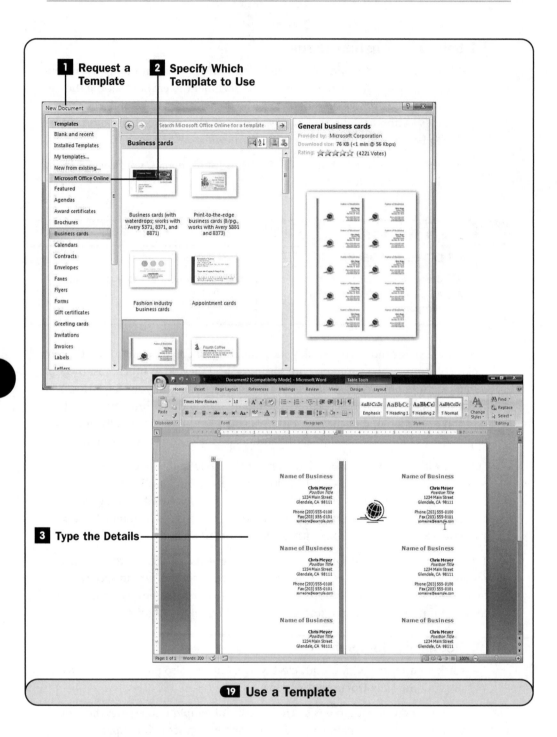

1 Request a Template

2 Specify Which Template to Use

3 Type the Details

19 Use a Template

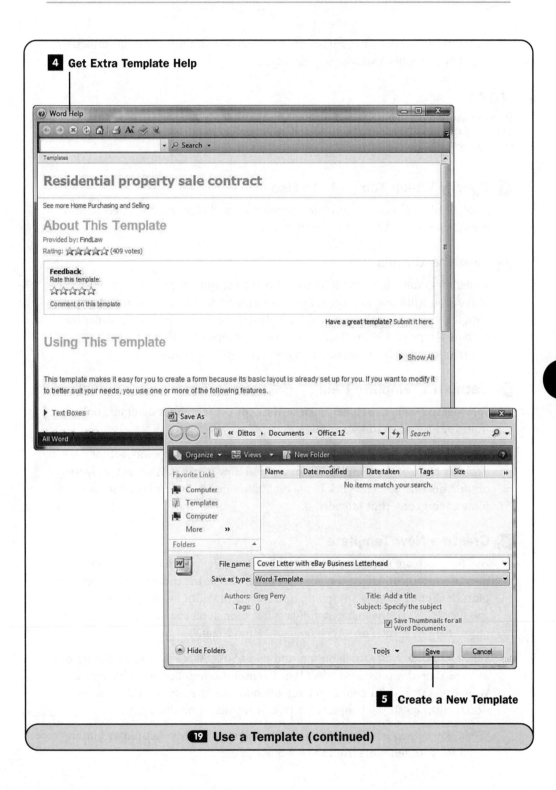

4 Get Extra Template Help

5 Create a New Template

19

templates from that category are stored there) and displays a list of business card templates from which you can select.

▶ **NOTE**

If you've saved templates to your computer, you can click **My Templates** toward the center of the **New Document** window and select one of your own stored templates to begin with.

2 Specify Which Template to Use

Scroll until you locate a template you want to start with, click to select it, and then click **Create**. Word displays that template.

3 Type the Details

Sometimes data will be filled in, so in the case of some business card templates, you will have to change the name and contact information. Other templates will not contain specific sample data or might offer placeholder text such as "[Type Last Name Here]" that you can replace with your specific information. Finish the document by filling in all the details.

4 Get Extra Template Help

Some templates are complex, such as the contract templates available online from your **New Document** window.

When you select some templates, Microsoft might display a window that explains more of the template's purpose and how to use it. Also, you may see an Internet link you can click to see additional information about the template or company that provided it.

5 Create a New Template

Feel free to create your own templates! For example, you might write many memos, so you can create a memo template. Create the model for the template, including the title, recipient, and subject areas, but don't add memo-specific text. Keep the text general. Feel free to include instructions to the user of this template, such as "[Type Body of Memo Here]."

When you click your **Office** button and select **Save As**, click to open the **Save as Type** drop-down list and select **Word Template** from the available items. Word saves your document as a template and uses the .dot filename extension to distinguish the template file from a regular Word document.

When you subsequently create a new file and click the **My Templates** button, you'll see your template from the list that appears.

19

4

Adding Lists, Tables, and Graphics

IN THIS CHAPTER:

Word provides the capability to add flair to your documents, through the use of bulleted lists and numbered lists, tables, charts, and graphics. With today's graphical technology, documents are far from text only, and you can easily add formatted graphics elements to get your point across to your audience.

So many of Word's features, such as bulleted and numbered lists, work automatically. You just begin typing the list and Word takes care of all the formatting and keeps track of the proper indention for you. When you want to return to regular text again, Word can easily return to regular paragraph mode.

▶ **TIP**

Word recognizes most lists in documents that you import from other word processors. For example, if you open a Microsoft Works document with a numbered list, Word recognizes the list and retains its formatting.

20

20   Add a Bulleted List

✔ BEFORE YOU BEGIN	→ SEE ALSO
13 Apply Paragraph Formatting	**21** Add a Numbered List

Office supports multiple levels of bulleted lists. Therefore, as you might do in an outline, you can indent portions of an already-bulleted list to create sublists.

Word makes bulleted lists easy to include in documents. You only need to type the list's items and click a button to convert that list to a bulleted list.

▶ **TIP**

Word supports several bullet styles, such as check marks and arrows.

1 Type the First Item

Anytime you want to begin a new bulleted list, simply type an asterisk (*) followed by a space and then the first line of your list. Do this on a new line. So, to start your list, type an asterisk, a space, and then the text for the first item in your list. Word recognizes that you're starting a bulleted list and converts the asterisk to a bullet symbol.

▶ **NOTE**

If Word doesn't create a bulleted list automatically, your AutoFormat options might not be set to allow automatic bullets. Click your **Office** button, select **Word Options**, click the **Proofing** tab, and then click the **AutoCorrect** button. Under **AutoFormat As You Type**, make sure that you've clicked to check the option labeled **Automatic Bulleted Lists**. (See **41** AutoFormat Your Document.)

2 Continue the List

You won't have to continue typing the asterisk after Word recognizes that you're typing a list. Word converts your asterisk to the bullet item on the first line and puts a bullet at the start of your next line so that you can continue typing. You only need to worry about your list items; Word takes care of the bullets and the indention.

3 Indent the List

When you want to create a sublist of bulleted items, press Tab after the bullet appears. Word indents the item to create the indented list and uses a different bullet symbol for the indented sublist. Keep typing the list, and Word keeps indenting the list, creating the sublist.

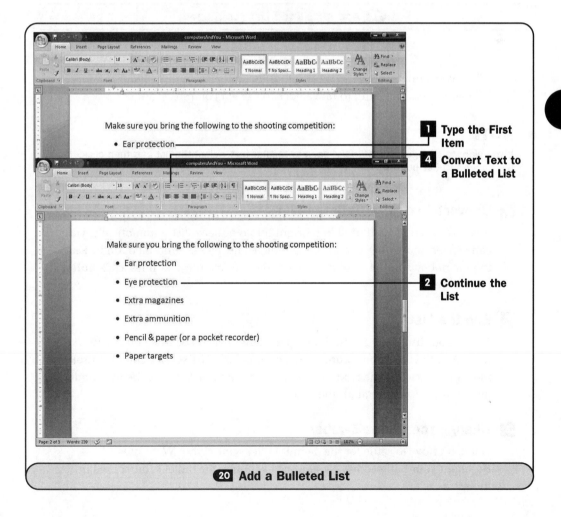

1 Type the First Item

4 Convert Text to a Bulleted List

2 Continue the List

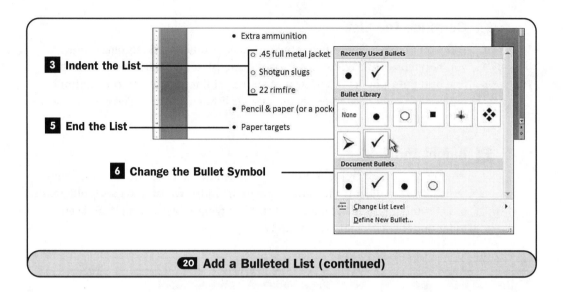

3 Indent the List

5 End the List

6 Change the Bullet Symbol

20 Add a Bulleted List (continued)

When you want to return to the original indention to continue your primary list items, press Shift+Tab to move back to the left column.

▶ **NOTE**

If you want to change a bulleted list back to regular text, select the list and then click the ribbon's **Bullet** button.

4 Convert Text to a Bulleted List

If you've typed items that didn't format into a bulleted list automatically, you can convert those lines of text into a bulleted list by selecting them and clicking the ribbon's **Bullet** button. To revert them to regular text lines, click **Bullet** once more.

5 End the List

To end your list, after the final item press Enter twice. The first Enter keystroke tells Word that you don't want to indent anymore. The second Enter keystroke moves the cursor to the next line, adding a blank line between the list's final item and your next regular line of text.

6 Change the Bullet Symbol

You don't have to settle for the default bullet symbol that Word uses. Highlight your bulleted list if you want to change the bullet symbol used in the list.

Click the down arrow to the right of the **Bullet** button to display your bullet library. As you point to the various symbols, Word's live preview feature shows you how your bullets will appear in your selected text. Click to select a bullet symbol and close the **Bullet** window.

▶ **TIP**

If you want to change only some of a list's bulleted symbols, such as the indented sub-lists, select only those portions of the list before clicking the **Bullets** button.

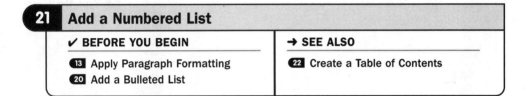

21   **Add a Numbered List**

✔ **BEFORE YOU BEGIN**

🔟 Apply Paragraph Formatting
🔟 Add a Bulleted List

➔ **SEE ALSO**

🔟 Create a Table of Contents

Office supports the use of numbered lists, which are indented lists with numbered items, in much the same way it supports bulleted lists (see 🔟 **Add a Bulleted List**).

Word handles not only the formatting of your numbered list but also the renumbering if needed. Therefore, if you add items anywhere within or after a numbered list, Word automatically updates the numbers to reflect the new items. If you delete an item from a numbered list, Word renumbers the remaining items so that the numbers order properly.

As with bullets, Office supports multiple, indented levels of numbered lists. Therefore, as you might do in an outline, you can indent portions of a numbered list to create sublists.

To start a numbered list, you only need to type 1. or i. or I. to signal to Word that you're typing the first item in a numbered list.

▶ **TIP**

You can use a closing parenthesis after the number instead of a period when typing the first item in a numbered list. Therefore, you can type 1) or i) or I) to start a numbered list.

After you type the first line in the numbered list and press Enter, Word recognizes the start of the numbered list, continues the numbering using the same format you used in the first item, and automatically indents the next line and adds its number so that you can quickly continue the list.

21

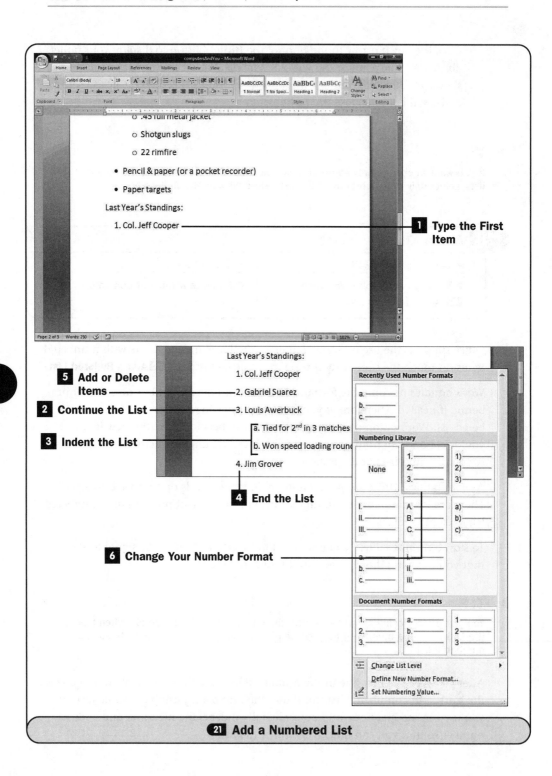

21

1 **Type the First Item**

5 **Add or Delete Items**

2 **Continue the List**

3 **Indent the List**

4 **End the List**

6 **Change Your Number Format**

21 Add a Numbered List

▶ **TIP**

Word supports several numbering styles, including letters; a "numbered list" might begin with A), B), C).

1 Type the First Item

When you want to begin a numbered list, simply type a number followed by a period or closing parenthesis, such as 1. or 1), followed by a space and then the first line of your list. Do this on a new line.

Word recognizes that you've begun a numbered list and continues the numbering as you type.

2 Continue the List

You won't have to continue typing the number after Word recognizes that you're creating a numbered list. Word puts the second number at the start of your next line so you can continue typing. You only need to worry about your list items; Word takes care of the numbers and the indention.

3 Indent the List

When you want to create a sublist of numbered items, press Tab after the number. Word indents the item and starts the numbering using letters in an outline format. Keep typing the list, and Word keeps indenting and creating the sublist.

When you want to return to the original indention to continue your primary list items, press Shift+Tab to move back to the left column and continue the numbering of the original list.

4 End the List

To end your list, after the final item press Enter twice. The first Enter keystroke tells Word that you don't want to indent anymore. The second Enter keystroke moves the cursor to the next line, adding a blank line between the list's final item and your next regular line of text.

5 Add or Delete Items

The true power of Word's numbered lists is Word's capability to renumber the entire list when you add or remove list items. To insert new items, put

21

your text cursor at the end of any item and press Enter. Word inserts a new line with the next number and renumbers all subsequent items accordingly. You may keep inserting new items; Word handles all the renumbering for you.

If you delete a line, Word renumbers the list to close the gap between the numbered items where you deleted the line.

6 Change Your Number Format

You don't have to settle for the default number that Word initially uses. Highlight your numbered list if you want to change the kind of number used in the list.

Click the **Home** ribbon's **Numbering** button's arrow to display the various number formats available. As you point to each one, your selected numbered list changes to reflect the new format. After you select a new format by clicking it, Word hides the **Numbering** window and changes your list to that new format.

22

▶ **NOTE**

If you want to change only some of a list's number style, such as an indented sublist, select only that portion of the list before selecting from the **Numbering** window.

22 Create a Table of Contents

✔ BEFORE YOU BEGIN	→ SEE ALSO
5 Edit Text	**23** Create an Index
17 Use a Style	

When you write for others, a *table of contents* provides easy access for your readers. They can quickly go to whatever subject, or chapter, they want to go to. Making a table of contents used to be tedious, but with Word, such a task is easy. If you make changes to your document, such as adding new chapters, you can easily regenerate the table of contents to keep it fresh.

▶ NEW TERM

Table of contents—A table in the front of many books that typically tells on which page number a book's chapters and other elements appear.

Generally, paragraphs to which you apply the built-in Heading 1 style will end up in your table of contents. With multiple heading styles, Heading 1, Heading 2, and so on, you have plenty of title, heading, and subheading styles with which to format your text. If any or all of these styles do not format paragraphs exactly the way you want them to, you can modify the styles. The important thing to note here is that if you do use the Heading 1 style, whether or not you've modified the style, Word considers each of those paragraphs to be part of the table of contents. All the contents should appear in the currently open document; otherwise, Word won't be able to locate the entries.

▶ NOTE

Word doesn't continually update a table of contents even when you use the Heading 1 style. After creating an initial table of contents, if you add more content to your document, click the **References** ribbon's **Table of Contents** button to generate a new table.

1 Find Text for the Table

Select one or more paragraphs that you want to include in your table of contents. If you're writing a book, generally such a paragraph will consist of the chapter titles and appendixes (if any).

▶ NOTE

If you formatted your introduction, chapter titles, and appendixes with the Heading 1 style, you don't need to reapply the style. You can apply additional heading styles such as Heading 2 and Heading 3 if you want subcategories in your table. For example, if you want chapter titles followed by section names to appear in your table of contents, you would format section names with the Heading 2 style.

2 Request the Heading 1 Style

If you've selected paragraphs to apply the Heading 1 style to, press Ctrl+Shift+S and select **Heading 1** from the **Apply Styles** dialog box.

You may continue applying the Heading 1 style to all paragraphs in your document that you want to include in the table of contents. As you apply the Heading 1 style, the format of those paragraphs typically changes to become boldface.

If you elected to include subcategories, apply the Heading 2 styles to them throughout your document.

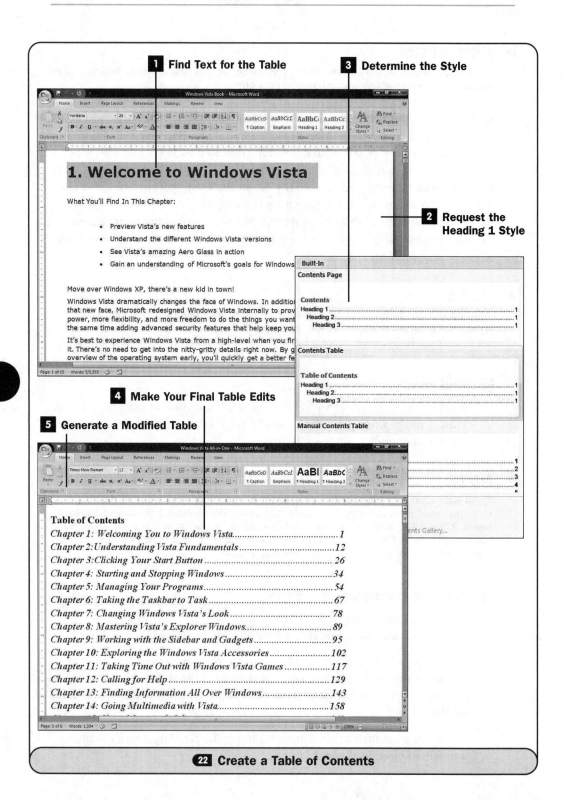

1 Find Text for the Table

3 Determine the Style

2 Request the Heading 1 Style

4 Make Your Final Table Edits

5 Generate a Modified Table

22 Create a Table of Contents

▶ **TIP**

Add chapter numbers in front of chapter titles so that your chapter numbers automatically appear in the table of contents.

3 Determine the Style

After you've applied the Heading 1 style to all the paragraphs you want to include in your table of contents, you can generate the table of contents. Move the text cursor to the beginning of your document (assuming that you want the table of contents to appear there).

Click the **References** ribbon's **Table of Contents** button to display a list of table of contents styles.

Select a table of contents style that most closely suits your needs. Word generates the table and places it at your cursor's insertion point.

4 Make Your Final Table Edits

You now must make final edits to the table of contents. You can format the table, put page breaks around it (using Shift+Enter), and add spacing between the lines if you want.

5 Generate a Modified Table

You can regenerate the table anytime you edit your document by clicking the **Table of Contents** button again.

---

23 Create an Index

✔ BEFORE YOU BEGIN	→ SEE ALSO
13 Apply Paragraph Formatting	**24** About Word Tables
22 Create a Table of Contents	

The longer your document, the more your audience will appreciate an ***index***. As you write, or after you've completed your document, you can mark any word in the document that you want to include in the index. Word can then generate the index showing the proper page numbers. If you make changes to the document, you can regenerate the index to keep it accurate.

▶ **NEW TERM**

Index—A table that appears in the back of some books that lists the page numbers of certain key words, people, and terms in the book.

At first, you might wonder why you have to do all the work of marking every index entry. Word is smart, but it cannot be smart enough to read your mind.

(Perhaps that's a feature being saved for Word 2010.) Word could never know which words you want to include in the index, so it's up to you to mark each of them. Unlike in the days of old, however, after you mark which words go in the index, your job is over because Word does the work of searching out the page numbers and generating the index.

▶ **NOTE**

A Word document can support multiple indexes. When you define index entries, you can determine to which of multiple indexes the entries are to go. Most documents have only a single index, however.

1 Locate Text for the Index

Highlight a word or phrase that is to appear in your index.

2 Mark the Entry

With the index entry selected, click the **Mark Entry** button on your **References** ribbon. You can also press Alt+Shift+X to do the same. The **Mark Index Entry** dialog box appears.

3 Set Up the Index Entry

Word places your selected text in the **Main Entry** area of the **Mark Index Entry** dialog box. You can edit the entry if you want. For example, you may have referred to the same entry in different ways throughout your document, perhaps using an abbreviation such as "CPU" in some places and spelling out the phrase as "central processing unit" elsewhere. In the **Main Entry** text box, you could change the entry to "CPU - Central Processing Unit," and as long as you did that everywhere you marked that index entry, one uniform entry will appear in your index for each occurrence of the phrase in your document.

Changing the entry is also useful for proper names you mark in your document that might begin with a first name but that you want to list in your index by last name. For example, if your document refers to Clint Eastwood and you want to place his name in your index (and if you don't, he will make your day, punk!), you might change the entry to "Eastwood, Clint."

▶ **NOTE**

To mark your index entries, Word adds a hidden code to each word. If you click your **Show/Hide** nonprinting characters button, you'll see the index codes. These codes don't normally print or appear on your screen unless you request to see them. When you first mark your entries, Word turns on the nonprinting characters to alert you to what is happening, but a quick click of your **Show/Hide** nonprinting characters button on your **Home** ribbon hides them again.

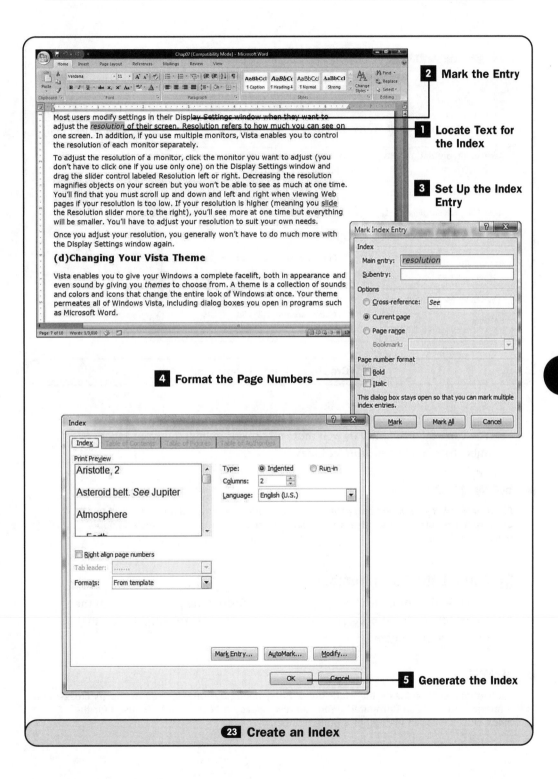

2 Mark the Entry

1 Locate Text for the Index

3 Set Up the Index Entry

4 Format the Page Numbers

5 Generate the Index

23

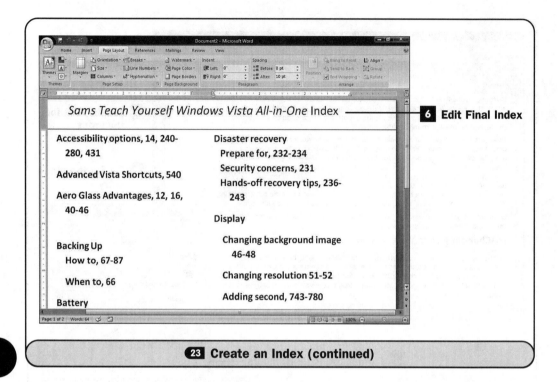

6 Edit Final Index

23 Create an Index (continued)

You can add a subentry as well that will appear indented in your index. Subentries create a *multilevel index*.

▶ **NEW TERM**

Multilevel index—An index entry that contains a primary term such as *fruit* and two or more secondary entries, offset to the right under the primary term, such as *apple*, *banana*, and *pear*.

4 **Format the Page Numbers**

Select **Bold** or **Italic** (or both) if you want to format the page number in the index differently from the surrounding page numbers. You might want to do this for proper names.

▶ **NOTE**

The **Options** section inside the **Mark Index Entry** dialog box enables you to specify cross-references (as in "See Computer"). You can also specify a bookmark to be used for the index entry's location instead of a page number.

5 **Generate the Index**

After you've defined all the entries, you make the request to Word to generate the index. Word compiles the index and places it at the cursor's current position.

In most cases, this means you will click to place your text cursor (the insertion point) at the end of your document and then click the **Insert Index** button on your **References** ribbon.

Word displays the **Index** dialog box, from which you can select index-formatting options and determine how you want your index to appear.

Click **OK** to generate the index.

6 **Edit Final Index**

After your index appears, you can edit the index to adjust formatting, such as the font and spacing, if you need to so that the index matches the format of the rest of the document.

24	**About Word Tables**	**24**

✔ BEFORE YOU BEGIN	→ SEE ALSO
5 Edit Text	**25** Create a Quick Table
13 Apply Paragraph Formatting	**26** Create a Table
	27 Manage Tables

Word's table-creation power shines when you see how easily you can compose customized *tables* of information in Word documents. Tables might contain numbers, text, graphics, or combinations of any of these. Each row and column intersection is called a *cell*. As you begin to use both Word and Excel (see **52** **Create a New Workbook**), you might want to embed part of an Excel spreadsheet into a Word table. Such embedded spreadsheets enable you, for example, to report financial data from within a Word report.

▶ **NEW TERMS**

Tables—Collections of information organized in rows and columns.

Cell—A row and column intersection in a Word or Excel table or worksheet.

With Word, you can easily create tables from your keyboard. You type a series of plus signs and hyphens, and Word will interpret that as the start of your table. For example, suppose you type the following:

```
+--------+--------+--------+--------+--------+--------+
```

Word then converts that to a one-row table with six columns. After you fill in the first row with values (pressing Tab and Shift+Tab to move between columns), Word inserts a new row for you.

Although typing the plus signs and hyphens is useful when you want a quick start to a table, you'll probably find that Word's other table tools are so powerful and simple to use that you'll probably use them most of the time to generate your tables.

Word includes several predefined *quick tables* that include calendars and other table formats you might want to begin with. The quick tables enable you to place a table into your document quickly and then make edits to the table as you need.

▶ NEW TERM

Quick tables—A collection of predesigned tables such as calendars and two-column lists that you can begin with.

24

You can also add an empty table to your document before typing anything. For example, you can request a 12-row, 5-column table formatted a certain way by using the **Table** button on your **Insert** ribbon.

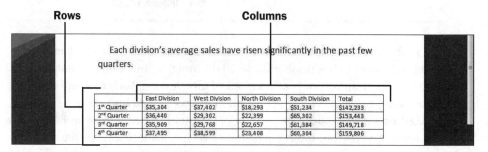

Rows   **Columns**

Each division's average sales have risen significantly in the past few quarters.

	East Division	West Division	North Division	South Division	Total
1ˢᵗ Quarter	$35,304	$37,402	$18,293	$51,234	$142,233
2ⁿᵈ Quarter	$36,440	$29,302	$22,399	$65,302	$153,443
3ʳᵈ Quarter	$35,909	$29,768	$22,657	$61,384	$149,718
4ᵗʰ Quarter	$37,495	$38,599	$23,408	$60,304	$159,806

This table contains five rows and six columns.

After you create a table, you can easily adjust its height and width by dragging one of the edges with your mouse. You can add and delete rows and columns, too. In addition, you can apply formatting attributes to your table to add color, highlighting, special fonts, and other format attributes that make a dull table look good. Word's live preview mode enables you to see what the format changes will look like before you apply them to your actual table. Also, if you select the entire table, you can make format changes to all the selected cells.

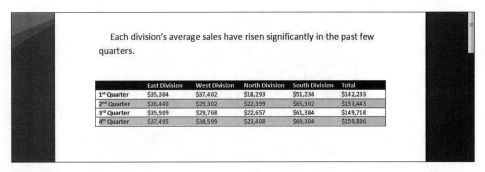

Each division's average sales have risen significantly in the past few quarters.

	East Division	West Division	North Division	South Division	Total
1ˢᵗ Quarter	$35,304	$37,402	$18,293	$51,234	$142,233
2ⁿᵈ Quarter	$36,440	$29,302	$22,399	$65,302	$153,443
3ʳᵈ Quarter	$35,909	$29,768	$22,657	$61,384	$149,718
4ᵗʰ Quarter	$37,495	$38,599	$23,408	$60,304	$159,806

One click of a button can format your table with colors and shading.

25 Create a Quick Table

✔ BEFORE YOU BEGIN	→ SEE ALSO
24 About Word Tables	**26** Create a Table
	27 Manage Tables

Word offers predesigned quick tables that you can quickly drop into your document and use as is or format to your liking. These tables include the following:

- Calendars
- Double-column tables
- Matrix tables
- Tables with subheads

A few mouse clicks are all that's required to insert these tables into your document. The tables look quite nice, especially the calendars, and if you use a quick table, you may not even need to change the formatting.

▪ Request a Quick Table

Click the **Table** button on your **Insert** ribbon, and then click **Quick Tables** to display the scrolling list of built-in tables.

▪ Choose a Quick Table

Scroll through the quick table list to find a table you want to insert into your document.

▪ Insert the Quick Table

Click to select the quick table you want to use. Word inserts the table into your document at the current insertion point.

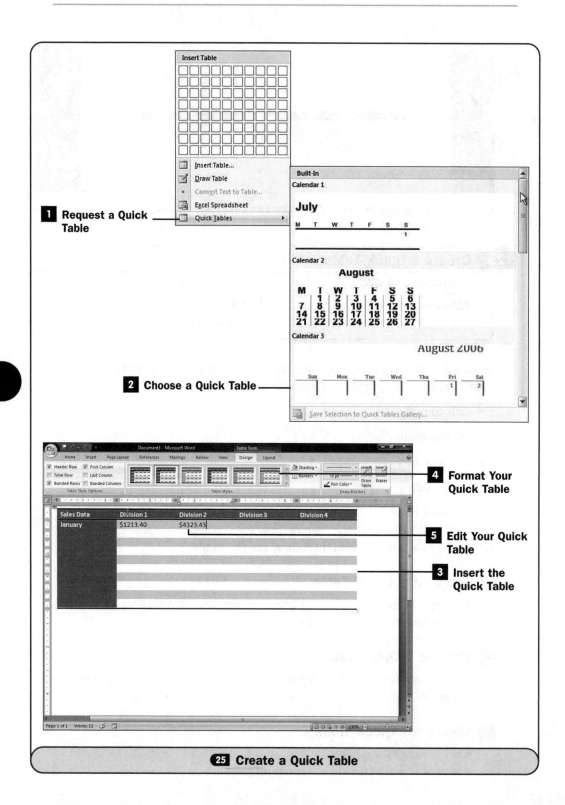

1 Request a Quick Table

2 Choose a Quick Table

4 Format Your Quick Table

5 Edit Your Quick Table

3 Insert the Quick Table

25 Create a Quick Table

4 Format Your Quick Table

Select the table style from the **Table Styles** section of your **Design** ribbon. As you point to each style, Word updates your quick table to reflect that style's format.

Click to select one of the styles to apply it to your quick table.

5 Edit Your Quick Table

Use Word's table-movement keys (see **27 Manage Tables**) and formatting commands to adjust the data and format of your quick table.

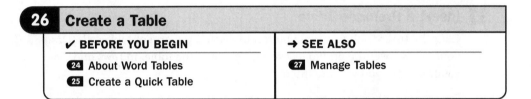

26 Create a Table

✔ BEFORE YOU BEGIN

24 About Word Tables
25 Create a Quick Table

→ SEE ALSO

27 Manage Tables

Word provides so many ways to create tables that the method you choose ultimately comes down to the one you prefer; there is not one method that is necessarily any better than another out of the different ways Word provides.

Word 2007's live preview ensures that your table looks the way you want it to look before you actually insert the table into your document. Of course, with Word's Undo feature, if you do insert a table that you don't care for, you can easily remove it and insert another that better serves your needs.

This task shows you the various ways to create Word tables. You'll then learn, in **27 Manage Tables**, how to navigate your tables.

1 Type to Create a Table

Open a new document to practice creating tables. Type a plus sign, followed by 10 hyphens. Type another plus sign and another 10 hyphens. Keep doing this until you type six sets and close with a plus sign. You can copy and paste these sets of hyphens instead of typing each one.

You have now typed what is needed to let Word know that you want to begin a new table.

▶ NOTE

If your cell is not wide enough to hold what you type, Word increases the cell height to hold more data. Word does not widen the cell. To widen the cell, see **27 Manage Tables**.

2 Complete the Lines

Press Enter after the final plus sign. As soon as you do, Word converts your line of plus signs and hyphens to one row of a table, designated by lines to form six columns.

After Word creates the first row of the table, it places your text cursor in the leftmost cell so that you can type the table's data. When you finish typing the data, press Tab to move to the next cell to the right. When you finish the row, press Tab again and Word will create the next row for you. If you press Enter instead of Tab at the end of a row, Word assumes that you're through with the table and will not add an additional row.

3 Insert a Premade Table

Click the **Insert** ribbon's **Table** button to display the grid of table cells. Drag your mouse over the grid to tell Word the size of the table, in rows and columns, that you want to insert.

For example, if you want to create a table with five columns and six rows, drag your mouse to highlight five columns and six rows of table cells. As you drag your mouse, a blank table appears in your document showing you the table being generated. When you release your mouse button, the table appears.

4 Format Your Table

When the empty table cells appear in your document, Word provides a series of table designs at the top of the ribbon. As you point to the table designs, your document's table updates to show what your table will look like if you select a design.

You can also designate shading and borders and table line width using the options that Word provides here.

5 Draw to Create a Table

Instead of letting Word insert your table, you can draw your table in the shape and size you want it to be.

Click where you want to create your table, and on the **Insert** ribbon, click the **Tables** group. Click the **Draw Table** button, and you'll notice that your mouse cursor changes to a pencil.

Drag your mouse to move the pencil. Start in one corner of your table, such as the upper-left corner, and drag your mouse down and to the right. As you do, Word draws your table's outline. You then can drag the pencil cursor across to make the table's rows and down to form the table's columns. Doing this enables you to position your table rows and columns at the width and height you want them to be.

▶ **TIP**

If you draw a table row or column line that you want to erase, click the ribbon's **Eraser** button and drag your mouse over the line you want to erase.

Drawing your table in this manner enables you to create rows that don't necessarily have all the columns in them. In other words, you can draw some rows to have five columns and other rows to have only one or two columns. Word follows your drawing to create whatever cell pattern you want your table to have.

After you finish drawing your table, you can format the table to look the way you want it to look.

6 **Create a New Table Style**

If you find yourself creating the same style of table multiple times, and the style is different from the table styles that Word's **Insert** ribbon provides, you can create your own table style and select it from the list of styles in the future.

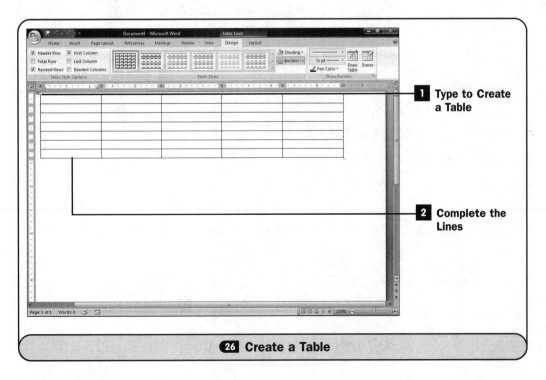

1 Type to Create a Table

2 Complete the Lines

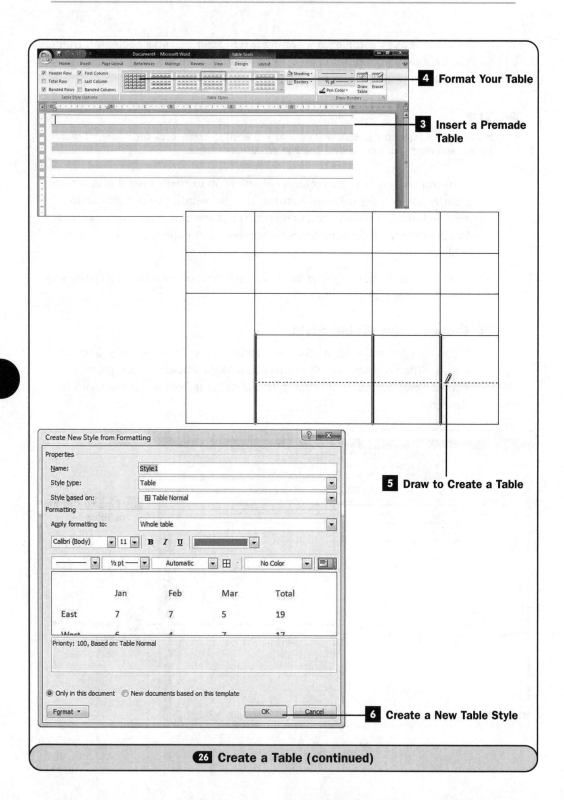

4 Format Your Table

3 Insert a Premade Table

5 Draw to Create a Table

6 Create a New Table Style

26 Create a Table (continued)

To create your table style, click the down arrow next to the list of available table styles and select **New Table Style**. Word displays the **Create New Style from Formatting** dialog box. Select from the options given to determine your table style and assign a name to your style in the **Name** text box. Subsequently, when you view table styles to format a new table, your style will appear in the available styles.

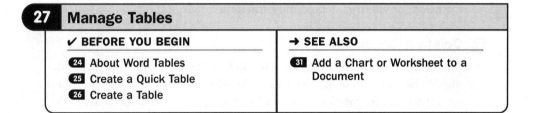

27 | **Manage Tables**

✔ BEFORE YOU BEGIN	→ SEE ALSO
24 About Word Tables	**31** Add a Chart or Worksheet to a
25 Create a Quick Table	Document
26 Create a Table	

After you're familiar with creating tables and formatting them, you'll still find yourself adjusting them as you work with them. Perhaps you need to add more rows or columns. Perhaps you want to make a quick adjustment to one of the column widths.

To put data into your table, you just go to the cell and type the data. Formatting a table and getting data into it is most of the battle because creating the table's outline is so simple. You will find that traversing a table differs somewhat from traversing regular text. Table 4.1 shows the keystrokes needed to traverse tables efficiently.

▶ **NOTE**

You can make a column width adjustment by dragging a column's edge on the horizontal ruler atop the document. Most users are more comfortable dragging the actual column edge to resize a column; a vertical line moves as you drag your mouse to show the new column size.

TABLE 4.1 Word's Table-Navigating Keystrokes

Press This...	To Move the Table's Cursor Here
Shift+Tab and left arrow	The preceding cell (your left arrow moves the cursor left until the cursor gets to the left edge of the cell, in which case the left arrow moves the cursor to the preceding cell)
Tab and right arrow	The next cell (your right arrow moves the cursor right until the cursor gets to the right edge of the cell, in which case the right arrow moves the cursor to the next cell)
Up arrow	The cell above the current cell
Down arrow	The cell below the current cell

1 Resize the Columns

Adjusting a column's size is extremely simple. Move your mouse pointer to an edge of the column you want to resize (to either increase or decrease the column width). The mouse pointer changes to a double arrow. Click the edge of the column and drag the column left or right. When you release the mouse, Word resizes the column to its new size. If you shrink a column's width too narrow, the text may not all fit on one line, and Word will be forced to double the height of the rows to hold the extra data.

2 Delete a Column

Select a column you want to delete by clicking the top line of that column. Right-click and a menu appears. Select **Delete Columns** to delete the column from the table. (If you first drag to select multiple columns, the **Delete Columns** command deletes all your selected columns.)

3 Insert a Column

Select an entire column when you want to insert a new column. Right-click and select **Insert** and either **Insert Columns to the Left** or **Insert Columns to the Right**, depending on where you want the new column.

27

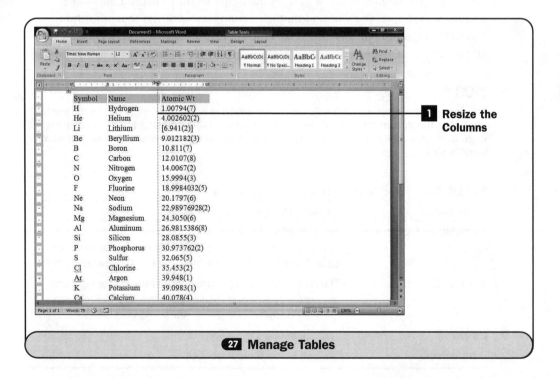

27 Manage Tables

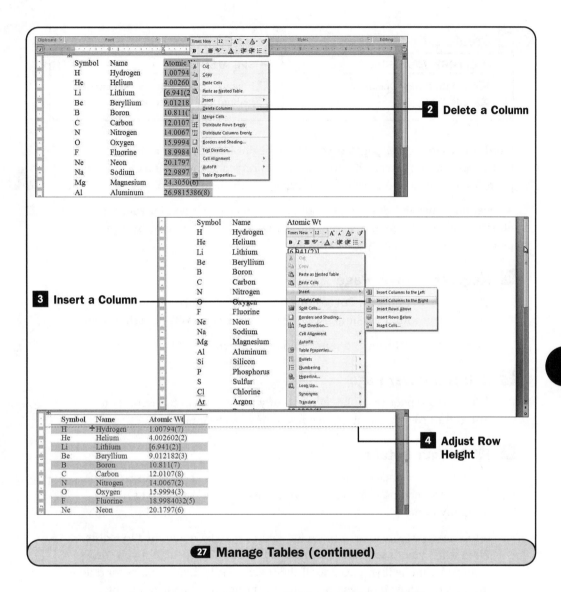

2 Delete a Column

3 Insert a Column

4 Adjust Row Height

27 Manage Tables (continued)

After the new column arrives, you'll fill it with data and adjust any column or table widths as necessary.

4 Adjust Row Height

Adjusting a row's height is as simple as dragging the row divider up or down. Click any row's dividing line and drag your mouse up or down to adjust that row.

▶ **TIP**

If you select the entire table, or select multiple rows in your table, you can drag one of the selected row's dividers up or down to adjust the height of all rows in the selection.

28 Create a Cover Page

✔ BEFORE YOU BEGIN	→ SEE ALSO
2 Create a New Document	**29** Insert Graphics into a Document
5 Edit Text	**40** About Building Blocks

Word can insert a cover page for you at the beginning of your document. No matter where your text cursor (the insertion point) appears when you request a cover page, Word creates and inserts the cover page at the beginning of your document.

A cover page includes sample text that acts as placeholder text for your name and other pertinent data. After inserting a cover page, you will need to change the placeholder text to reflect your own data.

28

1 Request a Cover Page

Click the **Insert** ribbon's **Cover Page** button. Word displays a gallery that presents you with a scrolling list of cover page designs you can select from.

Each cover page includes a name and description.

2 Select a Cover Page

Select a cover page from the gallery that you want Word to insert. Word inserts that cover page at the beginning of your document.

3 Fill In Your Details

Fill in the cover page details with your own specifics. In most cases, this requires adding a specific title and other information such as a company name.

If the cover page includes a place for your name, the name used to register Word when you or someone else installed Word will appear, but you can change the name if you need to. If the cover page includes a place for a date, the current date will appear, but you can change the date if you want.

4 Create Your Own Cover Page

If you find that none of the cover pages matches your needs well, you can create your own cover page and store that cover page in the gallery. The next time you request a cover page, your stored cover page will appear.

To add your own cover page to the gallery, create a cover page. You can add placeholder text, such as "[Title]" where each specific cover page's details are to go. You'll fill in those details subsequently after you insert the cover page.

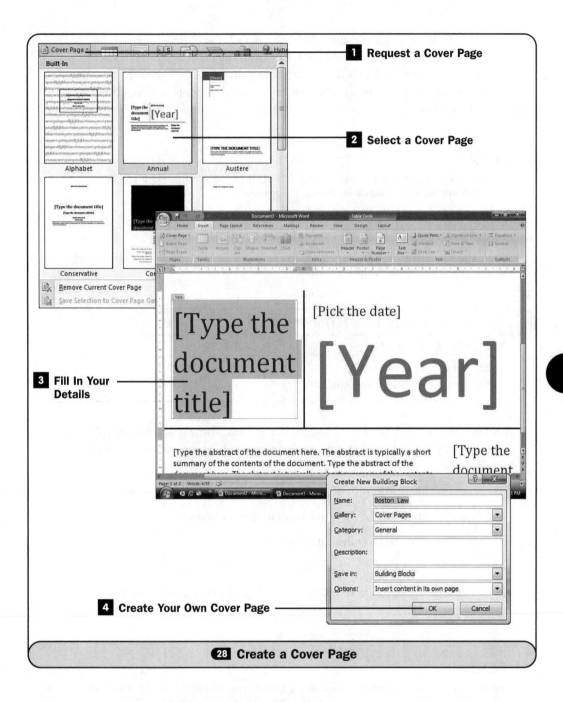

1 Request a Cover Page

2 Select a Cover Page

3 Fill In Your Details

4 Create Your Own Cover Page

28

Select the cover page and then click the **Cover Page** button again in the **Insert** ribbon. Select **Save Selection to Cover Page Gallery** to save your cover page. Word displays the **Create New Building Block** dialog box with **Cover Pages** selected as the **Gallery** entry. Assign a name to your cover page and click **OK**.

▶ **NOTE**

The cover page is just one of several kinds of *building blocks* that Word supports. See **40** About Building Blocks for more information.

▶ **NEW TERM**

Building blocks—Items related to Word elements, such as cover pages and styles, that you can store in galleries for later selection.

29 | Insert Graphics into a Document

✔ BEFORE YOU BEGIN	→ SEE ALSO
14 Set Up Page Formatting	**30** Draw with Word
15 Create a Multicolumn Newsletter	

Word enables you to put pictures in your documents. Those graphics images can have captions and borders, and you can specify how the text around such images wraps.

Word supports the inclusion of all the following kinds of graphics images:

- Graphics images from a file, such as bitmapped images
- Graphics images from Office's *gallery*
- Graphics images that you scan into your document
- Graphics images produced in Office's other products such as PowerPoint
- Excel charts

▶ **TERM**

Gallery—A collection of graphics supplied by Office programs that you can insert into your documents. Word can search online for graphics images from a database of thousands that Microsoft provides free of charge.

You can format your graphics images to appear on the left or right of text, or above or below the text in which you insert the graphics. You're not limited to placing a graphics image where you first anchor it, either; when you want to move an image, you just drag the picture to another location.

❶ Request a Picture

To insert a graphics image from a file, first place your text cursor close to where you want the image to go. Then display the **Insert** ribbon and click **Picture**. Locate a picture file on your computer or network. After you select the graphics image you want to place in your document, click the **Insert** button to insert the image.

▶ **NOTE**

Office supports all popular graphics file formats, including JPG, GIF, and BMP files.

❷ Adjust the Size

Your picture is selected so that you can make adjustments. Whenever a picture is selected, eight sizing *handles* appear around the picture that you can drag to increase or decrease the picture's size. In addition, the **Picture Tools** ribbon appears, offering one-click access to many common graphics-related tasks. (If you do not see the **Picture Tools** ribbon after clicking to select the picture, click the Format button located on the top row of your ribbon.)

▶ **NEW TERM**

Handles—Eight places that appear around selected pictures to allow you to resize the image without moving the image from its current place in your document.

After Word brings the graphics image into your document, you can make adjustments to suit your needs. Typically, Word imports graphics images and centers them at the location where you inserted them. By default, no text wraps to either side of the image, and the image often is not sized properly for your document.

❸ Place the Picture

If you want to embed the image inside text somewhere on the page, click the **Position** button to display the text wrapping positions where your picture can go. As you point to each option, Word's live preview mode shows you where the image will appear if you decide to click to choose that location.

▶ **TIP**

If you want to add a caption to your image, right-click the image and select **Caption** to display the **Caption** dialog box. You can add a sequential number before your caption so that you can reference all your images from the document by number.

29

▪ 4 Insert a Clip Art Gallery Item

You can insert one of Office's gallery images instead of importing your own graphics image. The gallery contains a collection of *clip art,* such as icons, simple art images, fancy numbers, buttons, and graphics borders, that you may want to use to spruce up your page.

▶ NEW TERM

Clip art—A collection of low-resolution art, supplied by Office, that you can use to decorate your documents.

You must display the gallery before you can drag items from the gallery into your document. To display the gallery, click the **Clip Art** ribbon button on the **Insert** ribbon to display the **Clip Art** task pane.

▪ 5 Request a Specific Image

Type a word to search for in the **Search For** text box and click **Go**. For example, you could type parrot if you wanted to look for a clip art image of a parrot. Click **Go** to see all the images Microsoft locates online. Click the arrow to the right of the image you want to insert and select **Insert**. Word inserts the clip art image.

29

▪ 6 Change the Style

Select from the list of styles across the top of the **Picture Tools** ribbon to change the style of the picture, such as by adding a border. You can also adjust the picture border by clicking to open the **Picture Border** button.

▶ TIP

If you're going to send the document to another person via email, click the **Compress Pictures** button before saving your document to reduce the size of your document's images.

The **Picture Tools** ribbon appears whenever you click to select a graphics image, whether that image is an actual picture or a clip art image.

▪ 7 Add a Picture Caption

To add a caption under your selected picture, click the **References** ribbon button. (Click **Exclude Label from Caption** if you don't want Word to place a label such as "Figure 1-" before your picture.) Type a caption and select from the **Position** list box to choose where you want the caption to go. After you add a caption, Word returns you to the **Picture Tools** ribbon with your picture still selected.

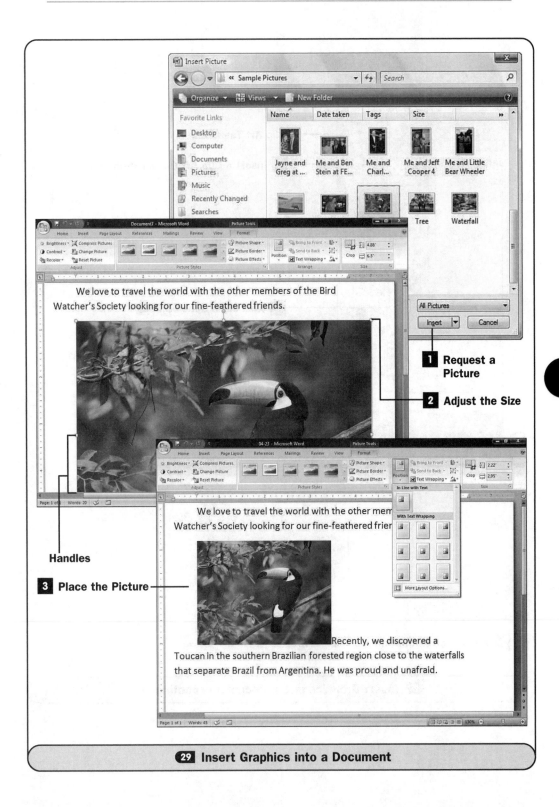

1 Request a Picture

2 Adjust the Size

Handles

3 Place the Picture

We love to travel the world with the other members of the Bird Watcher's Society looking for our fine-feathered friends.

Recently, we discovered a Toucan in the southern Brazilian forested region close to the waterfalls that separate Brazil from Argentina. He was proud and unafraid.

29 Insert Graphics into a Document

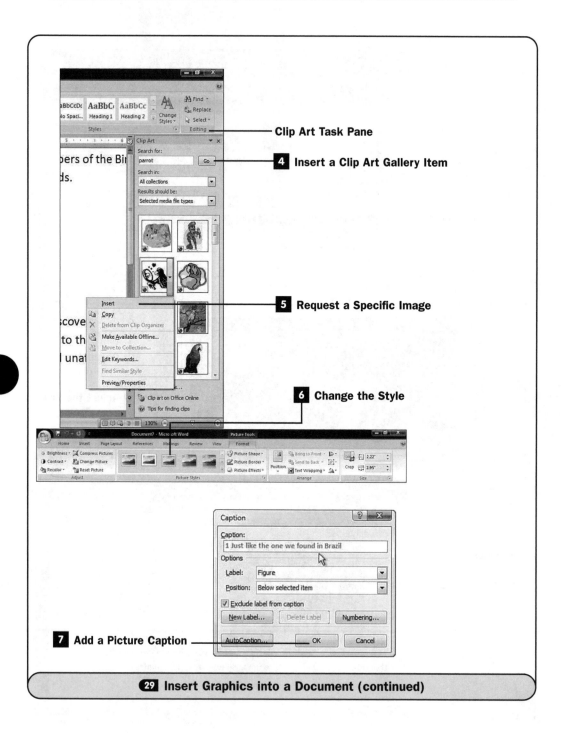

Clip Art Task Pane

4 Insert a Clip Art Gallery Item

5 Request a Specific Image

6 Change the Style

7 Add a Picture Caption

29 Insert Graphics into a Document (continued)

---

30 Draw with Word

✔ BEFORE YOU BEGIN	→ SEE ALSO
29 Insert Graphics into a Document	**31** Add a Chart or Worksheet to a Document
	49 Add WordArt to a Document

If you don't have graphics images to insert into your documents, you can draw your own! Word supports drawing tools with which you can create the following:

- Lines
- Rectangles
- *Polygons*
- Curves
- Freeform art
- Arrows
- *Flowcharts*
- *Callouts*
- Stars and banners

▶ NEW TERMS

Polygon—A multisided shape.

Flowchart—A drawing that shows an ordered flow of some process, such as the procedure an invoice goes through from blank form to final, or the steps a computer program takes to perform a task.

Callout—A caption that points to an item to describe that item.

Using one of the drawing tools usually requires only that you select the tool you want to use, click your mouse where you want the shape to begin, and then click your mouse where you want the shape to end.

1 Request a Drawing

Display your **Insert** ribbon. The **Shapes** group at the ribbon's leftmost edge forms the shapes available to you in Word.

2 **Display Additional Shapes**

Click the down arrow next to the **Shape** group to see a list of more shapes available to you. Word updates the **Recently Used Shapes** section to include any recent shapes you might have drawn.

3 **Create a New Drawing**

With the **Shape** box opens, click to select **New Drawing**. Word defines a rectangular drawing area in your document where you can put shapes. You can drag any of the rectangular area's corners or edges to shrink or expand the size of your drawing area.

▶ **NOTE**

Notice that your ribbon changes to display Word's **Drawing Tools**. As long as you work on your drawing, the ribbon remains here to provide tools you'll use for drawing and editing your drawing.

30

Click on one of the shape buttons, such as one of the lines, to draw the shape. Your mouse pointer changes to a cross-hairs pattern showing where your line will begin.

To draw a shape, click where you want the shape to begin. For example, after you've selected a line shape, click once on your document to anchor the line's starting point. Drag your mouse in the direction you want the shape to go, and when you release your mouse, the shape will appear in your document. The shape will have resizing handles around it. You may click any handle to resize the shape. For example, you can extend or shorten a line by dragging one of its two endpoint resizing handles in or out. You can also move a shape to a different location by moving the mouse pointer over the shape until your mouse cursor changes to show four arrows pointing in the compass directions. Drag the shape to where you want it to go.

Continue clicking to select shapes and place them on your drawing area. If you ever draw a shape that you don't want, click to highlight that shape's resizing handles and press the Delete key to remove the shape.

4 **Use the Scribble Tool to Draw Freeform**

Click to select the **Freeform** shape. You can drag the **Freeform** drawing shape to any position. A line follows your movement, drawing as you drag your mouse.

You can continue adding shapes in a like manner. The shapes don't replace actual drawing, but they give you a foundation to make simple drawings.

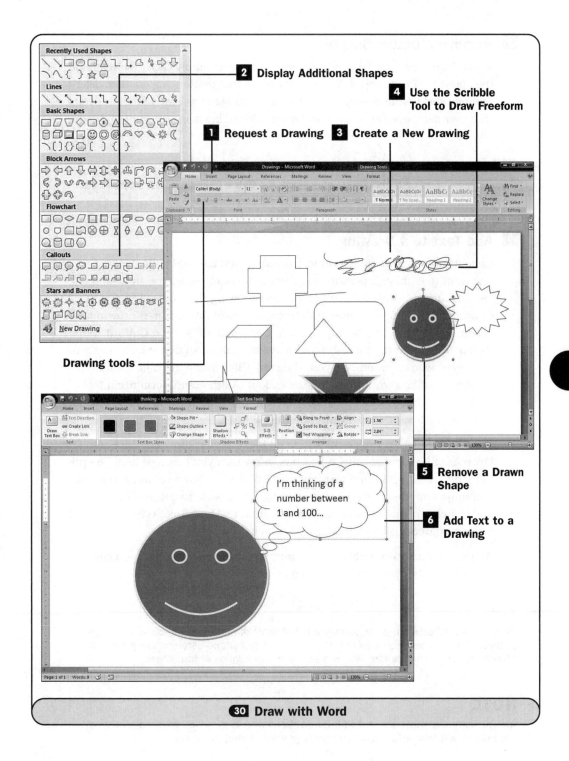

2 Display Additional Shapes

4 Use the Scribble Tool to Draw Freeform

1 Request a Drawing **3** Create a New Drawing

Drawing tools

5 Remove a Drawn Shape

6 Add Text to a Drawing

I'm thinking of a number between 1 and 100...

30

30 Draw with Word

5 Remove a Drawn Shape

If you decide you don't want a shape you've created, simply click to select it and then press the Delete key. If you have drawings that overlap one another, determining exactly what is selected can be tricky; study the resizing handles as you click over the shapes to ensure that you've selected the item you want to delete.

▶ **TIP**

If you change your mind about a deletion, click the **Quick Access** toolbar's **Undo** button (or press the undo shortcut key, Ctrl+Z).

6 Add Text to a Drawing

Callouts are often useful to add to a drawing. You can add callouts to text you want to highlight, perhaps to accent a discount paragraph in a sales letter. You can use a callout as a text balloon showing that someone on your drawing is speaking. For more traditional technical and business drawings, callouts are useful for labeling items. To add a callout, select a **Callout** shape tool, add the callout, and resize and move the callout so that it hovers exactly where you want it to land on your drawing. Click inside the callout and type whatever text you want to use for the callout. All the usual formatting tools work on the callout's text, such as italic and boldface. If the callout is too large for the text you type, resize the callout box.

The **Callout** tool isn't the only way to add text to your drawing. Click the **Draw Text Box** tool to draw a text box into which you can type text. The primary difference between a text box and a callout is that a callout has a line pointing to another item the text refers to. If you want to get really fancy, you can change the color of the text box from the **Text Box Styles** ribbon group that appears when you've added a text box.

All the tools across the ribbon constantly update to reflect things you can do to whatever shape you've just placed or selected.

▶ **TIP**

Click the **3-D Effects** button to display a list of three-dimensional effects you can apply to the various shapes you've added. Click to select any shape before clicking the **3-D Effects** button to change the three-dimensional appearance of that shape.

▶ **NOTE**

Always work to express and not to impress. Don't overdo graphics, or the busyness of the images will take away from the message you're trying to convey.

30

31   Add a Chart or Worksheet to a Document

✔ BEFORE YOU BEGIN	→ SEE ALSO
29 Insert Graphics in a Document	**52** Create a New Worksheet
	82 Add a Chart to a Worksheet

Office's electronic worksheet program Excel produces excellent charts and graphs. In many documents, you'll need to include a chart and possibly a spreadsheet to make a point more clear. Business reports, for example, are full of charts, spreadsheets, and text, all working together to demonstrate the financial health of a company.

You'll find that copying charts and worksheets (also called *spreadsheets*) into a Word document is extremely simple to do. Both require that you start in Excel, because Excel is the source of such charts and spreadsheets. All you need to do is select the chart or spreadsheet and drag or copy it into your document. Word recognizes the copied chart or spreadsheet, and you can resize and format the chart or spreadsheet using Word's tools.

▶ **NEW TERM**

Spreadsheet—Another name for an electronic worksheet such as you might create or edit with Excel.

▶ **TIP**

If you have dual monitors or can position both Word's and Excel's windows on the same screen, you can drag a selected chart from Excel to Word without using the Clipboard.

31

1 Create and Select Excel's Chart

Start Excel and create or load the spreadsheet that contains a chart you want to copy to your Word document. Select the entire chart by clicking it to display its resizing handles.

2 Copy to the Clipboard

Press Ctrl+C or click the **Copy** ribbon button to copy the chart to the Windows Clipboard.

3 Paste the Chart into Word

Return to your Word document and click where you want the chart to appear. Generally, plan to give the chart plenty of room. In other words, you'll usually give the chart the full margin width. Even so, the chart will probably come into your document too wide.

Press Ctrl+V (or click the **Paste** ribbon button) to paste the chart into your Word document.

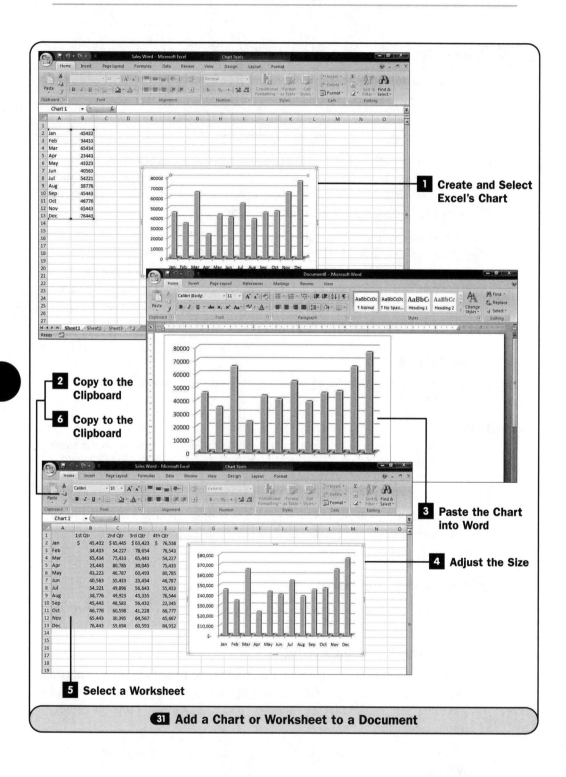

31

1 Create and Select Excel's Chart

2 Copy to the Clipboard

6 Copy to the Clipboard

3 Paste the Chart into Word

4 Adjust the Size

5 Select a Worksheet

31 Add a Chart or Worksheet to a Document

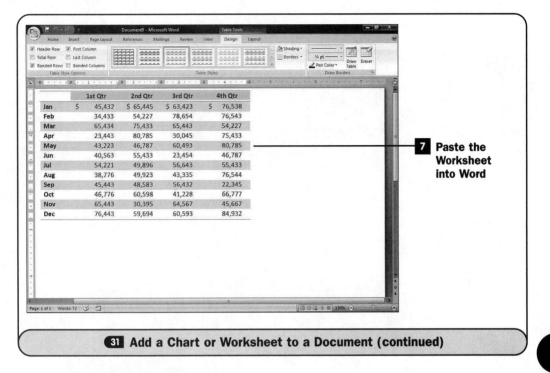

7 **Paste the Worksheet into Word**

31 Add a Chart or Worksheet to a Document (continued)

31

4 Adjust the Size

Drag the chart's resizing handles to adjust the chart's size.

5 Select a Worksheet

To bring an Excel worksheet into a Word document, you must start in Excel. Open the worksheet you want to copy to the Word document. Select the entire worksheet or just the portion of the worksheet you want to copy to Word.

6 Copy to the Clipboard

Press Ctrl+C or click the **Copy** ribbon button to copy the spreadsheet to the Windows Clipboard.

7 Paste the Worksheet into Word

Return to your Word document and click where you want the worksheet to appear. Click the **Paste** ribbon button (you can also press Ctrl+V) to paste the worksheet into your Word document.

▶ NOTE

If your worksheet columns have arrows indicating data-sorting buttons (see **89** About Excel Databases), those column-sorting buttons won't appear in the resulting Word worksheet after you import it.

5

Using Word's Advanced Features

IN THIS CHAPTER:

If you've read some of the earlier Word tasks, you already know that Word provides tremendous power and a lot of features. The capability to display a live preview of a format change before you actually apply that format is an advanced concept hardly found in any software before Word 2007.

Word provides even more advanced features than you've already experienced if you've read the tasks previous to this. Despite being considered advanced, these features are simple to use. In addition to enabling you, for example, to look up definitions and translate foreign words, Word works behind the scenes, automatically making corrections as you type. This chapter provides you with the tools you'll need to take your words to their next level and to create powerful and correct documents.

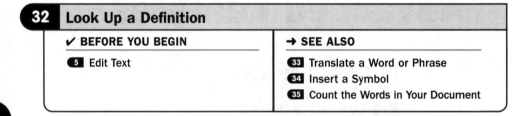

32 | Look Up a Definition

✔ BEFORE YOU BEGIN	→ SEE ALSO
5 Edit Text	**33** Translate a Word or Phrase
	34 Insert a Symbol
	35 Count the Words in Your Document

32

It's a wonder that all early word processors didn't support the lookup of definitions. Only recently have major word processors provided such a feature. When writing, what better tool can one want?

Fortunately, Word 2007 supports the lookup of definitions with ease. When you want to know what something means, just ask Word.

1 Locate a Word to Define

Highlight the word you want to define.

2 Research the Word

Display the **Review** ribbon. Click the **Research** button to look up the highlighted word. The **Research** task pane appears on the right edge of your screen.

3 Select Your Research Tool

Click to display the drop-down list box labeled **All Reference Books**. Word opens a list of dictionaries, thesauruses, websites, and other research locations you might be interested in.

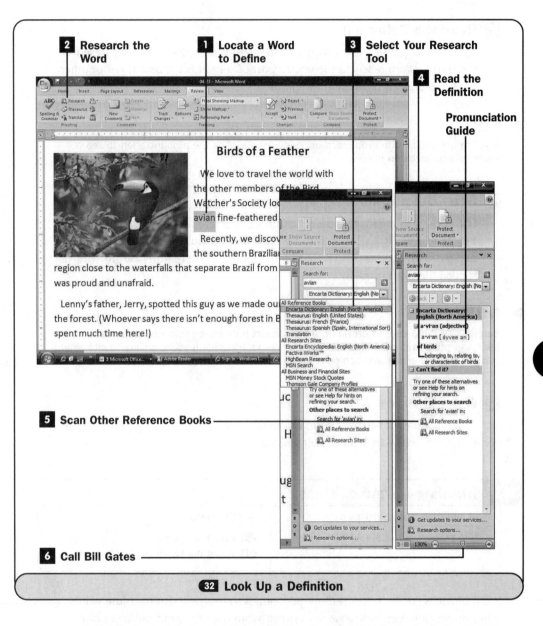

2 Research the
Word

1 Locate a Word
to Define

3 Select Your Research
Tool

4 Read the
Definition

Pronunciation
Guide

5 Scan Other Reference Books

6 Call Bill Gates

32 Look Up a Definition

Select **Encarta Dictionary: English (North America)** if you're in the United
States and working on an English definition. Encarta is a Microsoft product.

▶ **NOTE**

Obviously, if you're in a different country, you might select a different dictionary. If you
aren't writing in English, you certainly won't select the Encarta dictionary. Your default
country and language will almost certainly display a different dictionary that is more
appropriate to your location.

4 Read the Definition

After a brief pause, your selected word's definition appears in your **Research** task pane. Word tells you the word's part of speech (such as a noun or adjective) and offers a pronunciation guide.

▶ **TIP**

If you're unfamiliar with pronunciation guide marks, click the pronunciation to see a guide to pronunciation marks.

5 Scan Other Reference Books

If you want to see more than a definition, click the options under **Other Places to Search**. Occasionally, a word won't appear in the default dictionary, so you'll need to search these other places if you're fairly certain you've spelled the word properly.

▶ **NOTE**

Surprisingly, Word doesn't provide a way to insert a definition into your document. Microsoft might not allow this due to copyright restrictions. If you're willing to cite where you got the references, you can copy and paste the definition into your document.

6 Call Bill Gates

Call Bill Gates at Microsoft and ask him to include an audio pronunciation of dictionary words in Word's next version.

---

33 | **Translate a Word or Phrase**

✔ BEFORE YOU BEGIN	→ SEE ALSO
32 Look Up a Definition	**34** Insert a Symbol
	35 Count the Words in Your Document

Word provides you with translation dictionaries so that you can translate words and phrases from one language to another. Word does this with online resources (as with definitions; see **32 Look Up a Definition**), so you need an Internet connection for this feature to work. Word can even translate entire documents for you.

The number of languages Word translates to and from might surprise you. Keep in mind that machine translation is still in its infancy; Word does an adequate job at the translation. Actually, for a machine, Word does a fine job, but keep in mind that Word is a literal computer program. In spite of the fact that Microsoft's online translation tools are some of the leading edge tools available today, a person can

2 Research the Word or Phrase   **1** Locate a Word or Phrase to Translate

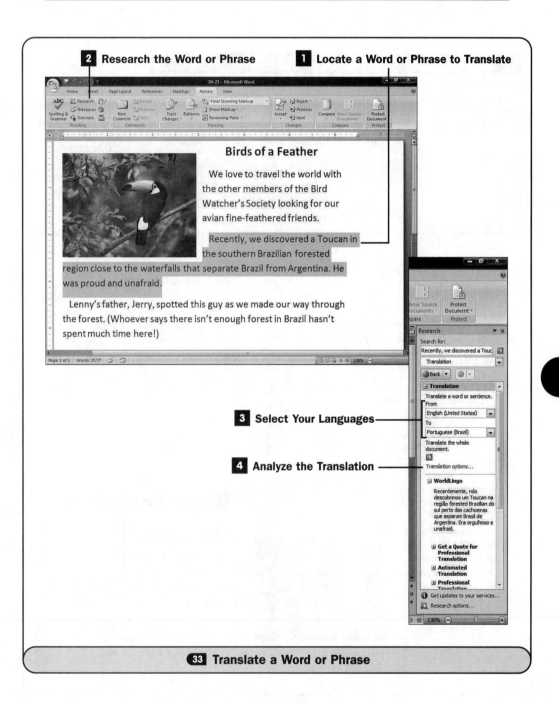

3 Select Your Languages

4 Analyze the Translation

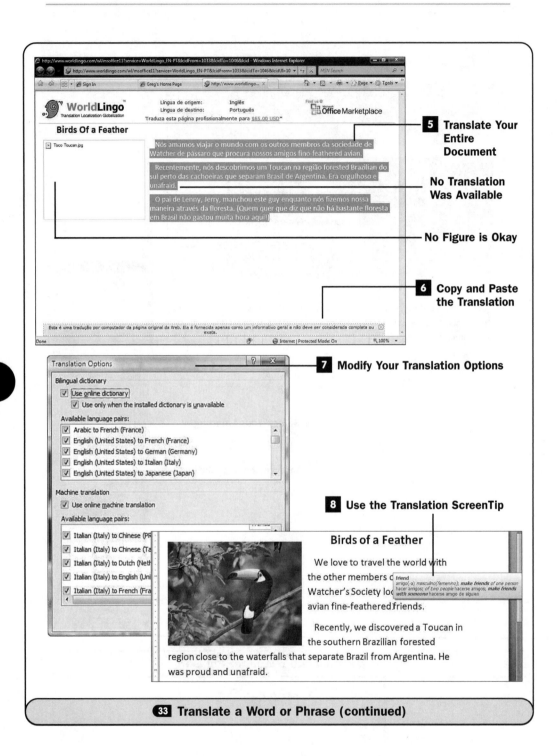

5 Translate Your Entire Document

No Translation Was Available

No Figure is Okay

6 Copy and Paste the Translation

7 Modify Your Translation Options

8 Use the Translation ScreenTip

33

33 Translate a Word or Phrase (continued)

still translate far better than a computer. A person has the innate ability to understand language nuances. Therefore, after you translate a word or phrase, do your best to study the translation, and if you have any knowledge of the target language, look over the translation as best you can to help ensure that your translated words convey the meaning you intended.

1 Locate a Word or Phrase to Translate

Highlight the word or phrase you want to translate.

2 Research the Word or Phrase

Display the **Review** ribbon. Click the **Translate** button to begin the translation of your highlighted phrase. The **Research** task pane appears on the right edge of your screen and the translation begins.

3 Select Your Languages

If Word doesn't guess correctly at the target language you want to translate, select a different language from the **To** list and click the green button to the right of your phrase in the **Search For** text box.

4 Analyze the Translation

Look over the translated phrase and make sure that it conveys your desired tone. Obviously, the more you know about the target language, the better you will be at this. If you're completely ignorant of the target language, you'll have to accept Word's translation. (Most of the time you'll be safe in doing this.)

5 Translate Your Entire Document

If you decide you want to translate your entire document, make sure that your target language is selected properly, and then click the green button under the heading **Translate the Whole Document**. After a dialog box for confirming the translation appears, Word sends your document to a website named WorldLingo.com to complete the translation.

▶ NOTE

The translated document won't display pictures you may have embedded in your Word document.

6 Copy and Paste the Translation

After the translation appears, open a new Word document and copy and paste the translated text from the website to your document. Again, be sure to review the translation. The more important the translation is, the more critical it will be for you to check it somehow. Some words will not be translated because they don't happen to appear in the translation dictionary. Word will underline the words that are spelled incorrectly.

▶ NOTE

Information appears on the WorldLingo.com website on professional translation services. You can hire a translator to translate your documents, and the fee is based on the number of pages to translate. For an important translation, this fee might be worth the cost to you.

7 Modify Your Translation Options

Click the **Translation Options** link in your **Research** task pane's center section to display the **Translation Options** dialog box. There you can modify options and select which languages should, or should not, appear as options in your translation window.

After selecting the options appropriate to you, click **OK** to close the dialog box.

8 Use the Translation ScreenTip

Click the **Translation ScreenTip** button on your **Review** ribbon to set a default language used to translate individual words in your document. After you've selected a language from the available languages in the drop-down list, when you rest your mouse pointer over a word in your document, Word pops up a translation tip showing you the word in the translated language and uses of that word in the language.

34

34 **Insert a Symbol**	
✔ **BEFORE YOU BEGIN**	→ **SEE ALSO**
5 Edit Text	**35** Count the Words in Your Document

Computers don't just work with letters and numbers. In the global economy in which we live, computers must be able to support a wide array of special characters. Those special characters include not only international monetary symbols but also characters from other languages that might not exist in your native tongue.

With Word, you can insert any special character into your documents. All these special symbols don't appear on your keyboard, so you must use a different means to insert them. In this task, you will see how Word makes doing so simple.

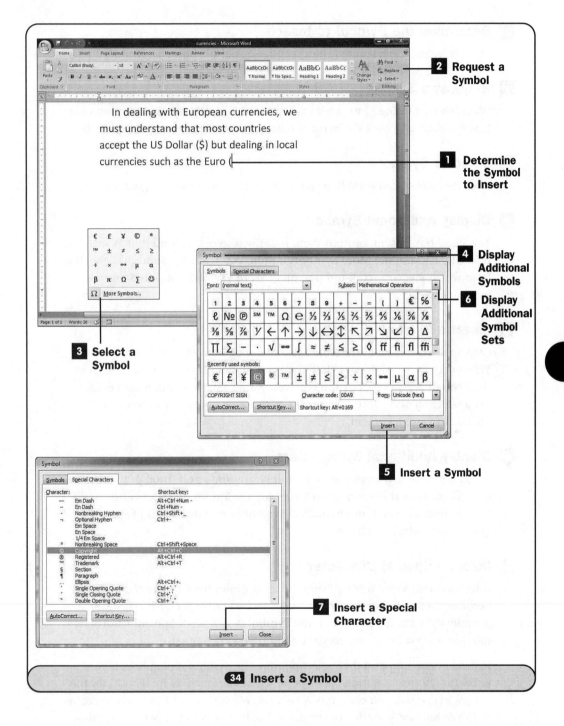

2 Request a Symbol

In dealing with European currencies, we must understand that most countries accept the US Dollar ($) but dealing in local currencies such as the Euro (

1 Determine the Symbol to Insert

4 Display Additional Symbols

6 Display Additional Symbol Sets

3 Select a Symbol

34

5 Insert a Symbol

7 Insert a Special Character

34 Insert a Symbol

1 Determine the Symbol to Insert

Open or create the document that requires a special character symbol.

2 Request a Symbol

When you get to the place where you need to insert the symbol, display your **Insert** ribbon and click the **Symbol** button. Word displays a list of symbols.

3 Select a Symbol

Click the symbol you want to insert. Word places the symbol in your document.

4 Display Additional Symbols

The small box of symbols that Word initially displays isn't all that Word offers. By clicking the **More Symbols** button, you open the **Symbol** dialog box from which you can scroll through all of Word's symbols and find one you want to insert.

5 Insert a Symbol

Click to select a symbol from the **Symbol** dialog box and then click **Insert**. When you do, Word doesn't close the **Symbol** dialog box; instead, it leaves the **Symbol** dialog box open in case you want to insert additional symbols. Keep selecting and clicking **Insert** for as many symbols as you want to include in your document.

6 Display Additional Symbol Sets

If you don't see a symbol you want to insert as you scroll through the **Symbol** dialog box, click the down arrow to display the **Subset** drop-down list. You'll find geometric shapes, mathematical symbols, and other kinds of symbol groups from which to choose.

7 Insert a Special Character

It appears that Word distinguishes the term *symbol* from *special character* because the **Symbol** dialog box includes tabbed pages for each. This isn't actually the case. If you click on the **Symbol** dialog box's **Special Characters** tab, you'll see a list of symbols and their keyboard shortcuts.

Instead of opening and then selecting from the **Symbol** dialog box, if you know the shortcut keystroke of a special character, such as Alt+Ctrl+C for the copyright symbol, you can press Alt+Ctrl+C when you want to insert the copyright symbol into your document instead of first having to open the **Symbol** dialog box. You can return to the **Special Characters** dialog box page if you need a refresher on the special character shortcut keystrokes available.

34

35 Count the Words in Your Document

✔ BEFORE YOU BEGIN	→ SEE ALSO
5 Edit Text	**38** About Hyphenation
	44 Add a Footnote or an Endnote

1 Get Page and Word Counts

2 Get a Selection Word Count

3 Include Text Boxes, Footnotes, and Endnotes

4 Get Page, Word, Character, Paragraph, and Line Counts

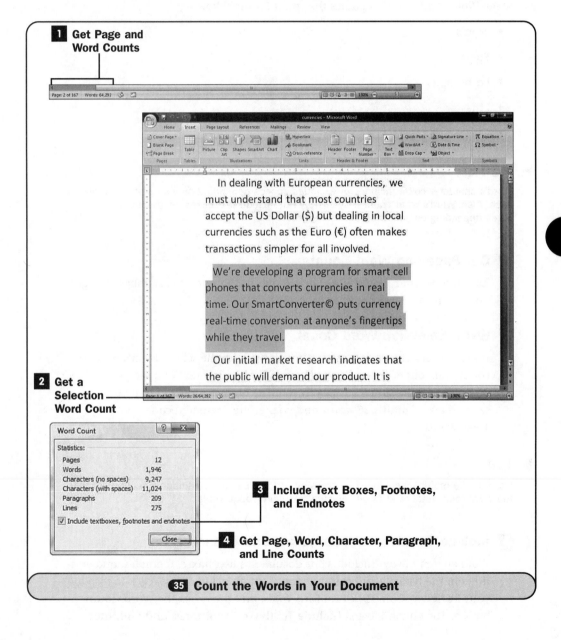

35

As you write, you'll sometimes need to know statistics about your document. How many words are there? How many letters? How many pages?

Writers for newspapers and magazines often have a word limit. Books are planned in advance, so the page count and word count must fall within a certain range.

Word provides these kinds of statistics for you and updates the counts as you write. Word continuously updates the count for the following:

- Words
- Pages
- Paragraphs
- Lines
- Characters

▶ NOTE

Word's character count includes or excludes spaces depending on your stated preference. Also, Word's word count may or may not include text boxes, footnotes, and endnotes depending on your stated preferences.

35

1 Get Page and Word Counts

As you type, your Word status bar updates to show you the number of pages and words that your document contains.

2 Get a Selection Word Count

When you select text, your status bar shows both the selected text's word count and your document's word count. If you select text and see "Words: 26/1,946" for the status bar's word count, Word is telling you that your selected text contains 26 words and your entire document contains 1,946 words.

▶ TIP

If you make multiple selections by pressing Ctrl as you select additional sections of text, the word-count total reflects all selected text word-count totals.

3 Include Text Boxes, Footnotes, and Endnotes

Word doesn't always include your document's text boxes, footnotes, and endnotes in the typical word count. If you want to include those, click to display your **Review** ribbon, click **Proofing Tools**, and then click the **Word Count** button. The option labeled **Include Textboxes, Footnotes, and Endnotes** appears. Click to check the option, or click to uncheck the option, depending on your needs.

4 Get Page, Word, Character, Paragraph, and Line Counts

As you can see from the **Word Count** dialog box, Word continuously updates the number of pages, words, characters (with or without spaces), and lines in your document as you type. Check the **Word Count** dialog box as often as you want to keep tabs on your writing's statistics.

▶ **NOTE**

Notice that the Word Count dialog box displays a character count that includes spaces and one that excludes spaces.

---

36   Use Drop Caps

✔ BEFORE YOU BEGIN	→ SEE ALSO
5 Edit Text	**39** Add a Watermark
12 Apply Character Formatting	

36

It seems as though great books in history start with a ***drop cap*** character. The large, first-letter lead-in works to add flair and style to a book, adding a respectable dimension.

▶ **NEW TERM**

Drop cap—A large starting letter or word, sometimes twice the size of the other letters of the same paragraph, that provides a visual starting point for paragraphs of text.

As with most of its offerings, Word enables you to add drop caps to your documents. You control how the drop cap falls on the line and how it is formatted. Drop caps look cool, but as with any formatting feature, don't overuse drop caps. Use them sparingly when the document deserves them.

1 Determine a Drop Cap Character

Select the letter in your document that you want to convert to a drop cap letter. Usually, this will be the first character in your document's text (not the title or heading).

▶ **NOTE**

If you select an entire word or phrase, Word converts all that selected text to a drop cap.

36

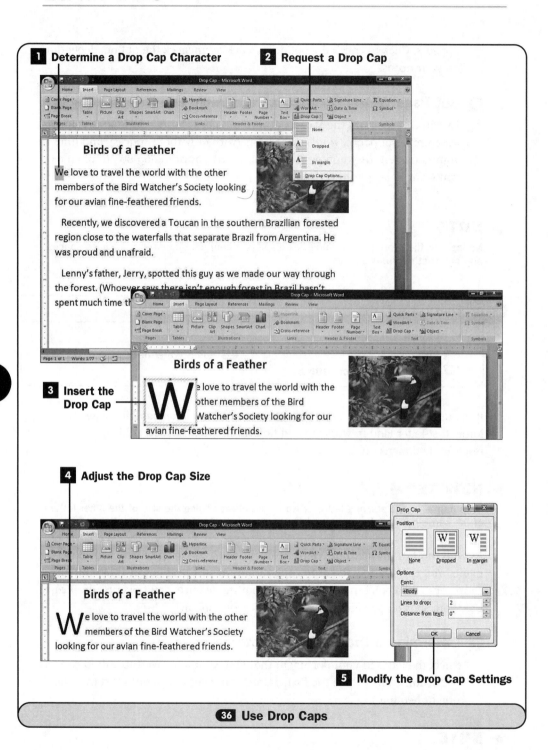

1 Determine a Drop Cap Character

2 Request a Drop Cap

3 Insert the Drop Cap

4 Adjust the Drop Cap Size

5 Modify the Drop Cap Settings

36 Use Drop Caps

2 Request a Drop Cap

Click to display your **Insert** ribbon. Click the **Drop Cap** button to display the drop cap options. The pictures on the drop-down button show you two of the available drop cap formats. You can insert a dropped letter that aligns with your left margin or offset the drop cap so that all text in the rest of the paragraph aligns to the right of the drop cap letter.

▶ TIP

As you point to each drop cap option, your text changes to reflect that selection.

3 Insert the Drop Cap

Click to select the drop cap you prefer. The selected letter (or word if you selected an entire word for the drop cap) expands and fills the drop cap space.

4 Adjust the Drop Cap Size

Sizing handles appear around your drop cap letter. You can drag to adjust the size of the letter so that it suits your needs. For example, if the drop cap spans three lines and you want it to span only two, you can drag the lower-right corner of the drop cap up and to the left to shrink its size to span only two lines of the text.

37

5 Modify the Drop Cap Settings

If you click **Advanced** from within the **Drop Cap** drop-down list available to you when you click the **Insert** ribbon's **Drop Cap** button, Word displays the **Drop Cap** dialog box, with which you have more precise control over the placement of your drop cap. You can specify the number of lines the drop cap is to span as well as the distance from the surrounding text and the font used.

---

37 | **Use AutoCorrect to Improve Your Typing**

✔ BEFORE YOU BEGIN	→ SEE ALSO
4 Type Text into a Document **8** Check a Document's Spelling and Grammar	**41** AutoFormat Your Document

---

Word's *AutoCorrect* feature acts like a helpmate looking over your shoulder as you type. If you make an error, the AutoCorrect feature can quietly and quickly correct it (depending on the error).

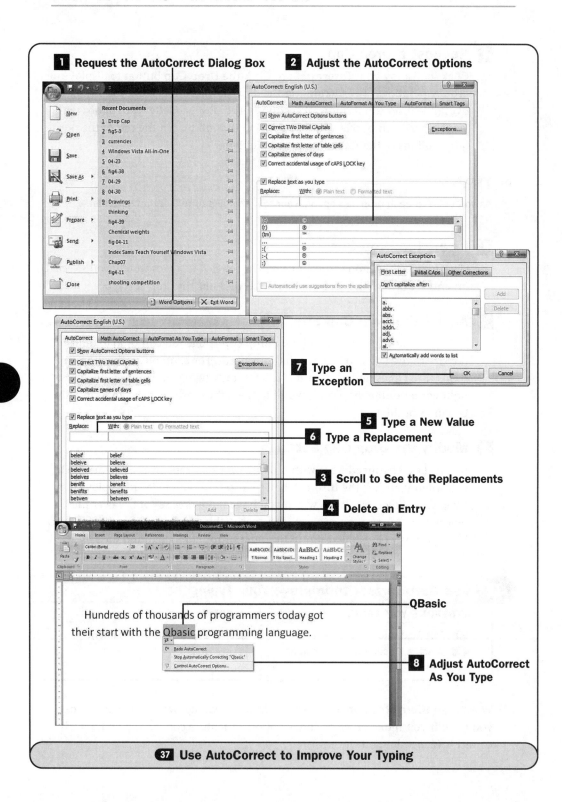

1 Request the AutoCorrect Dialog Box

2 Adjust the AutoCorrect Options

37

7 Type an Exception

5 Type a New Value

6 Type a Replacement

3 Scroll to See the Replacements

4 Delete an Entry

QBasic

Hundreds of thousands of programmers today got their start with the Qbasic programming language.

8 Adjust AutoCorrect As You Type

37 Use AutoCorrect to Improve Your Typing

▶ NEW TERM

AutoCorrect—Word's capability to make adjustments and corrections as you type.

Word gives you complete control over the way it handles AutoCorrect entries. You can modify the correction list, add your own corrections that you want Word to make, and add to a list of exceptions so that Word stops correcting things you don't want corrected.

If you find Word correcting certain words and phrases that you don't want corrected, you can add those words and phrases to Word's exception list.

1 Request the AutoCorrect Dialog Box

Click the **Office** button and select **Word Options** to display the **Word Options** dialog box.

2 Adjust the AutoCorrect Options

Click **Proofing** to display Word's proofing tool options. Click the **AutoCorrect Options** button to display the **AutoCorrect** dialog box. (See **41 AutoFormat Your Document** for information on how to use the AutoFormat tabbed pages.)

3 Scroll to See the Replacements

Scroll down the list to see all the replacements that Word will make on your behalf. Many of the replacements replace common misspellings, such as *believe* for when you accidentally type *beleiv*.

4 Delete an Entry

If you want Word to stop making one of the replacements, select that entry in the list and click the **Delete** button on the right side of the dialog box. For example, you may be writing a book and want to designate your headings using a common format such as A-heads, B-heads, C-heads, and so on, indicating each succeeding level of subheadings throughout the text. If you prefix your third-level headings with (c), Word immediately replaces the (c) with the copyright symbol, unless you delete that entry from the table.

5 Type a New Value

To add your own AutoCorrect entries, click the **Replace** text box and type your value there. This will be the value you want Word to replace.

6 Type a Replacement

Type the value you want to replace the other one with in the **With** text box. Click the **Add** button that appears on the right side of the dialog box when you finish the entry.

37

7 Type an Exception

If you regularly use a lowercase abbreviation that you don't want Word to capitalize, click the **Exceptions** button to display the **AutoCorrect Exceptions** dialog box.

Type the exception abbreviation in the **Don't Capitalize After** text box. If you regularly use a word with two initial capital letters, such as *QBasic*, click the **INitial CAps** tab and type your exception in the **Don't Correct** text box.

8 Adjust AutoCorrect As You Type

When Word corrects something as you type, most of the time you'll want to let Word make the correction. This becomes even truer as you modify the AutoCorrect options to suit the way you write.

When Word does make a correction, you're not stuck with that correction, however. When you notice that Word makes an automatic correction and it's not a correction you want made, move your text cursor back over the word. Word puts a blue underline under the letter that triggered the automatic correction.

Point to the blue line, and Word displays an arrow that produces a drop-down list from which you can choose. Select from the list to tell Word that you want the correction reversed, or that you want Word to stop making the correction in the future, and you can select **Control AutoCorrect Options** to display the **AutoCorrect** dialog box again, where you can make more extensive changes.

38 About Hyphenation

✔ BEFORE YOU BEGIN	→ SEE ALSO
5 Edit Text	**41** AutoFormat Your Document
15 Create a Multicolumn Newsletter	
37 Use AutoCorrect to Improve Your Typing	

Word will automatically hyphenate your document as you type. You can turn on or off hyphenation depending on your requirements. For example, when you're submitting magazine articles, most editors do not want you to hyphenate your submitted manuscript. The magazine's typesetting program will handle that to match the magazine's column widths. Therefore, if you were submitting an article to a magazine, you would want to turn off Word's hyphenation before starting to write.

With hyphenation, when a word is too long to fit at the end of a line, Word will hyphenate the word for you. Word uses a smart hyphenation algorithm to hyphenate the word properly according to the language's requirements. As with most of Word's features, you can control Word's hyphenation by specifying the following:

- Request automatic or manual hyphenation

- Specify optional hyphens

- Hyphenate a portion of your document

- Insert a *nonbreaking hyphen*

- Set the maximum amount of space allowed between a word and the right margin without hyphenating the word

▶ NEW TERM

Nonbreaking hyphen—A hyphen you always want displayed in a word or phrase or number. Word is never to break the word or phrase or number at that hyphen when it reaches the end of a line.

To request automatic hyphenation so that Word inserts needed hyphens as you type, display the **Page Layout** ribbon, and click the **Hyphenation** button in the **Page Setup** group. A list of options appears. Click **Automatic** to turn on automatic hyphenations, and Word will subsequently hyphenate as you type.

*Use the **Hyphenation** dialog box to control your document's hyphenation.*

To insert an optional hyphen, press Ctrl+hyphen where you want the optional hyphen to appear. You won't see the hyphen unless you click the **Show/Hide** button to view nonprinting characters. Word respects your hyphen request, and if the word falls at the end of the line and needs to be hyphenated, Word will hyphenate at the point of your optional hyphen even if that means it has to ignore a more standard hyphenating location.

Suppose that you want to include an optional hyphen in the word *superamalgamated.* Instead of letting Word hyphenate the word as *superamal-gamated* or *superamalga-mated,* you might prefer the word be hyphenated *super-amalgamated* if the word ever requires hyphenation. After typing *super,* you press Ctrl+hyphen before completing the word. (Again, you won't see the embedded hyphen unless you've shown nonprinting characters.) If Word ever has to hyphenate the word at the end of the line, Word will see your optional hyphen request and hyphenate there.

To hyphenate only a portion of your document, select that portion and then display the **Page Layout** ribbon and click **Hyphenation** in the **Page Setup** group. Select **Automatic** from the drop-down list, and Word will hyphenate only your selected portion of the document.

When you've requested a manual hyphenation, Word will prompt you each time a hyphen is required. If you elect to hyphenate, Word inserts the hyphen. If you deny the hyphenation request, Word moves the entire word down to the start of the next line. To set up manual hyphenation, display the **Page Layout** ribbon and click **Hyphenation** in the **Page Setup** group. Select **Manual**, and Word starts the hyphenation and begins hyphenating, requesting your permission each time the hyphenation is required. Word displays a **Hyphenation Is Complete** dialog box when finished.

A nonbreaking hyphen is most useful when typing numbers such as Social Security numbers, telephone numbers, or part numbers. When typing the number, instead of pressing your keyboard's hyphen key at the hyphen, press Ctrl+Shift+hyphen. So to type 1073-7-2220, you would type 1073 and then press Ctrl+Shift+hyphen and then type the 7 and then press Ctrl+Shift+hyphen and finish with 2220. Word will *always* display the number as 1073-7-2220 and will never break the number if it falls close to the end of a line of text.

If you want to shrink or expand the area Word uses at the end of a line for hyphenation, display the **Page Layout** ribbon and click **Hyphenation** in the **Page Setup** group. Select **Hyphenation Options** and change the **Hyphenation Zone** to a larger or smaller value.

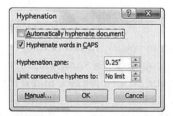

Adjust the spacing that Word uses at the end of a line for its hyphenation.

► **TIP**

Use the **Limit Consecutive Hyphens To** option to limit the number of sequential lines Word can place hyphens on. Some documents, such as narrow-column documents, end up with too many hyphenated lines. You might request that Word use hyphens in no more than two consecutive lines of text. If a third line would use a hyphen, Word won't hyphenate that line but moves the complete word to the start of the next line.

39 Add a Watermark

✔ BEFORE YOU BEGIN

3 Open an Existing Document
29 Insert Graphics into a Document
30 Draw with Word

→ SEE ALSO

49 Add WordArt to a Document

2 Request a Supplied Watermark   **1** Enter Print Layout View

4 Remove a Watermark

3 Apply the Watermark

Watermark

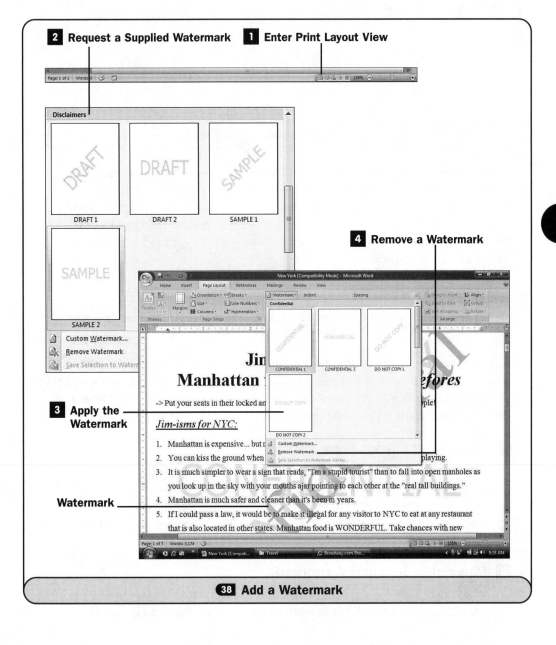

38 Add a Watermark

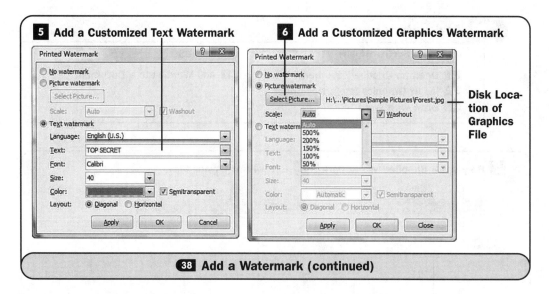

5 Add a Customized Text Watermark   **6** Add a Customized Graphics Watermark

Disk Location of Graphics File

38 Add a Watermark (continued)

A *watermark* is useful for adding a light background image to a document. Some people use watermarks as part of their stationary. Such a watermark might include a company logo. Others use watermarks for indicating a document's place of origin or perhaps labeling draft copies with the letters *DRAFT* diagonally down the page or perhaps putting *TOP SECRET* across the page to remind readers of a document's confidentiality.

▶ NEW TERM

Watermark—Text or a graphics image that appears behind text. A watermark is lighter than the foreground text so that it doesn't cover any of the wording.

In Word, if a document includes a watermark, you will see the watermark when you print the document. When editing a document with a watermark, you will see the watermark in Word's Print Layout or Full Screen Reading views (see **3** **Open an Existing Document** for more information about Word's views).

1 Enter Print Layout View

Before working with watermarks, make sure that you're using the correct Word view. Click the **Print Layout View** button to enter Word's Print Layout view, where you'll be able to see the watermark after you apply it. (You can also view watermarks from the Full Screen Reading view, but you cannot edit your document in that view.)

2 Request a Supplied Watermark

Word offers a few watermarks from which you can select. Display your **Page Layout** ribbon and click **Watermark** in the **Page Background** group. The scrolling list of common watermarks includes Draft and Urgent watermarks that you can apply to your document.

▶ **NOTE**

Surprisingly, Word does not offer a live preview of watermarks. To see how a presupplied watermark will look in your document, you'll have to apply a watermark and view the results. Your **QuickAccess** toolbar's **Undo** button will easily remove a watermark you've added if you change your mind.

3 **Apply the Watermark**

Click to select a watermark. The watermark will appear in your document's background. Assuming that your document had text or graphics before you inserted the watermark, the watermark should be light enough that you can see your text and graphics without problems.

4 **Remove a Watermark**

If you added a watermark in a previous editing session, your **Undo** command won't remove the watermark. To remove a document's watermark, click the **Page Layout** ribbon's **Watermark** button and select **Remove Watermark** to remove your document's watermark.

39

5 **Add a Customized Text Watermark**

You can add your own text to use for a watermark. Click the **Page Layout** ribbon's **Watermark** button and select **More Watermarks**. Word displays the **Printed Watermark** dialog box.

To add custom text, click to open the **Text** drop-down list box or type your own text in the **Text** text box. You then can adjust the font, size, color, and diagonal or horizontal layout of the watermark. For text such as **Top Secret**, you might want your watermark's color to be bright red to gain extra attention.

▶ **NOTE**

In most cases you'll want to keep the **Semitransparent** option selected so that your document text and graphics show through your watermark. Without the **Semitransparent** option checked, your watermark might be dark enough to overwrite your document's details.

▶ **TIP**

Even though Word doesn't provide a watermark live preview, you can usually see the result of your custom watermark. Click **Apply,** and you'll almost always see your watermark on your document, but the **Printed Watermark** dialog box won't close. You then can adjust the watermark and click **Apply** again to see your changes. Only after placing a watermark you approve of do you click **OK** to anchor the watermark in place.

⬛6 Add a Customized Graphics Watermark

You can add your own graphics image to use for a watermark. Click the **Page Layout** ribbon's **Watermark** button and select **More Watermarks**. Word displays the **Printed Watermark** dialog box.

To add a custom image, click to select **Picture Watermark** and click the **Select Picture** button. Locate the picture you want to use as the background watermark. Optionally, you can adjust the scale, or relative size, of the image to grow or shrink the watermark on your page. Keep the **Washout** option selected unless you want the graphics image to be more prominent and risk making your document's text and graphics more difficult to see.

▶ NOTE

You cannot use Word's drawing shapes or WordArt (see ⬛49 **Add WordArt to a Document**) as an actual watermark because the **Printed Watermark** dialog box won't recognize them as watermark figures. You can use these items as watermarks, however, by manually placing them on your page and lightening them up enough for your document's text and graphics to show through.

⬛40 About Building Blocks

✔ BEFORE YOU BEGIN	→ SEE ALSO
⬛28 Create a Cover Page	⬛42 About Headers and Footers

Building blocks are new in Word 2007. Actually, the name and the capability to shift some elements into a category called building blocks are new with Word 2007, but most users of previous versions of Word will be familiar with what building blocks can do. For example, if you've used Word's *AutoText* feature before, you'll understand using a building block in the same way you used AutoText previously because Word 2007 groups AutoText entries into the overall group called building blocks.

Building blocks save you time. Instead of re-creating or retyping the same document elements over and over, you save the elements in your building block library and insert one when you need one.

▶ NEW TERMS

Building blocks—Formatted text, such as a cover page, name and address block, or stationary letterhead that you store in Word's building block library.

AutoText—Text you've stored in Word's default template file (Normal.dot, **which loads automatically every time you create a blank document**) and assigned a name to. You store text that you want to reuse often as an AutoText entry. Type the AutoText name and press F3 to insert the expanded text.

Not only do you create new building blocks that suit your needs, but Word supplies several common building blocks you might find useful. All building blocks are available from your **Insert** ribbon.

*Most of your building blocks are located on your **Insert** ribbon.*

When you insert a cover page, you're actually inserting a stored building block. When you insert a header or footer (see **42** **About Headers and Footers**), you're inserting a building block. The building block might be one that Word supplies or one that you've saved in the past.

► **NOTE**

When you select a cover page, a header, a text box, or any number of other items stored in your library of building blocks, Word refers to those items by name and not by building blocks. In other words, you select from the Cover Page Gallery and the Text Box Gallery even though all these items technically reside in your *building block library.*

► **NEW TERM**

Building Block Organizer—The location where Word stores all your individual building blocks.

Therefore, to add to your building block organizer, you'll add specific elements from their ribbon buttons. To add a new cover page to your building block organizer, for example, you'll create a cover page, click the **Insert** ribbon's **Cover Page** button, and select **Save Selection to Cover Page Gallery**.

Locating your building block organizer isn't as straightforward as locating most of Word's features. To see all the items in your building block organizer, display your **Insert** ribbon, click the **Quick Parts** button, and select **Building Blocks Organizer**. Word displays your **Building Blocks Organizer** screen. Scroll through the list using the Gallery column as a guide to learn what each building block is used for.

40

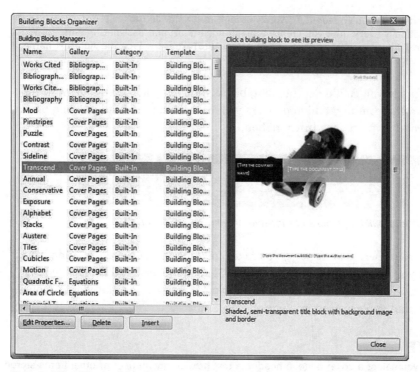

40

Your Building Blocks Organizer contains all building block elements in Word, including Word's supplied building blocks as well as the ones you create and add to the building block collection.

You'll rarely add to your Building Blocks Organizer directly. In other words, instead of adding a cover page to your Building Block Organizer from the **Building Blocks Organizer** dialog box, you'll click the **Cover Page** button and select **Save Selection to Cover Page Gallery** to add a cover page to your Building Blocks Organizer.

It's not obvious how to add AutoText to Word 2007. If you routinely place the same text in documents, such as your name and address or letterhead or a closing or legal disclaimer, you can save that formatted text in your Building Blocks Organizer and quickly insert the text when you need it later.

Select the text and display your **Insert** ribbon. Click the **Quick Parts** button and select **Save Selection to Quick Part Gallery**. Word displays the **Create a New Building Block** dialog box. Give your text a name, such as LegalShort, click to open the dialog box's **Gallery** entry, select **AutoText**, add an optional **Category** and **Description** if you like, and click **OK**. The next time you want to insert that formatted text into your document, type its name, such as LegalShort, and press F3 to replace the name with the full, formatted text.

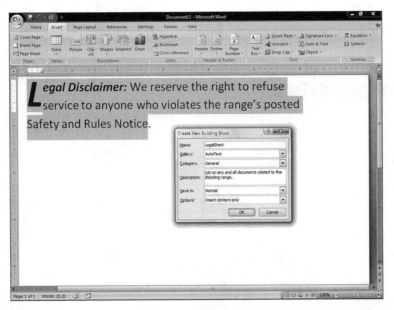

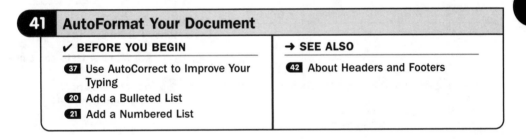

AutoText entries make typing and formatting routine text as simple as pressing F3.

41

41 | AutoFormat Your Document

✔ BEFORE YOU BEGIN	→ SEE ALSO
37 Use AutoCorrect to Improve Your Typing **20** Add a Bulleted List **21** Add a Numbered List	**42** About Headers and Footers

Many of Word's tools work in the background to make your writing as well formatted as possible. Word will check your spelling and grammar and even correct typing mistakes (see **37** **Use AutoCorrect to Improve Your Typing**).

Word will also automatically format your document as you type. Word can ensure that your bulleted lists look nice and uniform and that common fractions that you type out such as 1/2 immediately convert to a symbol such as ½. Also, Word can change straight quotes into custom, rounded quotes, sometimes called *smart quotes*.

▶ NEW TERM

Smart quotes—The rounded quotes that curl in or out, depending on whether they begin or end a quoted phrase. Both single quote marks and regular quotations can be smart quotes. The term originally started with Word and applies to a word processor's capability to recognize whether a quote mark should be open or closed.

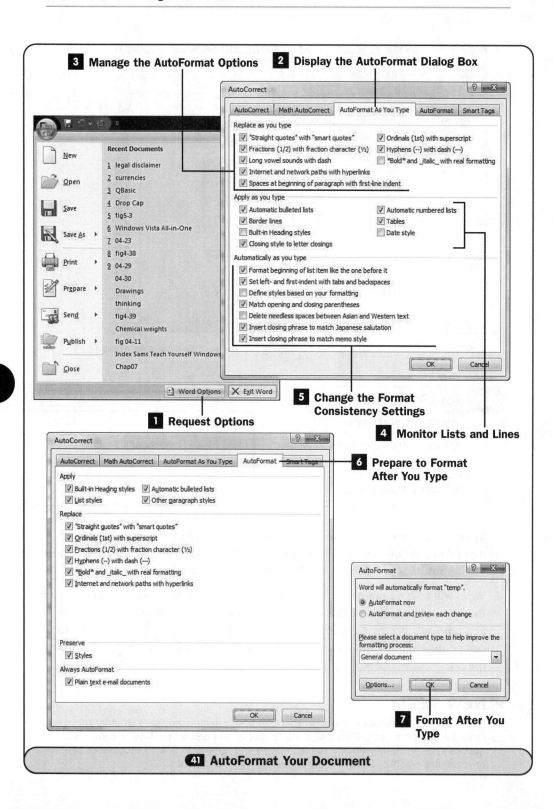

3 Manage the AutoFormat Options

2 Display the AutoFormat Dialog Box

5 Change the Format Consistency Settings

1 Request Options

4 Monitor Lists and Lines

6 Prepare to Format After You Type

7 Format After You Type

41 AutoFormat Your Document

1 Request Options

You manage AutoFormat-related commands from one of the **Word Options** pages. Click your **Office** button and select **Word Options** to display the **Word Options** dialog box.

2 Display the AutoFormat Dialog Box

Click the **Proofing** tab and then click the **AutoCorrect** button to display the **AutoCorrect** dialog box. Click the **AutoFormat As You Type** tab to change the way Word formats text as you type.

3 Manage the AutoFormat Options

When you first install or work with Word, most of the **AutoFormat** options will be selected. For example, the option labeled **Internet and Network Paths with Hyperlinks** will be selected. That means that any time you type an Internet web address such as www.BidMentor.com, Word will change the text to a link that is clickable and that takes you straight to the related website.

4 Monitor Lists and Lines

The **Apply as You Type** section of your **AutoCorrect** dialog box determines how much Word helps you create bulleted lists, numbered lists, tables, lines, and so forth.

Normally, when you start typing a numbered list by typing 1. on a line followed by a space and text, Word senses that you're creating a numbered list, and when you press Enter at the end of the line Word automatically starts the second item in the list with the number "2." (See **21 Add a Numbered List.**)

Also, Word creates a table for you when you start a table by typing plus signs with hyphens between them, such as +——+——+——+, which Word converts to a three-column table. Also, Word will change a row of five or more hyphens to a straight line across the page.

You can retain or reject any of these automatically formatted routines by clicking to check or uncheck the appropriate options.

5 Change the Format Consistency Settings

The section titled **Automatically as You Type** includes several consistency settings. Word will format a list of items like the first item in the list you type; for example, if you begin typing "(a) Apples" and press Enter, Word starts the next line with "(b)" followed by a space to prepare you for the second item in your list. Also, Word will monitor grammatical formatting issues,

41

such as ensuring that you have matching opening and closing parentheses in a document.

6 Prepare to Format After You Type

Depending on your needs, you might want Word to apply your AutoFormats after you type a document instead of as you type it. This might be a rare case, but suppose that you receive a document attached to an email that you didn't write but that you want to use. If you want to apply your specific AutoFormat settings to that document, you need a way to apply the AutoFormat procedure on completed documents.

Click the **AutoFormat** tab of the **AutoCorrect** dialog box to see the formatting elements available after you type a document. Click to check or uncheck the options as you prefer.

7 Format After You Type

The way you apply an AutoFormat to a document isn't as clear as most other features are in Word 2007. As a matter of fact, it seems as though you must resort to previous versions of Word's menus to access this feature.

Press Alt+O and then press A to simulate selecting from the **Format, AutoFormat** menu of previous versions of Word. Word displays the **AutoFormat** dialog box so that you can accept or reject each format change or apply your AutoFormat settings to your entire document at one time.

▶ NOTE

Word 2007 supports the previous Word versions' menu structures. Therefore, until you familiarize yourself with Word's ribbon, you might want to use the old menu keystrokes to get to the commands you need.

---

42 About Headers and Footers

✔ BEFORE YOU BEGIN	→ SEE ALSO
14 Set Up Page Formatting	**43** Add a Header or Footer
16 About Styles, Themes, and Templates	

Headers and *footers* can give your documents a consistent appearance. You can select certain pages to receive headers and footers. Word also supports the use of odd- and even-numbered headers and footers. For example, you might want a page number to appear in the upper-right corner of the header on odd pages and in the upper-left corner of the header on even pages. You can put both a header and a footer on a page or use only one or the other.

▶ NEW TERMS

Header—Text that appears at the top of every page in a section or document.

Footer—Text that appears at the bottom of every page in a section or document.

Headers and footers can contain graphics, so you can, for instance, place your company's logo at the top of every page. Word also supports the use of *fields*, such as page numbers, the time, the date, and even chapter numbers. When you insert one of these fields, Word inserts the actual value. If your document, for example, is 50 pages, the pages will automatically display 1 through 50. If you delete a page from your document, Word instantly renumbers the pages.

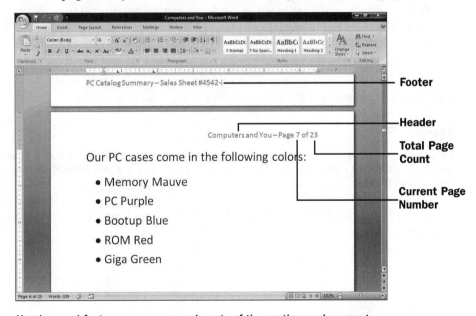

Headers and footers appear on each page of the section or document.

▶ NEW TERM

Fields—Placeholders in your documents that Office fills in with actual values, such as page numbers, the time, and the date.

Word comes with several predesigned headers and footers. You can also add your own. The headers and footers are part of your Building Blocks Organizer (see **40** *About Building Blocks*), so you can reuse ones you create and store.

When you're editing a document that has a header and footer, Word lightens the header and footer areas to indicate that they are protected. You cannot change a header or footer unless you first double-click that header or footer. Doing so brings the header or footer into clear view and places the cursor inside the header or footer area. Word requires that you specifically request an edit to a header or footer by double-clicking it so that you don't accidentally change the text inside a header or footer while editing the rest of the document.

43   Add a Header or Footer

✔ BEFORE YOU BEGIN	→ SEE ALSO
11 About Paragraph Breaks and Tabs	**44** Add a Footnote or an Endnote
42 About Headers and Footers	

43

Word's header and footer capabilities provide you with the tools you need to add predesigned headers and footers quickly and easily to your document's pages. Each header and footer is saved in the page's current section. If your document has multiple sections, your document can have multiple headers and footers, too. Word updates the fields in your headers and footers as needed, such as when a page number changes or if the date is included in a header or footer.

▶ **TIP**

Sometimes you won't want a header or footer to appear on a page. Simply insert a new section for that page and don't add the header or footer (see **11** **About Paragraph Breaks and Tabs**).

Here are some of Word's more common fields that you can use in your headers or footers:

- Date
- Time
- Page number
- Page count
- Author

The page number and page count fields can be combined to create a header or footer that reads, for example, "Page 4 of 17."

Section Number   Field Name   **1** Request a Header

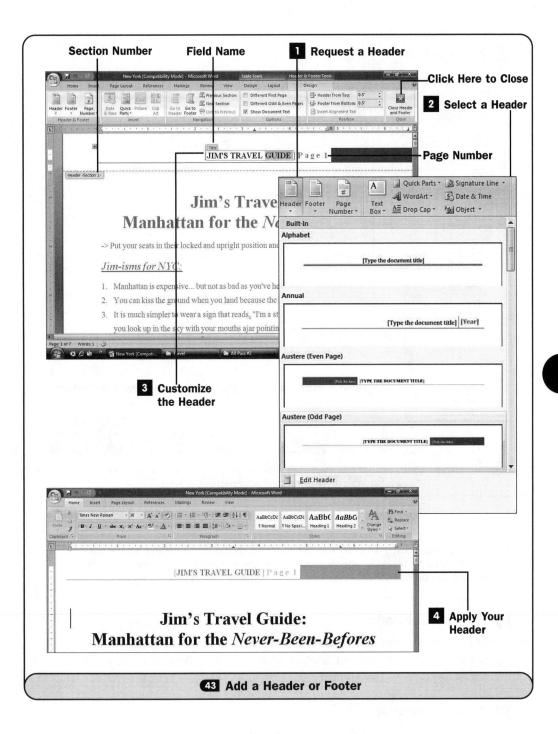

3 Customize
the Header

4 Apply Your
Header

43

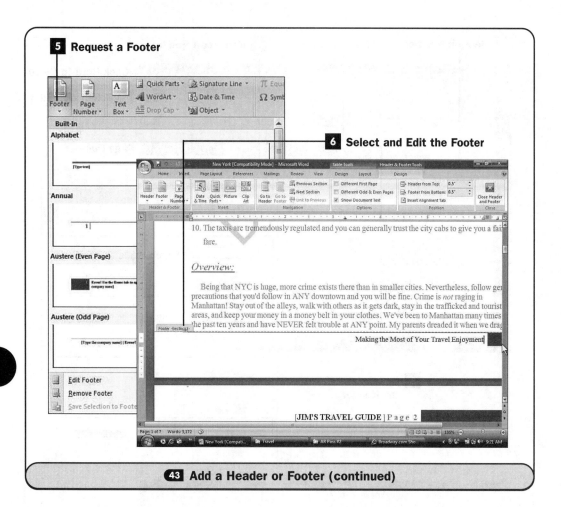

43 Add a Header or Footer (continued)

▶ TIP

You can make sure that a header or footer is unique to the first page in your document (as you might do for a cover page on which you might not want page numbers to appear) by selecting the **Different First Page** option when editing your header or footer.

1 Request a Header

Display your **Insert** ribbon and click to open the **Header** list. Word displays a scrolling list of predefined headers, as well as any custom headers you or someone else may have added.

2 Select a Header

Click to select one of the headers. Word will insert the header and place your cursor in the header area, where you can edit the fields.

3 Customize the Header

Change the fields as needed. As you click on each field, Word displays the field name, and you'll replace the field placeholder text inside the brackets.

Word also displays the current section number in case your document has different sections. For multisectioned documents, you can insert a different header in each section.

Your ribbon changes to reflect the fact that you're editing a header. You can adjust how far the header appears from the top of the page, as well as whether you want a different header on odd and even pages.

▶ **NOTE**

Books often use a different header atop odd and even pages. The header for even-numbered pages might be the title, and the odd-numbered header might include the chapter or author name. This book uses Task names for the odd pages header text.

4 Apply Your Header

Click your ribbon's **Close** button or just double-click inside your document's text to anchor the header and bring the editing focus back to your document's text.

If you want to make changes to your header, double-click the area inside the header, and Word will bring the editing focus back to the header and change your ribbon to include header-editing commands.

5 Request a Footer

You'll insert a footer in much the same way as a header. The footer, of course, appears at the bottom of your document pages.

Display your **Insert** ribbon and click to open the **Footer** list. Word displays a scrolling list of predefined footers as well as any custom footers you or someone else may have added.

6 Select and Edit the Footer

Click to select one of the footers. Word will insert the footer and place your cursor in the footer area, where you can edit the fields.

Change the footer fields as needed. As you click on each field, Word displays the field name, and you can replace the field placeholder text inside the brackets.

Word also displays the current section number in case your document has different sections. For multisectioned documents, you can insert a different footer in each section.

43

Your ribbon changes to reflect the fact that you're editing a footer. You can adjust how far the footer appears from the top of the page as well as whether you want a different footer on odd and even pages.

▶ **TIP**

As you type text for your header and footer, all of Word's character-formatting operations work on the header and footer text. You're not stuck with the character formatting that the predesigned headers and footers provide.

As with the header, when you click the **Close** button or just double-click inside your document's body of text, Word shades the footer section and returns your editing focus to your document's text. If you want to make changes to your footer, double-click the footer area, and Word brings it back into editing focus again.

44

44	**Add a Footnote or an Endnote**

✔ **BEFORE YOU BEGIN**

42 About Headers and Footers
43 Add a Header or Footer

In addition to headers and footers, Word supports the inclusion of *footnotes* and *endnotes* in your documents. A footnote differs from an endnote in that it appears only on the page in which it's referenced. An endnote appears at the end of your document, referenced somewhere in the text.

You can place both footnotes and endnotes in your documents. After you set up footnotes or endnotes, Word takes over the administration of them. Therefore, if you add a footnote between two others, Word renumbers all the footnotes accordingly. The same goes for endnotes, so if you delete an endnote, Word renumbers all the other endnotes affected by the deletion.

▶ **NEW TERMS**

Footnotes—Notes at the bottom of a page referenced by numbers somewhere on the page.

Endnotes—Notes at the end of a document referenced by numbers somewhere within the body of the document.

When you're ready to insert a footnote or an endnote, a footnote or endnote number appears at the location in the text where you inserted the footnote or endnote.

Word takes care of sequentially numbering footnotes and endnotes for you as you add them. If you remove a footnote or an endnote, Word renumbers the remaining footnotes and endnotes accordingly. When you hover your mouse pointer over a footnote or endnote number, Word pops up the text that goes with that footnote or endnote so that you don't have to keep jumping to the bottom of the page or to the end of your document to see what the number represents.

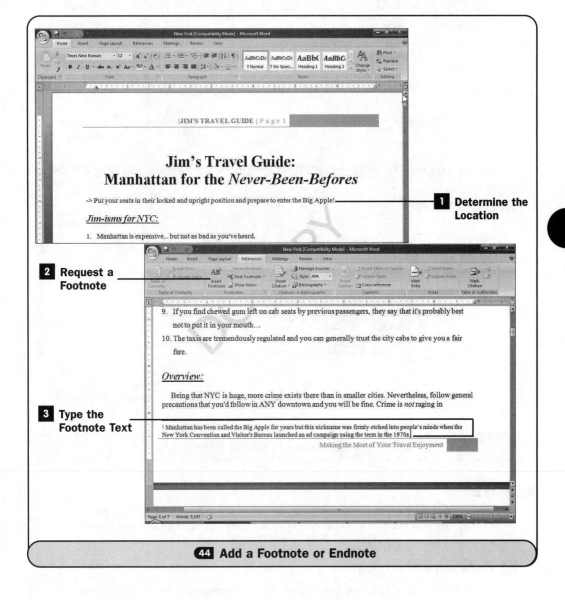

1 Determine the Location

2 Request a Footnote

3 Type the Footnote Text

44 Add a Footnote or Endnote

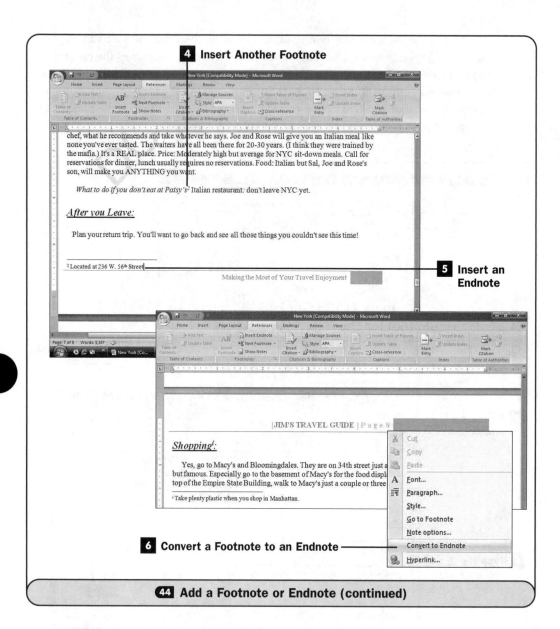

4 Insert Another Footnote

chef, what he recommends and take whatever he says. Joe and Rose will give you an Italian meal like none you've ever tasted. The waiters have all been there for 20-30 years. (I think they were trained by the mafia.) It's a REAL place. Price: Moderately high but average for NYC sit-down meals. Call for reservations for dinner, lunch usually requires no reservations. Food: Italian but Sal, Joe and Rose's son, will make you ANYTHING you want.

What to do if you don't eat at Patsy's[2] Italian restaurant: don't leave NYC yet.

After you Leave:

Plan your return trip. You'll want to go back and see all those things you couldn't see this time!

[2] Located at 236 W. 56th Street

Making the Most of Your Travel Enjoyment

5 Insert an Endnote

[JIM'S TRAVEL GUIDE] P a g e 8

Shopping[1]:

Yes, go to Macy's and Bloomingdales. They are on 34th street just a but famous. Especially go to the basement of Macy's for the food displ top of the Empire State Building, walk to Macy's just a couple or three

[1] Take plenty plastic when you shop in Manhattan.

Cut
Copy
Paste
A   Font...
Paragraph...
Style...
Go to Footnote
Note options...
Convert to Endnote
Hyperlink...

6 Convert a Footnote to an Endnote

44 Add a Footnote or Endnote (continued)

▶ **NOTE**

By default, Word numbers footnotes with regular cardinal numbers such as 1, 2, and so on. Word can also number endnotes with Roman numerals such as i, ii, and so on.

1 Determine the Location

Click inside your document where you want a footnote or an endnote place-holder to go. The placeholder will become a sequential number (or some other text that you will specify) attached to the footnote or endnote. For your first footnote, the number will be 1, and the footnote numbered 1 will always apply to that placeholder. An endnote placeholder numbered 21 will refer to an endnote with the same number. Again, these numbers update automatically if you insert or remove footnotes and endnotes from among others.

2 Request a Footnote

Display your **References** ribbon and click to display the **Insert Footnote** button. Word instantly jumps to the end of your page and adds a number to indicate the footnote number (the first of which will be 1).

3 Type the Footnote Text

Type your footnote text to the right of the footnote's number.

▶ NOTE

If you add a footnote to a multicolumned document, the footnote appears at the bottom of the column where you placed the footnote's anchor.

4 Insert Another Footnote

After you finish typing your footnote's text, scroll back up to your text and click to locate the next place you want to insert a footnote. When you click the **Insert Footnote** button, Word again takes you to the bottom of the page, automatically numbers the new footnote, and places your text cursor so that you can type the footnote text.

▶ NOTE

You can insert footnotes as you type or after you've finished creating a document.

5 Insert an Endnote

Inserting endnotes is virtually identical to inserting footnotes. Click to locate the place where you want to insert the endnote, display your **References** ribbon, and click **Insert Endnote**. Word jumps to the bottom of your document, inserts an endnote number, and places the text cursor next to it so that you can type the text of the endnote.

When you finish typing the endnote, scroll back up to the place in your document where you had inserted the endnote and continue editing.

44

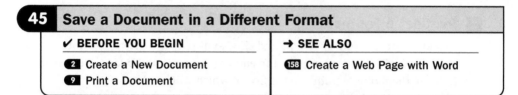

6 **Convert a Footnote to an Endnote**

Right-click over any footnote and select **Convert to Endnote** to request that Word move the footnote to the end of your document and renumber all footnote and endnotes and their references accordingly.

45 **Save a Document in a Different Format**

✔ BEFORE YOU BEGIN	→ SEE ALSO
2 Create a New Document	**158** Create a Web Page with Word
9 Print a Document	

45

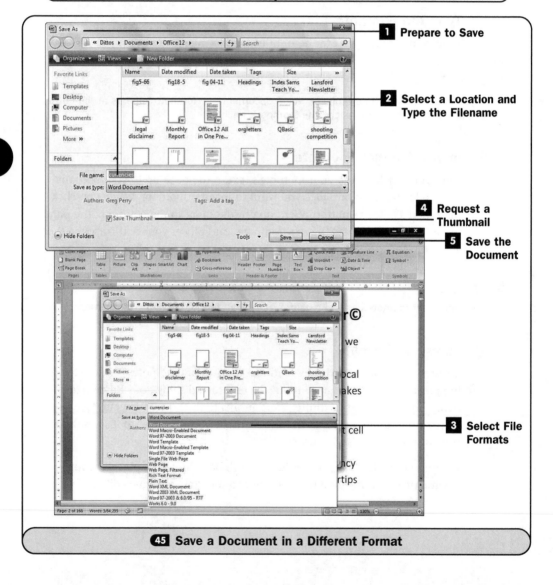

1 Prepare to Save

2 Select a Location and Type the Filename

4 Request a Thumbnail

5 Save the Document

3 Select File Formats

45 Save a Document in a Different Format

Word's native document format is new and differs from previous versions of Word formats. Instead of the .doc filename extension, Word 2007 uses .docx (the *x* is related to the *XML* format) for its native format.

▶ NEW TERM

XML—A machine-independent text format for documents on the Internet as well as offline that is compatible with a high number of programs and is customizable.

You might need to save a Word document in a different format. Perhaps you have friends who still use Word 2003 or earlier. You can also save Word documents as web pages. This task shows you how to save Word documents in any format Word supports.

▶ NOTE

When you save in different file formats, Word uses a different filename extension depending on the format. Therefore, you can have a document with the same filename in various formats; only the filename extension will differ among them.

1 Prepare to Save

When you are ready to save your document, click your **Office** button and click the **Save As** button. Word displays the **Save As** dialog box.

2 Select a Location and Type the Filename

Click to change the location of your saved file if you don't want to use the default location. Type your document's filename in the **File Name** text box.

3 Select File Formats

Click the down arrow next to the **Save as Type** drop-down list box to display all the file formats that Word supports.

Click to select one of the file formats. If, for example, you have Microsoft Works but not Word on your laptop, you could save your document as a Works file and email it to yourself. Retrieve your email on your laptop, and you'll be able to start Works and edit the file on your laptop.

▶ NOTE

Keep in mind that if you save the document using both the native Word document format (.docx) and another format, changes you make to one file will not be reflected in the other file.

▶ TIP

You can save Word documents in PDF or XPS formats if you download the Save As PDF or XPS Add-In here: http://r.office.microsoft.com/r/rlidMSAddinPDFXPS.

45

4 Request a Thumbnail

When you save a file, Word automatically clicks to select the option labeled **Save Thumbnails for All Word Documents**. Assuming that Windows Vista's Aero Glass feature is enabled, you can see a live preview of your document in Windows Explorer's thumbnails, when you press Alt+Tab to move between open windows that have your Word documents in them, and when you hover your mouse pointer over a taskbar button that represents an open Word document. If you don't want to save a thumbnail for Word documents, click to uncheck this option. If you don't use the Aero Glass feature, for example, there is no reason to consume extra disk space and time to create the thumbnail images for your Word documents.

5 Save the Document

Click the **Save** button to save your Word document in your converted file format.

---

46 About Mail Merge

→ **SEE ALSO**

47 Write Form Letters with Mail Merge
48 Print an Address on an Envelope or a Label

Word offers powerful *mail merge* tools for those who want to mail personalized documents to family, friends, and business associates. After you have a *data source* of contacts, sending a personalized document to them (often in the form of a letter addressed to them, for example) is simple.

▶ **NEW TERMS**

Mail merge—The process of creating a generic document and personalizing it with name and contact information from an outside data source.

Data source—A store of names, addresses, or other information you'll use to personalize an otherwise generic form letter.

Most people use mail merge to send personalized letters to contacts stored in some kind of name and address data source. Your source might be from Outlook or a Microsoft Access database. You can also type names and addresses directly into a Word document using a specific format and personalize letters so you address each contact individually in each letter.

You'll use Word's **Mailings** ribbon for your mail merge work.

Word's Mailings ribbon contains all the mail merge tools you'll need.

To perform a mail merge, you must create or select a data source, create a form letter called the **main document,** and then print each personalized letter for each contact in your data source. Basically, one personalized letter will print for each contact in your source list.

▶ **NEW TERM**

Main document—Your form letter document that contains placeholder fields for the recipients' name, address, salutation, or any other elements you want to replace in each letter with a corresponding field in the final letter.

▶ **TIP**

Word includes a mail merge wizard that guides you through the creation and printing of a mail merge. Even mail merge pros resort to Word's wizard to walk them through the steps and to produce their mailings.

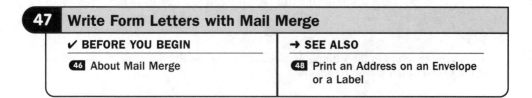

47 **Write Form Letters with Mail Merge**	
✔ **BEFORE YOU BEGIN**	→ **SEE ALSO**
46 About Mail Merge	**48** Print an Address on an Envelope or a Label

Given that mail merge is a more complex procedure than, say, formatting a paragraph, Microsoft included a mail merge **wizard** to help you through your mail merge sessions. Although the wizard is great for beginners who have never done much mail merging in the past, even the pros use the wizard, so don't think of it as a crutch.

▶ **NEW TERM**

Wizard—A step-by-step prompting that guides you through a process such as performing a mail merge. Word's mail merge wizard's steps appear in the task pane.

After you use the wizard for a while, you might want to adjust the way you perform a mail merge and use the specific buttons on the **Mailings** ribbon more. Most of the time, though, you'll probably resort to the wizard since it guides you through each mail merge so well.

1 Request a Mail Merge

Display your **Mailings** ribbon and click the **Start Mail Merge** button to display a list of options. Click to select **Step by Step Mail Merge Wizard**. Word opens the **Mail Merge** task pane and begins to guide you through your mail merge.

2 Specify the Mail Type

Tell Word the kind of document you want to use for the mail merge. For example, if you were sending emails to everybody in an email contact list, you would select **E-mail Messages**. Probably you'll most often send letters for which you want the recipient's name and address filled in, so in that case you click to select **Letters** if that option isn't already selected for you.

Click **Next: Starting Document** to continue the wizard.

3 Specify the Main Document

Let Word know if you want to use the current document (which might be blank if you have not typed your form letter yet), use an existing document, or use a template. If you have never created a form letter before, you'll click to select **Use the Current Document** to use the current, blank document for your form letter's main document. (You'll fill in the details in a moment.)

47

▶ TIP

If you want to return to the wizard's previous step, click the **Previous** link at the bottom of the wizard's **Mail Merge** task pane.

4 Locate Your Data Source

Word needs to know the data source you're going to use for your current mailing's recipients. One of the most obvious places will be your Microsoft Outlook Contacts list, if you use Outlook. For a large data source, hardly any tool is better than Microsoft Access. Word can use either of these, plus a wide array of other common data sources, as your mail merge contacts list.

Word enables you to select from an existing list (again, the list of recipients can be from several kinds of data sources), or to specifically select from Outlook contacts, or perhaps you want to create a new list on-the-fly and begin using it. Obviously, the latter method is time-consuming and doesn't lend itself to easy editing later. An Outlook Contacts list or, better, a database data source such as a Microsoft Access database, makes for a far more manageable data set that can grow with your needs.

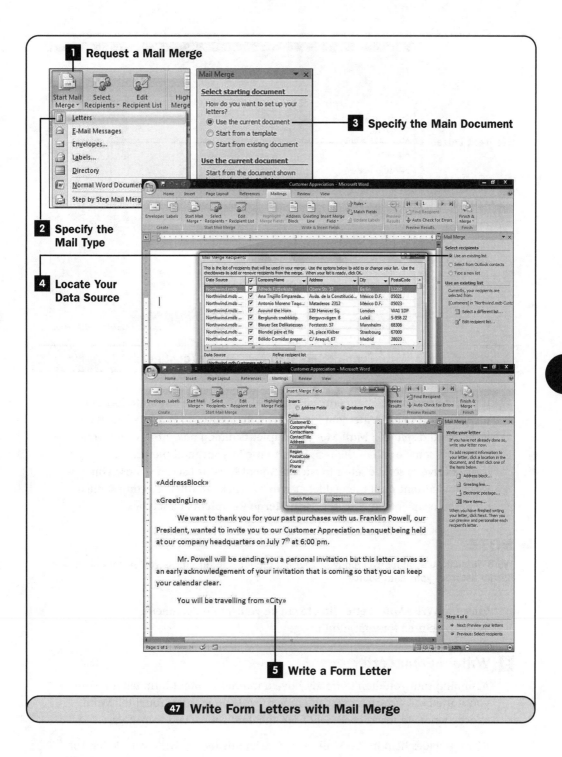

1 Request a Mail Merge

3 Specify the Main Document

2 Specify the Mail Type

4 Locate Your Data Source

5 Write a Form Letter

47

47 Write Form Letters with Mail Merge

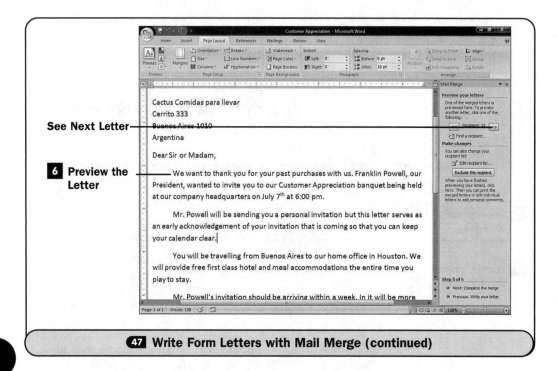

47 Write Form Letters with Mail Merge (continued)

If you're using an existing data source, click the **Browse** button to locate the file you want to use. After you locate the data source, such as an Access database, Word displays a **Mail Merge Recipients** dialog box, from which you can select some or all of the recipients to use in your mail merge. Word doesn't have to send a letter to each recipient in your list, only those you want the current mail-merged letter sent to. Click **OK** after selecting some or all of the recipients to close the **Mail Merge Recipients** dialog box.

▶ **NOTE**

Word defaults to sending everybody in your list the form letter unless you select only a partial list from your data source.

Click the **Write Your Letter** link to create your main document, or form letter, to be used for your mail merge.

5 Write a Form Letter

Assuming that you didn't already have a main document form letter before you started the wizard, now is the time to write your letter. You'll tell Word exactly where to insert each field from the data source you want to use.

Word provides help in the **Mail Merge** task pane as you write your letter. For example, if you want your letter to include the recipient's address, click the task pane's **Address Block** link. Word displays an **Insert Address Block** dialog box, where you can select the exact format you want to use for your recipient's address in your final letters. Word inserts a mail merge placeholder field, in this case <<AddressBlock>>, to indicate where the recipient's name and address will appear in the form letter.

You'll almost certainly want a greeting, so click the **Greeting Line** link to format your greeting the way you want it to look. The field used is <<GreetingLine>>.

▶ **NOTE**

Don't duplicate punctuation. If Word's predesigned field that you select, such as the greeting, includes a comma after the recipient's name, don't add your own comma after the <<GreetingLine>> field.

Type your letter, but when you want to address something personally about the recipient, click the **More Items** link and select the field you want to use. For example, if you reference the recipient's city in your letter, select the <<City>> field from the **Insert Merge Field** dialog box that appears when you click **More Items**.

When you finish typing your letter, click the **Next: Preview Your Letters** link to see the results of your efforts.

6 Preview the Letter

Word displays a finished letter with the first recipient's personal information filled in. Here you can see how your letter's formatting and flow look.

Click the >> button in the **Mail Merge** task pane to see the next recipient's details filled in. As you click through the list of recipients, look over each letter, especially if you're new to mail merging, to make sure that the spacing and format look good. You might, for example, realize that you allowed too much space between the recipient's return address information and the salutation; if so, click the **Previous: Write Your Letter** link to remove the spacing.

If you see a recipient you want to exclude, click the **Exclude This Recipient** button. Word will remove that recipient from the data source being used for your current mail merge session.

▶ **NOTE**

Word does not actually delete the recipient from your original data source but only from your mail merge session if you click **Exclude This Recipient**.

Click **Next: Complete the Merge** to finalize the mail merge and print your letters with each one personalized according to your specifications.

48 | Print an Address on an Envelope or a Label

✔ BEFORE YOU BEGIN

46 About Mail Merge
47 Write Form Letters with Mail Merge

→ SEE ALSO

151 Link to Office Data

Word makes it easy to print an address on an envelope or a set of mailing labels. You can quickly fill in a name and an address or grab addresses from a data source such as a Microsoft Access database (see **46** **About Mail Merge**) and print several envelopes or mailing labels in a single print run.

When printing multiple envelopes, it greatly helps if your printer supports the use of an envelope feeder. Otherwise, you'll have to hand-feed each envelope you want to print.

Mailing labels come in various shapes and sizes, as well as differing numbers on each page. Word can support all the common mailing label formats sold today, so make sure that the labels you use conform to the purpose of your use before settling on a certain kind. In other words, make sure that the labels you use are the right size, color, and style for whatever you want to use them for; Word can almost certainly adapt to whatever kind you select.

48

▶ TIP

Word supports the use of electronic postage through services such as Stamps.com and the post office. If you sign up for such a service, you can print postage directly onto your envelopes.

1 Request an Envelope

Display the **Mailings** ribbon and click the **Envelopes** button to display the **Envelopes** dialog box.

2 Enter the Address Information

If you're printing only one or two envelopes, you can manually type the recipient's name and address information in the **Delivery Address** field.

▶ TIP

Word will ask whether you want to use your return address information in the future so that you won't have to type it again.

3 Adjust and Print the Envelope

Click the **Options** button to specify the envelope size, font used on the envelope, and printing options from the **Envelope Options** dialog box.

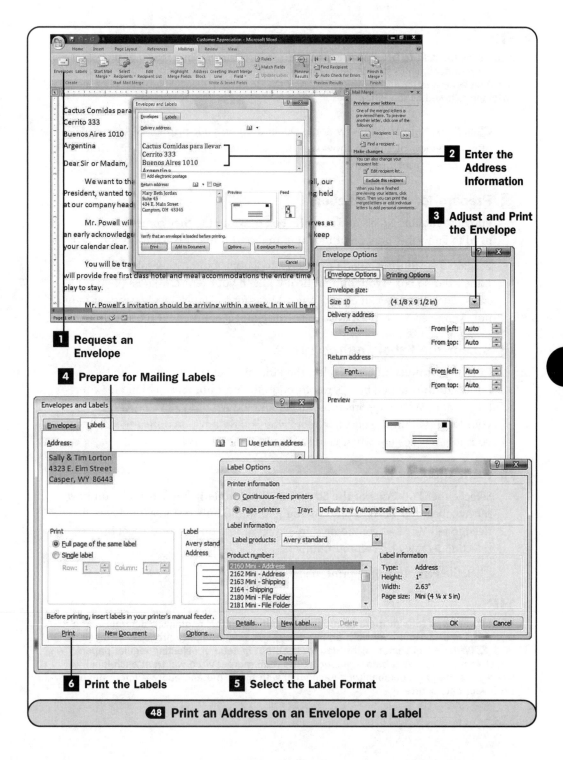

1 Request an Envelope

2 Enter the Address Information

3 Adjust and Print the Envelope

4 Prepare for Mailing Labels

5 Select the Label Format

6 Print the Labels

48 Print an Address on an Envelope or a Label

▶ **TIP**

If you click the **Add to Document** button, Word inserts an envelope "page" at the top of your current document with the recipient and return address information filled in. You can then write a letter in the lower portion of the document, select **Print,** and print the envelope followed by the letter.

Click **Print** to print your envelope. Depending on your printer, Word might offer a preview picture to show you how to load envelopes into your printer so that they print properly.

4 Prepare for Mailing Labels

Purchase mailing labels and save the box or wrapping they come in. You'll need to know the label's manufacturer and part number (such as Avery 2180).

Display the **Mailings** ribbon and click the **Labels** button to display the **Labels** dialog box. Word automatically fills in your return address (if you saved one), but you can change the address for the label. Obviously, you may not even need to print an address because labels are used for many things.

5 Select the Label Format

48

Click the **Options** button to select the kind of label you're using from the **Label Options** dialog box. Scroll through the part numbers looking for your label's part. Word supports most labels sold today, so if you've purchased your labels within the past few years, you should have no difficulty locating your labels. Click **OK** when you finish selecting the label.

6 Print the Labels

Select either **Full Page of the Same Label** or **Single Label** depending on how many labels you want to print. If you're printing only a single label, you'll need to tell Word where the next free label resides on the label sheet by selecting its row and column number.

Click the **Print** button to print the labels.

▶ **TIP**

What if you want to print more than one label but each label contains a different name and address or part number from an inventory? Use mail merge to produce the labels (see **47** **Write Form Letters with Mail Merge**), but instead of selecting regular paper, select your mailing label before producing the mail merge. Word will treat each label like a separate page, personalizing each label with the name and address information from your data source.

49 Add WordArt to a Document

✔ **BEFORE YOU BEGIN**	→ **SEE ALSO**
29 Insert Graphics into a Document	**158** Create a Web Page with Word
39 Add a Watermark	

Word offers *WordArt* when you want to display text in different shapes, colors, and styles to add pizzazz to your documents. For example, you could create an eye-catching title to place at the top of a menu for your Tasty Treats shop.

▶ **NEW TERM**

WordArt—Text you can bend, twist, and color.

WordArt enables you to produce fancy text messages without having to resort to a drawing package to obtain the letters. After you insert WordArt, you can drag resizing handles and format the WordArt to suit your needs.

1 Request the WordArt

Click where you want the WordArt to appear in your document. From the **Insert** ribbon, click the **WordArt** button to display the various WordArt styles available.

Word displays the **Edit WordArt Text** dialog box in which you specify the text and format to use.

2 Type Text for the WordArt

Type your text in the **Edit WordArt Text** dialog box. You can select a font for Word to use for your WordArt. Also, you can elect to apply boldfacing or italics to your text.

Click **OK** when you finish specifying the text, and Word inserts the WordArt into your document.

3 Adjust the Size

Click and drag the WordArt's sizing handles to adjust the WordArt's size.

4 Format the WordArt Specifics

Right-click and select **Format WordArt** to display the **Format WordArt** dialog box. Here you can specify exact measurements and determine how surrounding text is to wrap with the WordArt image.

Click **OK** to apply your format changes.

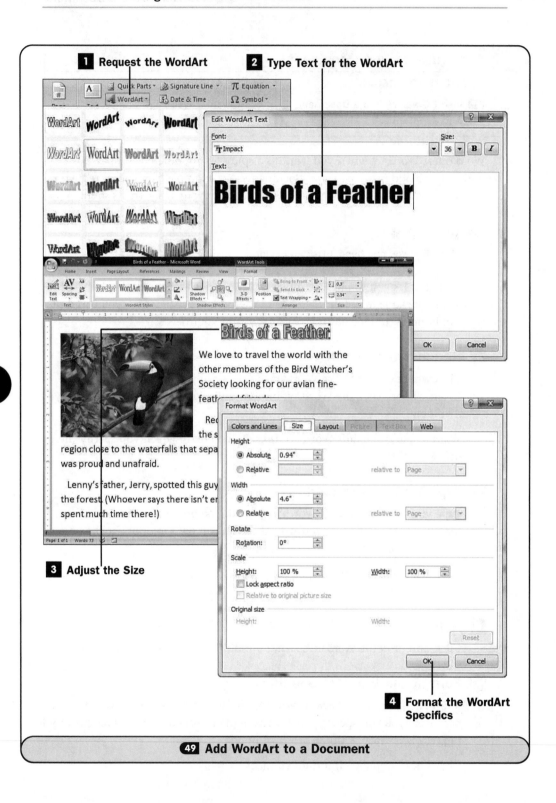

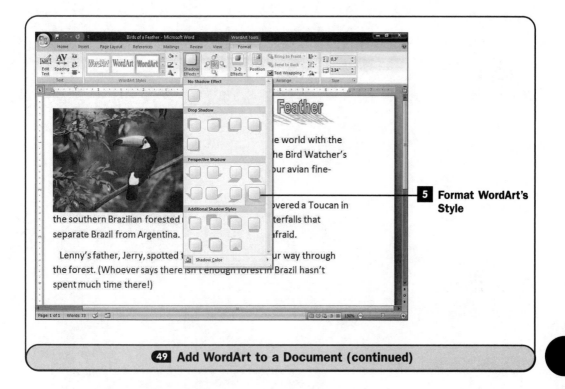

5 Format WordArt's Style

49 Add WordArt to a Document (continued)

49

5 Format WordArt's Style

When you click anywhere within your WordArt to select it and display its sizing handles, Word displays the **WordArt Tools** ribbon, from which you can format various WordArt designs.

For example, some WordArt looks good with a shadow effect. As you move your mouse pointer over the various effects and formats, your WordArt changes to show you what that effect will look like if you select it.

You can also change the WordArt's orientation and make the text run vertically instead of horizontally.

Finally, you can change the entire WordArt style to a different WordArt design by selecting from the **WordArt Styles** group.

PART III

Working with Excel Worksheets

IN THIS PART:

6

Getting to Know Excel

IN THIS CHAPTER:

This chapter introduces topics related to Excel, Office's **worksheet** program (sometimes called a **spreadsheet** program). Technically, a worksheet is a single document inside a **workbook,** but we often use the terms *worksheet* and *spreadsheet* and *workbook* interchangeably. It's confusing only when you first hear the terms, but their context often eliminates any confusion between them.

▶ NEW TERMS

Spreadsheet—Another name for a worksheet and often used as another name for workbook.

Worksheet—Numerical information presented in a tabular row and column format with text that labels the data.

Workbook—Office documents that contain one or more worksheets.

Microsoft Office's Excel is to numbers what Word is to text; Excel has been called a "word processor for numbers." With Excel, you can create numerically based proposals, business plans, business forms, accounting workbooks, and virtually any other document that contains calculated numbers. Those worksheets can contain graphics and charts, too.

50

If you are new to electronic workbooks, you may have to take a little more time learning Excel's environment than you have to take to learn other programs such as Word. Excel starts with a grid of cells in which you place information, not unlike Word's tables (see **24** **About Word Tables**). This chapter orients you to Excel by offering tasks that explain how to enter and edit data in Excel workbooks as well as how to navigate them.

50　About Worksheets and Workbooks

→ SEE ALSO

- **51** Set Excel Options
- **52** Create a New Workbook
- **60** Edit Cell Data

Excel enables you to create and edit one or more worksheets that you store in workbooks. Typically, people work with a single worksheet for simple applications, such as a worksheet that an investor might use to analyze a single stock investment.

Typically, Excel helps users prepare financial information, but you can manage other kinds of data in Excel, such as a project timeline. Excel even supports simple database routines (see Chapter 10, "Using Excel as a Simple Database"). If your project requires multiple closely linked financial worksheets, you'll keep those worksheets in one large workbook file.

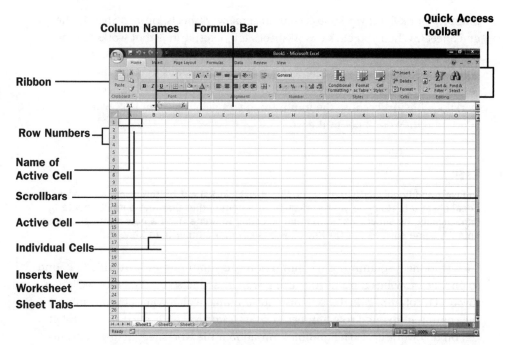

A worksheet is a collection of rows and columns that hold text and numbers.

A simple example may help solidify the difference between a *workbook* and a *worksheet* in your mind. A company with several divisions might create a workbook with annual sales for each division, and each division might be represented with its own tabbed worksheet inside the workbook. Anytime you create, open, or save an Excel file, you are working with a workbook. Often, that workbook contains only one worksheet. When that's the case, the terms *workbook* and *worksheet* really are basically synonymous.

All Excel files end in the .xlsx filename extension. Excel 2007 introduces a new file format to maintain compatibility with the XML standard, but Excel 2007 still reads and writes worksheets from previous versions (which primarily had the .XLS extension).

Your workbook name is the filename you assign when you save the file. You can save Excel worksheets in some non-Excel formats as well, such as comma-separated values (.CSV) and text (.TXT) formats, as well as the HTML format for displaying on web pages. To save your work, click your Quick Access toolbar's **Save** button, or click your **Office** button and select **Save**.

A worksheet is set up in a similar manner to a Word table (see **24 About Word Tables**), except that Excel worksheets can do much more high-end, numeric calculating than Word tables can.

Initially, blank Excel workbooks contain three worksheets, named Sheet1, Sheet2, and Sheet3. When you click a worksheet's tab, Excel brings that worksheet into view. Initially, you'll probably stay with one worksheet per workbook, so you'll typically never have to click the secondary worksheet tabs to bring the other worksheets into view. Most users leave the second and third worksheets in their workbook file just because the minor trouble in deleting them isn't worth the effort, and they don't get in the way.

▶ **TIP**

To insert additional worksheets, click the **Insert Worksheet** button. Excel adds an additional sheet tab. Rename your worksheet to a name other than the default Sheet# by right-clicking the sheet's name tab and selecting **Rename**. Type a new name and press Enter. A name such as 1st Qtr Payroll is easier to remember than Sheet3.

50

Each worksheet column has a column name; column names start with A, B, and so on. Each row has a number, starting with 1, 2, and so on. The intersection of a row and a column, called a cell, also has a name, which comes from combining the column name and row number, such as C4 or A1. A1 is always the top-left cell on any worksheet. The gridlines throughout the worksheet help you distinguish between cells.

Each unique cell name is sometimes called the *cell reference*, and it is unique for each cell in the worksheet. The active cell or cells are always highlighted with a dark border (**60 Edit Cell Data** shows how to select multiple cells). A cell's location, also known as its name or cell reference, appears in the Worksheet's Name box.

▶ **NEW TERM**

Cell reference—The name of a cell, composed of its column and row intersection, such as G14. This is sometimes called the cell address or cell name.

▶ **NOTE**

No matter how large your monitor is, you see only a small amount of the **Worksheet Area**. Use the scrollbars to see or edit information in the offscreen cells, such as cell M200.

51 Set Excel Options

✔ **BEFORE YOU BEGIN**	→ **SEE ALSO**
50 About Worksheets and Workbooks	**53** Open an Existing Worksheet
	60 Edit Cell Data
	73 Format Cells

Not everybody works the same way, so not every Excel user wants to use Excel the same way. By setting some of Excel's many options, you will make Excel conform to the way you like to do things. For example, you may want Excel to hide the gridlines that normally distinguish between rows and columns to reduce onscreen clutter. If so, Excel has an option to display or hide the gridlines.

As a matter of fact, Excel has an option for just about anything and everything, as you'll see in this task. The good news is that knowing about the options is less critical in Excel 2007 than in previous versions because you can customize so much about your worksheets using the ribbon atop your screen.

1 Display the Office Box

The **Office** button gives you quick access to file-related commands that used to be available in Excel's **File** menu. In addition, when you click the **Office** button, you'll have access to the **Excel Options** button that opens the **Excel Options** dialog box.

▶ **NOTE**

Most Windows programs have a menu with options that typically include commands such as **File**, **Edit**, and **View**. Until you get used to the way Office 2007 products operate, you'll find yourself using the old menu-based commands. Excel 2007 understands that you will do this and goes ahead and opens the **Excel Options** dialog box for you when you issue menu commands.

2 Select the Excel Options

Click the **Excel Options** button to display the **Excel Options** dialog box. From this dialog box, you change and set all the option settings within Excel.

If you use Windows Vista's *Aero Glass* graphics mode, your **Excel Options** dialog box window will have translucent borders that allow Excel's menu and toolbars to show through. If you don't run Aero Glass, your **Excel Options** dialog box window will have solid borders.

If you're fairly new to Excel, consider leaving all the options as is until you familiarize yourself with how Excel works.

51

3 **Change the Popular Options**

If the **Excel Options** dialog box doesn't open to the **Popular** tab, click
Popular. As the dialog box states, Microsoft considers these options to be the
most popular (which will be debatable by most Excel users).

You can elect to use the mini toolbar (see **59 Insert and Delete Rows and
Columns**), use the Live Preview feature (see **73 Format Cells**), show the
Developer tab on your ribbon (off by default), and select an Excel default
color scheme. You can also change your default username.

1 Display the Office Box

3 Change the Popular Options

Information Pop-Up

2 Select the Excel Options

51 Set Excel Options

51

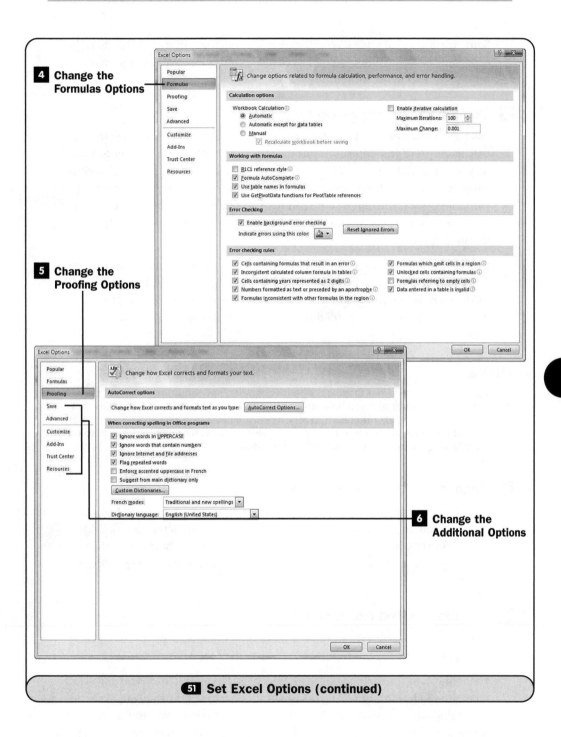

4 Change the
Formulas Options

5 Change the
Proofing Options

6 Change the
Additional Options

51 Set Excel Options (continued)

Some Excel options have a small, blue letter *i* enclosed in a circle to the right of them. Rest your mouse pointer over this information request, and Excel pops up a helpful description box of that option.

4 Change the Formulas Options

Click the **Formulas** tab to customize the way Excel handles formulas that it calculates. Here you adjust settings that you will become more familiar with as you learn and use Excel. For example, Excel recalculates an entire worksheet of data every time you change a single cell. For massive, complicated worksheets, this constant update can take a long time. You can elect to recalculate your worksheet, manually by clicking to select the **Manually** option (off by default).

Excel constantly monitors the formulas you enter to ensure that you're properly constructing them. Excel will issue an error if you enter a formula incorrectly, such as typing too many left parentheses without enough matching right parentheses. You can modify Excel's error-checking rules to weaken them somewhat.

51 ▶ **NOTE**

You won't routinely lower the threshold of error-checking, but sometimes you will be working on a worksheet and you have only partial formulas to work with right now that you will complete later. By turning off Excel's formula checks, you can enter your partial formulas now and complete more of your worksheet than you'd otherwise be able to do if Excel refused to allow improper formulas in its cells.

5 Change the Proofing Options

The **Proofing** category enables you to adjust AutoCorrect options. Excel can correct common errors as you type, such as incorrect punctuation, or flag repeated words with wavy underlines so that you'll spot them. From the **Proofing** options, you can adjust the way Excel looks over your shoulder, in effect.

6 Change the Additional Options

Continue viewing and changing the remaining options in the **Excel Options** dialog box. Click the tab that corresponds to the option you'd like to change.

You'll find tabs for saving your work under the **Save** tab. There you can select a default file format for saving documents, although you can always override the setting when storing any document. Another **Save** option that many find useful to change is the time interval for how long Excel waits before saving an AutoRecover document version. Some people feel that the default 10 minutes is too lengthy.

The **Advanced** tab offers advanced editing options such as how Excel handles sound and pop-up ScreenTips.

The remaining options allow you to perform less-common option changes such as customizing the icons on Excel's ribbon bar and allow you to view resources on the Web where you can get extra help.

When you're done reviewing and changing Excel options, click the **OK** button to close the **Excel Options** dialog box.

---

52 Create a New Workbook

✔ BEFORE YOU BEGIN	→ SEE ALSO
50 About Worksheets and Workbooks	**53** Open an Existing Worksheet
51 Set Excel Options	**78** About Excel Styles, Themes, and Templates
	81 Use an Excel Template

Excel offers two ways to create new workbooks: You can create a completely blank, new workbook (if you choose this approach, you must decide what to put in the workbook and where that information should go), or you can use a workbook template to open a preformatted workbook. **78** **About Excel Styles, Themes, and Templates** explains what templates are and how they apply to Excel worksheets.

Excel comes with several templates when you first install Office, and you can easily create a template to reuse later. This task shows you how to open a blank workbook. **81** **Use an Excel Template** explains how to create a new workbook based on a template you may have created and saved previously.

1 Request a New Workbook

When you first start Microsoft Excel, Excel displays a blank workbook with three empty worksheets named Sheet1, Sheet2, and Sheet3.

If you have been working in Excel and want to begin with a new workbook, click your **Office** button and select **New**. Excel displays the **New Workbook** dialog box.

▶ **NOTE**

Here is where the terms *workbooks* and *worksheets* can get confusing. Often you really just want to create a worksheet, a single sheet to lay out your data. Keep in mind that even a single worksheet must reside in a workbook. Therefore, when you want a new worksheet, you must request a new workbook first, and within that new workbook will be blank worksheets with which you can work.

52

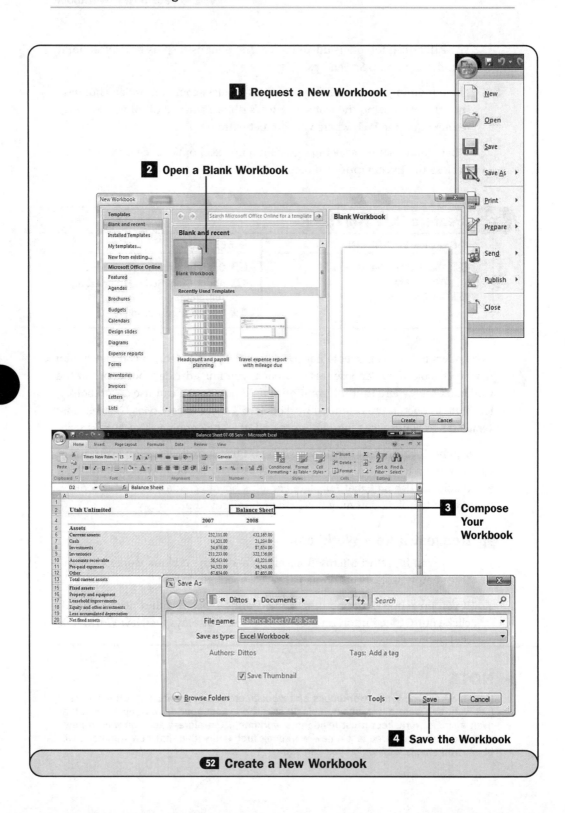

1 Request a New Workbook

2 Open a Blank Workbook

3 Compose Your Workbook

4 Save the Workbook

52 Create a New Workbook

2 Open a Blank Workbook

Click the **Blank Workbook** button to open a new, empty workbook with three worksheets inside.

All the other options on the **New Workbook** dialog box relate to available templates. For example, you can create a sales report worksheet based on the presupplied **Sales Report** template that you'll find by selecting from the list of online templates available in the **New Workbook** dialog box. The categories running down the left side of the **New Workbook** dialog box are additional templates you can use.

Obviously, a template saves you lots of formatting time, but unless your application matches that of one of the templates, you'll probably find it easier to create a new worksheet from scratch than to change one that Excel creates from a template.

3 Compose Your Workbook

Create your workbook in the blank work area of cells that Excel gives you. You'll enter text, numbers, and formulas, depending on the needs of your workbook. You can print your workbook (see **61** **Print a Worksheet**) at any time.

4 Save the Workbook

After creating your workbook, click the **Quick Access** toolbar's **Save** button and type the name of your workbook. Excel uses the filename extension `.xlsx` for your workbook. You can select another file format, such as **Excel 97-2003 Workbook**; doing so saves the workbook with the older Excel extension of `.xls`. Other file formats are also available (see **50** **About Worksheets and Workbooks**).

---

53 | **Open an Existing Worksheet**

✔ **BEFORE YOU BEGIN**	→ **SEE ALSO**
50 About Worksheets and Workbooks	**54** Enter Data into a Worksheet
52 Create a New Workbook	**60** Edit Cell Data

Opening an existing workbook to edit in Excel is simple. You tell Excel that you want to open a workbook file and then locate the file. Excel then loads the workbook into the row-and-column-based editing area.

Notice the name of this task, "Open an Existing Worksheet." Actually, when you open a worksheet, you're really opening a workbook that contains one or more worksheets (see **50 About Worksheets and Workbooks**). Given that so many Excel users interchange the terms *workbook* and *worksheet*, you might as well get used to that interchange if you're not already. So for the subsequent tasks, the term *worksheet* will often apply to the whole workbook file. Once in a while the distinction will be necessary (such as when referring to specific worksheets inside a workbook), and at that point the exact term will be used. Otherwise, you'll find it's not a big deal to interchange the words. If anything, the term *workbook* is used so infrequently for an Excel file that contains one or more worksheets that using *workbook* instead of the more general *worksheet* term can confuse some people even though it's more technically accurate in many instances.

1 Request a Worksheet File

Click your **Office** button to display the **Office** dialog box. Select **Open** to select from a list of worksheets. Excel displays the **Open** dialog box.

53

▶ **TIP**

Ctrl+O is the shortcut key to display the **Open** dialog box.

2 Navigate to Your Worksheet's Location

The worksheet that you want to open might not appear at the default location shown in the **Open** dialog box, so navigate to the folder in which the workbook you're looking for resides. If you're using Windows Vista, you can click the bread crumbs along the top of the **Open** dialog box, or if you're using an earlier Windows version, use the **Look In** drop-down list and traverse to your file.

3 Locate the File You Want

When you locate the folder that holds the workbook file, select the file you want to open. Then click the **Open** button to open the selected file in Excel's editing workspace. The **All Microsoft Office Excel Files** button enables you to select from only Excel files, but when you click this button, a list of other file formats appear that you can select from.

▶ **TIP**

Feel free to open more than one worksheet by holding down Ctrl while clicking multiple filenames. Excel opens each worksheet that you select in its own window.

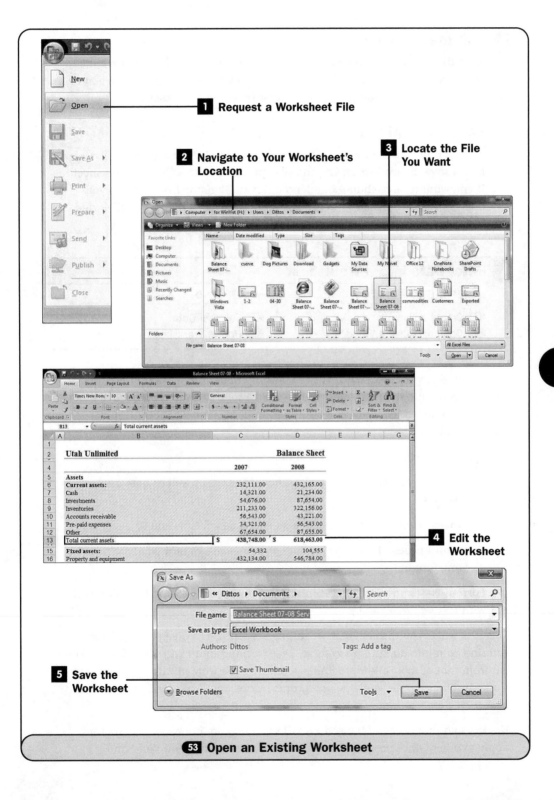

1 **Request a Worksheet File**

2 **Navigate to Your Worksheet's Location**

3 **Locate the File You Want**

4 **Edit the Worksheet**

5 **Save the Worksheet**

53

53 Open an Existing Worksheet

4 Edit the Worksheet

After the file opens in the Excel workspace, you can edit the file. Navigate to where you want to make edits (see **60 Edit Cell Data**), or move to the end of the document and add to it (see **54 Enter Data into a Worksheet**).

5 Save the Worksheet

After you finish with the worksheet, click the **Quick Access** toolbar's **Save** button to save the worksheet. You can also press Ctrl+S to save your worksheet. If you want to save changes under a different filename from the one you opened, click your **Office** button, select **Save As**, and enter a new filename before clicking the **Save** button.

---

54 Enter Data into a Worksheet

✔ BEFORE YOU BEGIN	→ SEE ALSO
52 Create a New Workbook	**60** Edit Cell Data
53 Open an Existing Worksheet	**61** Print a Worksheet

54

Often, entering worksheet data requires nothing more than clicking the correct cell to select it and then typing the data. The various kinds of data behave differently when entered, however, so you should understand how Excel accepts assorted data.

Excel works with the following kinds of data:

- **Labels**—Text values such as names and addresses, as well as date and time values.

- **Numbers**—Numeric values such as 34, –291, 545.67874, and 0.

- **Dates and times**—Excel accepts date and time values that you type in virtually any format.

- **Formulas**—Expressions that compute numeric results. (Some formulas work with text values as well.)

This task walks you through a short editing session just to give you a feel for entering data into an Excel worksheet. Keep in mind that Excel's interface is different from that of most other programs you may have worked with, unless you've worked with electronic workbook programs before. You'll be entering data in a row-and-column format.

Having said that, some of the editing skills you acquire in one Office program apply to other Office programs as well. For example, Excel and Word and

PowerPoint all support the use of themes (see **78** **About Excel Styles, Themes, and Templates**), and they can share themes between them. Obviously, Office's ribbon changes depending on which Office program you use, but most of its functions are similar across the Office programs. Therefore, if you know Word (the program most people learn first), Excel's interface won't be completely foreign to you.

1 Move the Active Cell

In a blank worksheet, click cell D5 to make it active. The cell's dark outline indicates that the cell is selected. Also, the cell name appears in the **Worksheet Area**.

2 Type Text into the Cell

Type ABC Co. into cell D5. To enter the text, simply type the text, and it appears both in the cell and in the **Formula** box toward the top of the screen. When you press Enter, the active cell moves down one row. Instead of Enter, you can press the right arrow button or Tab, and the cell to the right of the cell becomes active next.

By default, text always appears left-justified in a cell, although you can click one of the justification buttons to center or right-justify text in a cell. To correct a mistake, press Backspace and type the correct text.

54

▶ **NOTE**

You can change the action of the Enter key from within the **Excel Options** dialog box's **Advanced** tab.

If you press the Esc button at any point during text entry but before you move to another cell, Excel erases the text you typed in the cell and restores the original cell. In addition, you can press Ctrl+Z (for undo) or click your **Quick Access** toolbar's **Undo** button to back up to a cell's previous state.

3 Type a Long Title

Replace the text in cell D5 by typing Fiscal Year Report for the 1st Quarter. As you type, the text spills into cells E5 and F5 and finally ends in G5. The important thing to note is that only cell D5 holds the text value Fiscal Year Report for the 1st Quarter. Although it *looks* as though pieces of the title spill into the cells to the right, Excel is showing the full text in cell D5 because no values appear to the right of D5. If any data resided in cells E5, F5, or G5, Excel would not have shown the full value in D5.

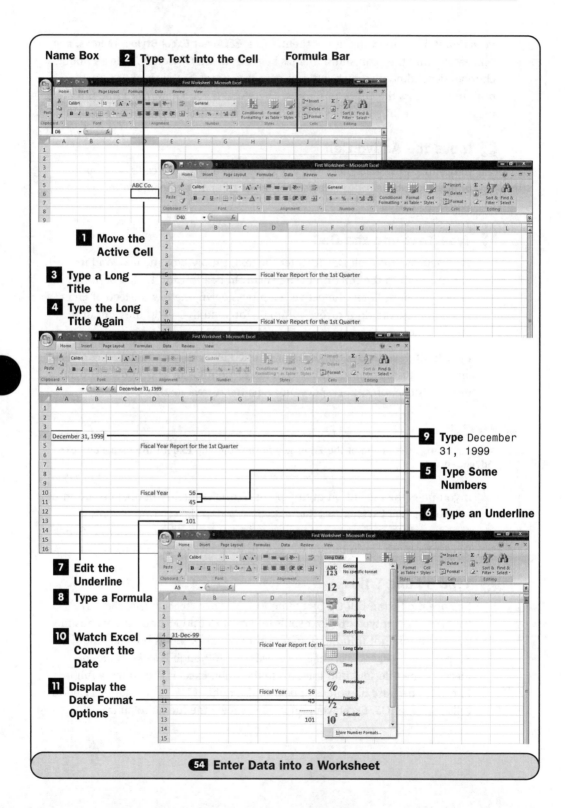

▶ **NOTE**

Depending on your AutoCorrect options, Excel might change "1st" to "1st" as you type it. You can turn off AutoCorrect features from the **Excel Options** dialog box's **Proofing** tab.

4 Type the Long Title Again

Move to cell D10 and type the same title, Fiscal Year Report for the 1st Quarter. As with cell D5, the full text shows because nothing appears in the cells to the right of D10.

As you begin to type the text, Excel automatically completes your entry thanks to a feature called AutoComplete. AutoComplete matches your text to input found elsewhere in that column. You can accept the proposed completion by press Enter or ignore the suggestion and continue typing.

▶ **NOTE**

You can turn off AutoComplete from the **Excel Options** dialog box's **Advanced** tab in the **Editing Options** section.

5 Type Some Numbers

54

Type the following numeric values into cells E10 and E11, respectively: 56 and 45. (Press Enter after typing the 45.) You'll see that as soon as you type cell E10's value, most of D10's long text goes away. The long text is still in cell D10, but Excel doesn't display the text because then you would be unable to see the number in cell E10.

Excel usually recognizes any entry that begins with an alphabetical character as text. Some textual data, such as price codes, telephone numbers, and zip codes, can fool Excel into thinking that you are entering numeric data because of the initial numeric value. Excel treats numeric data differently from text data when you type the data into cells. If you want Excel to treat a number (such as a zip code) as a text entry so that it does not perform calculations on the cell, precede the contents with a single apostrophe ('). For example, to type the zip code 74137, type '74137; the apostrophe lets Excel know to format the value as text. Knowing this enables you to enter text-based numbers such as zip codes and product codes that require a leading zero. Without the apostrophe, Excel interprets a value with a leading zero as a number and removes the zero and right-justifies the number.

Also notice that, unlike with text values, Excel right-justifies numeric values. You'll also see when you enter formulas that Excel right-justifies the results of those formulas.

6   Type an Underline

You can put a line, composed of hyphens, below the two numbers you just entered. Type '------- in cell E12 and press Enter. The dashed line doesn't look correct because Excel left-justified the line since the line is not numeric but text.

7   Edit the Underline

Click the cell with the underline to make it active. Then click the **Align Right** button in the ribbon's **Alignment** group. Excel right-justifies the underline so that it falls below the numbers properly.

8   Type a Formula

Type =E10+E11 in cell E13. You've just typed your first formula in Excel. The moment you press Enter, Excel displays the formula's answer instead of the formula itself.

Click cell E13 to make it active again. You'll see the formula in the **Formula** bar. So when you click a formula's cell, Excel shows you both the formula in the **Formula** bar and the value in the cell. If you want to change the formula, either press F2 to display the formula again inside the cell or click to edit the formula in the **Formula** bar.

54

▶ NOTE

For now, do not make changes to the formula but rather click cell E13 and press F2. Excel colorizes the formula and highlights each formula value's cell so that you can easily see the cells that compose the formula. Press Enter to keep the current value.

9   Type December 31, 1999

Type December 31, 1999 in cell A4.

10   Watch Excel Convert the Date

Excel converts your date to a different format. Excel converts the date to 31-Dec-99. Excel does retain the date's full value inside the cell and only the date's display appears in the new format.

11   Display the Date Format Options

Excel supports almost every national and international date and time format. To change the way Excel formats a date, click the drop-down list box labeled **General** to display a list of the various cell-formatting options.

You can select **Long Date** to change the date's display back to a longer format. You'll see more than you might have expected because Excel even shows the day of the week (Friday) to the left of the date.

As you've seen, when you type some values, Excel leaves their format alone (commonly this occurs when you enter routine numbers), and when you type some other values, such as text labels and dates, you may have to adjust the formatting so that the data appears the way you want it to.

---

55 | **About Moving Around Excel**

✔ BEFORE YOU BEGIN	→ SEE ALSO
54 Enter Data into a Worksheet	**56** About Excel Formulas

Your mouse and arrow keys are the primary navigation keys for moving from cell to cell in worksheets. Unlike Word, which uses an insertion point, Excel uses its active cell, the highlighted cell, to indicate your current position in the worksheet.

▶ **NOTE**

If you select multiple cells, the selection is considered to be a single set of active cells.

55

The active cell has a darkened border around it and accepts whatever data you enter next. As you press an arrow key, Excel moves the cell pointer in the direction of the arrow to a new cell, making the new cell the active one. After you begin typing inside a cell, the insertion point appears. Unlike in Word, though, the insertion point is not your primary means of traversing workbooks; rather, the active cell pointer is the dark border that moves over cells as you press arrow keys or that appears when you click cells with your mouse.

If you're working with a rather large worksheet, you might find the **Go To** dialog box useful. Press F5 to display the **Go To** dialog box, where you can select a range of cells that you might have previously named or enter a cell address, such as C141, to jump to that cell. You can also click any object in the **Go To** dialog box, such as a worksheet name, or select a range name to jump to.

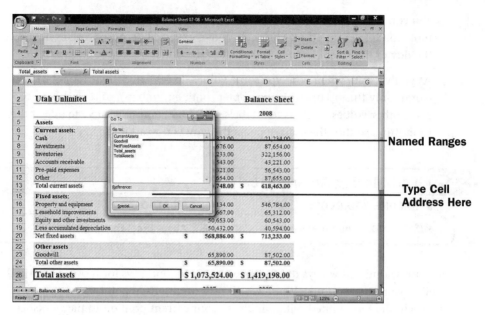

Use the Go To dialog box to jump around a worksheet quickly.

55

Instead of jumping to a cell address or selecting from a named range, you can jump to one of several other kinds of Excel elements. Click the **Go To** dialog box's **Special** button and select what you want to jump to. When you click **OK**, Excel jumps to that item.

Table 6.1 lists the most commonly used navigational keystrokes within Excel. Use your mouse to scroll with the scrollbars.

TABLE 6.1   Using the Keyboard to Navigate Excel

Press This Key. . .	To Move
Arrow keys	The direction of the arrow, one cell at a time
Ctrl+up arrow, Ctrl+down arrow	The topmost or bottommost cell that contains data or, if at the end of the range already, the next cell that contains data or the final cell possible in the current column
Ctrl+left arrow, Ctrl+right arrow	The leftmost or rightmost cell that contains data or, if at the end of the range already, the final cell possible on the current row
Page Up, Page Down	The previous or next screen of the worksheet
Ctrl+Home	The upper-left corner of the worksheet (cell A1)
Ctrl+Page Up, Ctrl+Page Down	The next or previous worksheet within the current workbook

56 About Excel Formulas

✔ **BEFORE YOU BEGIN**	→ **SEE ALSO**
50 About Worksheets and Workbooks	**58** Copy and Move Formulas
54 Enter Data into a Worksheet	**63** About Excel Ranges

Without formulas, Excel would be little more than a simple row-and-column-based word processor. When you use formulas, however, Excel becomes an extremely powerful timesaving, planning, budgeting, and general-purpose financial tool.

▶ NEW TERM

Formulas—Equations composed of numeric values and often cell addresses and range names that produce a mathematical result.

On a calculator, you typically type a formula and then press the equal sign to see the result. In contrast, all Excel formulas begin with an equal sign. For example, the following is a formula:

=4*2-3

The asterisk is an operator that denotes the times sign (multiplication). This formula requests that Excel compute the value of 4 multiplied by 2 minus 3 to get the result. When you type a formula and press Enter or move to another cell, Excel displays the result and not the formula on the worksheet.

When you type =4*2-3 into a cell, the answer 5 appears in the cell when you move away from the cell. You can see the formula in the **Formula** bar atop the worksheet if you click the cell again to make it active. When you're entering a formula, as soon as you press the equal sign, Excel shows your formula in the **Formula** bar as well as in the active cell. If you click the **Formula** bar first and then finish your formula there, the formula appears in the **Formula** bar as well as in the active cell. By typing the formula in the **Formula** bar, you can press the left- and right-arrow keys to move the cell pointer left and right within the formula to edit it. When you enter long formulas, this **Formula** bar's editing capability helps you correct mistakes you might type.

▶ TIP

Click the **Expand Formula Bar** button to the right of the **Formula** bar to increase the **Formula** bar's size to hold much longer formulas.

56

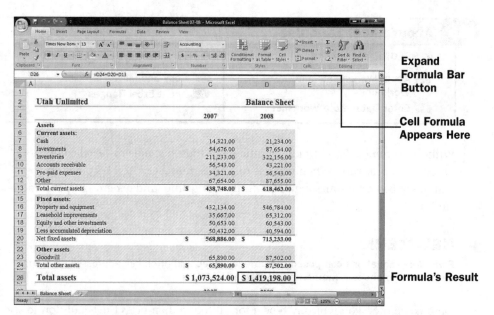

Expand Formula Bar Button

Cell Formula Appears Here

Formula's Result

Excel displays a formula's result in the cell and the actual formula in the Formula bar.

56

Table 6.2 lists the primary math operators you can use in your worksheet formulas. Notice that all the sample formulas begin with the equal sign.

You can combine any and all of the operators in a formula. When combining operators, Excel follows the traditional computer (and algebraic) *operator hierarchy model.* Therefore, Excel first computes exponentiation if you raise any value to another power. Excel then calculates all multiplication and division in a left-to-right order (the first one to appear computes first) before calculating addition and subtraction (also in left-to-right order).

TABLE 6.2   The Primary Math Operators Specify Math Calculations

Operator	Example	Description
^	=7 ^ 3	Raises 7 to the power of 3 (called exponentiation)
/	=4 / 2	Divides 4 by 2
*	=3 * 4 * 5	Multiplies 3 by 4 by 5
+	=5 + 5	Adds 5 and 5
−	=5 − 5	Subtracts 5 from 5

▶ NEW TERM

Operator hierarchy model—A predefined order of operators used when equations are being calculated.

The following formula displays a result of 14 because Excel first calculates the exponentiation of 2 raised to the third power and then divides the answer (8) by 4, multiplies the result (2) by 2, and finally subtracts the result (4) from 18. Even though the subtraction appears first, the operator hierarchy forces the subtraction to wait until last to compute.

```
=18 - 2 ^ 3 / 4 * 2
```

If you want to override the operator hierarchy, put parentheses around the parts you want Excel to compute first. The following formula returns a different result from the previous one, for example, despite the same values and operators used:

```
=(18 - 2) ^ 3 / 4 * 2
```

Instead of 14, this formula displays 2048! The subtraction produces 16, which is then raised to the third power (producing 4,096) before dividing by 4 and multiplying the result by 2 to get 2,048.

▶ NOTE

Formulas can contain cell addresses, cell names, and other values besides numbers. See **63** About Excel Ranges for more information about range names.

To add three cells together, you could type the following in another cell:

```
= D3 + K10 + M7
```

Excel adds the values in D3, K10, and M7 and shows the result in place of the formula. The cells D3, K10, and M7 can also contain formulas that reference other cells.

57	**Use Sum to Add Rows and Columns**
✔ **BEFORE YOU BEGIN**	→ **SEE ALSO**
54 Enter Data into a Worksheet	**66** About Excel Functions
56 About Excel Formulas	

Although an Excel worksheet can perform just about any mathematical calculation you'll ever need, one of the most common operations is adding values together. Most worksheets perform some addition. Addition is required to compute totals, subtotals, and grand totals. Addition is required to count items and to produce running tabular results.

Addition is so common that Microsoft placed a **Sum** button on your **Home** ribbon to add rows and columns. When you click **Sum**, Excel analyzes your worksheet to determine what kind of sum you need.

▶ **NOTE**

Excel actually inserts the Sum function into your worksheet when you click the **Sum** button. See **66** About Excel Functions to learn what Excel functions are and how to enter them yourself.

57

1 Enter Column Data for the Sum

Before you can sum data, that data needs to be part of your worksheet. Type a column of numbers you want to add together.

Click to place the cell pointer in the cell that is to hold the column total.

2 Request the Column Sum

Click the **Sum** button. Excel instantly verifies that you want to add the column of numbers.

When you first see Excel's response to clicking the **Sum** button, it might look somewhat confusing. The important thing to look at is the selected group of cells. Did Excel select the proper cells, the column of numbers, that you wanted to add together? If so (Excel almost always does this correctly), press Enter to finalize the total and display the total. Don't worry about the formula that begins with =Sum.

3 Enter Row Data for the Sum

The **Sum** button works just as well to add together values in a row. After you have a row of values to add together, click the **Sum** button again.

4 Request the Row Sum

Excel again will highlight the numbers it thinks should be included in the total. Verify that Excel analyzed your row properly, and press Enter to finalize the sum.

5 Select a Different Sum

Click the arrow to the right of the **Sum** button to see the other kinds of totals you can request from this single button alone. Excel can compute an average, count values, or locate the maximum or minimum values from the column or row you're working with.

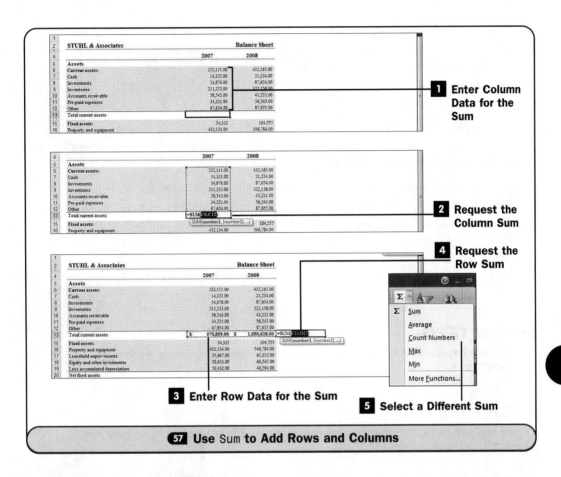

1 Enter Column Data for the Sum

2 Request the Column Sum

4 Request the Row Sum

3 Enter Row Data for the Sum

5 Select a Different Sum

57 Use Sum to Add Rows and Columns

58 Copy and Move Formulas

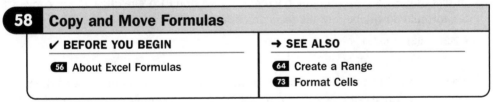

✔ BEFORE YOU BEGIN	→ SEE ALSO
56 About Excel Formulas	**64** Create a Range
	73 Format Cells

You can copy, move, and paste one cell into another using standard copy-and-paste tools such as the Windows Clipboard. When you copy formulas that contain cell addresses, Excel updates the cell references so that they become **relative references.** For example, suppose that you enter this formula in cell A1:

=A2 + A3

▶ NEW TERM

Relative reference—A cell that is referenced in relation to the current cell.

This formula contains two cell references. The references are relative because the references A2 and A3 change if you copy the formula elsewhere. If you copy the formula to cell B5, for example, B5 holds this:

```
=B6 + B7
```

The original relative references update to reflect the formula's copied location. Of course, A1 still holds its original contents, but the copied cell at B5 holds the same formula referencing B5 rather than A1.

A dollar sign ($) always precedes an absolute reference. The reference B5 is an absolute reference. If you want to sum two columns of data (A1 with B1, A2 with B2, and so on) and then multiply each sum by some constant number, for example, the constant number can be a cell referred to as an *absolute reference.* That formula might resemble this:

```
=(A1 + B1) * $J$1
```

▶ NEW TERM

58

Absolute reference—A cell reference that does not change if you copy the formula elsewhere.

▶ TIP

For cell references, the letters are not case-sensitive. You can type a3, and Excel converts it to the cell reference A3.

In this case, J1 is an absolute reference, but A1 and B1 are relative. If you copy the formula down one row, the formula changes to this:

```
=(A2 + B2) * $J$1
```

Notice that the first two cells changed because when you originally entered them, they were relative cell references. You told Excel, by placing dollar signs in front of the absolute cell reference's row and column references, not to change that reference when you copy the formula elsewhere.

$B5 is a partial absolute cell reference. If you copy a formula with $B5 inside the computation, the $B keeps the B column intact, but the fifth row updates to the row location of the target cell. For example, if you type the formula

```
=2 * $B5
```

in cell A1 and then copy the formula to cell F6, cell F6 holds this formula:

```
=2 * $B10
```

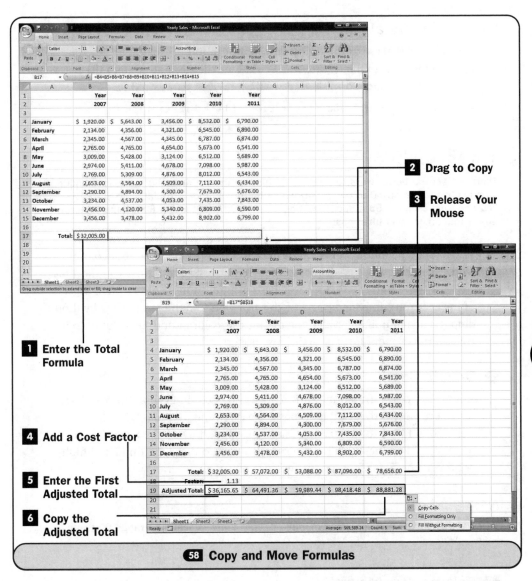

2 Drag to Copy

3 Release Your Mouse

1 Enter the Total Formula

4 Add a Cost Factor

5 Enter the First Adjusted Total

6 Copy the Adjusted Total

58

58 Copy and Move Formulas

You copied the formula to a cell five rows and five columns over in the worksheet. Excel did not update the column name, B, because you told Excel to keep that column name absolute. (It is always B no matter where you copy the formula.) Excel added 5 to the row number, however, because the row number is relative and open to change whenever you copy the formula.

▶ **TIP**

Most of the time, you'll use relative referencing. If you insert or delete rows, columns, or cells, your formulas remain accurate because the cells that they reference change as your worksheet changes.

1 Enter the Total Formula

For this worksheet, assume that you want a formula for each past year and projected years into the future. You would type the formula to total the first year in cell B17. One formula that would total this year would be

`=B4 + B5 + B6 + B7 + B8 + B9 + B10 + B11 + B12 + B13 + B14 + B15`

▶ **TIP**

There are several better ways to total a column. The most tedious but easiest to understand is this step's way. One better way would be to type this formula: `=Sum(B4:B15)`. You can even click the **Sum** button in most cases. **66** **About Excel Functions** explores Sum() and other Excel functions.

When you type long labels such as month names, sometimes your column won't be wide enough to display all the characters. Excel warns you that this cell's contents aren't fully displayed with a small triangle along the right side of the cell. You can widen cells like this that you find are too narrow by dragging the dividing line between the too-narrow column and the column to its right to make enough room to display properly.

2 Drag to Copy

After you type a formula in cell B17, you can copy that cell to the Windows Clipboard with Ctrl+C and then paste the cell into C17, then D17, then E17, and finally F17. Excel offers an easier way, though. Drag the lower-right corner of cell B17, where you'll see a small square, to the right, and Excel highlights each empty cell along the way as you copy.

▶ **NOTE**

When you drag your mouse across multiple cells, you are indicating a range that you want to work with.

3 Release Your Mouse

After you release your mouse button over cell F17, you will see that Excel totals all five columns for you where you copied the total formula. You may have to adjust column widths if all the data doesn't display. Excel displays only pound signs (#) if there is not enough room to display a number fully.

▶ **NOTE**

Look at the **Formula** bar for cell F17. You'll see that Excel copied the formula from B17 using relative addressing. It wouldn't make sense to put the total for column B in cell F17. When Excel saw that you wanted to copy the formula, and because the formula contains relative cell references, Excel copied the formula as though it referred to cells relative to B17.

4 Add a Cost Factor

To demonstrate absolute cell addressing, add a cost factor of 1.13 below Year 2007's total. You then can multiply the total to create an adjusted total in cell B19. If you also want to multiply the remaining totals by the adjustment factor, you *cannot* use relative addressing for the cost factor. In other words, if you multiply cell B17 by cell B18 and store the result in B19 with the formula =B17*B18, and then copy that formula to cell C19, cell C19 would hold this formula: =C17*C18. However, C18 is blank! So Excel would multiply C17 by zero, which is not the correct adjustment factor.

▶ NOTE

The figure's cells are formatted to display dollar signs in some places and not in others. **73** **Format Cells** explains how to format cells the way you want them to look. The labels for Factor and Adjusted Total are right-justified (with the **Align Right** button); however, they first enter their respective cells left-justified because they contain text.

5 Enter the First Adjusted Total

To enter the correct adjusted total in cell B19, you would type =B17 * B18.

If you use absolute addressing in cell B18 (that is, B18), when you copy it to the remaining years, all the cells you copy to will also use B18 instead of a different cell for the factor.

▶ TIP

You don't need to leave spaces around operators such as the multiplication operator (*) in formulas. Doing so makes the formulas easier to read and to check for errors, however.

6 Copy the Adjusted Total

To copy the adjusted total to the other years, you can copy with Ctrl+C and then paste with Ctrl+V into each year's adjusted total cell, but it's simpler just to drag the small square in the first cell's lower-right corner (the mouse pointer changes to a plus sign when you point to this square) across through the cells that are to receive the copied formula.

When you release your mouse after making such a copy with one or more absolute cell addresses in the range, the absolute address remains the same and the relative addresses inside the cells change. This sounds less obvious

58

than it is. In other words, when you copy the formula =B17 * B18 to cell C19, cell C19 gets this formula: =C17 * B18. Cell D19 gets =D17 * B18, and so on.

▶ **NOTE**

You can make only the row or only the column of a cell address absolute. In the cell reference M$15, the column named M is relative and will change if you copy a cell that contains this reference elsewhere, but the absolute row number, $15, will not change.

A formatting icon appears to the right of the final box you drag to. When you click this icon, Excel prompts you for formatting information. Excel can format the newly copied cells to look like the ones that you copied from, or Excel can copy without keeping the original formatting depending on your selection.

---

59 | **Insert and Delete Rows and Columns**

✔ BEFORE YOU BEGIN	→ SEE ALSO
54 Enter Data into a Worksheet	**60** Edit Cell Data

59

Inserting cells, as opposed to typing data inside a cell, requires that the existing worksheet cells move to the right and down to make room for the new cell. Perhaps you created a worksheet of employee salaries and failed to include the employees who work at another division. You can easily make room for those missing entries by inserting new cells. You can insert both new rows and new columns in your worksheets.

Of course, Excel also enables you to delete data you no longer need. You can easily clear a worksheet cell or delete rows and columns.

▶ **NOTE**

Excel enables you to add or delete as many rows and columns that you need to in one operation.

1 **Request a New Column**

To insert a column before another, click the column name that is to *follow* the new column. Then right-click your mouse, and a menu appears. Select **Insert**. Excel moves the worksheet's contents to the right by one column.

▶ **TIP**

To insert multiple columns, first select the number of columns you want to insert. Start with the column to the *right* of where you want Excel to insert the columns. Drag your mouse to select multiple column headings. After they're selected, right-click the selection of columns and select **Insert**. Excel inserts as many new columns as you've selected.

When you select a row or column and right-click to display the pop-up menu, Excel displays the mini toolbar. On the mini toolbar are common operations you'll often perform with selected rows and columns. You'll be able to select from the mini toolbar to apply simple formatting such as italics and boldfacing to your cell data, as well as add color to the cell's contents. The mini toolbar helps keep common operations close to selected data, but all the mini toolbar's features are available in a more comprehensive form on the ribbon across the top of your Excel window.

2 Determine How to Insert a Cell

To insert a cell before another, you must first consider the implications of what you're doing. Other cells reside in the worksheet. If, for example, you wanted to insert a cell before the final Adjusted Total value, how is Excel supposed to handle the value that's in the cell? Should Excel delete it, move it to the right, or move it down?

If other data were to appear to the right of a cell you try to insert, you must tell Excel how to handle the insertion. When you click to select a cell (or drag to select a range of cells) and right-click your selection and choose **Insert**, Excel displays the **Insert** dialog box. From the dialog box, you tell Excel whether you want the cells to the right of the newly inserted cell to shift down or to the right, or whether you want the entire row or the entire column moved so that all the data in the affected row or column moves.

3 Request a Row

To insert a row before another, click a row number that is to *follow* the new row. Then right-click your mouse, and a menu appears. Select **Insert**. Excel moves the worksheet's contents down by one row.

▶ **TIP**

To insert multiple rows, first select the number of rows you want to insert. Start with the row below where you want Excel to insert the new rows. Drag your mouse to select multiple row numbers. After they're selected, right-click the selection of rows and select **Insert**. Excel inserts as many new rows as you've selected.

59

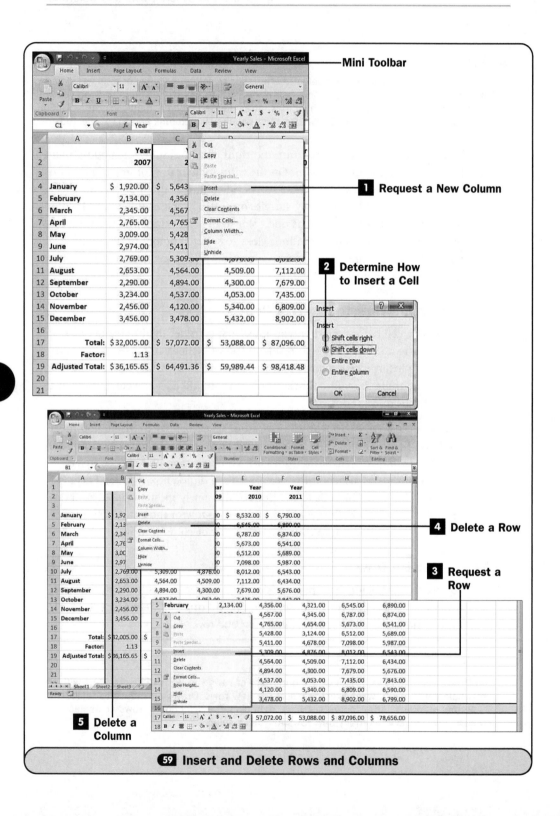

59   Insert and Delete Rows and Columns

4 Delete a Row

To delete a row, right-click the row number and select **Delete** from the menu.

To delete multiple rows, select all the row numbers you want to delete and right-click over the selection. Choose **Delete**, and Excel will delete those rows and move all the remaining rows below them up to fill the space. Keep in mind that deleting rows will affect other data and ranges and adjust your worksheet as the subsequent rows move up to fill in the gap.

5 Delete a Column

To delete a column, right-click the column name and select **Delete** from the menu.

To delete multiple columns, select all the column names you want to delete and right-click over the selection. Choose **Delete**, and Excel will delete those columns and shift all the remaining columns to the left to fill the empty space.

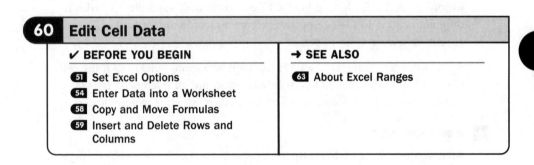

60 Edit Cell Data

✔ BEFORE YOU BEGIN	→ SEE ALSO
51 Set Excel Options	63 About Excel Ranges
54 Enter Data into a Worksheet	
58 Copy and Move Formulas	
59 Insert and Delete Rows and Columns	

60

Entering numeric data is error-prone at its best; the faster you edit cell values accurately, the faster you compose accurate worksheets. If you have already moved to another cell when you recognize that you have entered an error, you can quickly correct the mistake by editing the cell contents.

Deleting rows and columns differs from deleting specific contents inside cells. When you want to erase a cell's specific contents, the other cells to the right and below that cell don't shift to fill in the empty space (see **59 Insert and Delete Rows and Columns**).

To erase a cell's contents, you'll click the cell to move the cell pointer there and press F2 to edit the cell's contents. Press Backspace to erase the cell. Even quicker, you can press Ctrl+X or select **Edit**, **Cut** to remove the contents and send them to the Clipboard, where you can paste them elsewhere or ignore them.

1 Select a Cell to Change

Move the cell pointer to the cell you want to change.

2 Enter Editing Mode

Press F2 to enter Excel's editing mode. The cell's contents appear in the **Formula** bar, where you can edit them.

▶ **TIP**

As you edit, you'll also see the cell contents in the cell, of course, but most people find that the **Formula** bar provides an easier editing location.

3 View Cross-Referenced Cells

As you edit a cell, Excel highlights and colors other cells if your edited cell references other cells. A formula such as =C17*B18 (see **58 Copy and Move Formulas** for an explanation of the dollar signs in the B18 cell reference) references two cells: C17 and B18. When you edit a cell that contains this formula, Excel will highlight cell C17 one color and highlight B18 with a different color, and their respective references inside the formula will change to match those colors.

By coloring the referenced cells, Excel helps you more quickly spot the cells being referenced; instead of your having to locate all referenced cells by the cell address, you can locate them by their color, which is usually faster.

4 Save the Edit

After you've finished editing the cell, press Enter. Excel saves your changes in the cell unless you've made a formula error, in which case Excel returns you to the editing mode to correct the formula. (See **51 Set Excel Options** to learn how to adjust Excel's automatic formula-correcting capabilities.)

If you see an icon next to your edited cell that is an exclamation point (!) inside a yellow sign, click the down arrow to see your options. Excel constantly monitors what you do as you create and edit worksheets. If you enter a formula that differs greatly from several formulas around that cell, Excel pops up the warning exclamation point to let you know. Most of the time you will probably just ignore the warning, but if you did not mean to modify a formula so much that its pattern no longer matches those around it, you may need to edit the cell once more to correct the mistake.

▶ **NOTE**

Numerical mistakes are much easier to correct when you learn about them at their origin. If Excel didn't warn you of mismatched formula patterns, your final worksheet results would be incorrect and you would have a much tougher job trying to locate your mistake at that time.

60

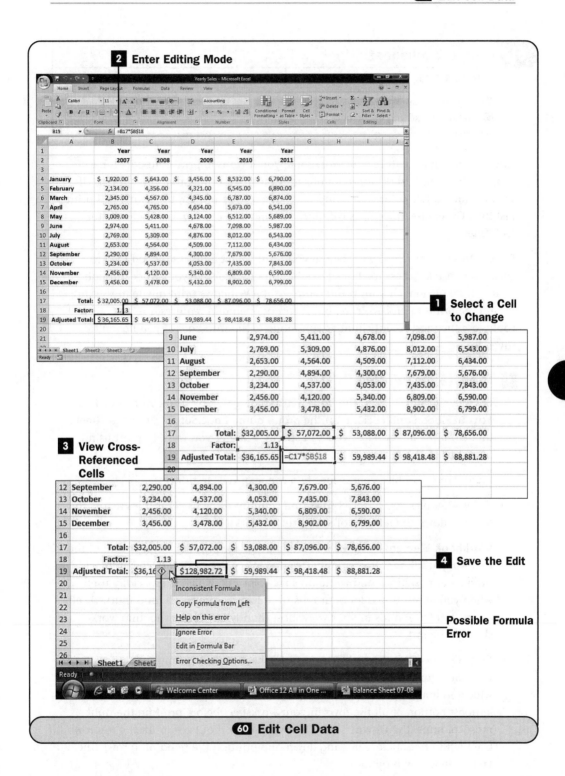

2 Enter Editing Mode

1 Select a Cell to Change

3 View Cross-Referenced Cells

4 Save the Edit

Possible Formula Error

60 Edit Cell Data

60

---

61 | **Print a Worksheet**

✔ BEFORE YOU BEGIN

52 Create a New Workbook
53 Open an Existing Worksheet

→ SEE ALSO

75 Set Up Excel Page Formatting

After you're done creating your workbook, you'll want to print it to paper. Excel supports the standard printing options that most Windows programs support. If your document has color charts and you have a color printer, the charts will print just fine. Otherwise, the charts will print in shades of black and gray (and still look fine!).

Be sure to save your workbook before you print it. Actually, it's a good idea to click your **Quick Access** toolbar's **Save** button often to save your work throughout your editing sessions. If your printer jams or the Windows print queue messes up during the printing process (rare, but it can happen and requires a reboot), you could lose the most recent changes you made to the workbook if you haven't saved it.

61

1 Prepare for Printing

Before you print, look at the **Page Setup** dialog box by displaying your **Page Layout** ribbon and clicking on the group name **Page Setup**. Click the **Sheet** tab. From the **Sheet** page, you can specify whether you want to print using any of the following options:

* **Print Area**—Enables you to specify a range of cells to print.

* **Titles**—Enables you to select rows and columns to be used for titles across the top and down the left side of your printed worksheet.

* **Workbook Elements**—Enables you to request the printing of any or all of the following: gridlines, draft quality (to save ink in your printer), row and column headings, black and white (to save color ink, which is especially useful when you're printing a lot of graphs from Excel), comments, and marked cell errors that Excel finds in your worksheet (handy for troubleshooting worksheet problems).

* **Page Order**—Determines how your worksheet prints over multiple pages. A worksheet rarely fits on a single piece of paper. For worksheets that are too wide and long to print on a single page, you can request that Excel print the leftmost portion of all the rows in your worksheet before printing the rightmost columns (the **Down, Then Over** option) or that Excel print the top rows from left to right before moving down and printing the remaining rows (the **Over, Then Down** option).

2 Request a Page Preview

Click your **Office** button and select **Print**. On the menu that appears, select **Page Preview**. Excel shows you how your current worksheet will look printed on paper.

If you want to print a different worksheet, you need to click that worksheet name before selecting **File**, **Page Preview**. It's easy to forget that a workbook can have multiple worksheets. When one does, you'll preview (and print) each worksheet individually.

3 Close the Preview

After you make sure that the previewed worksheet will print the way you want it to, press Esc or click the **Close Print Preview** button to return to your worksheet.

▶ TIP

Click the **Zoom** button on the **Print Preview** ribbon to zoom into your worksheet for easier reading of the details.

4 Prepare to Print

After you're satisfied that the worksheet is ready to print, select the **Print** option from the **Office** menu. The **Print** dialog box appears.

5 Select a Printer

Select the printer you want to print to using the **Name** drop-down list.

▶ TIP

If you have a fax modem, you can select your fax from the **Name** list to send your document to a fax recipient.

6 Select What to Print

Click to select either **All** or **Page(s)** to designate that you want to print the entire worksheet or only a portion of it. If you clicked **Page(s)**, type the page number or a range of page numbers (such as 2-5 or 1-10, 15-25) that you want to print.

61

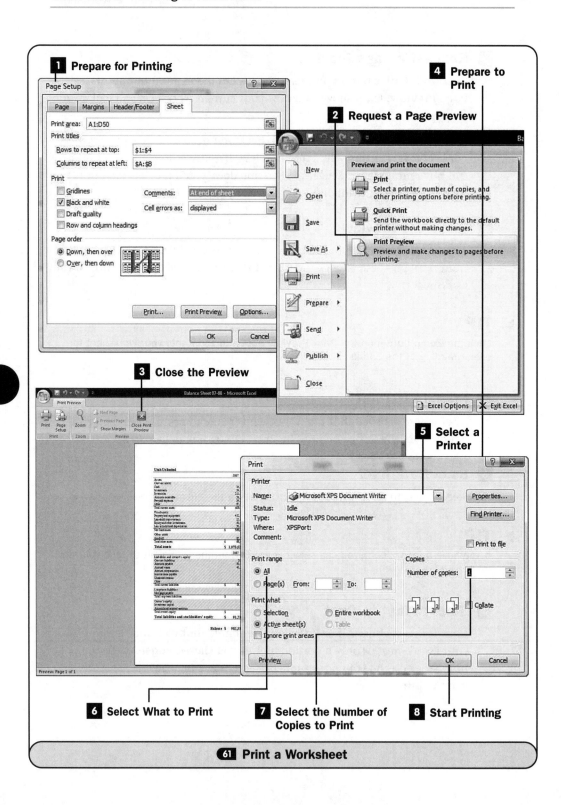

1 Prepare for Printing

4 Prepare to Print

2 Request a Page Preview

3 Close the Preview

5 Select a Printer

6 Select What to Print

7 Select the Number of Copies to Print

8 Start Printing

61 Print a Worksheet

7 Select the Number of Copies to Print

Click the arrow button next to the **Number of Copies** option to determine how many copies you want to print.

8 Start Printing

After you've determined how many pages and copies to print, click the **OK** button to print your worksheet and close the **Print** dialog box.

7

Working with Excel Data

IN THIS CHAPTER:

Here you will learn how to manage and organize your Excel spreadsheets to make them really work for you. You'll be surprised how Excel follows and updates formulas as you modify worksheet data. If you really want to master Excel, you must understand how to set up and work with cell ranges. By the time you finish this chapter, you will greatly enhance your Excel expertise. You will learn to use range names and references to produce more powerful Excel formulas and functions.

In addition to learning about Excel's range features, you'll see how Excel's built-in *functions* save you many steps when you need to perform calculations. By using functions, you'll leverage the use of common calculations such as averages and advanced calculations such as trigonometric calculations.

▶ NEW TERM

Functions—Built-in mathematical and logical routines that perform common calculations.

---

62 Find and Replace Data

62

✔ BEFORE YOU BEGIN	→ SEE ALSO
53 Open an Existing Worksheet	**67** Enter Excel Functions
55 About Moving Around Excel	

You'll find yourself working with small, single worksheets quite a bit in Excel because each sheet usually represents one aspect of a financial analysis, such as weekly sales figures for a division. Nevertheless, you'll also work with large spreadsheets quite often. Many times, a company needs to consolidate numbers from several regions, companies, or departments into a single spreadsheet. Therefore, you'll combine numerous smaller sheets into a spreadsheet and consolidate them, report totals from them, and analyze them against one another.

Whether you have one large sheet or multiple smaller ones, being able to locate numbers and text easily is important. Excel provides powerful find and replace tools you can use to locate and change the data you want.

▶ NOTE

Unlike with Word's find and replace tools, when you search for Excel data, Excel highlights the entire cell that contains the data. So if you search for the number 1 in a large spreadsheet, Excel locates and highlights the first cell (searching from left to right, row to row) that contains a 1, even if other numbers and text are in that cell.

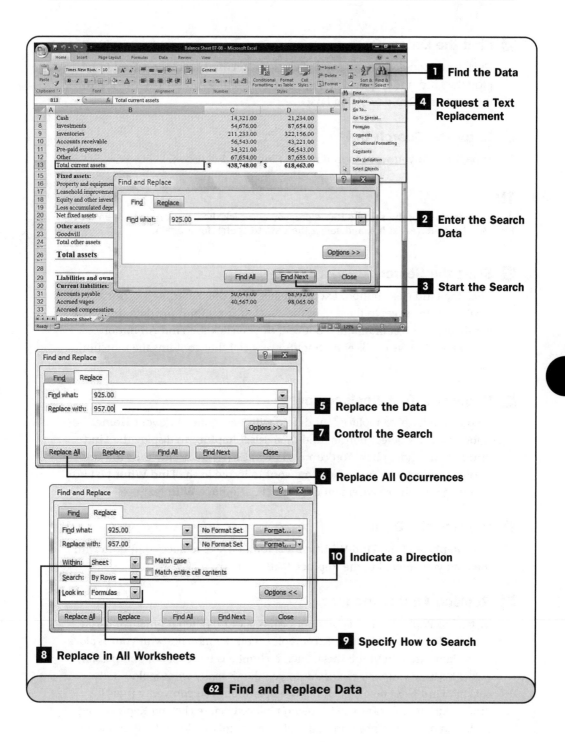

1 Find the Data

4 Request a Text Replacement

2 Enter the Search Data

3 Start the Search

62

5 Replace the Data

7 Control the Search

6 Replace All Occurrences

10 Indicate a Direction

9 Specify How to Search

8 Replace in All Worksheets

62 Find and Replace Data

1 Find the Data

Click your **Home** ribbon's **Find & Select** button, and then select **Find** to display the **Find and Replace** dialog box. You can also press Ctrl+F to display the **Find and Replace** dialog box.

2 Enter the Search Data

Type the data you want to find in the **Find What** text box.

▶ TIP

If you've searched for the same data before, you can click the down arrow to open the **Find What** drop-down list box and select the data to search for it again.

3 Start the Search

Click the **Find Next** button. Excel searches from the current cell cursor's position in the sheet to the end of the sheet. If Excel finds the data anywhere within a cell, Excel highlights that cell. (If you click the **Find All** button instead of **Find Next**, Excel highlights every cell that contains the matching data.)

62

4 Request a Text Replacement

If you want Excel to replace found data with new data, click your **Home** ribbon's **Find & Select** button, and then select **Replace** to display the **Find and Replace** dialog box. You can also press Ctrl+H to display the **Find and Replace** dialog box. Type what you want to locate in the **Find What** text box and then type the replacement data into the **Replace With** text box.

5 Replace the Data

Click **Replace**. If the **Find What** data is found, Excel replaces that data with the data you entered in the **Replace With** text box.

6 Replace All Occurrences

Instead of **Replace** (or after you perform one or more replacements), if you click the **Replace All** button, Excel replaces all the matches with your replacement data throughout the sheet. Such a change is more global and possibly riskier because you may replace data you didn't really want replaced. By clicking **Find Next** before each replace operation, you can verify that the proper data in the correct cell is being replaced before clicking **Replace**, but such a single-occurrence find and replacement takes a lot of time in a long spreadsheet in which much data needs to be replaced.

7 Control the Search

To control the way Excel searches the current sheet, or to enable Excel to search all sheets within the current spreadsheet, click the **Options** button. Excel expands the **Find and Replace** dialog box with additional options.

8 Replace in All Worksheets

Click to display the **Within** drop-down list to specify whether you want Excel to replace data in the current worksheet or in all the worksheets inside the currently open workbook.

9 Specify How to Search

Perhaps you want Excel to search only formulas for calculated results that match your search term. If so, click to select **Formulas** in the **Look In** drop-down list box. If you want Excel to search only in values and text you've typed, but not formulas, click to select **Values**.

▶ **NOTE**

Selecting **Formulas** enables Excel to locate your search term in either formulas or results. Selecting **Values** returns a match only if your search term is found in an actual number or text and not if it's the result of a formula.

10 Indicate a Direction

Although Excel normally searches from left to right and from the top row down, you can specify that Excel search completely down the first column of data before searching the second column, moving from column to column only after searching down the entire previous column. Click the **Search** drop-down list box to select the **By Columns** option if you want to search down an entire column before moving to the next one.

When you finish finding and replacing all the data for this search session, click the **Find & Replace** dialog box's **Close** button to close the dialog box and return to the sheet's work area.

▶ **NOTE**

Other search options exist, and you can try them when needed. For example, you can click **Format** to format your search data; Excel will consider the search to be found only if the data matches *and* the format of the data in the worksheet matches your specified format.

62

63 | About Excel Ranges

✔ BEFORE YOU BEGIN	→ SEE ALSO
58 Copy and Move Formulas	**64** Create a Range
	71 About Excel Limits

A selected group of cells composes a *range*. A range is always rectangular, and it might be a single cell, a row, a column, or several adjacent rows and columns. The cells within a range are always contiguous, but you can select multiple ranges at the same time. You can perform various operations on ranges, such as moving and copying. If, for example, you want to format a row of totals in some way, you first select the range that includes the totals and then apply the format to that range.

▶ **NEW TERM**

Range—One or more cells, selected adjacent to each other in a rectangular manner, that you can name and treat as a single entity or group of cells in formulas.

The next figure shows three selected ranges on a sheet. Excel lightly highlights ranges as you select them. You can describe a range by the cell reference of the upper-left cell of the range (an anchor point) and the cell reference of the lower-right cell of the range. As you can see from the figure, multiple-celled ranges are designated by listing the anchor point, followed by a colon (:), followed by the range's lower-right cell reference. Therefore, the range that begins at D11 and ends at F12 has the range of D11:F12. To select more than one range, in case you want to apply formatting or calculations to different areas of your worksheet at once, hold Ctrl while selecting each range.

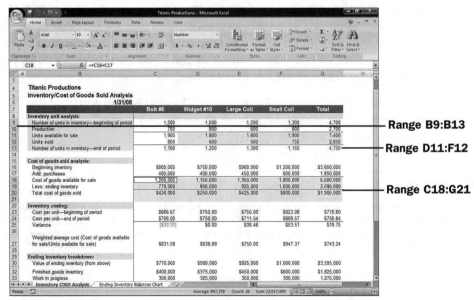

A worksheet can have multiple ranges selected at one time.

Keep in mind that a single cell, if selected, can be considered a range. So D5:D5 is a range composed solely of the cell D5. In this case, the anchor point is the entire range, which is only one cell.

The true power of Excel shows when you use ranges of cells, as opposed to specifying every cell by its cell address. (**64 Create a Range** explains how to name ranges.) Instead of referring to a range as F2:G14, you could name that range MonthlySales and then refer to MonthlySales in your formulas by name instead of having to type unintuitive cell references in formulas such as AD32:AJ210.

All the following are valid formulas. Cell references and range names appear throughout the formulas:

```
=(SalesTotals)/NumOfSales
=C4 * 2 - (Rate * .08)
=7 + LE51 - (Gross - Net)
```

When you enter formulas that contain range references, you can either type the full reference or point to the cell reference. If you want to include a complete named range in a formula (formulas can work on complete ranges), select the entire range, and Excel inserts the range name in your formula. Often, finding and pointing to a value is easier than locating the reference and typing its exact range address.

If, for example, you are entering a formula, when you get to the place in the formula that requires a cell reference, don't type the cell reference (such as G23); instead, point to and click on the cell you want to use in the formula, and Excel adds that cell reference to your formula. If you enter a formula such as =7 +, instead of typing a cell address of LE51 next, you could point to cell LE51 and press Enter to end the formula or type another operator to continue the formula. Immediately after typing the cell reference for you, Excel returns your cell pointer to the formula (or to the **Formula** bar if you are entering the formula there) so that you can complete the formula.

63

▶ **TIP**

Range names are absolute. If a formula in one cell refers to a range named Commission, Excel considers the reference to be absolute (see **58 Copy and Move Formulas**). Also, you never use the dollar sign when referring to a range as you could when making cell addresses absolute (such as F17).

After you assign a name to a range, you don't have to remember that range's address, such as R31:T65, when you use it in formulas. Suppose that you are creating a large worksheet that spans many screens. If you assign names to cells when you create them—especially to cells that you know you will refer to later during the worksheet's development—entering formulas that use those names is easier to remember and type. Instead of locating a cell to find its address, you need only to type its name when entering a formula that uses that cell.

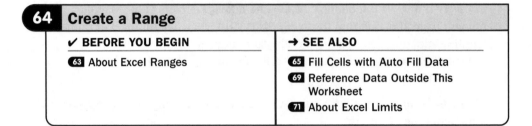

To name a range, you only need to select a range and assign a name to it. Excel supports the naming, renaming, and deleting of range names. After you've named a range of cells, you no longer have to refer to that group of cells by their cell addresses.

▶ **TIP**

64

Give your ranges meaningful names. The name **PayrollFeb** is obviously a better name than **XYZ** for payroll data for February. The better you name ranges, the fewer errors you'll type in your sheets because you'll more accurately refer to cells.

Excel keeps track of your ranges and changes them as needed. If you insert a cell in the middle of a range, or even entire rows and columns somewhere inside a range, Excel reassigns the range name to include the expanded cell range. This also holds true if you delete cells from inside a range. (If you delete only cell contents, the range is unaffected.)

1 Select a Range

Click the initial anchor cell in a range you want to define. While holding down your mouse button, drag your mouse to the last cell in the range. Excel highlights the cells within the range as you drag the mouse.

2 Request a Range Name

Right-click the range and select **Name a Range** from the menu. The **New Name** dialog box appears. This is where you name ranges and manage them.

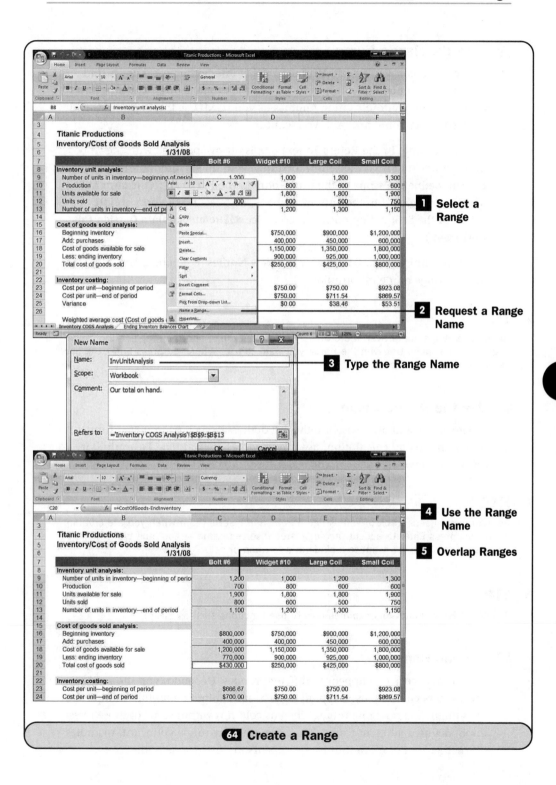

1 Select a Range

2 Request a Range Name

3 Type the Range Name

4 Use the Range Name

5 Overlap Ranges

64 Create a Range

3 Type the Range Name

Type a name for your selected range in the **Name** text box. Do not include spaces in the range name. Click **OK** to add the name to your worksheet. A worksheet can contain as many names as you need. Use the **Comment** field to describe the name further if you want to.

The range name in the **Refers To** text box is always prefixed with the worksheet's name and separated from the range with an exclamation point (!). You can define the scope of the range name, whether local to the current worksheet or global to the entire workbook, by selecting the appropriate option in the **Scope** drop-down list box. (See **69** **Reference Data Outside This Worksheet.**)

When you finish, click **OK** to close the **New Names** dialog box. You can now use the range name in formulas.

▶ TIP

To create a range name even more quickly, select the range and then replace the range address in the **Name** box with the name you want to use. When you press Enter, the new name appears in the **Name** box.

64

4 Use the Range Name

Where you would otherwise use the cell addresses, such as in a Sum() function or inside any calculation, use range names instead. The **Formula** bar always displays the range name inside formulas.

▶ NOTE

AutoComplete keeps track of your range names and inserts them when you are creating a formula; press Enter to accept the suggested inserted name or continue typing if that's not the range name you want to include in a formula or cell.

▶ TIP

66 **About Excel Functions** explains how to use functions such as Sum().

5 Overlap Ranges

Two or more cells can appear in different ranges. Depending on the kind of sheet you're creating, overlapping range names might be useful. Multiple rows might compose one range, whereas columns within some of those rows might define a different range. You can name any range you want, regardless of whether part or all of that range appears in other range names.

Name as many ranges as you can because the more range names you create, the less error-prone your sheets will be. By referring to ranges by name, you are less likely to make a mistake than if you reference the cells within that range by their addresses.

---

65 Fill Cells with Auto Fill Data

✔ BEFORE YOU BEGIN	→ SEE ALSO
52 Create a New Workbook **60** Edit Cell Data	**67** Enter Excel Functions

---

Excel often predicts what data you want to enter into a sheet. By spotting trends in your data, Excel uses educated guesses to fill in cell data for you. Excel uses *Auto Fill* to copy and extend data from one cell to several additional cells.

▶ NEW TERM

Auto Fill—The automatic placement of values in sheet cells based on a pattern in other cells.

One of the most common data fills you perform is to use Excel's capability to copy one cell's data to several other cells. You might want to create a pro forma balance sheet for an upcoming five-year period, for example. You could insert a two-line label across the top of each year's data. The first line would contain five occurrences of the label Year, and the second line would hold the numbers 2008 through 2012. After entering all the data in year 2008's column, you would only need to select that column and drag to fill in the remaining columns.

65

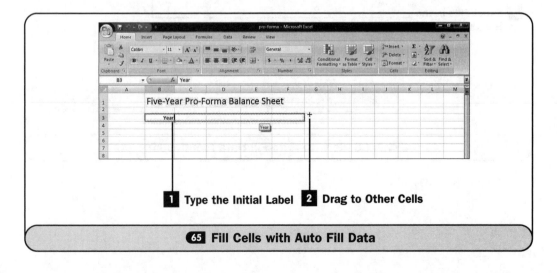

1 Type the Initial Label   **2** Drag to Other Cells

65 Fill Cells with Auto Fill Data

65

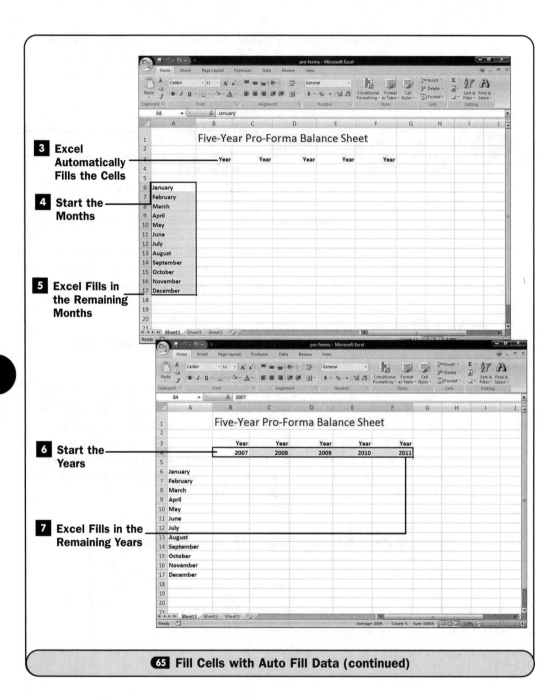

3 Excel Automatically Fills the Cells

4 Start the Months

5 Excel Fills in the Remaining Months

6 Start the Years

7 Excel Fills in the Remaining Years

65 Fill Cells with Auto Fill Data (continued)

Even if the only fill that Excel performed was this copying of data across rows and columns, the data fill would still be beneficial. Excel goes an extra step, however: It performs smart fills, too. Excel actually examines and completes data you have entered.

Using Excel's fill capability to enter the years 2008 through 2012 across the top of the sheet requires only that you type 2008 under the first Year title and type 2009 under the second title. Select both cells and then drag the fill handle right three more cells. When you release the mouse button, Excel fills in the remaining years.

▶ **TIP**

Excel not only fills in numbers in sequences but also can determine sequential years and other sequences (such as extending cells containing 3, 6, and 9 to new cells that hold 12, 15, 18, and so on). Excel also extends days of the week and month names. Type Monday in one cell and drag the *fill handle* to let Excel finish the days of the week in every cell you drag to.

▶ **NEW TERM**

Fill handle—A small black box, at the bottom-right corner of a selected cell or range, that you drag to the right (or down or up) to fill the range of data with values related to the selected range.

Excel 2007 introduces the **Fill** button on the **Home** ribbon. You can click to select a cell to begin the fill and then click the **Fill** button and select a direction to fill. Dragging your mouse is still the simplest and most intuitive way to fill a range of cells.

65

1 Type the Initial Label

Type your first label, such as Year. This will be the value you will fill succeeding cells with. Although you could copy the value to the Clipboard with Ctrl+C and then paste the value to other cells with Ctrl+V, the fill handle is quicker to use, as you'll see next.

2 Drag to Other Cells

Click and drag the cell's fill handle to the rest of the cells in which you want the label to appear. As you drag the fill handle to the right, Excel highlights each cell that will receive the filled data. Excel pops up a small box showing you the contents of the fill.

3 Excel Automatically Fills the Cells

When you release your mouse button, Excel fills the remaining cells in the range with your label. Excel fills with numeric data, too, not just text inside cells. When you drag *integers,* Excel extends the range by increasing the integer by one. (Click the icon that Excel places to the right of the filled cells if you want to change the way Excel formatted the fill cells.)

▶ **NEW TERM**

Integers—Numbers without decimal points, such as 0, –52, 164, and 435 (also called *whole numbers*).

4 Start the Months

To see how smart Excel's fill capability is, you can type a month name and drag that month's fill handle across or down the sheet to fill in the rest of the months.

5 Excel Fills in the Remaining Months

When you release your mouse, Excel fills in the remaining month names for you.

6 Start the Years

Type the initial year such as 2008. Type the next year. Excel uses the pattern you've established (adding one to each year).

Click to select both years and drag the fill handle from 2009's year cell to the right.

7 Excel Fills in the Remaining Years

When you release your mouse, Excel fills in the remaining years by incrementing the years for you as far as you allow the fill.

66

66	**About Excel Functions**
✔ **BEFORE YOU BEGIN**	→ **SEE ALSO**
57 Use Sum to Add Rows and Columns	67 Enter Excel Functions
63 About Excel Ranges	
64 Create a Range	

Entering individual formulas can get tedious. Suppose that you wanted to add all the values in a column of 100 cells. You would type a formula such as =F2+F3+F4+. . . and would likely run out of room in the cell before you completed the formula. In addition, such long formulas are likely to produce errors when you have to type so much.

Fortunately, Excel includes several built-in functions that perform many common mathematical calculations. Instead of writing a formula to sum a row or column of values, for example, you could use the Sum() function.

The debate rages as to whether one should write a function name with parentheses following its name, such as Average() or just Average. This book will generally use the parentheses because it's more obvious to you that a function is being referenced as opposed to a cell name when the parentheses appear. Also, Excel always converts functions to uppercase, but when discussing functions, for the sake of readability, this book will often capitalize the first letter only. You can do the same, but when you type Average(dataRange) into a cell, Excel converts it to AVERAGE(dataRange).

When actually typing a function inside a cell, you'll almost always use the parentheses because they are required. A function accepts zero or more **arguments,** and those arguments go inside the parentheses. A function might need zero, one, or more arguments, depending on how much information the function needs to do its job. When using multiple arguments in a function, separate the arguments with commas. If a function contains only a single argument, do not use a comma inside the parentheses. Functions generally manipulate data (numbers or text), and the arguments inside the parentheses supply the data to the functions. The Average() function, for example, computes an average of whatever list of values you pass in the argument. Therefore, all the following compute an average from the argument list:

```
=Average(18, 65, 299, $R$5, 10, -2, 102)
=Average(SalesTotals)
=Average(D4:D14)
```

66

▶ **NEW TERM**

Arguments—Values appearing inside a function's parentheses that the function uses in some way to produce its result.

▶ **TIP**

When you begin to enter a formula, ToolTips appear as you type the formula's name to help guide you through the formula's required contents. When you type =A into a cell, the ToolTip displays functions beginning with A. As you continue typing the v and e, Excel narrows down to the =AVERAGE() function. You can scroll through the list of ToolTip choices and press Enter when you see the function you want to use.

As with some functions, Average() accepts as many arguments as needed to do its job. The first Average() function computes the average of seven values, one of which is an absolute cell reference. The second Average() function computes the average of a range named SalesTotals. No matter how many cells compose the range SalesTotals, Average() computes and displays the average. The final Average() function shows the average of the values in the range D4 through D14 (a columnar list).

Functions improve your accuracy. If you want to average three cell values, for example, you might be tempted to type something like this:

```
=R2 + R4 + R6 / 3
```

That formula, however, does *not* compute an average! Remember that the operator hierarchy forces the division calculation first. If you use the Average() function, as shown next, you don't have to worry as much about the calculation's hierarchy:

```
=Average(R2, R4, R6)
```

The Sum() function is perhaps the most common function because you so often total columns and rows. Instead of adding each cell in a row or column individually, you could more easily enter the following function:

```
=Sum(R2:R45)
```

▶ **NOTE**

66

The **Sum** button actually places the Sum() function inside its target cell. (See **57** **Use Sum to Add Rows and Columns.**)

▶ **TIP**

When you insert rows within a Sum() range, Excel updates the range inside the Sum() function argument list to include the newly inserted values.

You can use functions inside other formulas. Combining functions with range names will make your formulas highly readable. The following formula might be included in a cell that works on sales totals:

```
=CostOfSales * Sum(Qtr1, Qtr2, Qtr3, Qtr4) / SalesFactor * 1.07
```

Table 7.1 describes common built-in functions for which you'll find a lot of uses as you create spreadsheets. Remember to start every formula with an equal sign and to add your arguments to the parentheses, and you are set.

TABLE 7.1 Common Excel Functions

Function Name	Description
Abs()	Computes the absolute value of its cell argument. (Good for distance- and age-difference calculations.)
Average()	Computes the average of its arguments.
Count()	Returns the number of numerical arguments in the argument list. (Useful if you use a range name for the argument list.)
Max()	Returns the highest (maximum) value in the argument list. (Useful if you use a range name for the argument list and you need to pick out the highest value.)
Min()	Returns the lowest (minimum) value in the argument list. (Useful if you use a range name for the argument list and you need to pick out the lowest value.)
Pi()	Computes the value of mathematical pi (requires no arguments) for use in math calculations.
Product()	Computes the product (multiplicative result) of the argument range.
Roman()	Converts its cell value to a Roman numeral.
Sqrt()	Computes the square root of the cell argument.
Stdev()	Computes the argument list's standard deviation.
Sum()	Computes the sum of its arguments.
Today()	Returns today's date (requires no arguments).
Var()	Computes a list's sample variance.

67 Enter Excel Functions

✔ BEFORE YOU BEGIN

57 Use Sum() to Add Rows and Columns
66 About Excel Functions

→ SEE ALSO

68 Use Excel's Function Wizard

67

Computing totals is so common that Excel makes the Sum() function even easier to use by placing the **Sum** button on the **Formula** bar. Just click a blank cell below or to the right of a range of values, click **Sum**, and Excel computes the sum and writes the proper Sum() function for you. The **Sum** button also drops down a list of other common functions such as Average(), Count(), Max(), and Min(). (See **57 Use Sum to Add Rows and Columns.**)

You'll have to type the remaining functions yourself when you want to use them, but doing so is far from a chore. **66 About Excel Functions** lists some of the most common functions you'll use. For the rest, use Excel's Help feature to find the function you want to use and then type that function and its arguments to get the result you want.

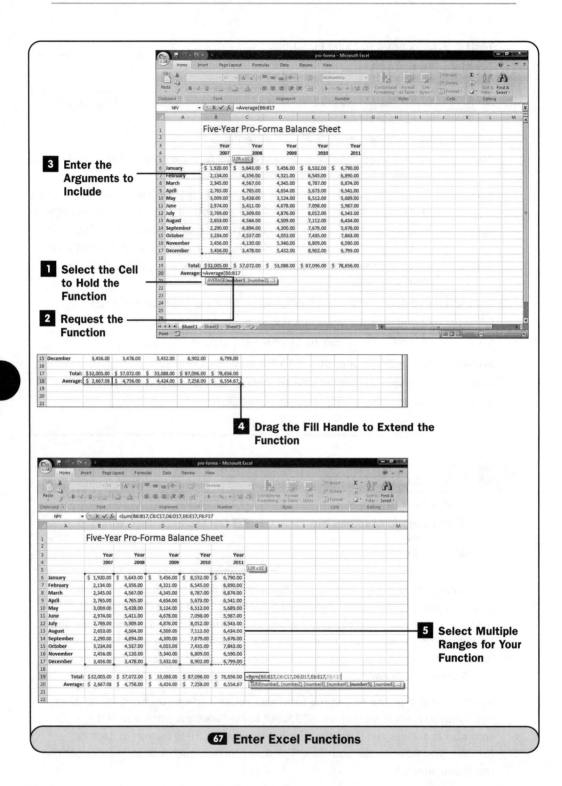

3 Enter the Arguments to Include

1 Select the Cell to Hold the Function

2 Request the Function

4 Drag the Fill Handle to Extend the Function

5 Select Multiple Ranges for Your Function

67

67 Enter Excel Functions

❶ Select the Cell to Hold the Function

Click to select the cell you want to contain the result of the function.

❷ Request the Function

Type an equal sign (=) followed by the name of the function.

❸ Enter the Arguments to Include

Type an open parenthesis and then type or select the values you want to include in the function, followed by a closing parenthesis. A border appears around any cell or range to be included in the equation. For the popular Sum() function, your task is simplified again because Excel proposes a range as soon as you enter the Sum() function name (or click the **Sum** button, which does the same thing). If Excel guesses wrongly, drag to adjust the selection to a different range of cells.

After the range or set of arguments is correct, press Enter to accept the function. The result of the function then appears in your cell.

▶ TIP

The status bar at the bottom of your work area provides a quick way to see the result of common functions on-the-fly. Simply select a range, and your status bar automatically displays an average, count, and sum of the selected cells.

▶ NOTE

As with formulas and text labels in cells, you can press F2 to edit the function, its arguments, or a formula that uses the function.

❹ Drag the Fill Handle to Extend the Function

As with any other formula or cell label, you can drag the formula's fill handle whose cell contains a function, such as Average() or Count(), to another cell to extend that formula.

❺ Select Multiple Ranges for Your Function

You can select multiple ranges before typing the final parenthesis to finish your function. When typing an argument, move your mouse pointer or use your arrow keys to select a range and press comma (,). Then select another range and press comma (,). Keep selecting ranges until you've included every range you want to use in the function. Press the closing parenthesis to finish the function and view the result.

67

68 Use Excel's Function Wizard

✔ BEFORE YOU BEGIN

66 About Excel Functions
67 Enter Excel Functions

→ SEE ALSO

70 Work with Dates and Times

1 Request the Function Wizard   **2** Select a Category

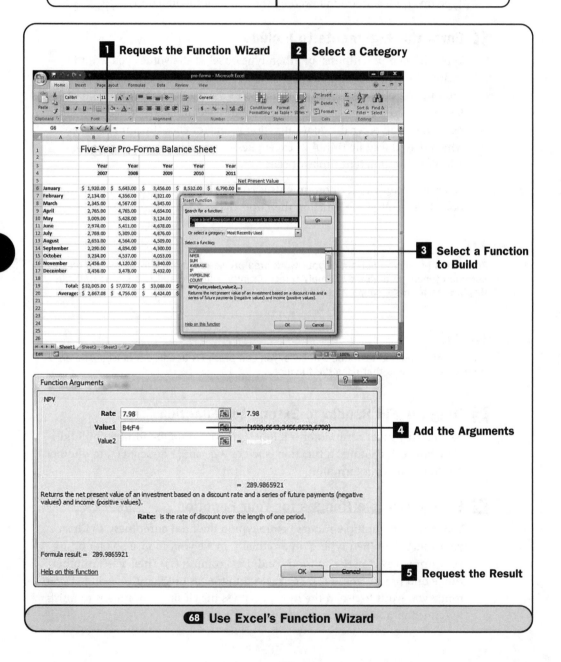

3 Select a Function to Build

4 Add the Arguments

5 Request the Result

68 Use Excel's Function Wizard

Some functions require more arguments than a simple cell or range. Excel contains many financial functions, for example, that compute loan values and investment rates of return. If you want to use one of the more advanced functions, or if you're unsure exactly which arguments are required for a function you're about to use, be sure to take advantage of Excel's Function Wizard that displays the **Insert Function** dialog box, with which you can build all your functions.

With the Function Wizard, you can do the following:

- Select from a list of functions organized by category

- Build your functions one argument at a time

From the **Insert Function** dialog box, you don't need to memorize long function argument list requirements. The dialog box works like a wizard, helping you build your functions without having to remember the nitty-gritty details of all the arguments.

▮ Request the Function Wizard

Click the cell you want to hold a function and then click the **Function Wizard** button.

▮ Select a Category

Select the category from which you want to write a function. For example, if you want to compute the net present value of a series of cash flows, you would first select the **Financial** category and scroll down until you reach the **NPV** function entry.

▶ NOTE

If you're unsure of a category, type a brief description in the **Search for a Function** text box at the top of the **Insert Function** dialog box. Excel will display a list of functions related to your search terms.

▮ Select a Function to Build

When you see the function you want to use in the **Select a Function** list, double-click to select that function name. Excel displays a list of fields to match every argument that function needs in the **Function Arguments** dialog box.

For example, if you selected the **NPV** function (net present value), Excel displays the fields that match the NPV() argument list: rate of return, and one or more values representing the cash flow. As you add arguments, Excel displays

68

the current result in the **Function Arguments** dialog box's lower area. Click **OK** when you finish entering the function's arguments.

4 Add the Arguments

You can type values directly into the argument list (such as a discount rate) or click to select a range in your worksheet to use as an argument. Click the argument you want to enter and then either type or select the argument.

5 Request the Result

After building your function and specifying its arguments, click **OK** to see the result. Excel places the completed function in the cell you selected in step 1.

---

69 Reference Data Outside This Worksheet

✔ **BEFORE YOU BEGIN**	→ **SEE ALSO**
54 Enter Data into a Worksheet	77 Conditionally Format Data
60 Edit Cell Data	

69

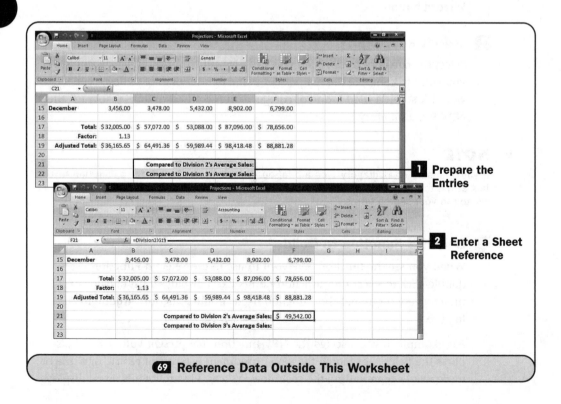

1 **Prepare the Entries**

2 **Enter a Sheet Reference**

69 Reference Data Outside This Worksheet

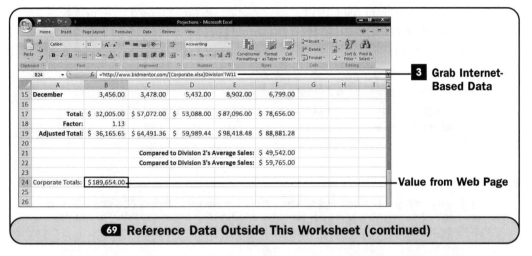

3 Grab Internet-Based Data

Value from Web Page

69 Reference Data Outside This Worksheet (continued)

If all your data resided in the current sheet, referencing other cells would be simple. You'd only need to know the other cell's address, such as D4. What if the cell is in another sheet inside the current spreadsheet? If Sheet1 needs to reference cell G6 in a worksheet named Sheet3, you cannot use the simple G6 reference to grab Sheet3's G6 cell contents.

▶ **TIP**

If you routinely use multiple worksheets within workbooks, consider renaming the default worksheet names of Sheet1, Sheet2, and Sheet3 to names that are more meaningful, such as Division1Sales, Division2Sales, and Division3Sales. Right-click the worksheet name's tab and select **Rename** to rename, insert, or delete any sheet.

Perhaps the data you need isn't even in another sheet but resides across your network somewhere. Or, perhaps, the data resides across the world, accessible from the Internet. That's no problem for Excel. You can insert network addresses and web address links anywhere in a spreadsheet to display data from that location. An Excel calculation doesn't care whether the data comes from the current worksheet or from a different worksheet in the workbook; Excel grabs the data and calculates with it.

1 **Prepare the Entries**

Set up your sheet so that it's ready for entries from other sheets and even from other locations. Of course, you can always add the labels after you reference data from other locations, too.

2 **Enter a Sheet Reference**

To reference a cell from another sheet, preface the cell address with the sheet's name followed by an exclamation point. For example, to display in the current sheet the value from cell G19 of a sheet named Division2, you'd type the following value in the current sheet's cell:

```
=Division2!G19
```

Excel locates the value in cell G19 of the sheet named Division2 and places it in the current cell. Remember that without the preceding equal sign, Excel would think you were typing a text label instead of requesting that Excel place the contents of Division2's cell G19 in that spot.

▶ **TIP**

Excel doesn't limit you to displaying values from other worksheets only. You can also use values from other worksheets in your formulas and function argument lists. For example, the following duration function uses arguments from three other worksheets:

```
=Duration(Region1!G45, Accounting!PValue, Finance!FutValue*.9)
```

Two of the values are range names given to individual cells: PValue and FutValue.

70

3 Grab Internet-Based Data

If you want to reference a value from a spreadsheet stored on the Internet, feel free to do so. Obviously, an always-on Internet connection is best for such a reference. Otherwise, Excel will dial your modem connection to get the value every time you recalculate the spreadsheet.

Use the following pattern:

```
='http://www.YourDomain.com/[Worksheet.xlsx]Sheet1'!Cell
```

That's quite a mouthful! Here is one such example:

```
='http://www.bidmentor.com/[Corporate.xlsx]Division'!W11
```

To read such a long reference, it helps to begin at the right. This references cell W11 in the sheet named Division in a spreadsheet named Corporate.xlsx on a website named www.BidMentor.com; keep in mind that you must enclose the web page reference inside single quotation marks and enclose the actual Excel workbook name in square brackets.

70	**Work with Dates and Times**	
✔ **BEFORE YOU BEGIN**		→ **SEE ALSO**
54 Enter Data into a Worksheet		**73** Format Cells
67 Enter Excel Functions		

Excel supports almost every national and international date and time format. Excel converts date and time values that you type to a special internal number that represents the number of days since midnight January 1, 1900. Although this strange internal date representation of days since 1-1-1900 might not make sense at first, you'll use these values to compute time between two or more dates. You can easily determine how many days an account is past due, for example, by subtracting the current date from the cell in the worksheet that contains the due date.

If you enter a date in a longer format, such as July 4, 1976, Excel typically (depending on your settings) converts the date to another format (such as 4-Jul-70). You can enter a date, a time value, or both. You can format the date and time values you enter (see **73** **Format Cells**) to take on any format you want.

▶ **TIP**

Excel's date and time functions are useful for calculating durations for past-due and other calculations related to date and time values.

1 **Enter This Moment**

Type =Now() in a cell. When you press Enter, Excel converts the function to the computer's currently set date and time. You can use this to calculate values based on this moment, such as the number of days old you are.

▶ **TIP**

Remember that Now() and the other date functions operate as number of days since January 1, 1900. Therefore, when you add or subtract dates, the result is always a number of days.

2 **Determine How Many Days Old You Are**

Enter your birth date. Type the date in any format. Although you can format the date using the **Number** group on your **Home** ribbon, don't worry about the format now; concentrate on what occurs when you use date arithmetic.

Subtract your birth date from the current date to determine how many days old you are. Excel might decide to use a date format for the resulting cell; if so, change the format to **Number** by clicking and selecting from the drop-down list box in your **Home** ribbon's **Number** group.

Digits to the right of the decimal indicate partial days since midnight of your birth date.

70

70

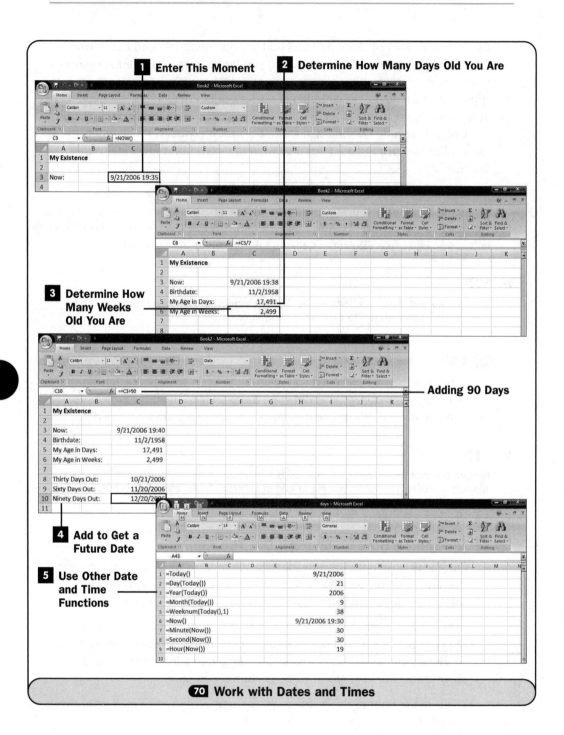

1 Enter This Moment

2 Determine How Many Days Old You Are

3 Determine How Many Weeks Old You Are

Adding 90 Days

4 Add to Get a Future Date

5 Use Other Date and Time Functions

70 Work with Dates and Times

3 Determine How Many Weeks Old You Are

Because the dates work in days, you can divide your age in days by seven to determine approximately how old you are in weeks.

4 Add to Get a Future Date

What will be the date one month from today? Sure, it's simple to look at a calendar, but when you write general-purpose spreadsheets, you've got to be able to apply such formulas to dates to age accounts receivables and other calculations.

By adding 30, 60, and 90 to today's date, you can display the date when future payments will come due. Excel understands that different months have different numbers of days in them, so adding 60 to April 12 properly returns June 11 and not June 12.

▶ **NOTE**

Generally, you'll use date formats to hide the time when you work with date arithmetic. Multiply time values by 24 to obtain the number of hours represented. When you subtract two date and time values, if you multiply by 24 you'll get the number of hours represented. For example, subtract a cell containing your birth date from a cell containing today's date, and then multiply the result by 24 to learn how old you are in hours.

5 Use Other Date and Time Functions

Several date and time functions are available to make working with dates and times simpler. Today() returns the date only (without the time, unlike Now()). Day() returns the day of the month of whatever date you use as its argument. Weeknum() returns the week number (within the year, from 1 to 52) of the date inside its argument list. Weeknum() requires two arguments: a date and either 1 or 2 to indicate that the start of the week is Sunday or Monday, respectively. Month() returns the month number of its date argument. Year() returns the year of the date given as its argument. You'll use these functions to pick off what you want to work with in another formula or label—the day, month, or year by itself instead of the complete date.

Second() returns the second number of its time argument. Minute() returns the minute number of its time argument, and Hour() returns the hour number of its time argument.

▶ **TIP**

You can enter a time value, a date value, or both. If you don't enter a date with a time value, Excel displays only the time in the cell.

Days() requires two date arguments and returns the number of days (and partial days) between two dates. Therefore, to determine the number of days between today and Easter, you could enter the following:

```
=Days(Eastersunday(Year(Today())+1); Now())
```

Although at first glance this appears convoluted, it's a simple set of arguments.

71   About Excel Limits

✔ **BEFORE YOU BEGIN**

50 About Worksheets and Workbooks

52 Create a New Workbook

69 Reference Data Outside This Worksheet

→ **SEE ALSO**

87 Import and Export Worksheet Data

89 About Excel Databases

71

Microsoft designed Excel 2007 to perform well for you whether you have a small amount or a large amount of data to work with. Excel has been around for about two decades, and Microsoft has improved it, added features, and continued to hone its speed since version 1.0.

The question often comes up as to how large a worksheet can be. With disk space and being able to reference data outside the current worksheet (see 69 **Reference Data Outside This Worksheet**), you're not really limited in any way because you can always link to another worksheet if you run out of room on your current one.

Nevertheless, it's good to review some of Excel's limits from time to time. It's possible, for example, if you use Excel as a simple database program, that your data could eventually exceed Excel's capability to handle it. At that time, you would have to move to a data-specific application such as Microsoft Access. (See 89 **About Excel Databases**.)

Table 7.2 lists some of Excel's limitations. You can peruse the table to get an idea of what Excel does and doesn't allow.

▶ **NOTE**

Some of the ranges are so vast that this actually reads more like a table of capabilities than limits.

TABLE 7.2 Some Excel Limitations

Feature	Maximum Allowable Limit
Open workbooks	Bounded by your computer's memory space
Worksheet size	1,048,576 rows by 16,384 columns
Column width	255 characters
Row height	409 *points*
Page breaks	1,026 horizontal and vertical
Cell characters	32,767
Print preview pages	65,556
Header or footer	255 characters
Workbook sheets	Bounded by your computer's memory space
Unique cell styles	64,000
Fill styles	32
Unique font types	1,024 global finds available for use and 512 maximum allowed for each workbook
Names in a workbook	Bounded by your computer's memory space
Windows in a workbook	Bounded by your computer's memory space
Linked worksheets	Bounded by your computer's memory space
Zoom range	10% to 400%
Undo levels	100
Data form fields	32
Filter drop-down lists	10,000
Formula length	8,192 characters
Selected ranges	2,048
Function arguments	255
Nested levels of functions	64
Date range	January 1, 1900 to December 31, 9999
Largest time value	9999:59:59
Data series in a chart	255
Data points in 2-D chart	32,000
Data points in 3-D chart	4,000
Users who can open shared workbook	256

▶ **NEW TERM**

Point—1/72 of an inch.

8

Formatting Worksheets with Excel

IN THIS CHAPTER:

Excel makes it easy to make even simple worksheets look professional. Excel can quickly format your worksheets within the boundaries you select. With Excel 2007's live preview, you can see how formatting changes will look before you apply them. If you apply them and then change your mind, no problem, because Undo puts things back the way they were.

If you want to format your spreadsheet by hand, the formatting commands you learn in this chapter will enable you to pinpoint important data and highlight it. Others can then look at your spreadsheets and easily find your highlighted information.

Throughout this chapter, you'll learn how to change the appearance of your spreadsheets so that they look as good as possible. Specifically, you will learn how to select from a list of professional formatting styles, how to format selected cells and ranges, how to apply themes to your worksheets, and how to leverage your spreadsheet designs so that you can reuse them with little trouble.

72

72   Freeze Row and Column Headers

✔ BEFORE YOU BEGIN	→ SEE ALSO
54 Enter Data into a Worksheet	**74** Center a Heading over Multiple Columns

Often, you'll enter lots of data into a spreadsheet—perhaps sales figures daily, for example. As you add more and more data, your sheets will grow to be quite large. Perhaps at the end of each month, quarter, or fiscal year, you close your books so that you can consolidate the data and begin anew the next time period.

Until you restart the data entry for the next period, the data continues to expand and might end up consuming more than one screen, which can lead to a problem. If you initially put labels across the top of the sheet to label the columns and put labels down the left side to label the rows of data, when you page down or move too far to the right, the column and row headings will scroll off the screen.

To keep track of the purpose of your sheet's values, you can freeze the scrolling of row and column headers so that those headers remain on the screen while the rest of the data scrolls under or to the right of them.

▶ **TIP**

You can freeze as many contiguous rows or columns as you need. For example, your worksheet title and column headings might span three rows. All rows below those three frozen rows will scroll up and down, but the three will remain in place so that you'll know what the columns represent.

1 Determine the Rows to Freeze

Select the row that *follows* the row (or rows) you want to freeze. For example, if you want the top row with column headings to remain in place no matter how much data falls below it, select the second-from-the-top row by clicking the row number.

2 Freeze the Rows

Display your **View** ribbon and click **Freeze Panes** to freeze all rows below the selected row.

▶ **TIP**

If you want to freeze only the top row, you don't need to select it first. You only need to select **Freeze Top Row** from the **Freeze Panes** drop-down list. The same is true if you want to free the leftmost column; you would select **Freeze First Column**.

3 Scroll Down

Scroll down the sheet. The frozen row (or rows) remains in place while the data below scrolls upward. No matter where you are in the worksheet, you know the labels that go with the data because the headings are never scrolled off the screen.

▶ **TIP**

Excel inserts a thick line between the frozen rows (or columns) and the data so that you'll know where the break occurs.

4 Unfreeze the Rows

To unfreeze rows or columns you've frozen, select **Unfreeze Panes** from the **Freeze Panes** list. You don't need to select rows or columns first to unfreeze them.

5 Freeze Columns

To freeze one or more columns, click the column name of the column that falls to the right of the last column you want to freeze. When you again select **Freeze Panes** from the **Freeze Panes** button's drop-down list, Excel

72

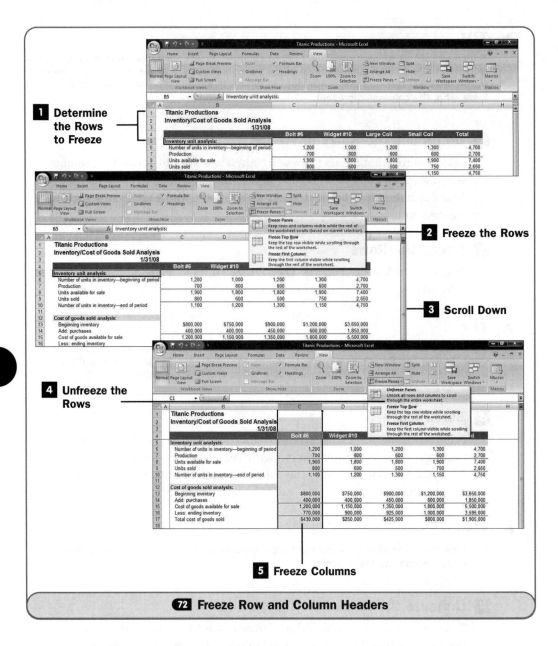

1 Determine the Rows to Freeze

2 Freeze the Rows

3 Scroll Down

4 Unfreeze the Rows

5 Freeze Columns

72

72 Freeze Row and Column Headers

freezes the column (or columns) so that when you scroll to the right, the column titles remain on your screen.

▶ **TIP**

If you want to freeze both row and column headings, click to select the cell that intersects the row and column following the headings you want to freeze before selecting **Freeze Panes**.

73	**Format Cells**	
✔ **BEFORE YOU BEGIN**		→ **SEE ALSO**
54 Enter Data into a Worksheet		**75** Set Up Page Formatting
		77 Conditionally Format Data
		78 About Excel Styles, Themes, and Templates

You can format individual cells to make them look just the way you want. From simple italics and boldfacing to a colorful selection of themes and styles you can choose from, Excel gives you many ways to create attractive worksheets. You won't just format cells. Sometimes you need to adjust the way a row or column looks by adjusting the row height or column width. Sometimes you'll want to format a range of data as a table that stands out from the rest of your worksheet.

Excel's live preview enables you to preview what most formatting selections will do before you actually apply the format to your cell or to your entire worksheet.

▶ **NOTE**

Whatever format you can apply to a cell, you can also apply to a range or to your entire worksheet. Select what you want to format and then select the formatting command.

73

1 Select the Area to Format

Select the cell, range, or entire worksheet that you want to format. Probably you'll want to format your worksheet in sections, a range at a time. That's because often headings and titles will appear one way, but the data inside the worksheet's data areas should look another way.

▶ **NOTE**

Ctrl+A is the shortcut key that selects your entire worksheet.

2 Format the Selected Area

Select from the **Font** list to choose a new font for your selected cells. As you scroll your mouse pointer over the available fonts, Excel's live preview updates your worksheet to show you what the resulting change will look like.

You can also change the text size and format, such as boldface and italic. Select from the **Fill Color** tool to change the background color of your selected cells, and select from the **Font Color** tool to change the color of the selected text. The **Alignment** group in your **Home** ribbon enables you to adjust the left, centered, or right alignment of the selected data.

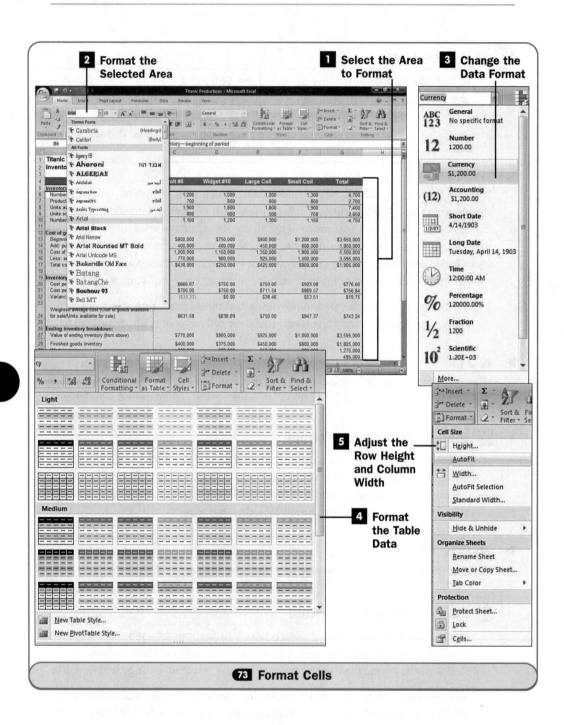

73 Format Cells

▶ **NOTE**

After increasing or decreasing the font used for data or text in a row, you'll often have to adjust the row's height.

3 Change the Data Format

Click to open the ribbon's **Number** drop-down list to change the way Excel formats your data. If you've selected a range of dollar amounts, perhaps you want to select the **Currency** format. If you've selected dates, you might want to adjust the way the date format appears.

▶ **NOTE**

Unlike with most other formatting changes, Excel does not use a live preview mode when you select from the **Number** group's drop-down list. You must apply the format and then click your **Quick Access** toolbar's **Undo** command if you don't want to keep the changes. Some changes, such as applying Excel's **Currency** format, cause data to widen enough that you widen the columns to display the dollar signs and commas.

4 Format the Table Data

To make some of your data stand apart from the rest of your worksheet in a table, you can click the **Home** ribbon's **Format as Table** button to display a list of table styles and colors you can apply to the selected data.

▶ **NOTE**

Previous to Excel 2007, you would use the **AutoFormat** command to format table data. Excel 2007's ribbon puts these table-formatting styles closer to you with the **Format as Table** button.

73

5 Adjust the Row Height and Column Width

If you want to increase or decrease the height of a row, just drag the row divider up or down for that row. To increase or decrease any column width, click to drag a column divider left or right. You must click to drag within the column names or row numbers area to adjust the height and width; you cannot drag the sheet's gridlines to make height and width adjustments.

If you shrink a column too small, Excel displays ### to let you know that there's not enough room for the data to show completely. Your data will still be stored inside the column completely, but the value cannot show until you increase the width of the column.

▶ **TIP**

You can increase or decrease every character in your entire worksheet by the same percentage factor. Press Ctrl+A to select your entire worksheet, and click your **Home** ribbon's **Increase Font Size** or **Decrease Font Size** buttons to increase or decrease the size of every font in your worksheet at once.

Clicking **Format** allows you to select from a list of common formatting options that enable you to set specific row heights or column widths for selected ranges, use *AutoFit* to adjust columns to their data, and hide and unhide cells, among other options. When you select from the list, Excel displays a small dialog box in which you can type the needed value.

▶ NEW TERM

AutoFit—The capability of Excel to adjust a column's width to accommodate the widest data value in that column.

▶ TIP

Excel enables you to change an entire worksheet's overall appearance at one time (see **78** About Excel Styles, Themes, and Templates).

74 Center a Heading over Multiple Columns	
✔ **BEFORE YOU BEGIN**	→ **SEE ALSO**
73 Format Cells	**75** Set Up Page Formatting

74

If you want to center a title over multiple columns, you might find that you have trouble adjusting the title just right. You must first type the title into the most central column over the sheet below. Even then, the title usually doesn't align properly, so you must go back and edit the column, inserting spaces, until the title is just right.

This problem occurs because one usually thinks about centering the entire width of a document. But Excel handles text cell by cell. If you center text in a cell, it's centered within that cell but not within the entire worksheet. Another challenge in creating a heading is adjusting the data below the heading so that it doesn't look crowded. Those who learned about formatting with a word processing program might expect Excel to make room for a heading by adding some extra space. Excel, however, doesn't work that way.

To center a heading so that it spans multiple cells of data, you must *merge* the cells. Merging two or more cells lets you align text across those cells. If, for example, your worksheet contains eight columns, you can create a heading and merge it across eight cells so that the heading is centered over the entire worksheet.

▶ NEW TERM

Merge—To combine two or more cells so that the contents of the cells can be centered or otherwise aligned across the width or length of all the cells.

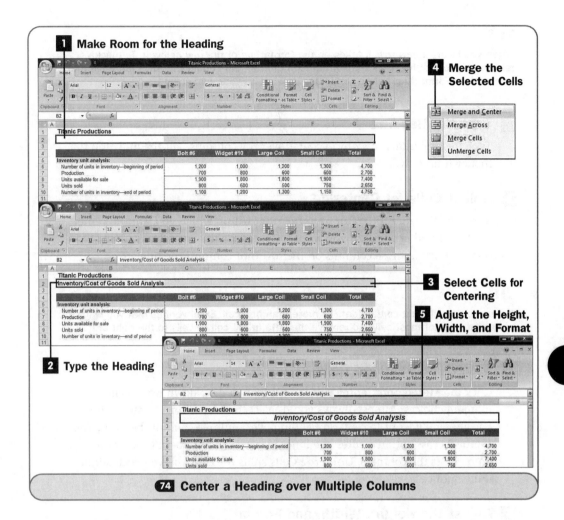

74 Center a Heading over Multiple Columns

▶ **NOTE**

The **Align Center** button does not accomplish what you want by itself when you attempt to center a title over multiple columns. The alignment (or justification) buttons align text only within single cells, not across multiple cells.

1 Make Room for the Heading

When you create your spreadsheet, leave room atop the columns for the title. It's best to create the columns, enter some or all of the data, and finally adjust the column widths before worrying about a centered title. You can also type a title atop these columns as a placeholder and then perform the actual centering after you finish the spreadsheet's columns.

▶ **TIP**

When you insert a new row, it takes on the formatting of the row below it. To quickly remove any formatting, click the Format icon that appears under the row's left edge and select **Clear Formatting** before continuing to work on your worksheet.

2 Type the Heading

Type the title that you want to center over the columns. Put the title atop the first column only.

3 Select Cells for Centering

Select the title and the columns to the right within which you want to center the title. In other words, if you want to center the title over five columns, select all five of those columns on the row that contains the title.

▶ **TIP**

If you merge cells that contain data in more than one cell, Excel verifies that you want to merge into the leftmost cell and remove the data in the cell or cells to the right of it.

4 Merge the Selected Cells

Click the **Merge and Center** button to display a drop-down list of cell-merging choices. Almost always you'll select the **Merge and Center** option because you'll want to center a heading over multiple columns below it. The **Merge Across** option creates one long, merged cell but doesn't center the data across the columns. **UnMerge Cells** splits the cells you've selected into individual cells.

5 Adjust the Height, Width, and Format

Depending on how your cells were formatted, you might have to make some adjustments to the format, height, or width of the newly merged cell.

---

75 | Set Up Page Formatting

✔ BEFORE YOU BEGIN	→ SEE ALSO
42 About Headers and Footers **73** Format Cells **74** Center a Heading over Multiple Columns	**77** Conditionally Format Data

You will often need to make format changes to your entire spreadsheet. Perhaps you want to change the printed margins on the page. You may want to add a background color or even put a border around the sheets.

The **Page Layout** ribbon contains Excel options that enable you to modify your worksheet's format. Any changes you make to the current page apply to all pages in your worksheets.

1 Display the Page Options

Click to select the **Page Layout** ribbon to see your page-formatting options. From this ribbon, you can format your themes (see **78** **About Excel Styles, Themes, and Templates**), set margins, set page and section breaks, add background images, insert watermarks (see **39** **Add a Watermark**), and adjust the entire worksheet's indentation and spacing.

▶ TIP

As with character formats, don't overuse background colors. You should use a colored stationary in your printer for best effect if you want to print on a colored background.

If you want to print a header or footer with your worksheet, use the **Insert** ribbon's **Header** and **Footer** buttons. (See **43** **Add a Header or Footer** for more information; Excel uses the same steps as Word to add headers and footers to printed documents.)

75

2 Adjust Your Margins

Click the down arrow under the **Page Layout** ribbon's **Margin** button and select from the several available margin settings that appear. Word offers common settings, and you'll usually find one you want to use.

3 Specify the Margin Measurements

If the ribbon's provided margin options aren't to your liking, select **Custom Margins** to display the **Page Setup** dialog box. You can enter precise margin settings for each margin, as well as adjust additional page settings such as the orientation while there.

4 Adjust the Paper Size

When you change the type of paper you use in your printer, such as going from letter size to legal, you'll need to select the proper **Size** option, such as **Legal**, from the **Size** list. If you use a nonstandard paper size, one that is not letter, legal, or one of the other options in the **Size** list, click **More** to display the **Page Setup** dialog box's **Paper** page.

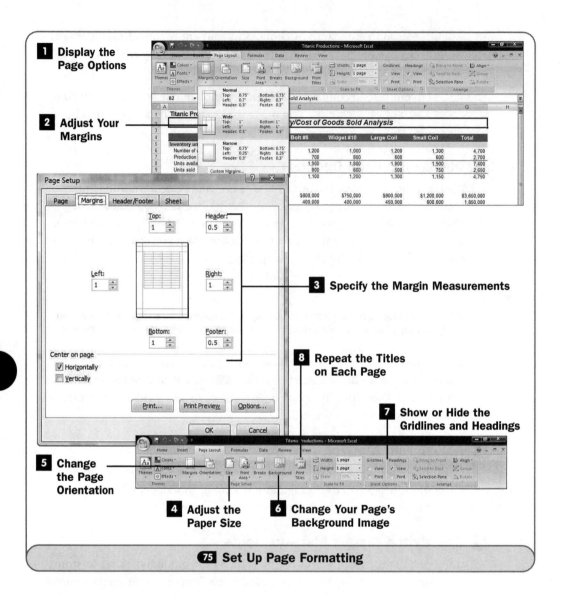

1 Display the Page Options

2 Adjust Your Margins

3 Specify the Margin Measurements

8 Repeat the Titles on Each Page

7 Show or Hide the Gridlines and Headings

5 Change the Page Orientation

4 Adjust the Paper Size

6 Change Your Page's Background Image

75 Set Up Page Formatting

75

5 Change the Page Orientation

You also may want to change the orientation of your printed page from portrait to landscape. Use the ribbon's **Orientation** button to select the proper orientation for your paper.

Worksheets are often wide, and you'll find that you prefer the landscape orientation more often than with Word or PowerPoint.

6 **Change Your Page's Background Image**

Click the ribbon's **Background** button to select a background image to add to your printed worksheet.

7 **Show or Hide the Gridlines and Headings**

Select from the **Gridlines** and **Headings** options to let Excel know whether you want to print the cell gridlines and headings when you print your worksheets. Select either **View** or **Print**, or both, to determine whether gridlines and headings will appear during printing, while viewing on the screen, neither, or both.

8 **Repeat the Titles on Each Page**

Clicking the **Repeat Titles** button opens the **Page Setup** dialog box's **Sheet** page, where you can specify one or more rows and one or more columns to repeat at the top of each printed page. These headings and row titles help those who read your printed worksheet by repeating titles that label the data.

---

76 | **Attach a Comment to a Cell**

76

✔ BEFORE YOU BEGIN	→ SEE ALSO
61 Print a Worksheet	**78** About Excel Styles, Themes, and
62 Find and Replace Data	Templates

You've seen the yellow sticky notes that some people plaster all over their desks. The reason for their popularity is that these notes work well for reminders. You can put them on just about anything, and although they stick for a while, they come right off without removing what's underneath and without leaving sticky gunk behind.

Excel offers the electronic equivalent of these notes. You can attach notes to cells inside your spreadsheets. The notes can remain yours alone, meaning that you don't print them when you print the sheets, or you can print the notes for others to see when you print the spreadsheet's contents.

▶ **TIP**

Suppose that you notice an anomaly in a report, such as a division's forecast being lower than expected. You can attach a note to that cell to follow up and find out where the problem lies.

1 **Select a Cell for the Comment**

When you want to attach a note to a cell, click to select the cell.

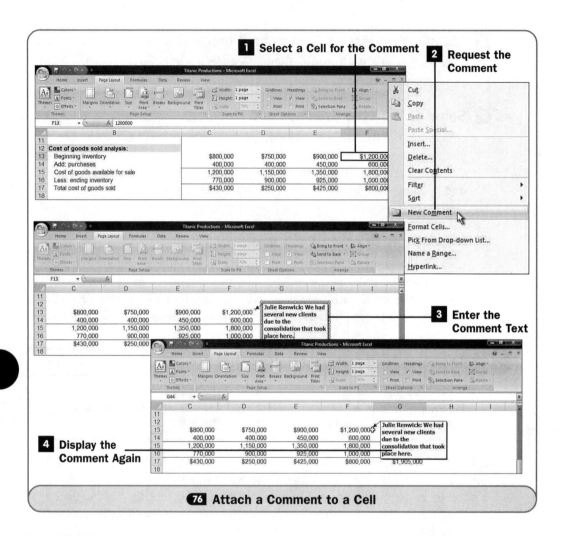

76 Attach a Comment to a Cell

▶ **NOTE**

You can attach a note only to a single cell only, not to a range of cells.

2 Request the Comment

Right-click the cell and select **New Comment** from the pop-up menu to request a comment. Excel then displays the yellow note box beside the cell with a callout pointing to the cell the comment goes with. The name of the person using the worksheet appears at the top of the comment, although you can press **Backspace** to erase the name.

3 Enter the Comment Text

The text cursor appears inside the comment so that you can type the comment's text. As you type, the comment expands to make more room if needed. You can also drag the comment's edges to expand or contract the size of the comment.

4 Display the Comment Again

After you press Enter after typing the comment, you go about working in your spreadsheet as usual. Excel indicates which cells contain comments by displaying a small red box in each cell's upper-right corner that contains a comment. To see any cell's comment, hover your mouse pointer over that cell, and Excel displays the comment.

▶ **TIP**

To edit the comment, right-click the cell, select **Edit Comment**, and edit the text that appears. Move the cell pointer to a different cell to hide the note.

---

77   **Conditionally Format Data**

✔ BEFORE YOU BEGIN	→ SEE ALSO
73 Format Cells	**84** Protect Worksheet Data
75 Set Up Page Formatting	**86** Ensure Valid Data Entry

77

Conditional formatting enables you to make your spreadsheets respond to the data they contain. When certain conditions arise, you can draw attention to particular cell entries by automatically making those cells display differently from the cells around those exceptions.

▶ **NEW TERM**

Conditional formatting—The process of formatting cells automatically, based on the data they contain. When the data changes and triggers a predetermined condition, Excel automatically changes the cell's format.

Most often, users place conditional formats on cells that they want to watch (for example, for extraordinarily high or low conditions that might require special attention).

The way you indicate whether a condition is met is to specify a value and a condition that must become true before the format takes place. Here's a list of the available conditions:

- Less than

- Greater than

- Equal to

- Not equal to

- Less than or equal to

- Greater than or equal to

- Between (requires two values for the condition)

- Not between (requires two values for the condition)

■ Request Conditional Formatting

Click to select the cell or range on which you want to apply a conditional format.

Select **Conditional Formatting** from the **Home** ribbon. A list of conditional formatting options appears.

■ Enter the Format Conditions

When you request a special format for a cell after a certain condition is met, that format points out to anyone viewing the worksheet that the condition has triggered. The format means that you are more likely to notice the exception of the data.

Click to select **Highlight Cells Rules**. Select the condition, such as **Less Than**. If the cell's value ever goes below the value you enter next to the condition, Excel changes the cell's format to match the style you select. (The **Between** condition requires two values for its condition to be matched.)

When you select **Less Than**, you are requesting that Excel highlight the cell if and only if the cell's value goes below a certain value. Excel displays the **Less Than** dialog box. Enter a value that will trigger the condition. For example, if you type 600000, Excel will format the cell with your requested format if and only if the value in the cell falls below 600,000.

Choose a setting you want Excel to use for the data's format if the condition is met by data within the cell. Anytime the data changes to make the condition true, Excel applies that format to the cell.

■ View Your Worksheet Again

The conditional format dialog box can become large when specifying multiple conditions. A **Shrink** button resides in the dialog box.

Click the **Shrink** button, and Excel temporarily shrinks the dialog box to a thin line so that you can view the spreadsheet again.

Click the **Shrink** button again to return the dialog box to its original size so that you can complete the formatting. After setting up the conditional format, click **OK** to apply it.

77

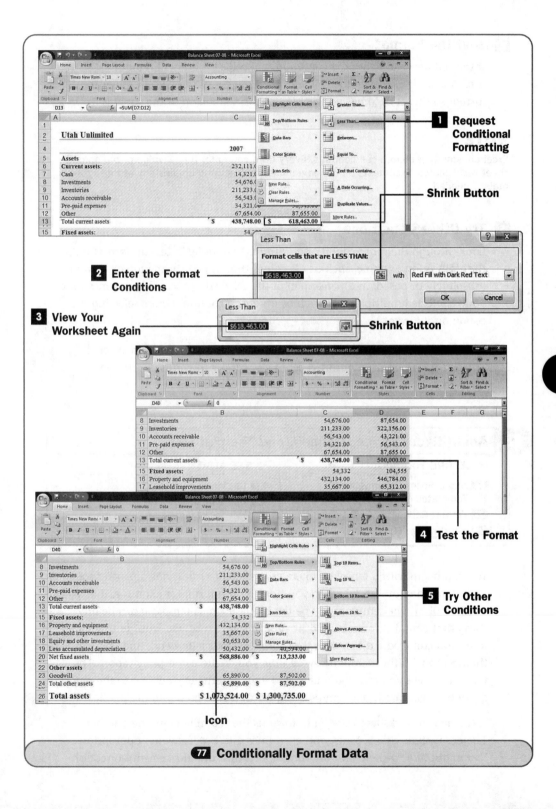

1 Request Conditional Formatting

Shrink Button

2 Enter the Format Conditions

3 View Your Worksheet Again

Shrink Button

4 Test the Format

5 Try Other Conditions

Icon

4 Test the Format

If the cell never matches the condition, the cell's format will remain unchanged. If, however, the cell does pass the condition, Excel applies the format so that it becomes noticeable to anyone looking at the spreadsheet.

▶ **NOTE**

Excel constantly monitors cell contents. Every time you enter a new value or the spreadsheet recalculates, Excel tests all the conditional formats and applies any of those formats if needed.

5 Try Other Conditions

Look through the other conditional formats available. Excel can format data that falls at an extreme, such as all values that appear in the top or bottom (absolutely or based on a percentile) of the selected range. (This assumes that you've selected multiple cells, such as an entire column, before selecting the conditional format.)

Excel also can display colored data bars across data that meets a specific criteria, and even display from a set of icons if a value falls in a range you specify.

78

78	About Excel Styles, Themes, and Templates

✔ BEFORE YOU BEGIN	→ SEE ALSO
16 About Styles, Themes, and Templates	79 Use an Excel Style
73 Format Cells	80 Use an Excel Theme
75 Set Up Page Formatting	81 Use an Excel Template

You can begin with a template to create a worksheet that has a prearranged look. Templates are useful when you have a data form, for example, that you need to fill in. The template will be the blank form. A template can be anything that contains formatting or text or graphics that you want to use again later. You can create a template that contains your letterhead, and you can then begin with that template every time you create a company report. The template keeps you from having to add your letterhead and logo to the report every time you produce a company report that is to go out to the public.

A theme is a worksheet-wide set of formats that complement one another. Themes include colors, fonts, and even lines and borders when appropriate. You might have a theme for internal reports that are marked with a reddish color to indicate an internal document, whereas all public documents won't have the red outlines and highlights on the titles. A theme you select or create would apply that reddish appearance to the internal documents you wanted to mark as such.

A style in Excel applies to a cell or a range of selected cells. For example, you might create a GrandTotal style that you always want to apply to your reports' bottom-line totals. Another style might apply to cells you designate as subtotals. An Excel style is the set of formats you've applied to a cell or range, such as boldfacing, italics, color, and alignment.

▶ **NOTE**

16 About Styles, Themes, and Templates defines styles, themes, and templates. These formatting elements are uniform in the way they work across Word, Excel, and PowerPoint.

By using templates, themes, and styles, you reduce the amount of work you have to do to create your worksheets.

Themes are associated with entire worksheets. Styles are usually associated with ranges of cells within a worksheet. A template is to an entire worksheet what a style is to a selected cell. When creating one worksheet that's to look like another that you often create, such as a Cost of Goods report that requires special formatting, you can elect to use a Cost of Goods template you've already set up with the all the headings, report columns, and your company logo across the top. You then need only to fill in the details. Changing the theme of the Cost of Goods Sold report does not affect any of the data or layout of the report but only the colors, fonts, and other formatting elements.

78

▶ **NOTE**

Given that a theme is not related in any way to your worksheet contents, all Office applications can share themes. If you create or standardize on a theme in Excel, you can apply that theme to PowerPoint and Word as well so that all your documents share the same overall feel. The theme is the message feeling you want to portray.

It's important to remember that a template is a model for a worksheet. A style is often a model for smaller blocks of a worksheet such as a cell or selected cells. A template may contain several styles. If you want to use a style that's available to your current worksheet, you can easily select that style and apply it to selected cells.

Excel offers several preset styles you can apply to your worksheets' cells, and you can create your own. You can see the predefined styles by clicking **Cell Styles** on your **Home** ribbon.

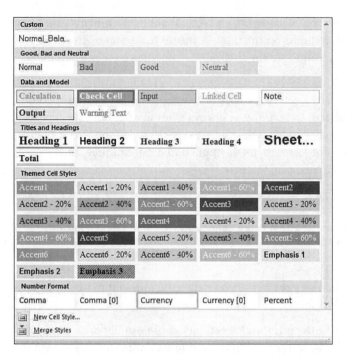

79

Excel supplies several predefined styles for your worksheet cells.

▶ **TIP**

Although you can use the same specific themes across Office applications, you cannot use the same styles or templates given that the Office programs work with different kinds of data. Nevertheless, the other Office products do support styles and templates. Learning the mechanics of Excel's styles and templates prepares you to understand how to create and work with styles and templates in the other Microsoft Office applications.

79   Use an Excel Style

✔ BEFORE YOU BEGIN	→ SEE ALSO
78 About Excel Styles, Themes, and Templates	**80** Use an Excel Theme
	81 Use an Excel Template

Using an Excel style is simple. You apply a style to selected cells to format those cells with the style's preset formatting. Excel comes with several styles, and you can add your own.

Suppose that you routinely create income statements for various departments. You might develop three separate sets of character formats that work well, respectively, for the title of the income statements, the data that composes the body of the income statements, and the profit or loss line at the bottom of the income statement.

Instead of defining each of these cell formats every time you create the income statement, you can create three styles and store the styles under their own names (such as IS Heading, IS Data, and IS ProfitLoss). The next time you create the income statement, you need only to select a style such as IS Title before typing the title. When you then type the title, the title looks the way you want it to look without your having to take the time to designate a format.

One of the easiest ways to apply a style is to click your **Home** ribbon's **Cell Styles** button. Excel displays a large list of cell styles you can choose from.

▶ **TIP**

Not only does Excel supply many styles you can use, but also you can define your own styles from cells you select.

1 Select a Cell for the Style

When you want to apply a predefined style to text, first select the cell or range. The format of the cell will completely change depending on which style you apply, but the data inside the cell will not change.

79

2 Display the Available Styles

Click your **Home** ribbon's **Cell Styles** button to display available styles.

The names of styles that you can apply to your selected cells then appear.

3 Select the Style

As you point to each style, Excel's live preview mode shows what your selected cells will look like when you apply that style.

Click to choose a style that you want to apply to the selected range. Excel applies the style immediately to your selected text. If you want to try a different style, choose another with the cells still selected.

4 Select a Formatted Range

You can easily add your own styles. You add styles to Excel's list of styles by example. In other words, format a cell or range to match a style you want to create, and then tell Excel to create a new style based on that format.

To add the new style to the list of styles, format your cell or range of cells to match the new style you want to create. Keep the cell or range selected.

79

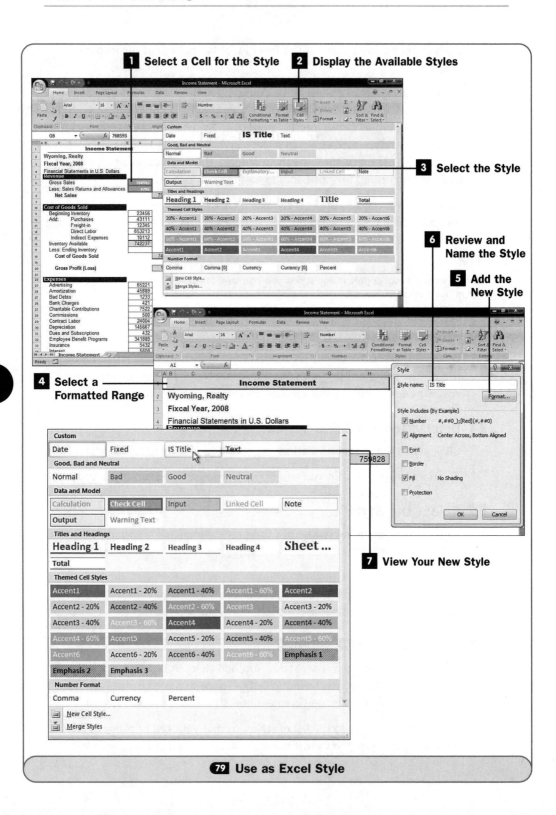

1 Select a Cell for the Style   **2** Display the Available Styles

3 Select the Style

6 Review and Name the Style

5 Add the New Style

4 Select a Formatted Range

7 View Your New Style

79 Use as Excel Style

5 Add the New Style

Click the **Cell Styles** button again to display Excel's cell styles.

Instead of selecting a style, select **New Cell Style**. Excel displays the **Style** dialog box.

6 Review and Name the Style

If your selected cells are formatted according to the style you want to create, type a name for the style in the **Style Name** text box and click **OK**. If your selected range requires additional formatting before you save it as a new style, click the **Format** button to display the **Format Cells** dialog box and adjust the formatting. When you click **OK** to close the **Format Cells** dialog box and click **OK** to close the **Style** dialog box, your cell style will be saved.

7 View Your New Style

Click the **Cell Styles** button again to display Excel's cell styles. Your new cell style will appear under the **Custom** heading.

▶ **NOTE**

To delete a style, right-click the style name and select **Delete**. You can also right-click to select **Modify** when you want to change a style you've saved.

80

80 Use an Excel Theme

✔ BEFORE YOU BEGIN	→ SEE ALSO
73 Format Cells	**81** Use an Excel Template
78 About Excel Styles, Themes, and Templates	
79 Use an Excel Style	

When your worksheet takes on the characteristics of a certain theme, the colors, format, pagination, and overall look and feel adhere to that theme's standards. Themes apply to your entire worksheet, and you can implement the same theme across all your Microsoft Office applications.

▶ **TIP**

If you design a theme that matches your company brand colors, logo style, and approved type styles, and then you apply that theme to all your Office documents including Word documents and Excel worksheets and PowerPoint presentations, you'll help solidify your company's brand recognition for all who see any document produced by your company.

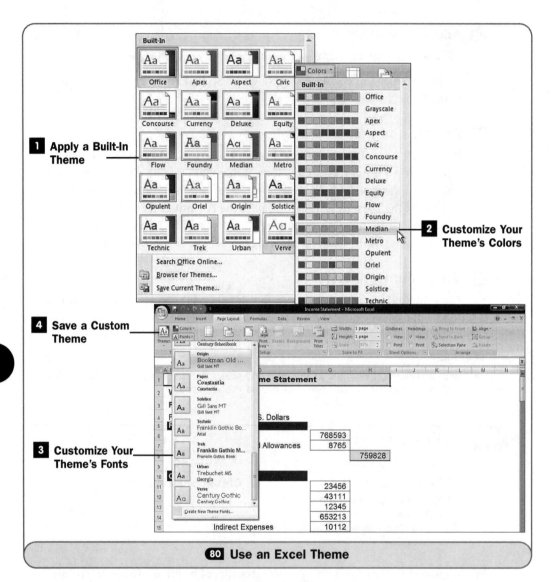

80

1 Apply a Built-In Theme

2 Customize Your Theme's Colors

4 Save a Custom Theme

3 Customize Your Theme's Fonts

80 Use an Excel Theme

Microsoft provides themes with Office and online, or you can design and save your own themes. Somewhere out there is probably a theme that's right for your needs. If you locate a theme that isn't quite what you want but is close, you can apply that theme, modify it to your liking, and then save the theme and reuse it afterward.

1 **Apply a Built-In Theme**

Open the worksheet you want to apply a theme to. You can apply a theme to a new, blank document, but you can see the applied theme's effects far better if you apply a theme to a worksheet you've already created.

Click to display your **Page Layout** ribbon, and then click the **Themes** button. Excel displays a scrolling list of built-in, supplied themes. As you point to the various themes, your worksheet's preview changes to reflect what each theme would look like if applied to your worksheet.

You can click the **Search Office Online** link to see what themes Microsoft makes available over your Internet connection.

After you click to apply a specific theme, your worksheet changes accordingly.

2 Customize Your Theme's Colors

The best way to create a customized theme is to begin with one that's close to your goal and then customize it.

Apply a theme that most closely matches your desired theme. In the **Themes** section of your **Page Layout** ribbon, select **Theme Colors**. A list of theme colors appears. Select a new theme color scheme or click **Create New Theme Colors** to create your own set. As you point to each set of possible theme colors, your document will update to reflect what that theme color will look like after you apply it.

3 Customize Your Theme's Fonts

To change the primary font used in your customized theme, click the **Theme Fonts** button to display a list of themed fonts. Again, Excel's live preview capability shows what each font selection will do to your worksheet as you point to each one.

4 Save a Custom Theme

After you specify the font and colors you want to apply to your new theme, and after you've looked over your worksheet to ensure that the theme's elements all work together to achieve the goals you had in mind, click the **Themes** button and then select **Save Current Theme**. Excel displays a **Save** dialog box in which you can name your new theme and save it.

In subsequent sessions, when you display a list of themes, your custom theme will appear in the list.

80

81   Use an Excel Template

✔ BEFORE YOU BEGIN	→ SEE ALSO
78 About Excel Styles, Themes, and Templates **79** Use an Excel Style	**87** Import and Export Worksheet Data

Templates almost make you think you're cheating when you want to create great-looking worksheets, because they are so simple and they do so much. Just a couple of mouse clicks put ready-made, preformatted worksheets at your fingertips. You still must supply the details because a template is only an outline (also called a skeleton or model) of a worksheet, but when you use a template, you hardly need to apply formatting or design considerations to the worksheets you create.

Starting with a completely blank worksheet might be a good idea for quick and simple worksheets, and you'll certainly do a lot of that. But for all else, start with a template if one exists that you want to use. If you find yourself creating rather complexly formatted worksheets routinely, you should create your own templates so that you have to generate all the formatting and worksheet layouts just the first time. If you create commonly used worksheets, such as balance sheets, income statements, budgets, and other routine financial statements, Microsoft has probably already supplied a template you can begin with to make your work go more smoothly and to make your worksheets look better from the start.

Templates contain formatting for complete worksheets. Some templates have same data, but you'll need to change that data to reflect your own situation. Some templates use placeholder text that you'll need to change to match your requirements.

All the Microsoft Office programs support templates. If you create a new worksheet without specifying a template, Excel uses a default template style to create the empty document and to set up initial font, margin, and other formatting-related details.

1 Request a Template

Click your **Office** button and select **New**. (You can also press Alt+F, N.) Excel displays the **New Workbook** window.

In the window's left pane is a scrollable list of template categories that contain several templates. When you select a template category such as **Budgets**, Microsoft looks online (and on your computer if any templates from that category are stored there) and displays a list of templates available within that category.

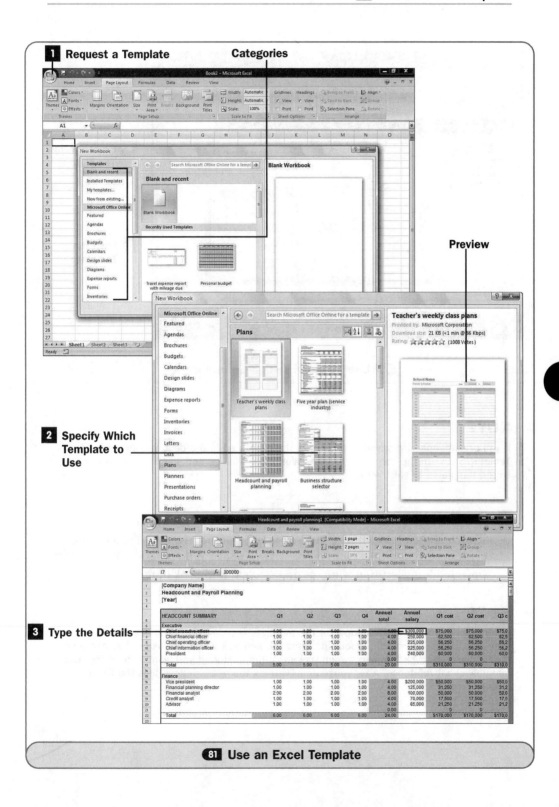

1 Request a Template

Categories

Preview

2 Specify Which Template to Use

3 Type the Details

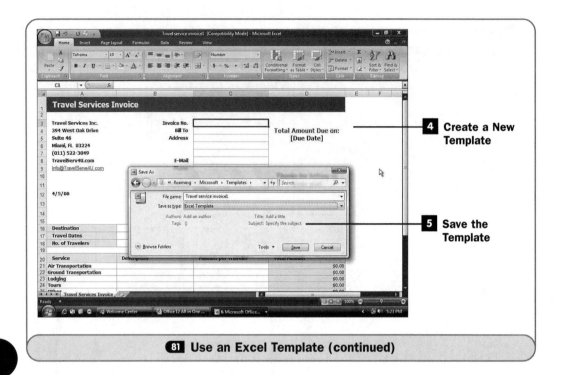

4 Create a New Template

5 Save the Template

81 Use an Excel Template (continued)

▶ **NOTE**

If you or someone else saved templates that you created in the past, you can click **My Templates** toward the center of the **New Workbook** window and select one of your own stored templates to start with.

2 Specify Which Template to Use

Scroll until you locate a template you might want to use. Click the template to see a worksheet preview in the **New Workbook**'s right pane. Click **Download** to select that template and create a workbook from it.

▶ **NOTE**

Excel often displays a help window for the template you download and use. The help window includes information about the template and tips on how to use it. You can print the help screen (click the help screen toolbar's **Print** button) if you want to print the help for subsequent reference. After you're done viewing the help window, click the **Close** button to close it.

3 Type the Details

Sometimes data will be filled in, so in the case of some business templates, you will have to change the data. Other templates will not contain specific sample data or might offer placeholder text such as [Company Name] that you can replace with your specific information. You must finish the worksheet by entering all its details after the template has produced an outline of your worksheet.

4 Create a New Template

Feel free to create your own templates! For example, you might produce different kinds of invoices, so you night want to produce a template for each type of invoice to make it easier to begin invoices subsequently.

To create a template, first create a worksheet that serves as a model for the template, including the title, company name, and common column and row titles, and apply whatever theme is appropriate for the overall look.

Keep the text general. Feel free to include instructions to the user of this template, such as [Per Diem Amount Here].

5 Save the Template

When you click your **Office** button and select **Save As**, click to open the **Save as Type** drop-down list box and select **Excel Template** from the available items. Excel saves your workbook as a template and uses the .dot filename extension to distinguish the template file from a regular Excel workbook.

▶ **TIP**

Document your templates by specifying the template author's name, title, and a few words in the **Subject** text box in the **Save As** dialog box. Then, anyone who uses a template and finds an error or requests a change can contact the template's author. Even more helpful would be to require the author's company phone extension with the name. (The **Author** and **Subject** fields are viewable from the Windows Explorer window.)

When you subsequently create a new file and click the **My Templates** button, you'll see your template in the list that appears.

81

9

Creating Advanced Worksheets

IN THIS CHAPTER:

A picture is worth a thousand words—and worth even more numbers! Your spreadsheet data might contain a ton of numbers, but many times you can present data better with a chart or graphic. The actual raw data supplied by a worksheet is accurate and vital information for analysis, but for trends and overall patterns, charts demonstrate the data's nature quickly and effectively. The data that those charts and graphs come from needs to be accurate and come from reliable sources, too. You need to understand how to import and export your Excel data and learn how to add error-checking to data-entry to ensure reliable information.

You can easily import graphics into your spreadsheets, as you might do, for example, with a graphics logo for your company or pictures of inventory items. The distinction between numbers, text, and graphics is blurred these days thanks to modern technology, and Excel handles virtually any data you want to store in a spreadsheet.

For peace of mind, you'll want to protect your worksheet contents so that you (or another user of your spreadsheet) don't accidentally overwrite something you shouldn't. You can protect cells to maintain their integrity. Excel's other capabilities, such as being able to check certain cells for accuracy, are explored in this chapter.

82

▶ **NOTE**

Data integrity is vital. If you enter bad data, the results will be wrong because Excel works with what you give it. As you create and design spreadsheets, protect cells with formulas and try to use data-entry validation for cells where data is typed to help ensure that your calculations are as accurate as possible.

82 Add a Chart to a Worksheet	
✔ **BEFORE YOU BEGIN**	→ **SEE ALSO**
65 Fill Cells with Auto Fill Data	**83** Insert Graphics into a Worksheet

Although Excel can produce professional-looking charts from your spreadsheet data, you don't need to know a lot about graphing to produce them. Excel 2007 greatly improved upon the previous Excel versions, giving you more control over how your charts look.

▶ **NOTE**

Many people call Excel's charts *graphs*. Most users use the terms interchangeably.

Instead, you'll simply tell Excel what data you want to see in the chart and select the type of chart you want Excel to produce, and Excel does the rest.

Table 9.1 describes some of Excel's more popular chart types. Different charts reflect different kinds of data. If you create one chart and realize that it's not the best type of chart to use, you can request that Excel switch to a different type.

TABLE 9.1 Excel's More Common Chart Types

Chart Type	Description
Area	Emphasizes the magnitude of changes over time.
Bar	Compares data items. A bar chart is a column chart with horizontal lines.
Column	Shows changes over time and compares values. A column chart is a bar chart with vertical bars.
Line	Shows trends and projections.
Pie	Compares the proportional size of items against the parts of the whole.
Stock	Illustrates a stock's (or other investment's) high, low, and closing prices.
XY (Scatter)	Shows the relationships of several values in a series.

▶ NOTE

Excel supplies 3-D versions of these chart types for use when you must chart data in multiple time periods or from multiple perspectives.

82

1 Select the Data to Chart

You must first tell Excel exactly what you want to chart. To do this, you must select one or more *data series* to use in the chart. A data series might be data values over a time period such as a month or year. One person's monthly sales totals (from a group of several salespeople's weekly totals) could form a data series. The entire company's yearly sales divided into monthly sales could be a series. Some charts can graph only a single series, such as a pie chart, whereas other charts can graph one or more data series, such as a line chart.

▶ NEW TERM

Data series—A single group of data that you might select from a column or row to chart. Unlike a range, a data series must be contiguous in a row or column with no empty cells in between.

When you select a data series, include labels in the series if available at the top or to the left of the series. Excel can use those labels on the chart to label what is being charted.

2 Request the Chart

Display your **Insert** ribbon to see your chart types in the **Charts** ribbon group. Select a chart you want to produce by clicking on a chart type and determining which type of chart you want to plot.

Excel analyzes your data and labels and makes assumptions about your chart's labels. (If Excel assumes incorrectly, you'll be able to edit the chart.)

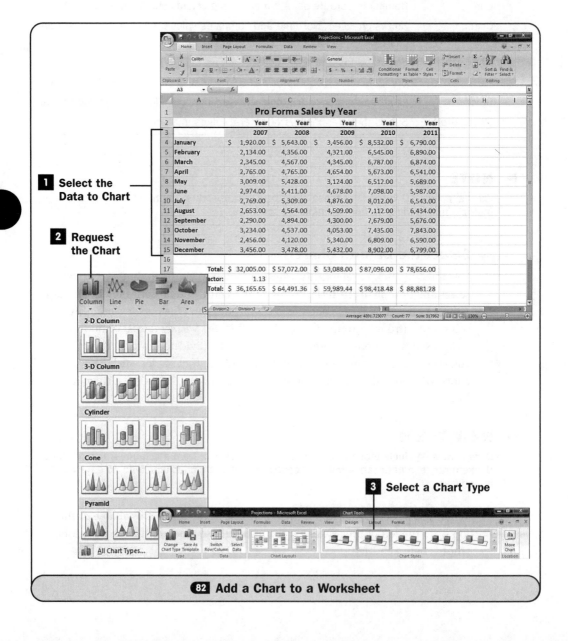

82

1 Select the Data to Chart

2 Request the Chart

3 Select a Chart Type

82 Add a Chart to a Worksheet

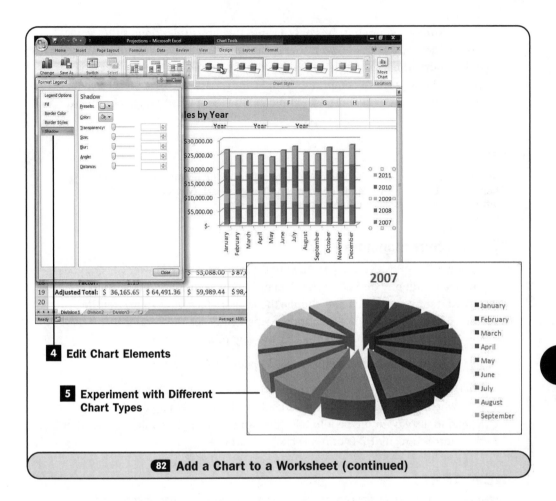

4 Edit Chart Elements

5 Experiment with Different
Chart Types

82 Add a Chart to a Worksheet (continued)

▶ **TIP**

Excel displays charts you build next to the current sheet's data. Move the chart to a different location by dragging its border. Resize the chart by clicking on a corner and dragging your mouse in or out. Move your chart to its own worksheet by right-clicking your chart, selecting **Move Chart,** and then selecting the **New Sheet** option and naming the chart's new worksheet that it will reside in.

3 **Select a Chart Type**

Scroll through the various charts offered and select the chart you want to build. Excel builds the chart and places it on your worksheet. In doing so, Excel also highlights your worksheet data with different colors to indicate labels and data.

If you didn't select a chart type that works well with your selected data, click your **Quick Access** toolbar's **Undo** button and select a different chart type.

If, for example, your chart has only 12 monthly gross sales figures that you want to graph, you would want to select a simple chart type and most likely a line chart. The line will show the direction and trend of the sales over the year. A chart type that compares multiple data series against others, such as a bar chart or an area chart, would make little sense when you're charting a single series.

▶ **TIP**

You can change the chart to a different type by right-clicking on the chart and selecting **Change Chart Type** from the pop-up menu. A **Change Chart Type** dialog box opens, from which you can select a different chart.

4 Edit Chart Elements

After Excel displays your chart (next to the data or in its own worksheet), you are free to edit any and all of the elements in the chart. By right-clicking the *legend,* for example, you can change the legend's format or source for the data. The resizing handles that appear when you click the various pieces of the chart enable you to resize the chart to any proportion you prefer.

As you select and change options, Excel updates the chart.

Click **Next** to continue building the chart. Excel displays one more dialog box, where you enter a title for your chart, indicate whether you want a legend to display, and type labels for the two (or three, depending on whether the chart is a regular 2-D or a 3-D chart) chart axes.

▶ **NEW TERM**

Legend—Tells a chart's audience what series each colored line or bar represents.

▶ **TIP**

If you elect to produce a 3-D chart, you can customize all 3-D aspects of it, such as its shading and rotation angle, by right-clicking the chart and selecting **3-D View** from the pop-up menu. Excel's **Format Chart Area** dialog box opens, showing various 3-D options you can adjust.

5 Experiment with Different Chart Types

When first mastering the nuances of Excel's charting capabilities, start with a single data series to get a feel for the charting dialog boxes and to learn the terminology. Then you can experiment with charting additional data series within the same chart to make data comparisons that sometimes are easier to study in chart form as opposed to lists of numbers inside a large worksheet.

82

83 | Insert Graphics into a Worksheet

✔ BEFORE YOU BEGIN	→ SEE ALSO
75 Set Up Page Formatting	**88** About Advanced Worksheet Printing
82 Add a Chart to a Worksheet	**90** Create an Excel Database

Excel enables you to put pictures in your spreadsheets. Perhaps you'll want to accent a motivational message next to sales figures or maybe insert your company's graphics logo at the top of the worksheet sheet.

▶ **NOTE**

Excel supports all popular graphics file formats, including JPG, GIF, and BMP files.

When you insert a graphics image, Excel displays the image in the worksheet. You'll almost always have to adjust the image size to fit the worksheet's design.

1 Request a Picture

To insert a graphics image from a file, click the cell where the image is to go and display your **Insert** ribbon. Select **Picture**. Excel displays the **Insert Picture** dialog box.

Select the image you want to insert into your worksheet and click **Insert**. Excel places the image in the cell.

▶ **TIP**

If you use Windows Vista's Aero Glass feature, the **Insert Image** dialog box shows thumbnail images of each picture you can insert. These thumbnail images help ensure that you select the correct picture the first time.

2 Adjust the Size

After Excel brings the graphics image into your spreadsheet, you will almost always need to make adjustments to suit your worksheet. Typically, Excel imports graphics images and centers them at the location where you inserted them. No text wraps to either side of the image because, unlike in a word processing document, a spreadsheet relies on the exact placement of data inside the rectangular grid. Therefore, you may even have to move the image so that it doesn't overwrite important data in your spreadsheet. You'll certainly need to resize it in most cases.

To resize your image, click to display the sizing handles and drag them in or out to decrease or increase the picture size. To move the image to a different location, click and drag the picture to where you want it.

▶ **NOTE**

Even though you clicked a cell before inserting the image, Excel doesn't actually place the picture in that cell. Excel uses that location for the image, but the image lies on a plane above your actual worksheet cells. You can move the picture to anywhere in your worksheet.

3 Adjust the Image

When you inserted the picture, Excel changed to the **Format** ribbon and displayed the **Picture Tools** there. You can use those picture tools to adjust the way your image appears. Click to select the picture and then click the ribbon's Format tab if you don't see the picture-editing ribbon.

For example, the **Picture Styles** button group allows you to adjust the picture's border and shape. As you point to each **Picture Styles** button, Excel's Live Preview shows you what your image will look like if you were to select each button.

After you select a different picture style, a yellow diagonal icon appears as one of the sizing handles. You can drag this diagonal box left or right to further change the picture's shape.

In addition, you can select from the **Picture Shape** button to display a long list of possible shapes. Below the **Picture Shape** button are **Picture Border** and **Picture Effects** buttons to provide additional image shapes and effects.

Click the **Crop** button to reduce your picture by removing parts of the image. You can also click to change the inserted picture's height and width by adjusting the size buttons to the far right of your **Format** ribbon.

▶ **TIP**

Use the picture-editing tools at the left of your **Format** ribbon such as **Brightness, Contrast, Recolor, Compress Pictures,** and **Change Picture** to adjust your image even more. If you over-edit, click the **Reset Picture** to back up one edit (acts as an **Undo** command).

4 Insert Clip Art

If you prefer to use something other than a photograph, you can access Microsoft's online clip art gallery and insert royalty-free images into your worksheets.

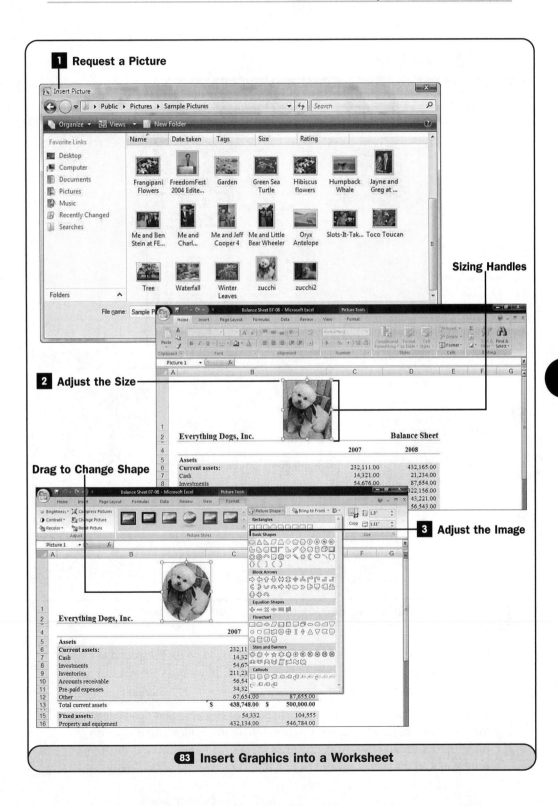

1 Request a Picture

Sizing Handles

2 Adjust the Size

Drag to Change Shape

3 Adjust the Image

83

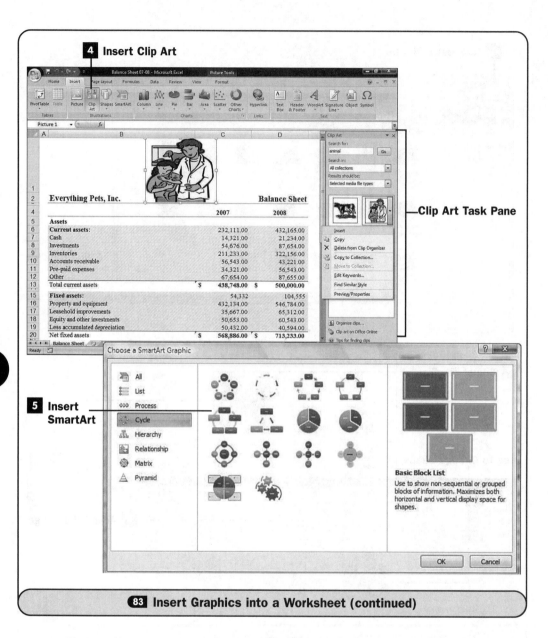

4 Insert Clip Art

Clip Art Task Pane

83

5 Insert SmartArt

83 Insert Graphics into a Worksheet (continued)

Click to select the cell position where the image is to go and display the **Insert** ribbon. Click the **Clip Art** button. Excel displays the **Clip Art** task pane to the right of your worksheet.

Type a word or phrase that matches the kind of clip art image you're looking for and click **Go**. Excel searches through Microsoft's online clip art gallery and displays images that match your search term. Scroll through the images until you find the one you want to use, and click the image to display a list of pop-up choices. Click **Insert**, and Excel inserts the clip art into your worksheet, where you can edit the art's size, placement, and look.

5 Insert SmartArt

Most of Microsoft Office 2007's applications support the use of *SmartArt.* You might have a need for such artwork in a worksheet. Perhaps you need to show a business relationship between two sets of data, or perhaps you keep track of an organizational structure in Excel using Excel's database features (see **90 Create an Excel Database**).

To select a SmartArt image to insert into your worksheet, display your **Insert** ribbon and click the **SmartArt** button. Excel displays the **Diagram Gallery** dialog box. Select the kind of diagram, such as an organization chart, that you wish to place in your worksheet. After Excel inserts the diagram, you can resize and move the diagram to the position you wish it to appear. Click any text boxes (labeled with **Click to add text**) to label the diagram.

▶ **NEW TERM**

SmartArt—Predesigned corporate and industrial images such as organizational charts, Venn diagrams, and data-flow patterns that you can insert in various Microsoft Office documents to enhance their message.

▶ **NOTE**

Most of the SmartArt images require room, so you'll probably want to partition off at least 20 rows and 8 columns initially to hold the SmartArt image.

84

84	**Protect Worksheet Data**
✔ **BEFORE YOU BEGIN**	➜ **SEE ALSO**
73 Format Cells	**85** Combine Multiple Cells into One
81 Use an Excel Template	**86** Ensure Valid Data Entry

When developing spreadsheet templates (see **81 Use an Excel Template**) or creating spreadsheets that others less savvy in Excel will work with, you may want to protect certain cells from being changed. This protection helps ensure that formulas do not get changed and that fixed data remains fixed.

In addition to protecting individual cells and ranges, you can add security by password-protecting entire workbooks to keep them secure and to limit access to them.

▶ **NOTE**

Cells inside a worksheet that you designate as protected are protected only if you also protect the worksheet.

1 Select the Cells to Protect

Select the cell or the range of cells you want to protect. These cells can contain data, be empty, or contain labels or formulas.

2 Request Cell Protection

On your **Home** ribbon, click to display the **Format** drop-down list and select **Lock Cell**. Excel locks the selected cells so that they cannot be changed after the worksheet is locked. After you lock the cells, you'll notice nothing different about them at first.

3 Protect the Sheet

Once again, click to display the **Format** drop-down list and select **Protect**. Excel displays the **Protect Sheet** dialog box. Enter an optional password and select each item you want protected from change. In other words, you might want to not only protect individual cells you declared as protected but also keep users from deleting columns and rows or changing the format of cells.

The password is optional. If you don't specify a password, the items you click to select in the **Protect Sheet** dialog box will be protected from change, but all that protection goes away as soon as any user displays the **Protect Sheet** dialog box again and clicks to uncheck the option labeled **Protect Worksheet and Contents of Locked Cells**. If you do specify a password, the protection cannot be changed except by someone who knows the password.

▶ **TIP**

Even if you create a worksheet that only you will edit, there are advantages to protecting certain cells from change. By protecting headings and titles, you keep yourself from inadvertently changing something that shouldn't be changed.

4 Check the Protection

After you protect your worksheet, attempt to change something that you protected. Excel should display a warning letting you know that what you're trying to do is not possible with the current protection turned on.

5 Remove the Protection

To remove the protection, you can display the **Review** ribbon and click **Unprotect Sheet**. If you used a password to protect your worksheet, Excel prompts you for the password. Otherwise, Excel removes the worksheet's protection.

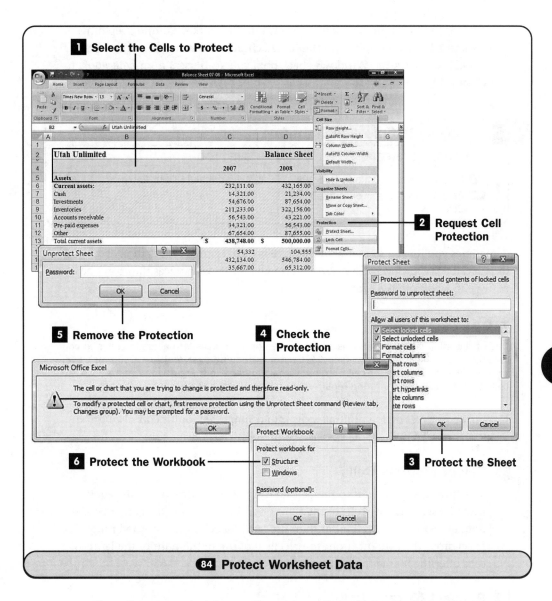

84 Protect Worksheet Data

The cells you marked for protection are still marked as such. Keep in mind that Excel protects cells you've marked only after you protect the worksheet (or the workbook).

6 Protect the Workbook

To protect the entire workbook and all sheets within it that have cell protection indicated, click the **Structure** check box. You should protect the workbook's structure to prevent the viewing of worksheets you may have hidden from view, keep users from moving, deleting, or editing worksheet names, prevent the insertion of new worksheets into the workbook, and keep other various edits from happening that could change the structure of the workbook. If you click the **Windows** check box, you keep users from being able to change the size and position of windows inside the workbook.

85 | Combine Multiple Cells into One

✔ BEFORE YOU BEGIN	→ SEE ALSO
72 Freeze Row and Column Headers **74** Center a Heading over Multiple Columns	**86** Ensure Valid Data Entry

Sometimes you'll need to merge multiple cells into a single cell. Perhaps you want to pad a label with several surrounding blank cells to add spaces that can't be easily removed from the label.

▶ **TIP**

85

One of the most common reasons to merge two or more cells into a single cell is to center titles over multiple columns (see **74** Center a Heading over Multiple Columns). Even so, you'll find many uses for cell merging when you need to merge two or more adjacent cells that don't fit the centering requirement for headings and titles.

Not only can Excel merge multiple cells into a single cell, but it can also turn a single cell with multiple values back into multiple cells once again.

1 Select Multiple Cells

Select the cells you want to merge into a single cell. Generally, this requires that you select empty cells to the right or to the left of one or more labels. If data appears in any cell other than the leftmost cell in the selected range, Excel drops the contents from those cells that are to the right of the leftmost cells after the merge takes place.

2 Request Merged Cells

In your **Home** ribbon's **Alignment** group, click the **Merge and Center** button to display a list of merge options. Select **Merge Cells**.

Excel merges your selected cells into a single cell. You can now format the merged cell just as you would a single cell—changing its alignment, its size, or the formatting of the text—to create a bolder or more useful label.

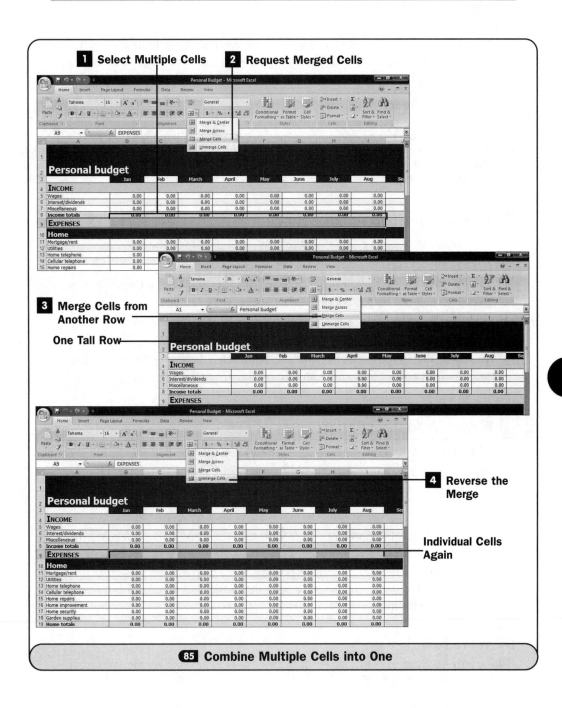

1 Select Multiple Cells   **2** Request Merged Cells

3 Merge Cells from Another Row

One Tall Row

4 Reverse the Merge

Individual Cells Again

85 Combine Multiple Cells into One

Working with a single cell is simpler because you only have to then format the one cell instead of constantly having to select multiple cells, many of which will be blank.

▶ NOTE

If you select cells from two or more rows to merge, Excel merges those cells' contents into a single cell on a single row. Usually, you'll want to merge only adjacent cells from the same row. There are times, however, when you'll want to combine two or more rows into a single, tall row to simplify editing and formatting of those rows.

3 Merge Cells from Another Row

If you need to merge two or more rows into a single row, select the adjacent rows.

In your **Home** ribbon's **Alignment** group, click the **Merge and Center** button to display a list of merge options. Select **Merge Cells**.

4 Reverse the Merge

To reverse the merge, select a merged cell and select **Unmerge Cells** from the **Merge and Center** button on your **Home** ribbon's **Alignment** group.

86

86	Ensure Valid Data Entry
✔ BEFORE YOU BEGIN	→ SEE ALSO
77 Conditionally Format Data	**87** Import and Export Worksheet
84 Protect Worksheet Data	Data

Not only can you conditionally format data so that the format changes based on data values (see **77** **Conditionally Format Data**), but you also can set up *data validity* rules to help maintain accurate spreadsheets. After you set up data validity rules, you or those who use your worksheets will be limited to what can be entered into certain cells.

▶ NEW TERM

Data validity—A check to determine whether data entered into a cell is valid, defined by a set of criteria that you set up.

Without data validity checks, anybody can enter any value into any cell (assuming that the cell is not protected). After you set up data validity checks, if someone violates any criterion you set up that you disallow, such as entering a negative payroll amount, Excel flags the entry as an error. If a user types a value that violates any data validity check you've set up, Excel displays an error message you define for that situation.

1 Select the Range to Validate

Select the cell or range that you want to create a data validity check for. For example, you may want to create a range of dates and disallow any entry into the range that is not a valid date.

To add the data validity check, click to display your **Data** ribbon and then click the **Data Validation** button to display the validation options.

2 Set Up Criteria

Click **Data Validation** to display the **Data Validation** dialog box.

The data validation rules that you set up on the **Settings** page are determined by the data type you allow in the selected cells. For example, if you select **Date** from the **Allow** list, you'll be able to specify that you want to allow only dates that fall between or before or after a certain date or dates. If you select **Text Length**, you can limit the number of characters possible in a text-based cell.

Keep the **Ignore Blank** option checked if you want to allow blanks in the range without the blanks violating the criteria. Unchecking the **Ignore Blank** option will trigger a data error if the user leaves a blank in the cell.

▶ **TIP**

If you want to clear all the options you've selected in the **Data Validation** dialog box and start again, click the **Clear All** button to quickly restore the defaults.

3 Specify an Input Message

Click the **Input Message** tab to display the dialog box's **Input Message** page in the **Data Validation** dialog box. Here, you set up a floating ScreenTip that appears whenever the user selects the cell. The title and message that you type in the **Title** and **Input Message** fields appear when the cell becomes active. The purpose of the **Input Message** field is to let your users know the kind of data you allow in the cell.

▶ **TIP**

Usually, cells don't require both a title and an input message if the criteria are simple. A title such as `Must be more than 0` is usually sufficient and doesn't need further clarification in the **Input Message** field.

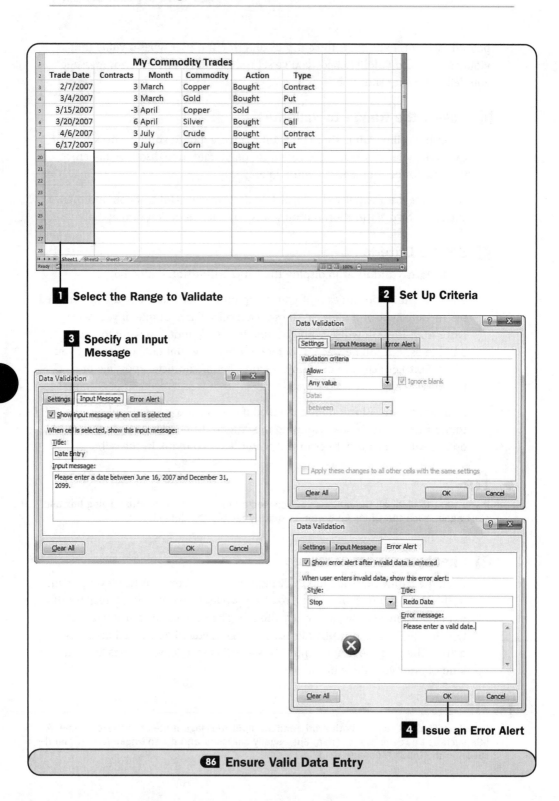

86

1 Select the Range to Validate

2 Set Up Criteria

3 Specify an Input Message

4 Issue an Error Alert

86 Ensure Valid Data Entry

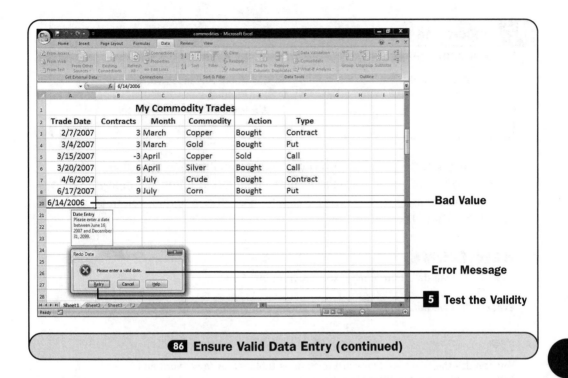

86 Ensure Valid Data Entry (continued)

86

4 Issue an Error Alert

The **Error Alert** page describes what happens if and when the user violates the criteria you set up on the **Settings** page. The **Style** field can be set to **Stop**, **Warning**, or **Information**, depending on what you want to happen when the violation occurs. When you select **Stop**, Excel disallows any entry into the cell until the user enters data that conforms to the criteria. **Warning** or **Information** allows the data but shows a pop-up dialog box with the title and error message you enter in the **Title** and **Error Message** fields of the **Error Alert** page.

5 Test the Validity

Test your data validity check by typing data in the cell. When you select the cell, the **Redo Date** message should appear, telling you what data the cell expects. If you enter a value that violates the criteria, Excel responds with a warning or a pop-up dialog box, depending on how you set up the error alert.

87 | Import and Export Worksheet Data

✔ BEFORE YOU BEGIN	→ SEE ALSO
61 Print a Worksheet	**88** About Advanced Worksheet Printing
	91 Import Data into an Excel Database

As with all the Office programs, Excel works well with data from the other Microsoft Office programs as well as common data formats that you *import* from other programs. If you want to use Excel data in another program, you must *export* the spreadsheet data.

▶ NEW TERMS

Import—To load data from a non-Excel program into Excel.

Export—To save data from Excel so that another program can use the data.

87

▶ TIP

You can use the Windows Clipboard to transfer tables to or from Word and PowerPoint. Just copy and paste the tables into Excel.

❶ Select a Source

Click to display your **Data** ribbon. In the **Get External Data** group resides Excel's data-importing features. To import a Microsoft Access database, for example, you would click **From Access**. To import a Web page, you would click **From Web**. To import from a text file, you would click **From Text**.

▶ NOTE

Each type of data file you import brings its own challenges. Excel will often make assumptions about your data, and you may have to edit your data after Excel imports it.

❷ Determine How to Import

Depending on the kind of file you want to import, Excel displays a different dialog box. For example, if you want to import a text file, Excel displays the **Text Import Wizard** dialog box and walks you through the three-step process of describing your text data, its format, and how you want that data to appear after it comes into Excel.

3 Specify a Different Source

To import data from a non-Access database or an XML file, you'll need to first click the **Data** ribbon's **From Other Sources** button to display a list of options to choose from. Each option steps you through the process of importing that kind of data.

▶ **NOTE**

The **Existing Connections** button produces a dialog box from which you can connect to live data sources such as Microsoft's **MoneyCentral** website.

4 Export Excel Data

To export a workbook to a non-Excel file format, click your **Office** button and select **Save As**. Excel displays the **Save As** dialog box.

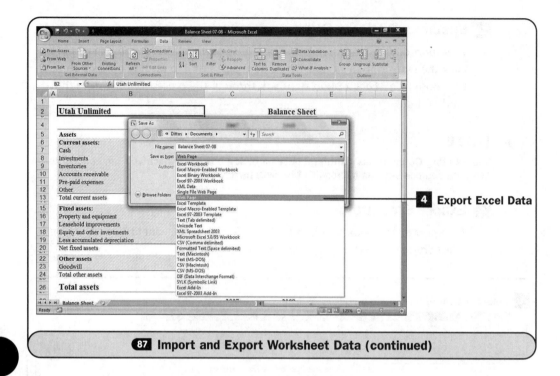

87

87 **Import and Export Worksheet Data (continued)**

Select the location where you want to save the exported workbook, and then click the down arrow next to the **Save as Type** drop-down list box to display all the export file formats that Excel supports.

Click to select one of the file formats. If, for example, you want to display a workbook on the web, you would save your workbook with the **Web Page** option and use an *FTP program* to transfer the page to your website.

▶ **NEW TERM**

FTP program—A program that transfers data to and from a web page. Stands for File Transfer Protocol.

▶ **NOTE**

When you save in different file formats, Excel uses a different filename extension depending on the format. Therefore, you can have a workbook with the same filename in various formats; only the filename extension will differ among them.

88 | About Advanced Worksheet Printing

✔ BEFORE YOU BEGIN	→ SEE ALSO
61 Print a Worksheet **75** Set Up Page Formatting	**94** Compute Table Totals and Subtotals

Printing Excel spreadsheets offers some challenges that other kinds of documents, such as Word documents, do not involve. For example, after you develop a comprehensive spreadsheet, you may want to print the spreadsheet with all its notes showing, perhaps even with formulas showing instead of values. Such reports serve as documentation to the spreadsheet and can help you pinpoint errors in the spreadsheet that might be more difficult to locate by searching and scrolling around the screen.

▶ **TIP**

Before printing, be sure to view a preview by clicking your **Office** button and selecting **Print** and then **Print Preview**. The preview ensures that your printed spreadsheet will look exactly the way you want it to look before you send the spreadsheet to paper.

The **Page Layout** ribbon offers some printing options. Before printing a worksheet, you should specify the print area so that Excel knows what to print. You might want to print only a portion of a worksheet (perhaps not include charts). Select the range you want to print and then click the **Print Area** button to select the **Set Print Area** option.

88

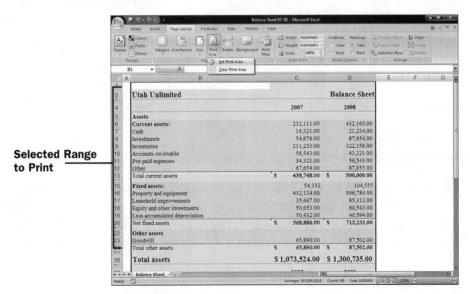

Selected Range to Print

You should specify the range to print by setting the print area before printing.

Click the **Print Titles** button to display the **Page Setup** dialog box. Here reside several print options you may want to specify depending on your current needs.

Normally, the gridlines that separate cells are suppressed during printing, but to help with your row and column alignment when studying large spreadsheets, you may opt to select the **Gridlines** option so that Excel prints the gridlines to paper.

In addition, Excel normally suppresses comments that you've attached to cells but will print those comments along with the rest of the spreadsheet if you click to select the **Comments** option. The **Comments** drop-down list box determines whether you want such notes printed at the end of the printed worksheet all together or as they appear on the actual worksheet, next to the cells that contain them.

If your worksheet has errors, you may want to print the error messages in the cells, leave the cells with errors blank on the printout, or perhaps see dashes or #N/A in their place. The **Cell Errors As** option offers these choices.

88

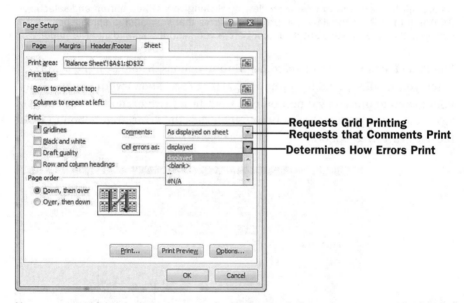

You can control just about any aspect of worksheet printing.

The **Print** dialog box itself enables you to print only a selected range. If, for example, you want to print only certain rows in your spreadsheet, select those rows and then click your **Office** button and select **Print** from the menu. Click the **Print** dialog box's **Selection** option before clicking **OK** to start printing your selected range.

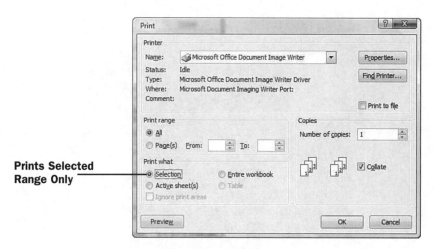

Excel can print only selected ranges if you want.

Prints Selected Range Only

▶ **TIP**

To print all the worksheets in your entire workbook instead of the current worksheet whose tab is active, click to select the **Entire Workbook** option on the **Print** dialog box before clicking **OK** to start printing.

88

10

Using Excel as a Simple Database

IN THIS CHAPTER:

Although Office includes a ***database*** program called Microsoft Access, Excel supports the use of simple database tables from which you can store, edit, sort, and
report from the data as though you were using a standalone database program.
Excel is useful when you have data to sort or store, but your needs don't require
the complications of a standalone database system such as Microsoft Access.

▶ NEW TERM

Database—A collection of data that is often organized in rows and columns to make
searching and sorting easy to do.

Everyone trudges through a lot of data at work and at home. With the prolifera-
tion of computers, information overload seems to be the norm. A database
application helps you organize your data and turn raw facts and figures into
meaningful information. Although Excel's primary job is to be an excellent worksheet program, Excel can provide some database-like capabilities so that you can
spend your valuable time analyzing results instead of trodding through rows and
rows of raw data. Suppose, for example, that your company keeps thousands of
parts in a Excel worksheet, and you need to know exactly which part sold the
most in Division 7 last April. Excel can supply the answer for you. By using Excel's
database features, you can quickly locate the data you need no matter how many
rows your data consumes.

89

This chapter introduces you to the world of databases with Excel. The nature and
use of databases are not difficult to master, but you must understand something
about database design (see **89** **About Excel Databases**) before you can fully master
Excel's capability to process database data.

89 About Excel Databases

✔ **BEFORE YOU BEGIN**	→ **SEE ALSO**
52 Create a New Workbook	**90** Create an Excel Database
	91 Import Data into an Excel Database
	94 Compute Table Totals and Subtotals

Before using a database, you need to learn how a database management system
organizes data. With Excel, you can create, organize, manage, and report from
data stored in your Excel worksheet.

▶ **NOTE**

Excel's row-and-column format makes it a useful tool as a database program and as a worksheet program. The difference between the two is how you access, change, and sort the data in the worksheet.

A database typically contains related data. In other words, you might create a home-office database with your household budget but keep another database to record your rare-book collection titles and their worth. In your household budget, you might track expenses, income, bills paid, and so forth, but that information does not overlap your book-collection database. Of course, if you buy a book, both databases might show the transaction, but the two databases would not overlap.

Technically, a database does not have to reside on a computer. Any place you store data in some organized format, such as a name and address directory, could be considered a database. In most cases, however, the term *database* is reserved for organized, computerized data.

When you design a database, consider its scope before you begin. Does your home business need an inventory system? Does your home business often need to locate a single sales contact from a large list of contacts? If so, an Excel database works well. Only you can decide whether the inventory and the sales contacts should be part of the same system or separate, unlinked systems. The database integration of inventory with the sales contacts requires much more work to design, but your business requirements might necessitate the integration. For example, you might need to track which customers bought certain products in the past.

89

If you need your database tables to relate to each other so that you can create reports that, for example, compare your spending on rare books printed before 1750 and after 1750, and show contact information for all dealers who sold you books that have appreciated in value in the past 12 months, you probably need a relational database such as Microsoft Access to handle that more challenging data organization.

▶ **NOTE**

Not all database values relate to each other. Your company's loan records do not relate to your company's payroll, but both might reside in your company's accounting database. You probably would keep these in separate Excel worksheets, although for a small company, one worksheet with multiple sheets representing separate databases might be manageable.

To keep track of data, you can break down each database sheet into **records** and **fields**. A database's structure acts just like an Excel worksheet because the rows and columns in a worksheet match the records and fields in a database. This similarity between databases and worksheets is why Excel works well for simple database management.

► **NEW TERMS**

Records—The rows in a database representing all the data for a single item. A single employee record would consist of one employee's data, such as employee number, first name, last name, address, birth date, hire date, and so on.

Fields—The columns in a database representing individual descriptions of the records. A field in an employee database might be the Last Name field or the hire data.

In the following figure, the database's records are the sheet's rows, and the fields are the columns. This database is a simple checkbook-register database; you usually organize your checkbook register just as you would organize a computerized version of a checkbook, so you will have little problem mastering Excel's concepts of records and fields.

90

Seven Records

Six Fields

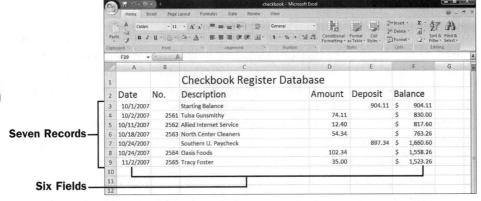

A database contains records and fields that correlate to Excel's rows and columns.

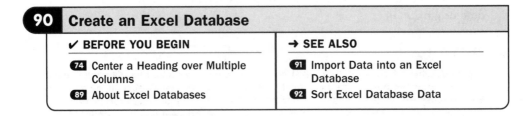

90 | Create an Excel Database

✔ BEFORE YOU BEGIN	→ SEE ALSO
74 Center a Heading over Multiple Columns	**91** Import Data into an Excel Database
89 About Excel Databases	**92** Sort Excel Database Data

You already know how to create an Excel database if you know how to create an Excel worksheet. A database consists of records and fields (see **89** About Excel Databases), and a worksheet consists of rows and columns that perform the same purpose as records and fields when you type data into them.

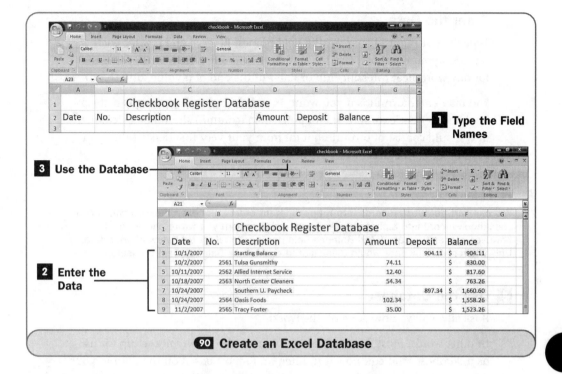

3 Use the Database

2 Enter the Data

1 Type the Field Names

90 Create an Excel Database

90

Each field in your database must have a name. The simplest way to designate a field name is to type a label atop each column in your database. That label, such as Address or DateHired, becomes the name of that field. A field contains as many values as you have records in the database. For example, if your database has 100 rows, your database has 100 records, and each field in the record contains 100 values. (Some may be left blank to designate missing data for those records.)

▶ **NOTE**

A field can consist of a calculated value that contains a formula based on other data in the record.

1 Type the Field Names

To create field names for your database, you only need to type a one-line label atop each column in your worksheet's database. First, though, label your worksheet with an appropriate title that describes the database you're creating.

▶ **TIP**

74 Center a Heading over Multiple Columns shows you how to center your database title in a wide column across the top of the fields.

2 Enter the Data

Type the data that falls under the field names. Reserve one row for each record in your database. Use the standard data-entry techniques you'd use for any worksheet (pressing Tab or Enter at the end of a value, and so on).

You may enter formulas if you want. In a database that represents a checkbook register, for example, the Balance field (column) should be calculated and should consist of a running total from your very first deposit that you used to set up the account in the first record.

▶ **NOTE**

You can sort database records into many different orders. For example, you can sort a checkbook record into alphabetical order based on whom you wrote checks to. This, however, makes the calculated Balance field nonfunctional for that view of your data. Only when sorted by date would a calculated checkbook Balance field be useful.

3 Use the Database

Basically, you've now done all the work!

91

In other words, most Excel worksheets you create are already set up for use as a database. You can now sort, filter, and report based on the data in your worksheet's rows and columns. Your ribbon's **Data** tab displays the data-related commands available.

▶ **NOTE**

If you've used a competing worksheet program, such as OpenOffice.org's Calc, you're used to converting worksheet to data tables before using database-like commands. Excel doesn't require such a conversion. As long as your worksheet has no blank columns or field names, you can apply both worksheet and database operations to your worksheet.

---

91   Import Data into an Excel Database

✔ BEFORE YOU BEGIN	→ SEE ALSO
89 About Excel Databases	**87** Import and Export Worksheet Data
90 Create an Excel Database	**92** Sort Excel Database Data

Although you can type data into an Excel database, if you already have that data stored elsewhere, you can usually import that data directly into Excel by first saving the data in a format Excel can read. For example, suppose that your company uses an Access database for its records and you want to import the customer table into Excel's database so that you can work with the data more easily. You would first export that customer table's data in Excel's *.xlsx* worksheet format and then open that worksheet in Excel.

After the table is open, you must define the data range and save the file as an Excel worksheet. See **87 Import and Export Worksheet Data** for help with importing non-Excel worksheets into Excel and **90 Create an Excel Database** for help with creating a worksheet you can use as a simple database.

▶ **NOTE**

A worksheet can have multiple data ranges, and they can overlap. Depending on how you want to sort or filter your data (see **93 Filter Data You Want to See**), you might overlap several columns, or fields, in several different range names.

1 Export Your Data

In Microsoft Access or wherever your data resides, export that data to an Excel worksheet. In Access, you can right-click over a table name, select the **Export** option, select the **Excel** format, and click **OK** to export the entire table.

▶ **NOTE**

You don't first have to export from the non-Excel program such as Access. Just click Excel's **From Access** or **From Web** or **From Text** or **From Other Sources** button to import data. The advantage to starting inside the original program is that you can selectively export some instead of all the data. Although you can import select data into Excel using the **From** buttons, doing so requires more guesswork than from the actual program.

2 Load the Data

While inside Excel, click your **Office** button and select **Open**. Select the exported data to load that data into Excel.

3 Format the Data

After you've imported the data, you might need to format that data into better-looking columns. Often, the columns are bunched together in Excel when the data came from a non-Excel source. If you imported data from Access, the Access field names become the column headings (the Excel database's field names), and you may have to adjust the column widths to be able to read the column headings.

1 Export Your Data

2 Load the Data

3 Format the Data

91

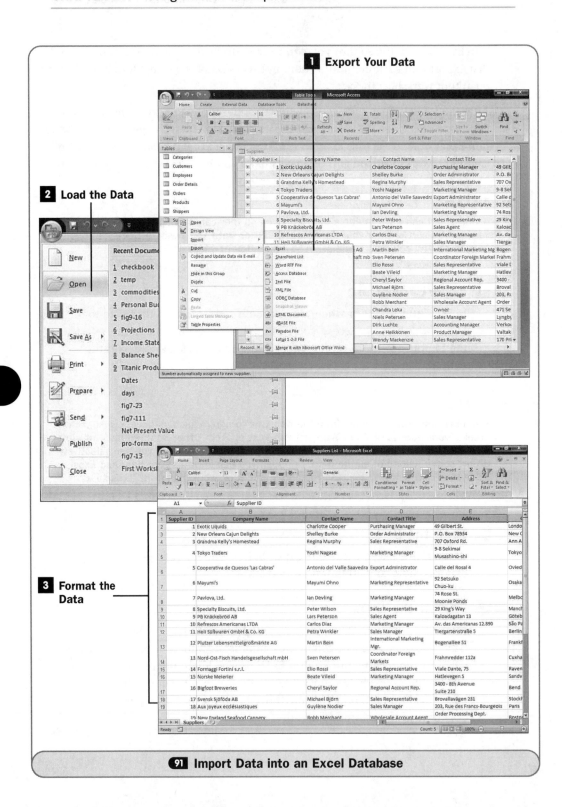

91 Import Data into an Excel Database

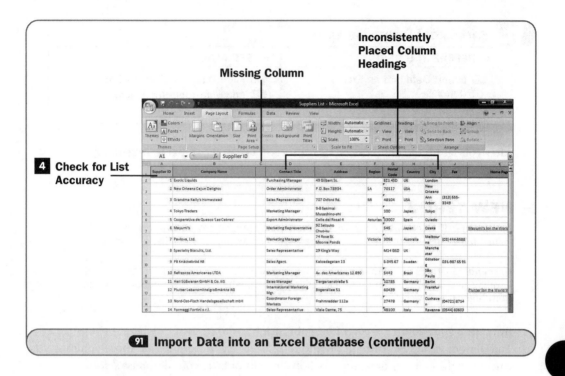

Missing Column

Inconsistently Placed Column Headings

4 Check for List Accuracy

91 Import Data into an Excel Database (continued)

91

▶ NOTE

Column headings are important when you're working with data, so if you imported data from a source that did not use column headings, you'll need to add them now.

4 Check for List Accuracy

An Excel database, as you know from **89 About Excel Databases**, consists of columns next to each other with row headings that you use as field names. If your data came from Access or some other database program, your data will almost certainly import properly into Excel, so you can treat the data as a regular worksheet or as a database table.

If your data does not come from a database program, you should review the imported data to be sure that column names run across the top of the table in a consistent manner and that no columns are separated from each other by one or more blank columns. You'll need to remove blank columns and make sure that a row of field names runs across the top of the entire imported worksheet before you can apply Excel's database operations to the sheet.

92   Sort Excel Database Data

✔ BEFORE YOU BEGIN	→ SEE ALSO
91 Import Data into an Excel Database	**93** Filter Data You Want to See
	94 Compute Table Totals and Subtotals

After you set up the database, you can sort on amounts or text in *ascending* or *descending* order.

▶ NEW TERMS

Ascending—The sort method in which lower values are sorted early in the list and higher values fall at the end of the list, as is the case with an alphabetical list of names.

Descending—The sort method in which higher values are sorted early in the list and lower values fall at the end of the list, as is the case when payroll amounts are sorted from highest to lowest.

By sorting your data, you can often gain insights into it, such as where the top and bottom values lie, without having to resort to extra work to find those values (such as writing `Max()` or `Min()` functions in cells outside your database's data range). Also, you can print parts of the list in zip code order as you might do when printing a list of names and addresses for a mailing.

▶ NOTE

When you sort a data range, you sort on one or more fields (columns), but all the data in all the rows of the data range sort along with your key sorting fields.

1 Prepare to Sort

After you've set up your Excel data as a proper table, with lists of columns next to each other and column titles across the row in one row, you're ready to sort the data in any manner you want.

Click the **Data** tab on your ribbon to display the **Data** ribbon to gain access to Excel's sorting operations.

2 Select the Sort Data

Set up your sorting criteria by pressing Ctrl+A to select your entire database. You never want to sort a single column even though you'll often sort *on* a single column.

In other words, if your data includes a City field and you want to sort your entire database alphabetically by each city's name, you can easily do so, but

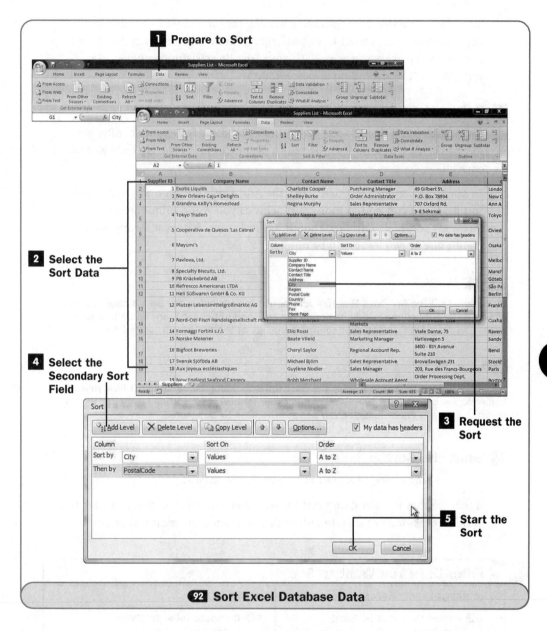

1 Prepare to Sort

2 Select the Sort Data

4 Select the Secondary Sort Field

3 Request the Sort

5 Start the Sort

92 Sort Excel Database Data

you will need to select the entire database or risk having only the City list be sorted without the matching row records in the other columns being sorted properly as well.

3 Request the Sort

Click the **Data** ribbon's **Sort** button to display the **Sort** dialog box. Select the column by which you want to sort by selecting from the **Sort By** drop-down list. Select the order from the **Order** list. If your sort column contains text, you'll almost always want to sort ascending alphabetically from *A* to *Z*, but you can sort descending as well. (If your **Sort By** selection is numeric, your sort order will be ascending or descending.)

4 Select the Secondary Sort Field

Sometimes you'll want to sort on multiple columns. For example, after you sort by the City column list, you might also want to sort on zip code within each city.

To select a secondary sort field, click the **Add Level** button and select another sort field. You can add as many sort fields as you want, although after two or three, the sorting is fairly redundant in most cases. For most sorting requirements, one or two levels will be ample.

▶ **NOTE**

Make sure that the **My Data Has Headers** option is checked in the **Sort** dialog box. Excel will respect your column headings during the sort and not count them as data to sort inside the data. Excel keeps your column headings at the top of your sorted data.

93

▶ **TIP**

Click the **Options** button to display the **Sort Options** dialog box and adjust how your sort behaves. You can request that Excel respect your letters' case, sorting lowercase letters before uppercase equivalents, or you can set the case to be ignored.

5 Start the Sort

Click the **Sort** dialog box's **OK** button to sort your data.

If you see that the sort didn't sort the way you wanted it to, you can click your **Quick Access** toolbar's **Undo** button and sort using different sort options.

93 Filter Data You Want to See	
✔ **BEFORE YOU BEGIN**	→ **SEE ALSO**
91 Import Data into an Excel Database	**94** Compute Table Totals and Subtotals
92 Sort Excel Database Data	

Databases can grow to be enormous. Without some way to filter the data, finding what you want is tedious. Excel's **Find and Replace** command works well enough to locate values that you want to find, but by being able to apply a filter to your database, you can actually hide data that does not currently interest you without removing that data from your database. When you're done with the filtered data, you can easily return to the full database view.

Excel supports several kinds of filters, two of which are the most common:

- *AutoFilter* filters, in which you specify values to filter by

- Filter by selection, a process in which you can specify a range of values to filter by

▶ NEW TERM

AutoFilter—An Excel database filter in which you select from a list of values to filter by and view.

▶ NOTE

If you delete or format cell ranges that include rows currently hidden by an AutoFilter, those rows are unaffected by the deletion or formatting. For more information on formatting cells, see **73** Format Cells; for more information on deleting cells, see **60** Edit Cell Data.

After you filter out the data you don't want to work with, you'll be left with a subset of your database. You can edit, sort, print, and save that subset of data.

1 Apply the AutoFilters

Click the **Filter** button on your **Data** ribbon. Excel adds arrows to the right of each of your column headings. (A subsequent click of **Filter** removes those arrows.) These arrows indicate that Excel's AutoFilter feature is active.

These arrows are the way you determine which data to filter.

2 Determine the Filter Value

Click one of the column's down arrows to open the filter list. Excel analyzes the data in that column and displays one of each item in the filter list with a check box to the left of each item.

Scroll through the list of filter values and deselect all data values you don't want to see. For example, if your data contains a CategoryID field and you only want to see data from categories 2, 4, 6, and 8, you would uncheck all other values such as 1, 3, and 5.

93

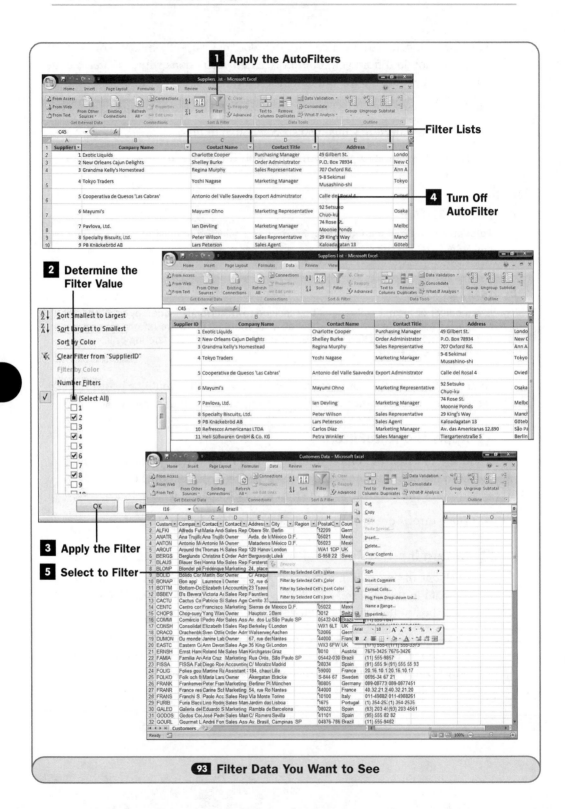

93 Filter Data You Want to See

6 Work with a Data Subset

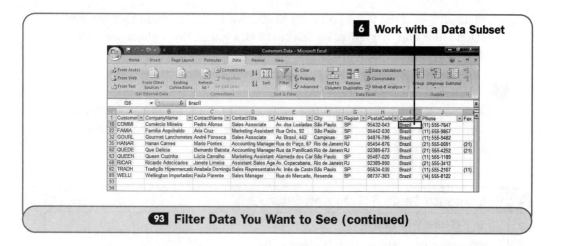

93 Filter Data You Want to See (continued)

▶ **NOTE**

If you select the **Number Filters** option, you can use comparisons to select filtered data. In other words, you can request filters based on values that are equal to, less than, more than, and between other values as well as select from other filter criteria such as the top 10 values in the database for that column.

93

3 Apply the Filter

Click the **OK** button to display the filtered data.

The data you filtered out isn't gone from your table permanently but only for the present. The subset of data you see appears so that you can print a report or otherwise work with that subset.

4 Turn Off AutoFilter

Click the ribbon's **Filter** button again to restore your database to its full set of values and to remove the subset from your screen.

5 Select to Filter

The AutoFilter method is simpler than filtering by selection, but sometimes the selection filter is more appropriate for your data.

Filter by selection works by example. Suppose that you want to display only those table records that contain a specific field value; for example, you need to work only with customer records from Brazil. If your customer table contains a Country field with scattered Brazil entries, you can filter out all those records that do *not* contain Brazil in their Country field column.

Right-click over the value you want to filter by. From the menu that appears, select **Filter** and then **Filter by Selected Cell's Value**. Excel filters away all data that does not match your selected value in that field.

6 Work with a Data Subset

A subset of data now appears in your worksheet. Click the ribbon's **Filter** button again to restore your database to its full set of values and to remove the subset from your screen.

---

94 Compute Table Totals and Subtotals

✔ **BEFORE YOU BEGIN**

91 Import Data into an Excel Database
92 Sort Excel Database Data
93 Filter Data You Want to See

94

When you're working with any kind of financial database information, the ability to calculate subtotals and totals, based on sorted data, becomes necessary. For example, you might want to see all the total sales from a given region or zip code. If any sales are down in one area, you can get your Marketing Department to step up their efforts in that area.

Excel can summarize database data for you based on several criteria, including these:

- **Sum**—The added total of data.

- **Count**—The number of items in the data range.

- **Average**—The calculated intermediate value in a range of data.

- **Min or max amounts**—The lowest or highest value in the data.

- **Product**—The multiplied result of the data values.

- **Count numbers**—Ordered by a count of inventory.

- **Standard deviation (of a sample or population)**—A statistic that measures how well dispersed values in a data range are.

- **Variance (of a sample or population)**—The square of the standard deviation used for statistical measurements.

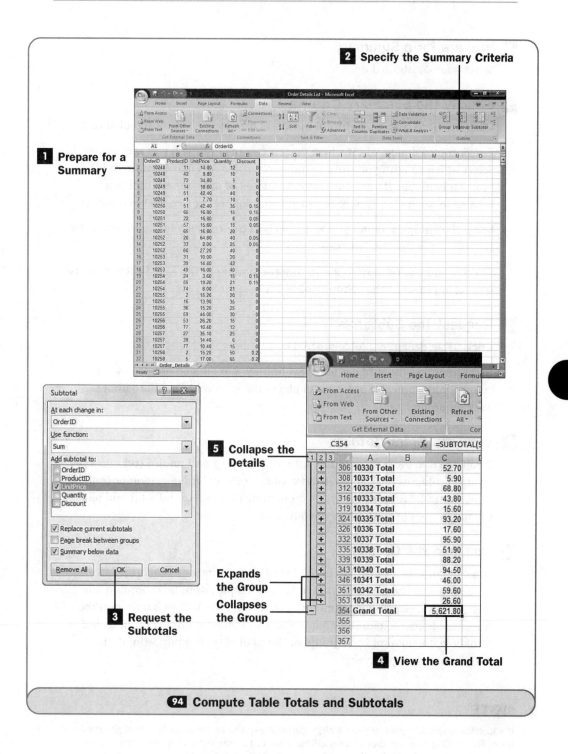

2 Specify the Summary Criteria

1 Prepare for a Summary

5 Collapse the Details

Expands the Group

Collapses the Group

3 Request the Subtotals

4 View the Grand Total

Subtotal

At each change in:
OrderID

Use function:
Sum

Add subtotal to:
☐ OrderID
☐ ProductID
☑ UnitPrice
☐ Quantity
☐ Discount

☑ Replace current subtotals
☐ Page break between groups
☑ Summary below data

Remove All   OK   Cancel

	A	B	C	D
306	10330 Total		52.70	
308	10331 Total		5.90	
312	10332 Total		68.80	
316	10333 Total		43.80	
319	10334 Total		15.60	
324	10335 Total		93.20	
326	10336 Total		17.60	
332	10337 Total		95.90	
335	10338 Total		51.90	
339	10339 Total		88.20	
343	10340 Total		94.50	
346	10341 Total		46.00	
351	10342 Total		59.60	
353	10343 Total		26.60	
354	Grand Total		5,621.80	

94

94 Compute Table Totals and Subtotals

1 Prepare for a Summary

Select your database data.

2 Specify the Summary Criteria

Click the **Data** ribbon's **Subtotal** button to display the **Subtotal** dialog box.

The **Subtotal** dialog box is where you specify the grouping you want to see. Select which column you want to group on in the **At Each Change In** list box. For example, if your data were composed of order details and you wanted to see subtotals of each order, you might select **OrderID** to group on.

Select the kind of subtotal you want, such as a sum or standard deviation, by selecting from the **Use Function** list box.

Select a numeric column to use for the subtotaling in the **Add Subtotal To** list by clicking to select the column you want to subtotal.

3 Request the Subtotals

Click **OK** to generate a table ordered by subtotals.

Excel computes the subtotal for the column you requested ordered by the column you wanted to order. Excel places the subtotal in boldface under each grouping.

4 View the Grand Total

Scroll down to the bottom of the data to view the grand total. Excel totals the grouped columns (or computes the variance or standard deviation or count or other grand total based on what you requested) into a grand total and places the grand total at the bottom of your data.

5 Collapse the Details

You can click the minus sign to the left of a row number to collapse that group's detail. The minus sign then becomes a plus sign. By collapsing various types of detail in your summary (by clicking the **1**, **2**, or **3** button at the top of the leftmost column of data), you can request a display of the grand total only, the total of each group, or the total of each group with all the details shown, respectively.

94

▶ **NOTE**

If you click a specific plus or minus sign, you will expand or collapse just that grouped item. By clicking specific groups throughout your data, you show only the data details you want to see while hiding the data you're currently uninterested in.

PART IV

Impressing Audiences with PowerPoint

IN THIS PART:

11

Learning About PowerPoint

IN THIS CHAPTER:

Have you ever wanted to wow your audiences with professional *presentations*? You can with PowerPoint. This chapter introduces you to PowerPoint, and you'll soon be designing and creating eye-catching and engrossing presentations. By using the predefined presentation tools of PowerPoint, you can generate good-looking presentations without worrying about design, format, and color details all the time. After PowerPoint generates a sample presentation, you need only follow a few simple procedures if you want to modify and tweak the presentation into your own unique version.

▶ NEW TERM

Presentation—A set of screens, also called *pages* or *slides*, that you present to people in a room or over the Internet.

The primary purpose of PowerPoint is to help you design, create, and edit presentations and printed handouts. Because PowerPoint provides a wide variety of pre-defined templates, you don't have to be a graphics design specialist to create good-looking presentations.

▶ NOTE

95

Keep in mind that the term *presentation* refers to an entire PowerPoint collection of slides (or pages), whereas the term *slide* or *page* refers to an individual screen within that presentation.

PowerPoint slides can hold many kinds of information. Here are a few of the things you can add to a PowerPoint presentation:

- Data you insert into PowerPoint, including text, charts, graphs, and graphics
- Word documents
- Live data from the Internet, including complete Web pages
- Excel worksheets
- Multimedia content such as video and sound files
- Graphics from graphics programs such as Adobe Illustrator

---

95 **About Presentation Creation in PowerPoint**

✔ BEFORE YOU BEGIN	→ SEE ALSO
16 About Styles, Themes, and Templates	**103** Review PowerPoint Templates
	104 Use PowerPoint Layouts and Themes

You'll almost always begin a new presentation the same way—you'll start PowerPoint and select a template or apply a *layout* to the slides. Although **16** **About Styles, Themes, and Templates** discusses Word-based templates, the nature of templates applies in PowerPoint too, and if you're unfamiliar with templates, you'll want to review that task. After you create an outline of a presentation with a template or by applying a layout, you will then fill in the presentation's details.

▶ **NEW TERM**

Layout—A master slide design that defines content on the slide. A layout contains placeholders to indicate where pictures and text appear on slides you apply that layout to. PowerPoint includes several layouts, and you can create your own.

In other Microsoft Office programs such as Word and Excel, it seems as though templates play a less vital role than they do in PowerPoint. In spite of their importance and power and ease of use, you'll often create a letter or another Word document without using a template. Worksheet formats can be so varied that even extensive worksheets are begun without initially using a template due to their unique nature. A presentation, however, often follows a similar pattern among its slides. To maintain consistency and professionalism, your presentation slides will often follow a similar format or look throughout your presentation. Therefore, keeping things uniform with a template or layout seems to be the best way to create a new presentation.

▶ **NOTE**

The AutoContent Wizard from previous PowerPoint versions is not available in PowerPoint 2007.

▶ **TIP**

Plan your presentations! Think about your target audience. Presenting identical information to two audiences might require completely different approaches. A company's annual meeting for shareholders requires a different format, perhaps, than the board of director's meeting. After determining your target audience, create a slide outline before you begin.

When you first start PowerPoint, it displays a blank presentation with a single slide showing. The layout is simple, with a title across the top and a subtitle below.

95

Slides Pane

Slide Preview

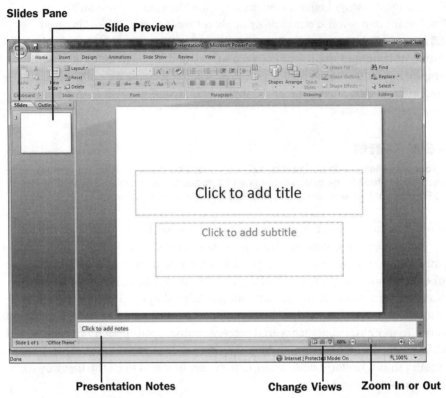

Presentation Notes   **Change Views**   **Zoom In or Out**

PowerPoint displays a blank presentation when you start the program; a simple layout defines the first slide's details.

If you want to begin with the slide PowerPoint gives you when you start the program, you will click to add a title and subtitle, and continue creating the presentation (see ⑩ **Enter Text into a Presentation**). After you fill in the text and possibly add a background image, you could apply a theme to the presentation and continue on to the next slide by clicking the **New Slide** button.

If you click the icon above the **New Slide** button, PowerPoint selects a slide layout and generates a new slide.

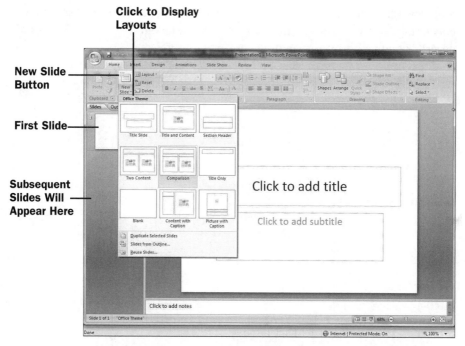

Click to Display
Layouts

New Slide
Button

First Slide

Subsequent
Slides Will
Appear Here

PowerPoint displays a blank presentation when you start the program; a simple layout defines the first slide's details.

95

To add a title to the second slide, you'll click **Click to Add Title** and type a title. Click **Click to Add Text** to add one or more bullet points to the slide. If you want to add something other than text in the title or body areas, click one of the six buttons in the center of the slide. Depending on what you click, you can add one or more of the following:

- **Table**—A worksheet-like table with rows and columns containing data.

- **Chart**—A graph showing data relationships.

- **Clip Art**—An image from the Microsoft online Clip Art gallery.

- **Picture**—An image from a graphics file.

- **SmartArt Graphic**—A diagram image from Microsoft's SmartArt Gallery such as an organization layout chart or a flowchart.

▶ **TIP**

PowerPoint's spelling checker will display a red wavy line under misspelled words in your presentation if you've requested spell-checking (see **96** **Set PowerPoint Options**).

Instead of clicking the **New Slide** button's icon, if you click the **New Slide** button's text with the down arrow to the left of it, PowerPoint displays the **Office Theme** drop-down list. The name *Theme* is misleading. What you see in the list are layouts from which you can select. When you select a layout, PowerPoint creates a new slide and you continue creating your presentation.

Available Layouts ———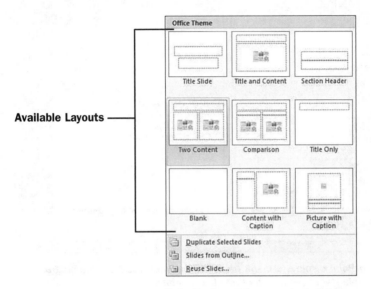

Select a layout for your next slide.

For a fancier presentation, you'll probably begin with a template. When you click the **Office** button and select **New**, PowerPoint displays the **New Presentation** window. If you want to begin with a completely blank presentation, you can click the **Blank Presentation** button, but to begin with a template, you should select a template.

The categories to the left of the **New Presentation** window provide a list of topics on which you can base your own presentation. For example, if you were creating a training presentation, you could click to display the available templates from the **Presentations** category, select **Training**, and then click to select one of the sample presentations that appear. One will be a training presentation for the old Outlook 2003. You can change the content to match your presentation. As is true with most of the template presentations, the Outlook 2003 presentation is professional looking, and you should be able to convert it to the subject you're teaching so that your topic portrays the same consistent and professional look.

95

Template Categories

Loads of templates provide you with ready-made presentations.

After you select a template, PowerPoint loads it and creates the presentation. Although a template is often referred to as a model without data, many PowerPoint templates come with full presentations inside them. You'll have a wealth of slide formats you can use and modify for your own presentation.

When PowerPoint first presents you with your new template-inspired presentation, a help window appears telling you about the presentation template and offering some advice on ways to change the template's presentation to suit your own needs.

▶ **NOTE**

You can personalize the presentation using the tasks described in the rest of this book. Some templates come with far more slides than you'll use. To delete a slide, right-click the slide in the left preview pane and choose **Delete Slide**. To add a slide, click the preview of the slide that is to come before your new slide and select either **Duplicate Slide** or **New Slide**.

▶ **TIP**

Your **Quick Access** toolbar's **Undo** command will undo any new slide creation or deletion if you change your mind.

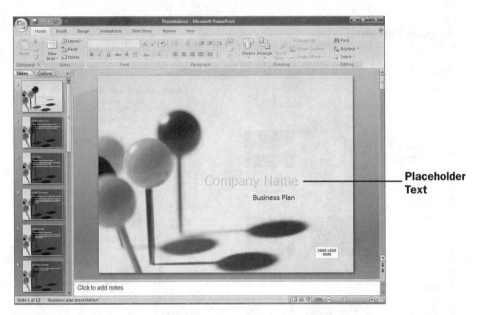

Placeholder Text

Your template will sport either placeholders for data or actual data you can personalize.

96

96 | Set PowerPoint Options

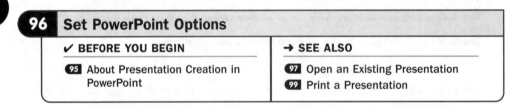

✔ BEFORE YOU BEGIN	→ SEE ALSO
95 About Presentation Creation in PowerPoint	**97** Open an Existing Presentation **99** Print a Presentation

Not everybody works the same way, so not every PowerPoint user wants to use PowerPoint the same way. By setting some of PowerPoint's many options, you will make PowerPoint conform to the way you like to do things. For example, you may want to change the color scheme that PowerPoint uses for its windows and ribbons or turn off the automatic spelling checker if your presentations contain a lot of technical jargon and abbreviations that the PowerPoint spelling dictionary might not recognize. The PowerPoint options enable you to set these and other PowerPoint aspects.

▶ TIP

Even if you're familiar with Excel or another Office set of options, initially scanning PowerPoint's options helps introduce you to PowerPoint so that you can learn the kinds of customization options available to you.

1 Display the Office Box

The **Office** button gives you quick access to file-related commands that used to be available in PowerPoint's **File** menu. In addition, when you click the **Office** button, you'll have access to the **PowerPoint Options** button that opens the **PowerPoint Options** dialog box.

2 Select PowerPoint Options

Click the **PowerPoint Options** button to display the **PowerPoint Options** dialog box. From this dialog box, you change and set all the option settings within PowerPoint.

If you use Windows Vista's Aero Glass graphics mode, your **PowerPoint Options** dialog box window will have translucent borders that allow PowerPoint's menu and toolbars to show through. If you don't run Aero Glass, your **PowerPoint Options** dialog box window will have solid borders.

If you're fairly new to PowerPoint, consider leaving all the options as is until you familiarize yourself with how PowerPoint works.

3 Change the Popular Options

If the **PowerPoint Options** dialog box doesn't open to the **Popular** tab, click **Popular**. As the dialog box states, Microsoft considers these options to be the most popular (which will be debatable by most PowerPoint users).

You can elect to use the mini toolbar (see **59 Insert and Delete Rows and Columns**), use the Live Preview feature (see **105 Change a Presentation's Background**), show the **Developer** tab on your ribbon (off by default), and select a PowerPoint default color scheme. You can also change your default username.

Some PowerPoint options have a small blue letter *i* enclosed in a circle to the right of them. Rest your mouse pointer over this information request, and PowerPoint pops up a helpful description box of that option.

4 Change the Proofing Options

The **Proofing** category enables you to adjust AutoCorrect options, request or reject automatic spell-checking, and change the way the spell-checking operates by modifying options such as flagging repeated words and ignoring words that contain numbers.

96

96

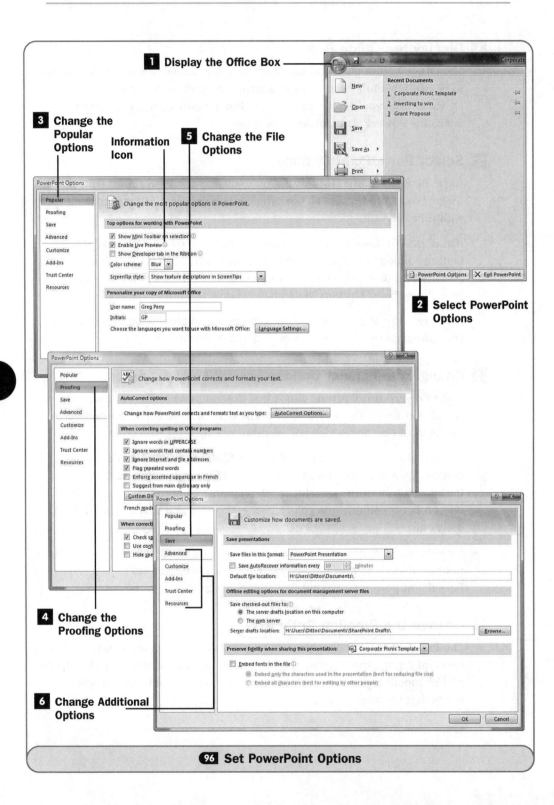

1 Display the Office Box

3 Change the Popular Options

Information Icon

5 Change the File Options

2 Select PowerPoint Options

4 Change the Proofing Options

6 Change Additional Options

96 Set PowerPoint Options

▶ **NOTE**

PowerPoint offers no grammar-checking capability. Presentations are often filled with bulleted items and short quips that are not grammatically correct but are completely acceptable as slide text during a presentation. A grammar checker would flag too much to be useful.

▶ **TIP**

If your presentations will contain a lot of text that you want to check the grammar on first, type the text into Word, and after Word checks the grammar, cut and paste the text into your presentation's slide. Proofread your text even if it passes PowerPoint's grammar and spell checker because those tools are reliable but aren't foolproof.

5 Change the File Options

The **Save** category enables you to adjust default file formats when storing your presentations. In addition, a useful option is being able to embed fonts in the presentation. If you routinely use specialized fonts in your presentations but present those presentations on other computers, or perhaps save presentations on websites for others to see, by embedding the fonts you use inside the presentation, you ensure that your audience will always see the text as you meant them to.

The drawback to embedding fonts in a presentation file is that your presentations will be larger and, therefore, slower to load over the Internet.

96

▶ **NOTE**

PowerPoint presentations are a useful way to get your message across over the web. You can introduce new products or teach others how to do something in a presentation because your viewing audience can step through the presentation a slide at a time at their own pace.

6 Change Additional Options

Continue viewing and changing the remaining options in the **PowerPoint Options** dialog box. Click the tab that corresponds to the option you'd like to change.

The **Advanced** tab offers advanced editing options such as how PowerPoint handles sound and pop-up ScreenTips.

The remaining options allow you to perform less-common option changes, such as customizing the icons on PowerPoint's ribbon bar, and view resources on the Web where you can get extra help.

When you're done reviewing and changing PowerPoint options, click the **OK** button to close the **PowerPoint Options** dialog box.

---

97   **Open an Existing Presentation**

✔ BEFORE YOU BEGIN	→ SEE ALSO
95 About Presentation Creation in PowerPoint	**98** Give a Presentation
96 Set PowerPoint Options	**99** Print a Presentation

When you open a document in most programs, such as Word or Excel, you usually start the program and then click the **Office** button and select **Open** from the menu. Opening a presentation from within PowerPoint is similar, but you must keep in mind that PowerPoint always creates a blank presentation and displays that new presentation's first slide whenever you start PowerPoint.

Fortunately, you don't have to close that blank presentation if you want to open another. After you open a presentation and it appears inside PowerPoint's editing area, the blank one goes away and is not located in another window somewhere.

▶ **NOTE**

Microsoft PowerPoint 2007 uses the .pptx filename extension.

97

1 Request a Presentation

Select **Open** from the **Office** Windows menu. PowerPoint displays the **Open** dialog box, from which you can open an existing presentation. Locate the place where the presentation resides and click to select a presentation. Click **Open** to load the presentation into PowerPoint. You can also select an existing presentation if it's name appears in the right pane labeled Recent Documents.

▶ **NOTE**

Windows Vista's live preview icons (available if you use the Aero Glass mode) do not display a presentation's first slide as you might expect. Instead, you see only a PowerPoint icon on a document for each PowerPoint presentation entry in the **Open** dialog box.

2 Edit or Run the Newly Opened Presentation

After PowerPoint loads the presentation, you are free to run (see **98 Give a Presentation**) or edit it.

3 Open Another Presentation

After you're inside PowerPoint, if you want to open a second presentation, click your **Office** button again to display the **Open** dialog box and select another presentation to open. PowerPoint enables you to open multiple presentations at one time, each in its own Windows window.

▶ **TIP**

You might want to open more than one presentation to copy and paste from one to another.

▶ **NOTE**

Depending on your screen's resolution and the details in a presentation's slide, you might need to zoom in or out by dragging the **Zoom** slider in PowerPoint's lower-right corner.

4 Change the Presentation's View

PowerPoint provides three view buttons to the left of the **Zoom** slider control. The Normal view shows one PowerPoint slide at a time in the large, center editing area. Slide Sorter view shows multiple thumbnails of your slides on the screen at one time. The Slide Sorter view is useful for seeing multiple slides at one time to get an overview of your presentation or perhaps to rearrange your presentation by dragging slides to different locations. The **Slide Show** button starts your presentation running (see **98** **Give a Presentation**).

5 Close the Presentation

When you finish giving or editing a presentation, close the presentation by clicking your **Office** button and selecting **Close**. This clears your PowerPoint editing area. If you made changes that you haven't yet saved, PowerPoint prompts you to save your changes before closing the current presentation.

97

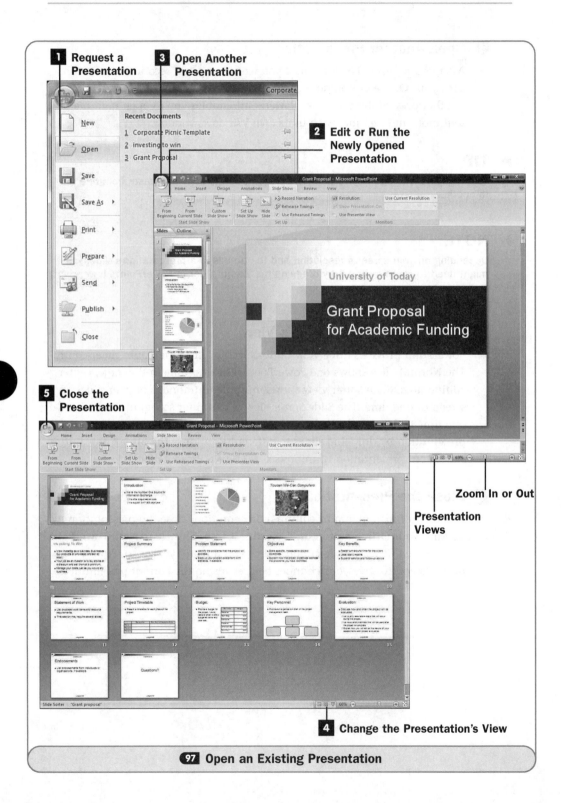

97 Open an Existing Presentation

---

98 | **Give a Presentation**

✔ BEFORE YOU BEGIN	→ SEE ALSO
95 About Presentation Creation in PowerPoint	**112** Make an Automatic Presentation
97 Open an Existing Presentation	

Unlike a Word document or an Excel spreadsheet, your PowerPoint presentation is active from the beginning. That is, your presentation is meant to move, from slide to slide, from beginning to end, and possibly back and forth, depending on the exact order you desire.

Therefore, your audience doesn't just read a static document or spreadsheet when they view your presentation. When you want to give your audience a PowerPoint presentation, you *run* the presentation. In PowerPoint terminology, when you run a presentation, you show your audience a *slide show*.

▶ NEW TERMS

Run—The act of showing your PowerPoint presentation to an audience so that the presentation moves from slide to slide. Also called *give* in this context.

Slide show—Your running presentation, given this name due to its slide-by-slide format.

You'll want to master some common presentation-controlling keystrokes before you give a presentation. When you master these keystrokes, you'll be able to step through your presentation, jump around the presentation, and control the entire presentation live. Table 11.1 lists the keystrokes you should know before running your presentation.

▶ TIP

If you use your mouse pointer in your presentation, it's simple to move forward one slide at a time by clicking anywhere on your slide with your left mouse button. Right-click to display a pop-up menu over the presentation for additional options you can control with your mouse. The lower-left corners of slides also have buttons you can click to manage your presentation.

1 Open Your Presentation

Click your **Office** button and select **Open** to display a list of presentations. Select the presentation you want to give.

TABLE 11.1   Using the Keyboard to Navigate Through Presentations

Press This Key . . .	To Do This
Page Down or N or Enter	Move forward through your presentation by one slide each time you press Page Down
Page Up or P or Backspace	Move backward through your presentation by one slide each time you press Page Up
Home	Move to the first slide in your presentation
End	Move to the last slide in your presentation
B or .	Instantly switch your presentation to a black screen or return from a black screen back to your running presentation
W or ,	Instantly switch your presentation to a white screen or return from a white screen back to your running presentation
Ctrl+S	Display the **All Slides** dialog box so that you can jump to any specific slide in the presentation
Esc	End your running presentation and return to the PowerPoint editing screen

98

▶ **TIP**

Most presentations are given in front of an audience, often from a laptop plugged into an overhead projector. Walk through this task of running your presentation before your audience arrives to ensure that you have the overhead connected properly to your laptop.

❷ Prepare Your Presentation for the Slide Show

After your presentation appears on the screen, click to display the **Slide Show** ribbon and click the **Set Up Slide Show** button to open the **Set Up Show** dialog box.

❸ Specify Slide Show Settings

Many of your **Set Up Show** dialog box settings are determined when you create your presentation, although you can always change them here at the **Set Up Show** dialog box. You'll be able to select all or just a range of slides (from the **From** options), as well as determine how your slide show will display (either in the default full-screen mode or in a smaller window with a lower resolution).

If the **Manually** option is unchecked, PowerPoint assumes that you originally created this presentation to display automatically, without intervention. If you're speaking and using the presentation to support your speech, you probably won't want the automatic changing of slides that occurs. Instead, you will want to move from slide to slide when you're ready to do so. If your

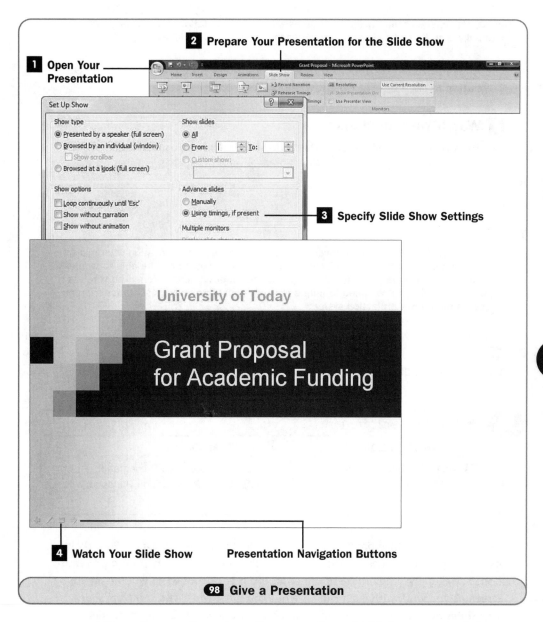

2 Prepare Your Presentation for the Slide Show

1 Open Your Presentation

3 Specify Slide Show Settings

4 Watch Your Slide Show   Presentation Navigation Buttons

98 Give a Presentation

audience has questions along the way or if you decide to cover a topic longer than you originally planned, you need full control over your presentation. So in such a case, ensure that **Manually** is checked.

▶ TIP

The default slide show setting is not **Manually** but is **Using Timings, if Present**. Unless you've added a timer to each slide (see **112** **Make an Automatic Presentation**), PowerPoint still relies on you to manually move the slides forward during your presentation. The **Manually** option ensures that the presentation will always move manually even if you have set timers on each slide for automatic viewing.

After you've set the options that suit your current presentation, click the **OK** button to close the **Set Up Show** dialog box.

▪4 Watch Your Slide Show

To start your slide show, click the **Slide Show** ribbon's **From Beginning** button. Excel starts the slide show by displaying the first slide in your presentation.

▶ **NOTE**

If you master Windows Vista's Network projection feature and the location where you're presenting has connected its room projects to a network, you should be able to wirelessly access the room's projector through your wireless Internet connection. If no wireless signal is available, you will need to plug a network cable into your presentation's laptop to access the room's projection system.

99

▶ **TIP**

The **From Current Slide** button enables you to start your presentation from any slide.

---

99 **Print a Presentation**

✔ BEFORE YOU BEGIN	→ SEE ALSO
95 About Presentation Creation in PowerPoint	**113** Add Notes to a Presentation
97 Open an Existing Presentation	**114** Create Presentation Handouts

---

Unlike the other Office programs, such as Word, Excel, and No Draw, PowerPoint users generally don't need to display a Print Preview before they print a presentation. The slide-by-slide nature of presentations means that what you see on your screen as you work with each slide is what you'll get when you print the slides. The **Slides** pane to the left of your PowerPoint window is like a print preview that's always visible to you.

▶ **TIP**

When you run your presentation on your monitor, you are in effect getting a preview of what each slide will look like when you print your presentation.

1 Request the Print Dialog Box

Click your **Office** button, click the right arrow next to **Print**, and select **Print** to display the **Print** dialog box.

2 Specify What to Print

You now are at the place, at the **Print** dialog box, where you determine the PowerPoint settings you need for printing what you want printed.

The **Print What** area determines what you want to print. Most audiences appreciate it very much when you print a copy of your presentation to hand out to the members. They will be able to concentrate on your speech and not worry about taking copious notes. Click to select the **Handouts** option to print multiple slides on one page (as opposed to a single slide per page, as will be the case if you leave the option at **Slides**). Change the **Slides per Page** option to determine how many slides will print on each sheet. Print as many as is readable; your audience should be able to read the slides, but you won't waste as much paper as you would if you printed one slide per page. **114 Create Presentation Handouts** explains how to produce effective audience handouts.

You may want to print only your speaker's notes at the bottom of your slides by clicking to select the **Notes Pages** option (see **113 Add Notes to a Presentation**). The notes will print under the slides you've attached them to. You might choose to print your presentation's outline. To do that, click to select the **Outline View** option.

If you're printing a large presentation, you might want to save some color ink by printing a grayscale or black-and-white version of your presentation for your audience. Use the **Grayscale** or **Pure Black & White** options in the **Color/Grayscale** area to print using only black ink.

3 Specify the Range to Print

The **Print Range** section determines which slides you will print. The **All** option prints all slides, whereas the **Current Slide** option prints only the slide that appeared in the center PowerPoint editing window when you requested the **Print** dialog box.

You can also print selected slides by entering slide number ranges in the **Slides** option. For example, you could type 1-3, 7, 11, 13-15 to print eight slides: slide 1, 2, 3, 7, 11, 13, 14, and 15.

99

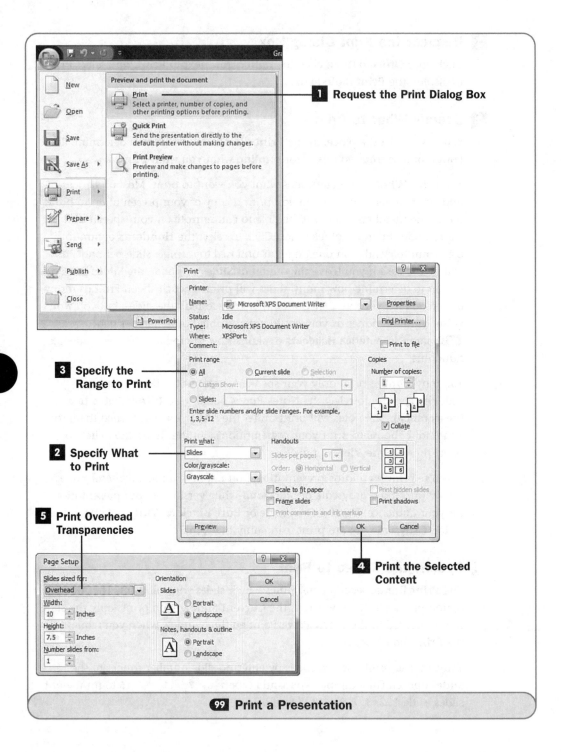

1 Request the Print Dialog Box

3 Specify the Range to Print

2 Specify What to Print

5 Print Overhead Transparencies

4 Print the Selected Content

99 Print a Presentation

4 Print the Selected Content

Click the **OK** button to print your selected slides and notes.

5 Print Overhead Transparencies

If you won't be using a computer projector but instead will be giving your presentation with a lower-tech overhead transparency projector, you can request that PowerPoint print your presentation's slides as overhead transparencies.

Click to display your **Design** ribbon and click the button to the right of the **Page Setup** group. The **Page Setup** dialog box appears. Select **Overhead** from the **Slides Sized For** drop-down list box. PowerPoint will optimize each slide to show best on an overhead transparency projection system.

▶ **TIP**

The **Page Setup** dialog box also enables you to specify landscape and portrait printing, as well as specify the exact print measurement for your slides in case you want to print onto a nonstandard page size.

99

12

Adding Flair to Your Presentations

IN THIS CHAPTER:

When you first learn PowerPoint, you should get a general overview of what presentations are all about and how to create them. Chapter 11, "Learning About PowerPoint," covers all those topics, and if you have never worked with PowerPoint, you may want to review the tasks in that chapter.

This chapter covers details such as how to add text to your presentation slides and how to format your slides to create a dazzling presentation. No matter how graphical you want your presentation to be, the presentation's words are what usually convey your information to your audience. The most important element on your slides will be the text, and this chapter focuses a lot of attention on how to place and format text.

You must enter and format text on the slides in a way that informs your audience without overwhelming them with too many special effects or too much text.

▶ **NOTE**

Not only is too much text difficult to read, but also presentation slides aren't designed to convey lots of textual information. That's your job as the presenter! Design your presentation to support and enhance the message you convey as you give your presentation.

100

100	**Enter Text into a Presentation**

✔ **BEFORE YOU BEGIN**	→ **SEE ALSO**
95 About Presentation Creation in PowerPoint	**101** Find and Replace Text
	102 Animate Text

Generally, you'll add text and edit your slides simply by clicking where the text is to go and typing the text. You can make edits directly on the slide and see the results of those edits as you make them.

To add text to a new slide, you must insert the new slide in your presentation. The new slide will hold the text you want to type. The layout you apply to the slide determines how your text appears and whether graphics might also appear with the text. When you want to edit some text, you'll actually be editing text within a text box that lies on a slide. To edit text in a text box, click that text box to activate it and to place the text cursor inside it.

PowerPoint displays the text box surrounded by sizing handles. PowerPoint treats a slide's title as a single object and the slide's bulleted set of items as another object. Both of these objects are text objects, and they will appear inside an editable text box when you click them.

▶ **NOTE**

If you've inserted an element other than text onto the slide, such as a graphics image, sound, or video clip, you can click that object and move, edit, or delete it.

Although PowerPoint's layouts define where text will go and how large that text will be, there will be many times when you want to change the text format to something else. You can control many factors related to your presentation's text, including the following:

- Choose the alignment (such as left and right justification)

- Change the text size

- Change the font

- Animate the text (as described in **102** **Animate Text**)

- Change the text to a 3-D format

If you've used other Office programs, such as Word, you'll feel at home with some of PowerPoint's formatting tools because the font-related options are similar to those of the other Office programs.

1 Request a New Slide

100

To insert a brand-new slide, click the down arrow at the bottom of the **Home** ribbon's **New Slide** button and select a layout that best matches the slide you want to insert.

A new slide appears in your PowerPoint editing area, and the **Slides** pane shows a thumbnail of the new slide. Depending on the type of layout you choose, placeholders will show you where to add text.

2 Add Text to the Slide

Click any placeholder. If the placeholder rests in a title area, you'll be able to add a title to the slide. If the placeholder resides inside a large text box, you will be able to add multiple lines of bulleted text to that area.

▶ **TIP**

You can request that the current date or time appear at the bottom or top of a slide by clicking the **Date & Time** button from the **Insert** ribbon.

3 Select the Text to Format

If you want to format any of the text on the slide, select the text. PowerPoint's mini toolbar appears, from which you can click to select common formatting options such as boldface, italic, text-alignment, font changes, and coloring of the text.

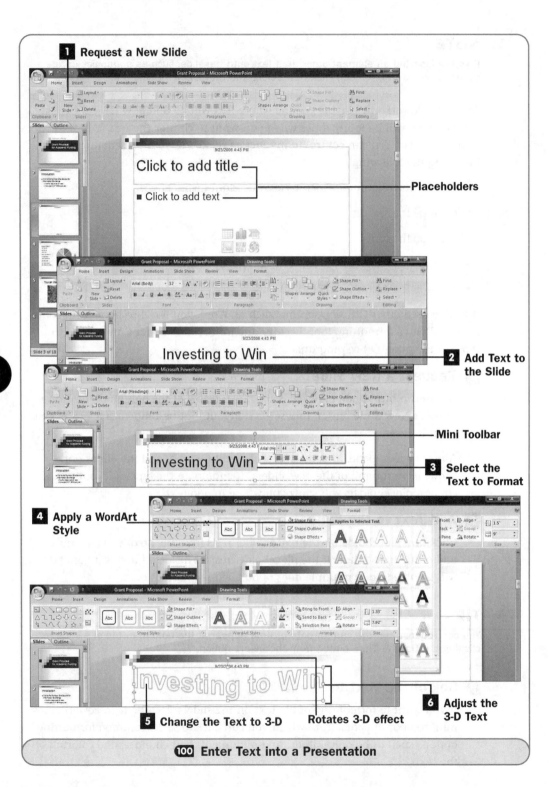

100

1 Request a New Slide

Click to add title

Click to add text

Placeholders

2 Add Text to the Slide

Investing to Win

Mini Toolbar

3 Select the Text to Format

Investing to Win

4 Apply a WordArt Style

5 Change the Text to 3-D   Rotates 3-D effect   **6** Adjust the 3-D Text

100 Enter Text into a Presentation

4 Apply a WordArt Style

The **Home** ribbon not only contains standard formatting buttons such as underlining and paragraph formats (many of which are also available on the mini toolbar), but it also enables you to turn your selected slide text into WordArt text and give your text a more dramatic look.

As you pass your mouse pointer over the **WordArt** option buttons, PowerPoint's live preview shows what the slide's text will look like if you were to apply that WordArt to the selected text by clicking the **WordArt** buttons or by clicking the down arrow to the right of the **WordArt** buttons and selecting from the list that appears.

▶ TIP

The **Text Fill** and **Text Outline** buttons to the right of the **WordArt** buttons enable you change the way the WordArt text appears.

5 Change the Text to 3-D

You can convert selected text to three-dimensional text by clicking the **Format** ribbon's **Text Effects** button and selecting from the list of 3-D formats that appears.

101

6 Adjust the 3-D Text

After you apply a 3-D effect to text, you can change the rotation angle of the text. With the 3-D text selected and the sizing handles appearing, you'll see that a green circle appears at the top of the center sizing handle. Click and drag the green circle left or right to adjust the rotation angle of the 3-D text.

---

101 Find and Replace Text

✔ BEFORE YOU BEGIN	→ SEE ALSO
95 About Presentation Creation in PowerPoint	**102** Animate Text
97 Open an Existing Presentation	

When you work with large presentations, being able to locate text quickly, either to edit the text or to verify its accuracy, is vital. You don't want to step through a presentation slide by slide until you find text you want to see.

As with all the Office programs, PowerPoint offers a powerful find-and-replace command that enables you to locate text you want to find. After PowerPoint locates the text, you can request that PowerPoint automatically replace it. If, for example, you realize that your company's vice-president's name is spelled *McGuire* instead of *MacGuire*, you can quickly make PowerPoint change all the misspelled instances of the name, even if you're about to start your presentation in the next minute. (Just make sure that you don't pass out those preprinted handouts of your slides!)

■ Find the Text

Click the **Find** button to display the **Find** dialog box.

▶ TIP

You can also press Ctrl+F to display the **Find** dialog box.

■ Enter the Search Text

Type the data you want to find in the **Find What** text box. If you've searched for the same data before, you can click the down arrow to open the **Find What** drop-down list box and select the data to search for it again.

101

■ Start the Search

Click the **Find Next** button. PowerPoint searches from the current position in the presentation to the end of the presentation. If PowerPoint finds the text anywhere in the presentation, it displays the first slide that holds that text. (Unlike Word and Excel, PowerPoint doesn't offer a **Find All** button in its **Find** or **Replace** dialog boxes.)

■ Replace the Text

If you want PowerPoint to replace found text with new text, click the **Home** ribbon's **Replace** button to display the **Replace** dialog box. Type the text to locate and the text to replace that located text within the **Find What** and **Replace With** fields.

▶ TIP

You can also press Ctrl+H to display the **Find** dialog box.

■ Replace All Occurrences

If you click the **Replace All** button, PowerPoint replaces all the matches with your replacement text throughout the slide. Such a change is more global and possibly riskier because you may replace text you didn't really want replaced. By clicking **Find Next** before you click the **Replace** button, you'll be sure that

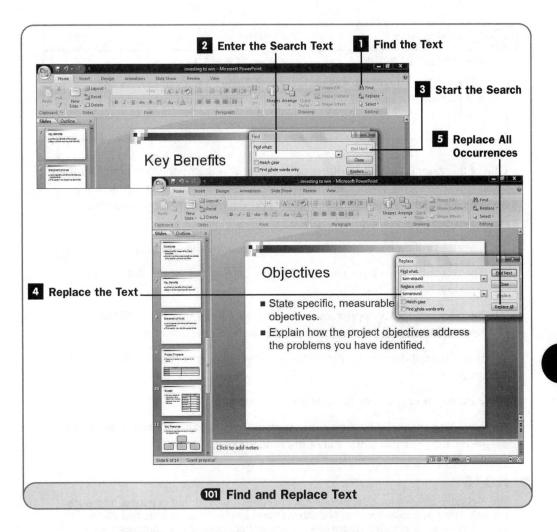

2 Enter the Search Text **1** Find the Text

3 Start the Search

5 Replace All Occurrences

4 Replace the Text

101 Find and Replace Text

the proper text is being replaced, but such a single-occurrence find-and-replacement operation takes a lot of time in a long presentation.

▶ TIP

You can click to select the **Replace** text box's **Find Whole Words Only** option if you don't want PowerPoint to find words that are contained within other words. If, for example, you want to find instances of the word *in*, you probably don't want to find every word that contains the letter combination *in*.

102 Animate Text

✔ BEFORE YOU BEGIN	→ SEE ALSO
100 Enter Text into a Presentation	**104** Use PowerPoint Layouts and Themes
101 Find and Replace Text	**110** Add Special Effects to a Presentation

One of the more interesting features of PowerPoint is its capability to animate the various text elements of your slides, producing an animated effect as the slide appears during the presentation. Consider how captivating your presentation could be when any of the following occurs:

- The title and then the rest of the text flies onto the slide from the side.

- The title falls down from the top while the bottom half of the slide rises up from the bottom edge.

- The slide's graphics appear and the text slowly fades into view. (**110 Add Special Effects to a Presentation** describes how to animate graphics.)

- Each bulleted item in the list comes onto the slide by each letter cartwheeling into view.

- Paragraphs of text fade in at different moments.

- The title of your slide bounces into view, and when it finally comes to rest at its anchored location, the rest of the slide appears.

▶ NOTE

The biggest problem with animation is not in getting it to work but in getting it to work too well. Don't overdo animation. Animated effects are fun to work with, and it's tempting to add all sorts of fades, cartwheels, wipes, and bounces. If you do, though, your presentation can become so top-heavy with animation that the message will be lost on your audience.

1 Select the Text to Animate

Click to select the text you want to animate. Opening titles make good candidates for animated text, perhaps with some music in the background as your presentation's title flies in from the side of the screen. Self-running presentations should have slightly more animation than presentations that you give, simply to keep the presentation from becoming stagnant. But even self-running presentations shouldn't overdo the effects at the expense of the content.

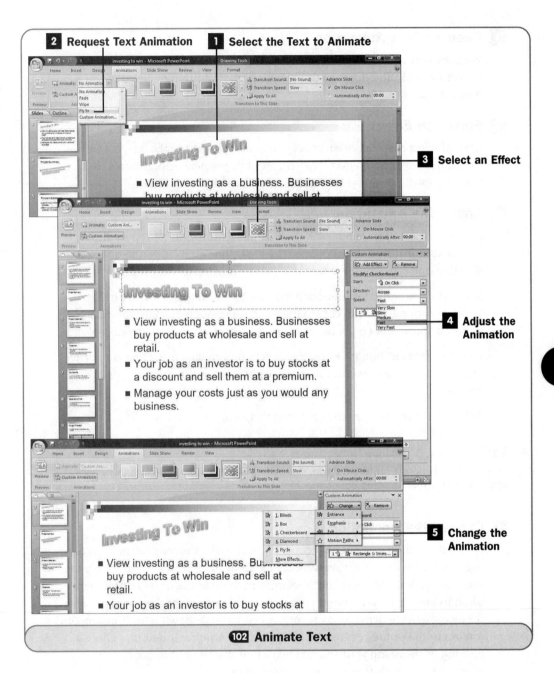

2 Request Text Animation   **1** Select the Text to Animate

3 Select an Effect

4 Adjust the Animation

5 Change the Animation

102

2 Request Text Animation

With the text still selected, click to display your **Animations** ribbon. Click the arrow to display the drop-down list box that's initially labeled **No Animation**.

3 Select an Effect

Click to select the animation effect you want the text to take on. As you run your mouse over each effect, PowerPoint's live preview demonstrates what that effect will do with your selected text.

4 Adjust the Animation

After you select animation, click the **Custom Animation** button to display the **Custom Animation** task pane. This task pane enables you to adjust the direction and speed of the animation you've applied to your slide.

Select how you want the animation to begin by selecting from the **Start** list. When presenting, you can click to trigger the animation or let the animation appear before or after other animation you may have added to the current slide.

The **Direction** list box indicates the direction from which the text is to arrive. The options in the **Direction** list vary depending on the animation you've applied.

Adjust the **Speed** to vary the animation's speed.

102

▶ **TIP**

As you select options from the **Custom Animation** task pane, PowerPoint's live preview shows you how your selected option modifies your text's animation.

5 Change the Animation

PowerPoint hasn't run out of tricks yet. Clicking the **Custom Animation** task pane's **Change** button displays lists of all kinds of options you can apply to the text. For example, text that flies in from the side might fly in and then begin to appear in a diamond pattern or perhaps in a checkerboard pattern, slowly (or quickly depending on your **Speed** setting) showing itself in random squares until the full text resides on your slide. Another interesting effect is growing or shrinking your selected text's font size when it appears on the screen, which emphasizes the message even more.

As you add animation to the rest of the slide (if you choose to), the additional text's animation effects also appear in the **Custom Animation** task pane. PowerPoint labels each animation with a number, both in the **Custom**

Animation task pane and on the slide. (Your audience won't see the animation numbers on the slide.)

By numbering the animations, you can more easily follow the order of the animation you're applying to your slides to adjust, remove, or add additional animation as you deem appropriate for your message.

---

103 Review PowerPoint Templates

✔ BEFORE YOU BEGIN	→ SEE ALSO
95 About Presentation Creation in PowerPoint	**104** Use PowerPoint Layouts and Themes
	105 Change a Presentation's Background

As **95** **About Presentation Creation in PowerPoint** explained, templates generally play a more important role in PowerPoint than in Word or Excel. You'll more often start with a template in PowerPoint due to the wide assortment of presentations available in PowerPoint's online template library. In addition, although different presentations are certainly unique in content, most presentations generally contain the same kind of slides: slides that contain easy-to-read text and graphics when appropriate.

This task is like a timeout for you during which you can explore the many templates available. The quality and content of PowerPoint templates might surprise you.

▶ **NOTE**

PowerPoint's template library contains not only presentation templates but also single slide templates. For example, you'll be able to insert a slide with the current month showing by selecting from the appropriate template.

1 Request a Template

Click your **Office** button and then click **New** to open the **New Presentation** window. If you were going to create a presentation from scratch, you would click the **Blank Presentation** to begin with a blank slate.

Creating a presentation from one that already exists is usually simpler. The templates include complete presentations with all their details that you can change, as well as presentations with placeholders where your details will go.

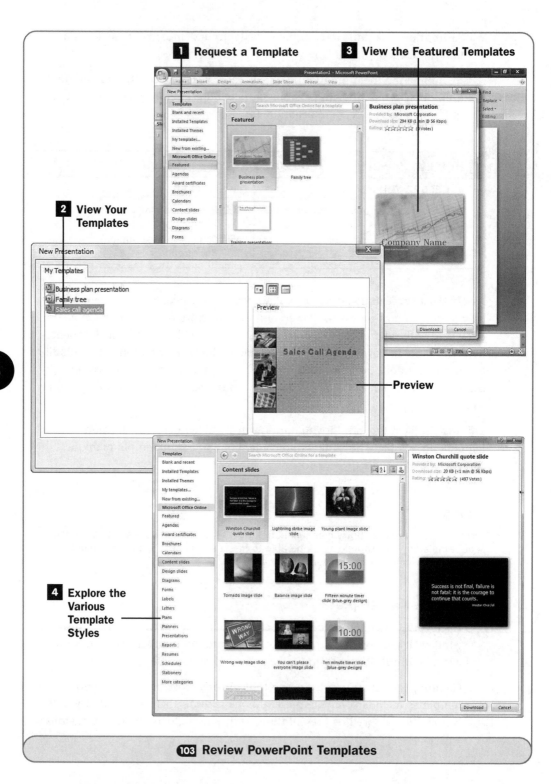

103 Review PowerPoint Templates

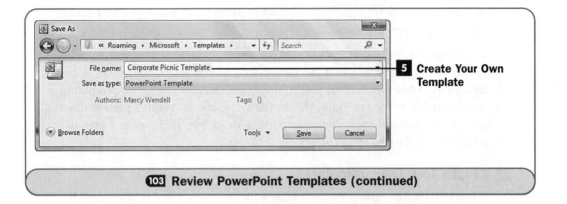

103 Review PowerPoint Templates (continued)

▶ **TIP**

If you click the **New from Existing** button, PowerPoint creates a new presentation from an existing presentation, in effect creating a copy of the existing presentation. After you make changes to the new presentation, PowerPoint won't allow you to overwrite the original file you used as a model.

2 View Your Templates

If you click the **My templates** button, PowerPoint displays the **My Templates** page with presentation templates on your computer. These include templates you've created as well as templates that PowerPoint installed on your computer. Clicking once over a template will often provide you with a preview of that template in the **Preview** area. You can click one of your templates and then **OK** to create a new presentation based on that template, or click **Cancel** to return to the **New Presentation** window.

3 View the Featured Templates

PowerPoint displays something different almost every time you display the **New Presentation** window in the **Microsoft Office Online** area. There you'll see featured templates and new templates that Microsoft placed on its template website. In addition, you'll find helpful online tips and web pages that you can browse by clicking the links in the **Microsoft Office Online** area.

▶ **NOTE**

If you click one of the links to web content, Internet Explorer opens to that page. PowerPoint's **New Presentation** window remains open.

4 Explore the Various Template Styles

Click through the template categories on the left of the **New Presentation** window to view the many templates available to you. You'll find complete presentations as well as presentations with placeholders where you can insert your own text and graphics.

You might be surprised at the kinds of presentations available to you. In addition to the usual training and teaching presentations, templates are available for creating schedules such as project timelines; resumes (useful for promoting yourself online when you fill in the details and place the resume presentation on a website); diagrams for various sporting, academic, and business presentations; agendas; and even calendars.

5 Create Your Own Template

When you create a new presentation, whether you've created it from scratch or from an existing template, you can turn that presentation into a new template. By doing so, you eliminate much of the formatting work the next time you want to create a similar presentation.

Prepare the presentation to be saved as a template by going through the slides and editing them to eliminate specific content and by placing placeholder text messages such as Bullet Point #1, Bullet Point #2, and Bullet Point #3 in the places you'll fill in when you use the template as the basis for a new presentation.

After you've finalized the presentation, click your **Office** button and select **Save As**. Name the template. For the **Save as Type** field, click to select **PowerPoint Template**. When you click **Save**, PowerPoint adds the template to your list of available templates.

104

---

104   Use PowerPoint Layouts and Themes

✔ BEFORE YOU BEGIN	→ SEE ALSO
16 About Styles, Themes, and Templates **103** Review PowerPoint Templates	**105** Change a Presentation's Background

---

A layout determines where text, graphics, charts, and other elements appear on an individual slide. A theme determines the look of an entire presentation's colors, fonts, and overall format. A layout is to a slide what a theme is to an entire presentation. Both specify the way a slide or overall presentation looks.

Themes are universal across Word, Excel, and PowerPoint. You can use predefined themes that come with PowerPoint, or you can define your own. If you create a company-wide theme, you can apply that theme to all your Microsoft Office documents to apply a standardized look.

◼ Select a Style for a New Slide

When you click your **Home** ribbon's **New Slide** button's lower half (with text and the arrow), PowerPoint opens a layout list from which you can select. When you click to select a layout, PowerPoint inserts a new slide at that location in your presentation with that layout.

▶ **TIP**

If you clicked the **Add Slide** button's top half with the icon, PowerPoint inserts a new slide into your presentation with the same layout as the slide that was showing before you clicked **Add Slide**.

◻ Change a Slide's Layout

You can change the layout used for any slide. If you just inserted a new slide and want to change the layout, right-click over an empty place on the slide, select **Layout** from the pop-up menu, and select a new layout.

You can also change a slide's layout that already has text and graphics, but the target layout may not retain all the original text and graphics if the target layout has no place for all the text and graphics you had on the slide originally.

104

▶ **NOTE**

A slide can hold text, graphics, charts, SmartArt, and videos. Your layouts determine where those elements go.

◻ Modify a Slide's Layout

After you apply a layout to a slide, you can adjust the size and positioning of that layout's elements.

Click any layout's field to display the sizing handles. You can drag a corner to resize the layout's field or click inside the field and drag your mouse to move that layout field to a different location on the slide.

▶ **TIP**

If you change your mind and want to restore the layout to its original state, right-click over an empty area on your slide and select **Reset**.

◻ Request a Theme

Click your **Design** ribbon to bring up a list of themes that you can apply to your presentation. Click the down arrow to the right of the ribbon's themes to see additional themes.

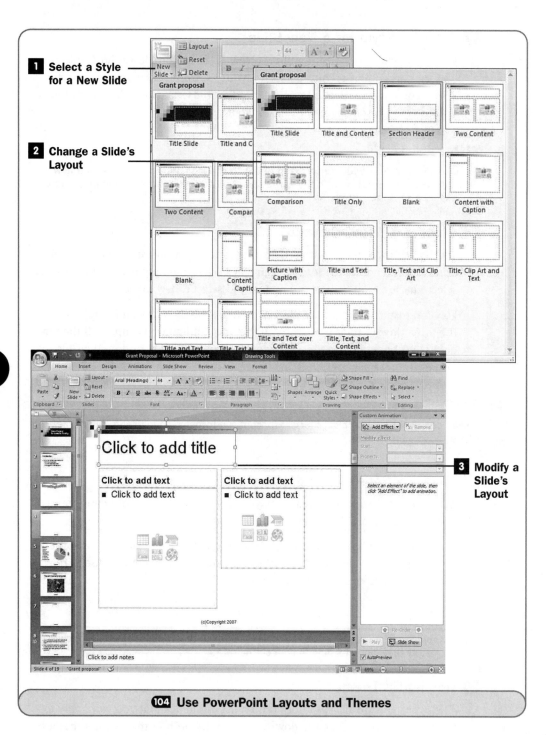

104 Use PowerPoint Layouts and Themes

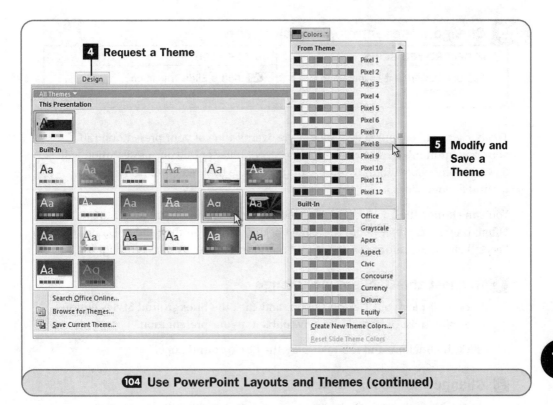

104 Use PowerPoint Layouts and Themes (continued)

As you move your mouse pointer over each theme, PowerPoint's live preview shows what your presentation will look like if you apply that theme.

5 Modify and Save a Theme

Select from the **Font**, **Colors**, and **Effects** buttons to the right of the **Themes** group on your **Design** ribbon to change individual theme elements. You might do this if you've used a theme that is close but not exactly the style you want your final presentation to take on.

After you've modified a theme to your liking, click the down arrow next to the ribbon's themes and select **Save Current Theme**. After you've named the theme, PowerPoint makes that theme available in the future so that you won't have to customize a different theme again to achieve the current look.

▶ **TIP**

Your new theme will be available for Excel and Word documents, too. Just click to select from their theme list to see and apply any theme you've created in PowerPoint.

105 Change a Presentation's Background

✔ BEFORE YOU BEGIN	→ SEE ALSO
104 Use PowerPoint Layouts and Themes	**111** Add a Slide Transition

The background of your slide provides the overall tone of your presentation. If your presentation's background appears in cool blue tones, your presentation will feel far more relaxed than if you use bright orange and red tones in the background of your slides.

You can change the background of a single slide or of your entire presentation. Often, presenters prefer to use the same background on all their slides. Doing so keeps their presentations consistent and maintains a similar mood throughout.

1 Request the Background Change

Click to display your **Design** ribbon, and click the **Background Styles** button to display a list of backgrounds available for your presentation.

Click the **Background** tab to display the **Background** page.

2 Change the Background

As you scroll through the background images, PowerPoint's live preview shows what your presentation will look like if you apply that background.

▶ **TIP**

You can elect to show no background (a white background) by clicking the first option called **Style 1**. This, in effect, removes the background from all your slides.

3 Customize the Background

Click the **Background** button at the bottom of the list of backgrounds to display the **Format Background** dialog box. The **Format Background** dialog box is where you can customize your presentation's background to include colors and images you want to place on all your presentation's slides.

The **Fill** options determine whether the slides' background will be filled with your selected color, and if so how that color (or colors) is to fill the background. You can request no fill (leaving a white background), a solid fill, or a *gradient* fill from one color to another. If you elect to perform a gradient fill, the **Format Background** dialog box's options increase so that you can adjust exactly how that gradient fill will occur. For example, you might want the gradient colors to change from one to another across your slides diagonally or

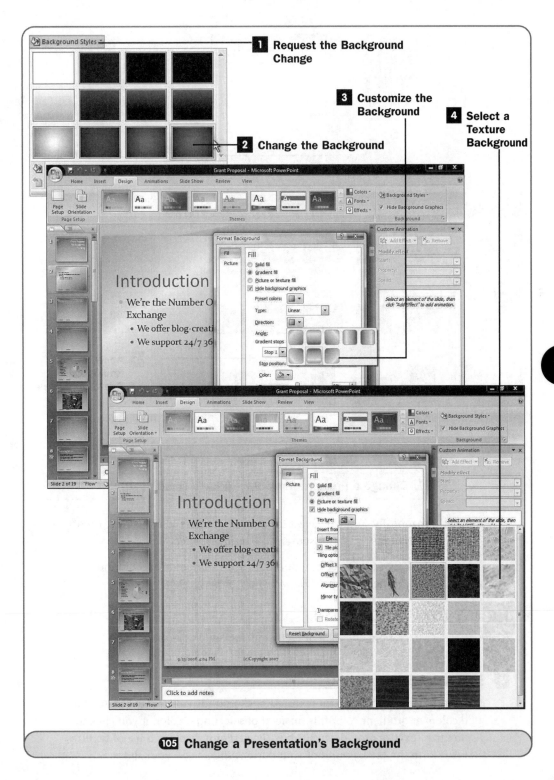

1 Request the Background Change

3 Customize the Background

4 Select a Texture Background

2 Change the Background

105

105 Change a Presentation's Background

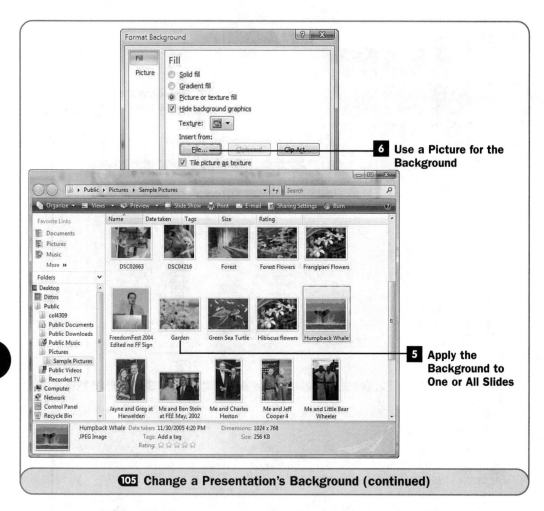

6 Use a Picture for the Background

5 Apply the Background to One or All Slides

105 Change a Presentation's Background (continued)

perhaps horizontally. You can select from a list of colors to use for the gradients, as well as adjust how transparent the gradient effect is.

The **Hide Background Objects** option determines whether background graphics you've placed on the slide will show or be hidden.

▶ **NEW TERM**

Gradient—A transition from one color or pattern to another on the same slide.

4 Select a Texture Background

PowerPoint comes with several textured backgrounds you can use instead of solid colors or gradient color fills. Instead of selecting a color, if you click to display the **Texture** drop-down list box, PowerPoint displays a list of textures that can form the background of your current slide or all your slides.

5 Apply the Background to One or All Slides

The way you close the **Format Background** dialog box determines whether the background is to apply to the currently selected slide or to your entire presentation's set of slides.

Click the **Close** button to apply the background to the current slide only. Click the **Apply to All** button to apply the background you've selected to your entire set of slides.

▶ **NOTE**

If you're used to previous versions of PowerPoint that used a *slide master* concept, you may be interested to know that PowerPoint 2007 does support a slide master. However, with the background tools on the **Design** ribbon, you really don't need to use a slide master to easily adjust a slide's background or your entire presentation's background.

▶ **NEW TERM**

Slide master—A slide that determines how certain elements, such as background color, will appear on all slides in a presentation.

6 Use a Picture for the Background

If you click the **Format Background** dialog box's **File** button, PowerPoint displays the **Insert Picture** dialog box, from which you can select a background graphic for your slides. You might want to place a watermark on your slides with your company name or logo, for example.

▶ **TIP**

A watermark with a copyright notice might be good to place on every slide before printing slide handouts. You can remove the copyright notice after you've printed the handouts so that it doesn't appear on every slide you present during your live presentation.

105

13

Making More Impressive Presentations

IN THIS CHAPTER:

The more pizzazz and flair you add to your presentations, the more responsive your audiences will be. PowerPoint will help you drive home your point with several advanced features. Your presentations won't be boring. You can add charts and import graphics to spruce up your presentations. You can also animate graphics and determine special slide transitions so that the movement from slide to slide follows the same tone as that of your presentation.

The notes feature enables you to add your own private speaker's notes to your slides so that you always remember important points you want to make. Your audience will also appreciate it when you print a copy of your presentation for them to take. PowerPoint doesn't stop with live presentations; you can create automated presentations that repeat themselves, and you can easily put your PowerPoint presentations on the Web for the world to view.

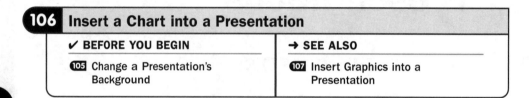

| **106** | **Insert a Chart into a Presentation** |

✔ BEFORE YOU BEGIN	→ SEE ALSO
105 Change a Presentation's Background	**107** Insert Graphics into a Presentation

106

A chart can summarize presentation data, and audiences often glean information from charts that they might not otherwise get from long lists of data or from your listing scores of numbers for them. So you'll often want to use charts in your presentations to make your data more available to your audience.

▶ **NOTE**

The term *chart* here is used in the same manner that Excel uses the term. A chart is a graph of data. You can also insert tables of data in an Excel slide by clicking the table icon instead of the chart icon.

▶ **TIP**

82 Add a Chart to a Worksheet, although an Excel-based task, describes charts and terminology related to them. If you are unfamiliar with Office chart types, take a few minutes to review this task.

1 Request a Chart

You can insert a chart in any slide. If the slide contains a chart placeholder (a small icon of a chart among a group of five other icons for table, clip art, picture, SmartArt, or video), double-click that placeholder to add the chart to the slide. PowerPoint displays the **Create Chart** dialog box.

▶ **NOTE**

The text prompt **Click to add text** goes away when you insert a chart into the slide instead of typing text in its place.

If the slide doesn't contain a placeholder, choose **Chart** from the **Insert** ribbon. PowerPoint opens the **Insert Chart** dialog box. When you select a chart, it will be inserted at your current cursor's position on the slide.

2 Select a Chart Type

Click to select a chart from the inventory of chart types in the **Create Chart** dialog box. Click **OK** to request that specific chart type.

3 Enter the Chart Data

The moment you request a chart, Excel opens on half your screen, with your slide showing on the other half. You must enter the data for the chart. PowerPoint sends Excel some sample data and titles to get you started.

▶ **TIP**

If you copy a chart from Excel, you can paste that chart directly onto a slide without entering the data.

4 Adjust the Chart

After you enter the data and close Excel, you can position and format the chart on your slide.

Select from the **Chart Layouts** group on your **Chart Tools Design** ribbon that appears. You can change any element of your chart, such as the legend location and the chart colors. You can even click the **Change Chart Type** button to change the type of chart displayed to another type using the same data.

Click on any chart element, such as the title, to move, resize, or change that element.

▶ **TIP**

82 **Add a Chart to a Worksheet** describes each chart type and the best use for each one.

106

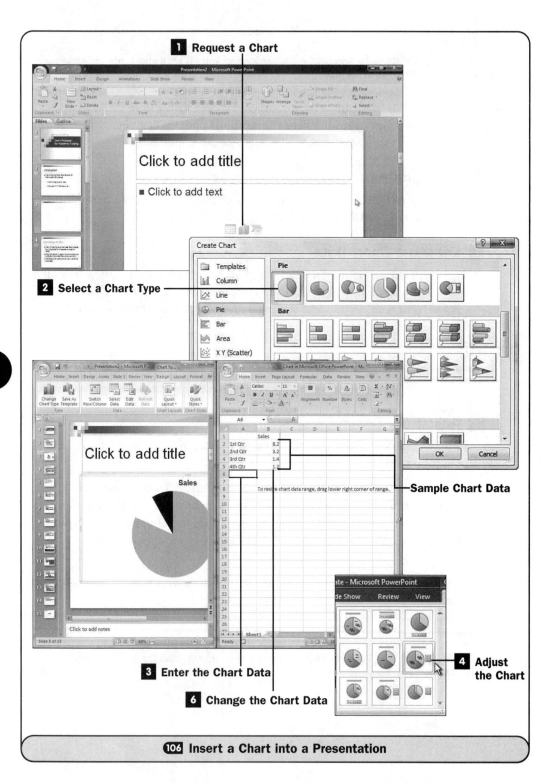

1 Request a Chart

2 Select a Chart Type

3 Enter the Chart Data

6 Change the Chart Data

4 Adjust the Chart

Sample Chart Data

106 Insert a Chart into a Presentation

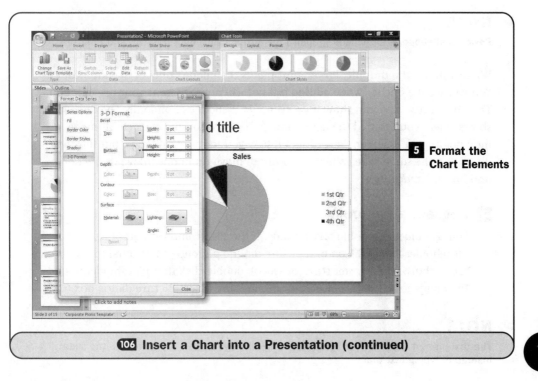

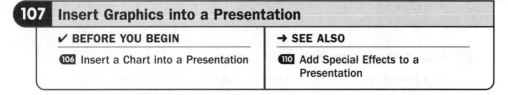

106 Insert a Chart into a Presentation (continued)

107

5 Format the Chart Elements

Right-clicking over any chart element produces a menu that includes a **Format** command. For example, right-clicking the legend displays the **Format Legend** dialog box, where you can adjust all aspects of those data labels, including whether or not they take on a 3-D appearance.

6 Change the Chart Data

Click anywhere on the chart and then click to display your **Design** ribbon when you want to change the data used in the chart. Excel opens once again, and you can change the data to change the chart.

107 Insert Graphics into a Presentation

✔ BEFORE YOU BEGIN	→ SEE ALSO
106 Insert a Chart into a Presentation	**110** Add Special Effects to a Presentation

PowerPoint enables you to put pictures throughout your presentation slides. Perhaps you'll want to stress your point when giving a motivational speech, for example, by showing a runner winning a race.

▶ **NOTE**

PowerPoint supports all popular graphics file formats, including JPG, GIF, and BMP files.

When you insert a graphic, PowerPoint places the image's anchor at that location. You will see the anchor when editing but not when you present your presentation. The anchor also does not show if you print your slides as handouts. The anchor shows where you inserted the actual image. The anchor and the actual image may not appear together, depending on how you format the image, but they will appear on the same slide. When you want to move an image, move its anchor and not the image itself.

❶ Request a Picture

You can place a graphic on any slide. If the slide contains a graphics placeholder (a small icon of a picture among a group of five other icons for table, chart, clip art, SmartArt, or video), double-click that placeholder to add the image to the slide. PowerPoint displays the **Insert Picture** dialog box.

▶ **NOTE**

107

The text prompt **Click to Add Text** goes away when you insert a picture into the slide instead of typing text there.

If the slide doesn't contain a placeholder, choose **Picture** from the **Insert** ribbon. PowerPoint opens the **Insert Picture** dialog box, and when you select a picture from a graphics file, PowerPoint places it at your current cursor's position on the slide.

▶ **TIP**

You can insert a clip art image instead of a picture from a graphics file by following these same steps and selecting from Microsoft's clip art gallery of images.

❷ Select a Graphics File

Click to select an image from your disk or another location such as a networked storage area you have access to. Click **Insert** to place the image in your slide.

❸ Adjust the Image Size and Location

After PowerPoint places the image on your slide, sizing handles appear around the image that you can click to resize. Clicking an edge where no sizing handles appear produces a four-sided arrow mouse cursor that you can use to move the image.

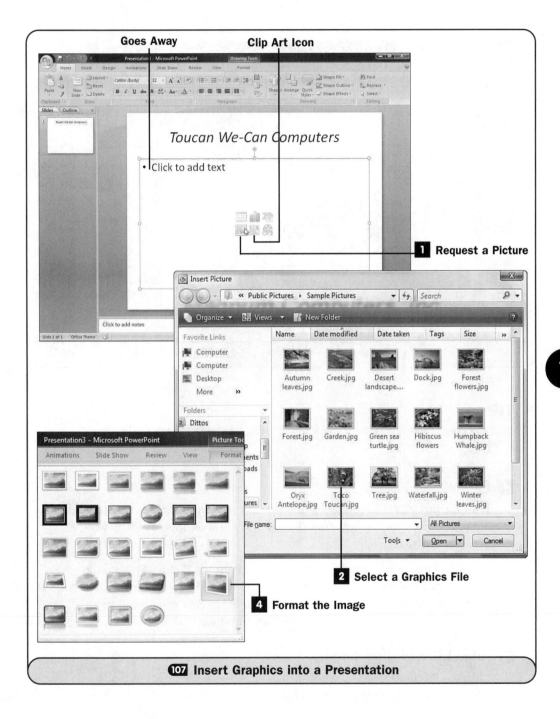

107 Insert Graphics into a Presentation

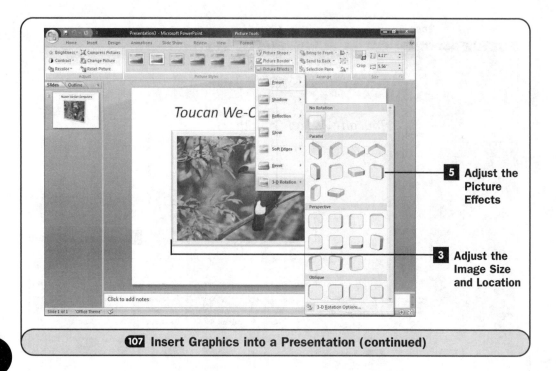

107 Insert Graphics into a Presentation (continued)

▶ **TIP**
Drag the green circle above the image's center sizing handle to change the image's rotation.

4 Format the Image

With the picture's sizing handles still showing, you can format various aspects of the image on the **Picture Tools Format** ribbon that appears whenever the image is selected.

You can change the picture style by selecting from the **Picture Styles** group. PowerPoint's live preview mode activates, and the picture updates as you run your mouse pointer over each picture style so that you'll know what the image will look like after you apply that picture style to it.

5 Adjust the Picture Effects

Click the **Picture Effects** arrow to display additional rotational and 3-D effects you can apply to your picture.

You can also change the border around the picture with the **Picture Border** button and adjust the picture's shape with the **Picture Shape** button. Other control buttons such as **Brightness** and **Contrast** appear across your ribbon as well.

▶ **TIP**

Select the **Compress Pictures** button to shrink the size of your presentation's pictures with slight denigration in their quality. This shrinks your presentation for those times when you want to send it to others attached to an email. You might want to keep two versions of your presentation, one with regular-size images and one with compressed images.

---

108 **Add a Presentation Header or Footer**

✔ BEFORE YOU BEGIN	→ SEE ALSO
95 About Presentation Creation in PowerPoint	**114** Create Presentation Handouts
98 Give a Presentation	

108

You can apply a header or footer to one specific slide or to all slides in your presentation. In addition, when you do add a header or footer to all the slides in your presentation, you can elect to hide the header and footer on your presentation's first slide. (Title slides often have no header or footer.)

At first glance, PowerPoint appears to support headers, but when you add one, you'll see that the "header" appears at the bottom of your slides beginning in the left margin. A footer falls at the bottom of a slide in the middle of slides. After you add a header, you can reposition the header so that it appears at the top of each slide if you want.

You may add the date, time, or slide number (referred to as the *page number*) in a header or footer area. When that slide appears during your presentation, the current date or time at that moment appears in the header or footer area. You may also add a header or footer with fixed text, such as a copyright message or company email and website.

1 **Request a Header or Footer**

Click to select the **Insert** ribbon and click the **Header & Footer** button to display the **Header and Footer** dialog box.

2 Select the Date and Time

To place the date and time in the slide's header, click to select **Date and Time** and be sure to click to select **Update Automatically**. You must also select the format for the date and time by clicking to open the date-formatting list box and selecting the format you want to use. If you want only the time to display, select a format that shows only the time.

3 Add a Fixed Header

Instead of adding the date and time, you can add your own header, such as a copyright notice. Click to select **Fixed** and type the message to be used for the header.

If you want to use both the date and time and a fixed message, the date and time will appear at the left edge of the bottom of each slide, and the fixed message must be a footer that appears in the center of each slide to the right of the date and time.

▶ **TIP**

108

PowerPoint displays the slide number of each slide in the slide's lower-right corner if you click to select the **Slide Number** option.

If you don't want your header and footer to show on your presentation's first slide, click to select the option labeled **Don't Show on Title Slide**.

4 Choose Which Slides Display the Header and Footer

Click the **Apply to All** button to apply your header and footer to all slides in your presentation (with the possible exception of the title slide if you chose not to apply the header and footer to your title slide). Click the **Apply** button to apply the header and footer only to the currently selected slide.

5 Select the Header and Footer for Notes and Handouts

Click the **Header and Footer** dialog box's **Notes and Handouts** tab to add headers and footers to your speaker notes and to slide handouts that you print. These can be the same as or different from your presentation slide's header and footer messages, although you apply the notes and handout headers and footers in the same manner as the slides' headers and footers.

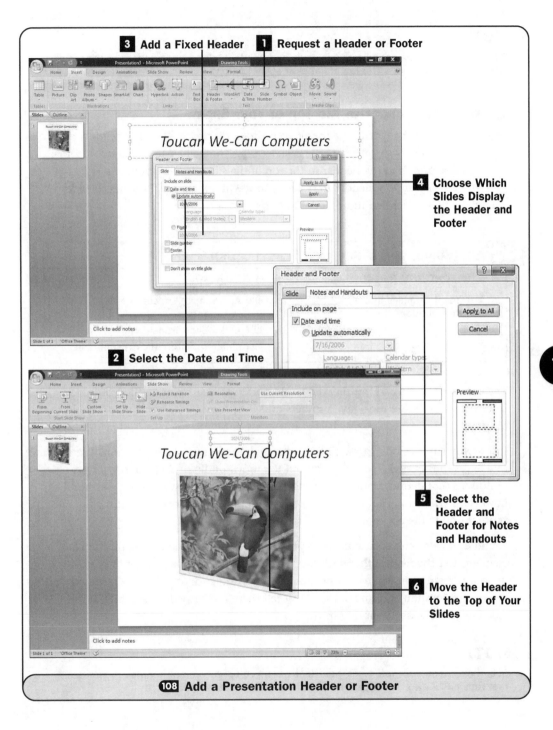

3 Add a Fixed Header   1 Request a Header or Footer

4 Choose Which Slides Display the Header and Footer

2 Select the Date and Time

5 Select the Header and Footer for Notes and Handouts

6 Move the Header to the Top of Your Slides

108

108 Add a Presentation Header or Footer

▶ **NOTE**

The headers that you define for your notes and handouts actually *do* appear at the top of the notes and handouts. The footers appear at the bottom.

6 **Move the Header to the Top of Your Slides**

To move your header to the top of your slides, display a slide that holds the header in the lower-left corner of a slide. Click the header to display its sizing handles, and drag the header to the top of the slide. Release your mouse where you want the header to reside, and it will appear up there on all slides where you've defined that header to appear.

---

109   **Add Sound and Video to a Presentation**

✔ BEFORE YOU BEGIN	→ SEE ALSO
107 Insert Graphics into a Presentation	**110** Add Special Effects to a Presentation
	111 Add a Slide Transition
	112 Make an Automatic Presentation

109

The computer world is a multimedia world and has been for more than a decade. Data consists of more than just numbers and characters. Data is active, it's audible, it's visual.

Just as you can overdo a presentation with too many graphics, extra-fancy fonts, and excess animations, you also can put too much audio and video in your presentations that detract from the message you want to portray. On the other hand, however, never think that a presentation is inappropriate for such multimedia content—quite the opposite!

Sound and video can spruce up your presentation. You can add those multimedia elements to activate an otherwise-static presentation. Perhaps you get to a point in your presentation where you need to tell your audience about a new training video your company produces. Don't just tell them but *show them* samples of the video as you describe your offerings.

▶ **NOTE**

Sound and video are even more important when you produce an automated presentation that runs on its own (see **112** Make an Automatic Presentation).

1 Request an Audio Clip

Click to display your **Insert** ribbon. To the right is a group labeled **Media Clips**. This is where you go to insert audio and video clips into your presentation.

2 Determine the Audio Source

Click the down arrow below the **Sound** button to display your audio options. You can insert sound from a sound file (such as a .wav file or an .mp3); insert a sound from Microsoft's Clip organizer gallery, which includes not only clip art images but also sound and video files; play a CD audio track (the CD must be in your CD-ROM drive to play the track at the time you add the audio and give your presentation), or record a new audio file using a sound recorder (you must have a microphone or audio input). Select Sound from Clip Organizer to open the Clip Art pane.

3 Describe How the Sound Starts

A sound can begin as soon as the slide appears in the presentation or only after you, the presenter, click the speaker icon that represents the sound. PowerPoint asks which you prefer.

109

▶ **NOTE**

For automatic presentations that run on their own, you'll want the sound to begin automatically.

4 Adjust the Sound Properties

When you click the speaker icon that represents the sound, PowerPoint changes to the **Sound Tools Options** ribbon, where you can control how the sound plays. You can loop the sound until you stop it during a presentation, play a long sound across many slides (meaning that the sound for the current slide doesn't stop when you move to the next slide), fix the sound's volume for play during the presentation, and limit the size of the sound file so that extra-large sounds (such as long MP3s) aren't included in the presentation, which is useful if you send your presentation as an email attachment or perhaps if you send your presentation to a web page that needs to load quickly.

5 Request a Video File

As with sound, you insert video clips into a presentation from the **Insert** ribbon. By clicking the down arrow on the **Movie** button, you determine whether you want to insert a video clip from an existing file on your computer or from Microsoft's online clip gallery.

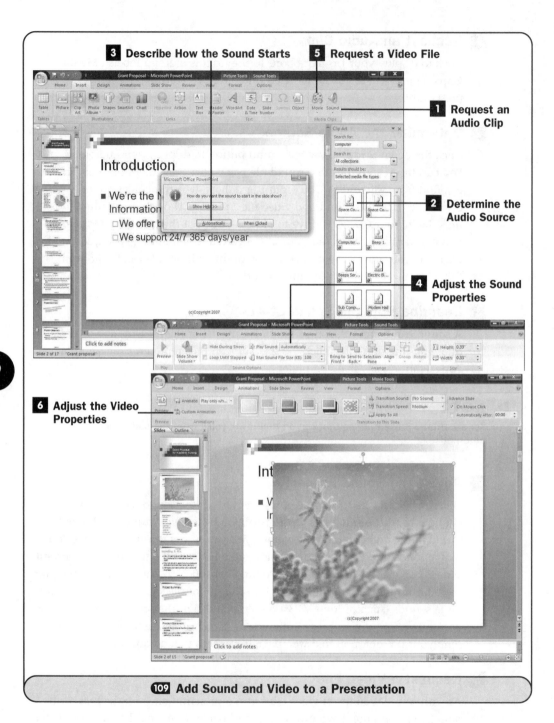

109 Add Sound and Video to a Presentation

▶ **NOTE**

A graphics image can be stored as a JPG file, a GIF file, or other kind of graphics image format available to the computer user. GIF files can be animated and are not always static pictures. That is why Microsoft's clip gallery includes several GIF images when you request a video.

6 Adjust the Video Properties

As with sound files, when you insert a video file into your presentation, PowerPoint needs to know whether you want the video to start automatically as soon as the slide appears during a presentation or only when you click the movie's image. (The image will show you the opening cell of the video.)

After you insert the video, or anytime thereafter when you click on the image that represents the video, your ribbon changes to the **Movie Tools Options** ribbon, where you can further refine the video's properties.

110	**Add Special Effects to a Presentation**

✔ **BEFORE YOU BEGIN**	→ **SEE ALSO**
102 Animate Text	**111** Add a Slide Transition
107 Insert Graphics into a Presentation	

110

Adding special effects to graphics and other presentation elements can really make your presentation come alive. You can make graphics images fly onto the screen, not unlike the animated text you can cause to roll into place (see **102 Animate Text**). As with any special effects, don't overdo them. Reserve them for when you want to make an impression at a particularly important part of your presentation.

▶ **NOTE**

You can apply special effects to many items. These are more pronounced than the simpler animated text you can also place in text boxes. Most often you'll apply animations to graphics images because they can fly in during a presentation at the request of your mouse click. (PowerPoint can begin an animation automatically, from a mouse click, based on a timer, or linked to another animation that comes before it.)

Here are just a few of the effects you can apply to graphics and other presentation elements with PowerPoint:

- The object flies in from outside the slide.

- A laser-like show produces the object.

- The object fades into place.

- The slide sparkles, slowly producing the object from the moving glitter.

- The object (graphics text works well here) snakes into the slide from one of the edges.

- The object spirals into place.

◼ Select a Presentation Element

Click to select an element in your presentation, such as a graphics image or a text box. You must first click to select the object before you can apply an effect to it.

◼ Request an Animation Effect

Click to display your **Animations** ribbon. The icons in the **Transition to This Slide** group affect your slide transitions (see ◼ **Add a Slide Transition**) and aren't intended as special effects for specific objects within your slide.

The **Animations** group to the left does affect the way your specific objects such as selected graphics images animate on the slide. Click to display a list of animations available for your image. Three simple animations appear at the top of the list: **Fade**, **Wipe**, and **Fly In**. As you move your mouse pointer over these options, PowerPoint's live preview shows how that effect will look if you were to select it for the image.

◼ Request the Custom Animation Task Pane

With the image still selected, click the **Custom Animation** button to apply more advanced animation effects. The **Custom Animation** task pane appears. You can close the **Slides** pane if you need a larger view of the current slide after the **Custom Animation** task pane opens.

▶ NOTE

Most of the special effects that appear in the **Animation Effects** dialog box are also available as slide transitions. See ◼ **Add a Slide Transition**.

◼ Select the Effect You Want

The **Add Effect** button contains four special-effects groups that you can add to the selected object. Click **Add Effect** to see each choice available.

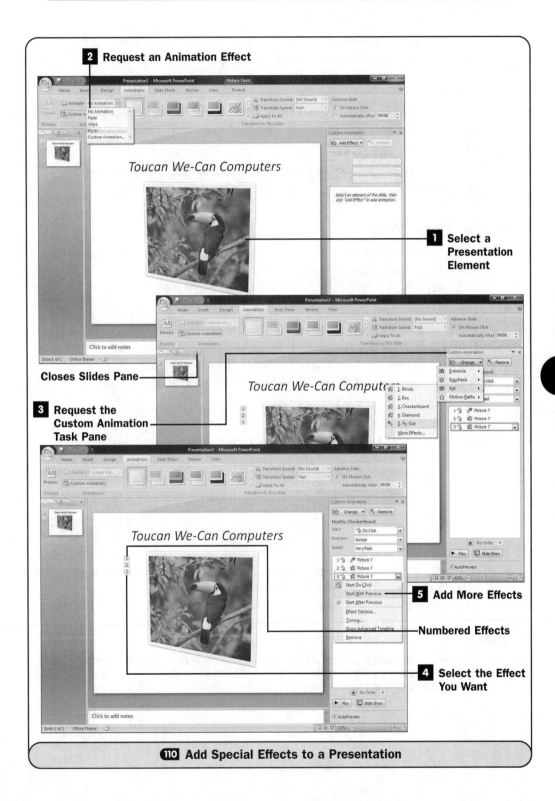

2 Request an Animation Effect

1 Select a Presentation Element

Closes Slides Pane

3 Request the Custom Animation Task Pane

5 Add More Effects

Numbered Effects

4 Select the Effect You Want

110

110 Add Special Effects to a Presentation

You can choose an **Entrance** effect to control how the selected object first appears (such as flying in from the left), an **Emphasis** effect to control how the object behaves on the slide (such as spinning in place), an **Exit** effect to control how the selected object leaves the screen (if you choose to remove the object after it's done with its special effect), and **Motion Paths** that add motion to the object (such as having the object move along an oval-shaped path).

These four special effects are organized into categories such as **Down** and **Checkerboard** to help you find and adjust the look of the animation.

5 Add More Effects

You can select multiple effects for the image. For example, you can select an entrance effect and an exit effect. If your slide contains multiple items, you can apply different special effects to the various elements on the slide.

Each time you add a special effect, PowerPoint numbers that effect and begins to build a list in the **Custom Animation** task pane. Each effect comes with a default **Start**, **Direction**, and **Speed** option, and you can change each of those to modify the way your special effect begins (such as with a mouse click), the direction of entry, and the animation effect's speed.

You can right-click over any item in the list of special effects to remove that particular special effect or to change it. Drag a special effect up or down if you want to rearrange the effects. (The **Re-Order** buttons toward the bottom also move selected effects up or down.) For example, you might inadvertently add an exit effect before adding an entry effect, and you would need to reverse the order of those effects.

▶ **TIP**

Each effect occurs when you select one, but to see all the effects for the slide, click the **Play** button in your **Custom Animation** task pane.

▶ **NOTE**

Click the **AutoPreview** button to turn off the automatic preview of each effect as you apply it. Sometimes the movement is distracting until you've applied a few special effects and can see the big picture of the start-to-finish effect.

111 Add a Slide Transition

✔ BEFORE YOU BEGIN	→ SEE ALSO
109 Add Sound and Video to a Presentation	**112** Make an Automatic Presentation
110 Add Special Effects to a Presentation	

Adding a transition between slides is very much like adding special effects to graphics and other objects on your slides (see **110** **Add Special Effects to a Presentation**). Instead of applying a special effect to a graphics image, you apply the special effect to the next transition. For example, a rolling transition would bring the next slide into view, during an automatic slide show or when you request the slide during a presentation, by rolling it in from one of the edges as it slowly overrides the previous slide.

You can apply a different transition to each slide throughout your presentation. In addition, you can apply the same transition to multiple slides. As with any special effect, don't overdo it because it's your presentation's message that is more important than the look of the physical presentation.

1 Select the First Slide for a Transition

Move to the slide that is to take on the transition. In other words, if you want the second slide in your presentation to appear on the screen through a special animated transition, display the second slide.

2 Request the Transition

Click to display the **Animations** ribbon. The **Transition to This Slide** group holds the transitional effects available to you.

3 Select a Transition

Move your mouse over any transition to watch a preview of that transition in your slide-editing area. Click the down arrow to the right of the screen icons to display an expanded list of transitions.

4 Modify the Transition

You can apply a sound to your transition's effect as well as change the speed of the transition and adjust how the slide transitions to the next slide with the other buttons in the **Transition to This Slide** group.

To apply a sound, click the down arrow and choose a sound. PowerPoint will play that sound as the transition occurs. The **Transition Speed** options allow you to adjust for a **Slow**, **Medium**, or **Fast** transition to the current slide.

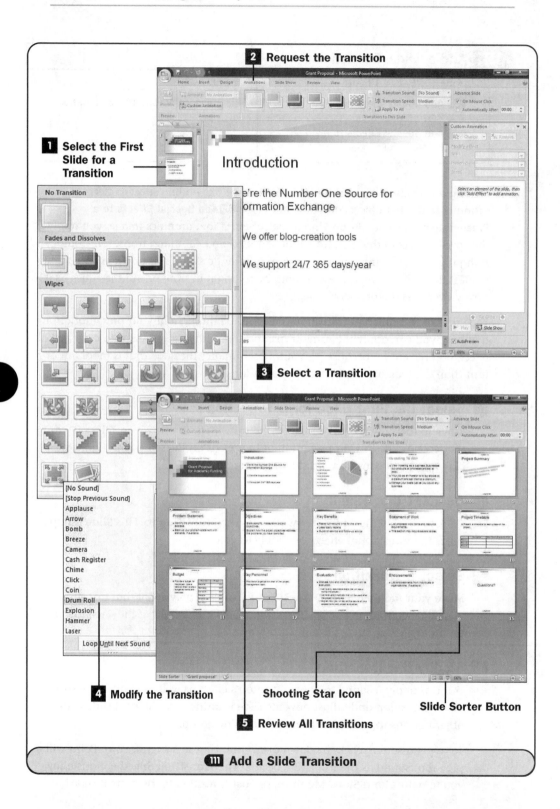

2 Request the Transition

1 Select the First Slide for a Transition

3 Select a Transition

4 Modify the Transition

Shooting Star Icon

Slide Sorter Button

5 Review All Transitions

111 Add a Slide Transition

▶ **TIP**

If you want to apply your transition to all slides in your presentation, click the **Apply to All** button. Generally, you shouldn't apply a spectacular transition to every slide due to the overuse of such an effect.

You can also control whether the transition occurs manually or automatically in the **Advance Slide** section. If you want the transition to occur automatically after a certain time, select the **Automatically After** option. In the text box, designate the amount of time the slide should stay onscreen.

▶ **NOTE**

If you're controlling your own presentation (as opposed to creating an automatic presentation), leave the **On Mouse Click** option checked so that the transition doesn't occur until you click the mouse button or press the spacebar during your presentation.

5 **Review All Transitions**

Review your slide show by running through it from the **Slide Show** ribbon. Make sure that your transitional effects work the way you want them to work.

If you click the **Slide Sorter** button, PowerPoint displays multiple slides from your presentation on your screen. Any slide with a shooting star icon is a slide that will transition when you first display that slide during your presentation. Clicking over that slide in your **Slide Sorter** view shows a thumbnail action of that slide's transition.

▶ **NOTE**

The shooting star icon appears both for slides with transitions defined and for slides with special effects applied. Clicking the icon activates both the transition and the special effect for your review if the slide contains both a transition and a special effect.

112 **Make an Automatic Presentation**	
✔ **BEFORE YOU BEGIN**	→ **SEE ALSO**
95 About Presentation Creation in PowerPoint	**115** Turn a Presentation into Online Web Pages
97 Open an Existing Presentation	

An automated slide show is useful for creating self-running demonstrations, product presentations, and conference information distribution. You can control each detail of a self-running slide show, add special and transition effects, and ensure that the show automatically runs within a given time frame.

▶ **NOTE**

The terms *kiosk* and *kiosk presentation* are other terms for automatic presentations that run without user control.

① Prepare the Slides for Automation

After you've designed your presentation's slides and added any transitions, click to display your **Slide Show** ribbon.

Determine which slides you want to use in the automatic presentation. Most often, you'll show all slides; but if you want to hide one or more slides, press Page Down to get to each slide you want to hide and click the **Hide Slide** button. (Clicking the button once again will display the slide.)

② Set Up an Automated Show

Click the **Set Up Slide Show** button to display the **Set Up Show** dialog box.

Here you determine how your slides will display. The default method is **Presented by a Speaker**, in which you as the presenter step through the slides in front of an audience. You can also select **Browsed by an Individual**, which displays the slide show in a window on the computer that an individual at the computer can step through. **Browsed at a Kiosk** sets up the slide show for full automation to run on its own.

Click to select the **Using Timings, If Present** option so that the presentation steps through its slides on its own.

The remaining options section of the **Set Up Show** dialog box enables you to select various options for your automated presentations, such as whether you want animations to show throughout the automatic presentation. Click **OK** to close the **Set Up Show** dialog box.

③ Add Optional Narration

If you'd like to speak over the slides as they advance, you can add narration to your slide show. Click the **Record Narration** button to display the **Record Narration** dialog box. After you test your microphone level and adjust the sound quality, click the **OK** button to start recording. PowerPoint prompts you to see whether you want to add narration to your entire presentation or only to the selected slide. As you record your voice over each slide, click your mouse or press Page Down to move through the presentation. Press Esc when you want to end the recording of your narration.

112

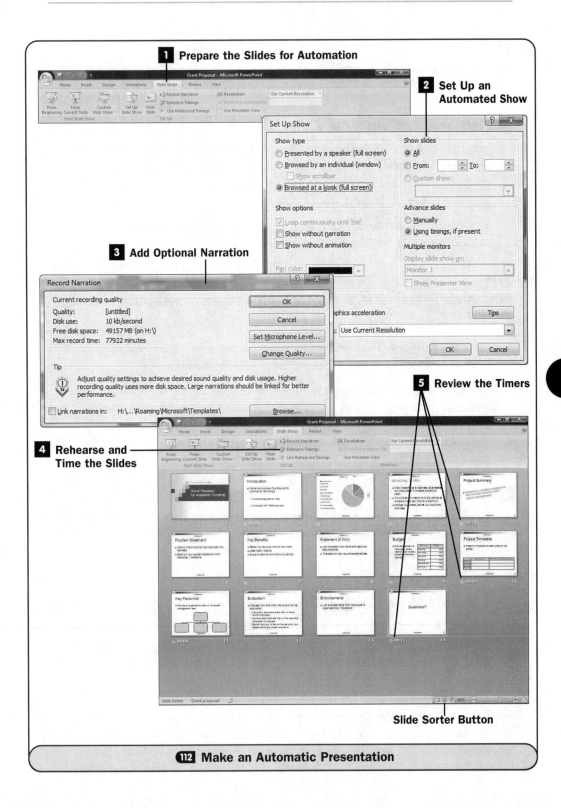

1 Prepare the Slides for Automation

2 Set Up an Automated Show

3 Add Optional Narration

4 Rehearse and Time the Slides

5 Review the Timers

Slide Sorter Button

112

112 Make an Automatic Presentation

▶ **TIP**

When you're recording voice on your computer, a headset microphone manufactured for computers produces superior results over hand-held microphones.

▪4 Rehearse and Time the Slides

You can walk through a slide show in real time, selecting exactly when you want the next slide to appear. As you rehearse the presentation in this manner, PowerPoint records the time frame that you use for each slide and prepares automatic transitions for you.

To rehearse the automatic presentation, click the **Slide Sorter** button to display your presentation from a bird's-eye view.

▶ **TIP**

You can easily rearrange slides by dragging them from one location to another while in the **Slide** view.

Click the **Rehearse Timings** button. Your presentation begins, and the first slide appears with a timer in the lower-left corner of your screen.

When the first slide has been on the screen as long as you want, press Page Down (or click your mouse). PowerPoint advances to the next slide, using a transition and sound if you've set them up, and that slide's timer begins. Continue clicking each slide's timer after each slide has appeared until the presentation ends.

▪5 Review the Timers

When you return to the **Slide Sorter** screen, each slide with a transition or special effect appears with a shooting star icon. The display time you've rehearsed for the slide also appears.

---

113 **Add Notes to a Presentation**

✔ BEFORE YOU BEGIN	→ SEE ALSO
99 Print a Presentation	**114** Create Presentation Handouts
100 Enter Text into a Presentation	**116** About Giving Presentations

---

PowerPoint's **Notes Page** view enables you to create and edit notes for you or your presentation's speaker. When you display the notes, PowerPoint shows the notes at the bottom of your slide while you work on your presentation. The **Notes Page** view shows the slide contents and, below that, a dialog box for your notes.

▶ **TIP**

Generally, the **Notes Page** view is best used for short reminders of things you want to remember for each slide. Don't plan to write your entire presentation's text in the note area because you'll get bogged down in the details (see **116** **About Giving Presentations**).

The **Notes Page** view is designed to allow printing of the notes for the speaker. However, the speaker can also display the **Notes Page** view during a presentation to eliminate paper shuffling. If your laptop has an output for an external monitor, as most do, you'll plug the overhead projector into that port. PowerPoint will send the slides to the projector, and your slides and notes will be visible on your laptop's screen as you walk through the presentation.

▶ **TIP**

If your **Notes Page** view's text is not large enough to read easily, expand the viewing area by dragging your **Zoom** control in the lower-right corner of your PowerPoint screen.

1 **Request the Notes Page View**

Click to display your **View** ribbon, and then click the **Notes Page** button to enter the **Notes Page** presentation view. Here you see the entire note area at the bottom of each slide.

2 **Begin Adding Notes**

Click the notes area of the slide that contains the placeholder text **Click to Add Text**. Type your notes that go with the current slide. You can apply all the usual text-formatting commands to your notes (see **100** **Enter Text into a Presentation**).

Press Page Down to move to the next slide and add notes where needed throughout the rest of your presentation.

▶ **NOTE**

You don't have to add notes after finishing a complete presentation. If you display the **Notes Page** view after creating each slide, you can add notes along the way.

3 **Print the Notes**

If you prefer to print your notes before a presentation so that you will have them instead of reading them from your laptop screen, print each slide and the notes that go with them by clicking your **Office** button and selecting **Print**. Select **Notes Pages** in the **Print What** section and click **OK** to start the printing.

113

113

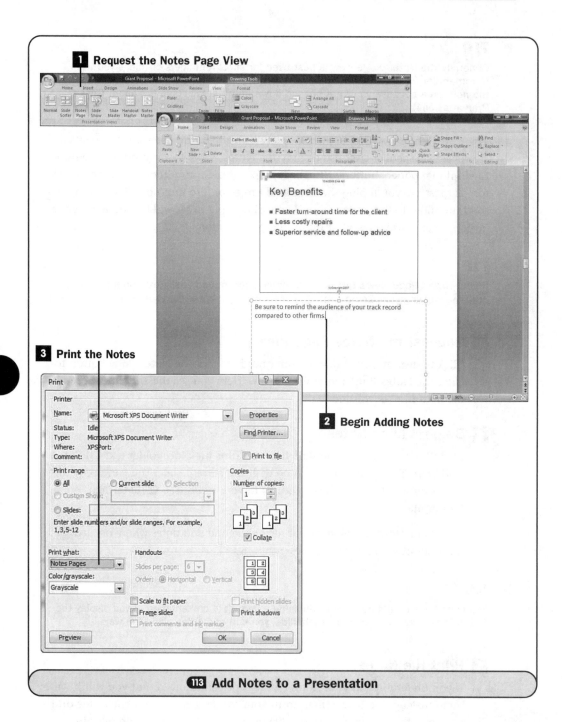

113 Add Notes to a Presentation

114 Create Presentation Handouts

✔ BEFORE YOU BEGIN	→ SEE ALSO
99 Print a Presentation	**115** Turn a Presentation into Online Web Pages

Handouts can benefit your audience because they can take home ideas and tips from your presentation. You control what goes into your handouts. You don't have to print every slide in the presentation. Doing so would only cost you paper and would not necessarily benefit your audience. Instead, select the slides that mean the most to your presentation.

Consider the following handouts as important, depending on your presentation:

- Your presentation's title, its goal, and your name

- Your contact information (website, phone number, email address, and so on)

- Critical ideas within your presentation

- Numerical examples the audience can study at their leisure

- Goals for the audience

- Take-home action items that the audience might want to do as a result of your presentation

- Products you or others sell that relate to your presentation and that will benefit your audience

1 Request Print Preview

Click your **Office** button and click the arrow to the right of the **Print** option. Select **Print Preview** to enter the **Print Preview** mode.

▶ **TIP**

You can specify how you want the printed handouts to appear elsewhere in PowerPoint, but the **Print Preview** mode seems to offer the simplest way of specifying your handout content.

2 Determine What to Print

Click the **Print What** option to display the number of slides for each printed handout.

▶ **TIP**

Three slides per page leaves ample room for your audience to write notes on the handouts you give them. PowerPoint provides the space and lines to write on at the left of each of the three slides on the printed page.

3 Select the Orientation

Depending on your slide content, you might need to change the print orientation from **Portrait** to **Landscape** in the **Orientation** drop-down list box.

4 Adjust the Handout Master

Every time you adjust the way a handout will look inside the **Print Preview** view, PowerPoint maintains the look of that handout in its *Handout Master*. The Handout Master determines how many pages print per handout page, specifies where the headers and footers go, and enables you to change the theme and background image of the handouts to differ from those in your presentation.

114

▶ **NEW TERM**

Handout Master—A slide that appears in the background of every presentation you create that determines how your printed handouts will look.

Click to display your **View** ribbon and click the **Handout Master** button to display the Handout Master slide. Select a theme, a background, and other options you want to apply to your handouts. When finished, click the **Close** button to close the **Handout Master** view and return to your presentation's slides.

▶ **NOTE**

You could begin determining how your handouts will look by going directly to the Handout Master slide instead of starting in the **Print Preview** view, but you'll need to do that only if you want to change more than the number of slides per page and adjust the header, footer, or page number. Otherwise, your **Print Preview** view is simpler to use.

5 Print the Handouts

Click to select your **Office** button and click the **Print** button. (You can also click the **Print** button on your **Quick Access** toolbar.) PowerPoint displays the **Print** dialog box. Make sure that the **Handouts** option is still selected in the **Print What** list box. Adjust the other print settings you desire, and click **OK** to begin printing the handouts.

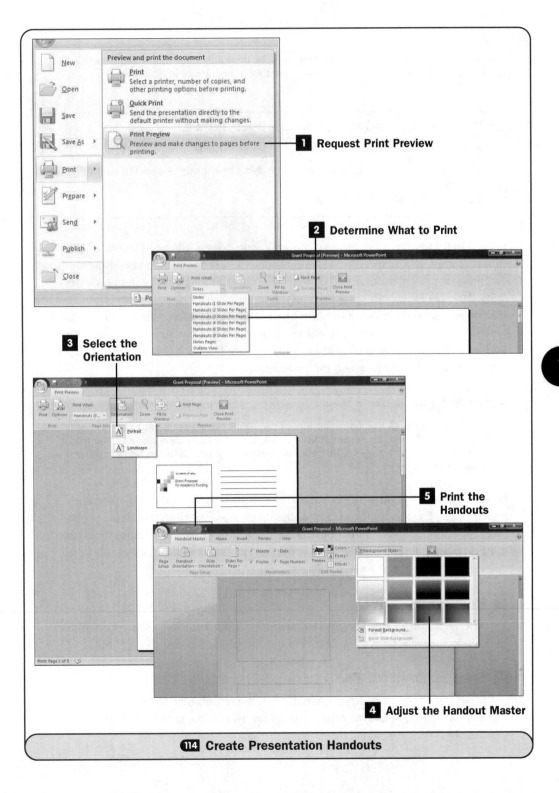

1 Request Print Preview

2 Determine What to Print

3 Select the Orientation

5 Print the Handouts

4 Adjust the Handout Master

114

114 Create Presentation Handouts

▶ **TIP**

The first time you print a presentation's handouts, print only one copy. Make sure that the printed pages are to your liking before printing the copies of the handouts.

---

115 Turn a Presentation into Online Web Pages

✔ BEFORE YOU BEGIN	→ SEE ALSO
95 About Presentation Creation in PowerPoint	**116** About Giving Presentations
97 Open an Existing Presentation	

115

Instead of a roomful of people, why not give your presentation to the world? You can, by turning your PowerPoint presentation into a set of web pages. After converting your presentation to web content, you must upload your pages to a *web hosting service* (which will probably be the same service, either in-house or out, that hosts your website currently) and link to the presentation. When your site's visitors click the link for your presentation, they can enjoy your presentation from their web browser. If the presentation is manual and not automatic, they can click forward and backward to watch the presentation.

▶ **NEW TERM**

Web hosting service—A company you hire or an inside computer support center that provides disk space where you can store web pages and other online content. You might even host your own web pages from your own computer if you have the knowledge and system software to do so.

PowerPoint makes it surprisingly easy to convert your presentation to an online presentation. The most difficult part of the process is uploading the online presentation and linking to it (neither of which is PowerPoint's role, but rather tasks you must do outside PowerPoint—or you can find someone who has the knowledge to upload and link to your presentation for you).

1 Request the Save

After you finish designing and reviewing your presentation, click your **Office** button and select **Save As**. PowerPoint displays the **Save As** dialog box.

2 Save as an HTML File

Select a location in which to save the online presentation at the top of the **Save As** dialog box. Type a filename in the **File Name** field and make sure that Web Page is selected in the **Save as Type** list box.

Two buttons appear in the dialog box, a **Publish** button and a **Change Title** button.

3 Change the Web Page Title

The **Change Title** button determines what will ultimately appear in the presentation's web page title bar during someone's view of your presentation. By default, the title that appears is the first text that appears in your presentation (other than header text). You can click the **Change Title** button to use a different title for the presentation's web page title.

4 Publish as a Web Page

Click the **Publish** button to determine how your presentation will appear on the Internet.

Here you determine options for the online presentation, such as whether you want to put the entire presentation online or only a range of slides. In addition, you can choose to display your speaker notes online with each slide or note.

▶ **NOTE**

Your speaker notes can be more critical when someone views your presentation online than they would be if you were presenting the slides yourself and speaking in front of an audience.

Choose the version of Internet Explorer and Netscape Navigator that you want your presentation to be compatible with. If you select the **Microsoft Internet Explorer 4.0 or Later** option (the default), your presentation will perform best if its web viewers are using Internet Explorer version 4 or later. Most will be using 4.0 or later. Use another option only if you know that your viewing audience generally won't have a later-model Internet Explorer (as might be the case on a school's intranet or perhaps in countries that aren't as up-to-date as the more industrialized nations are.

Always select a filename and location in the **File Name** field to save the web-based presentation onto your computer.

▶ **TIP**

Leave the **Open Published Web Page in Browser** option checked to review your presentation after PowerPoint converts it to the Web's HTML format.

115

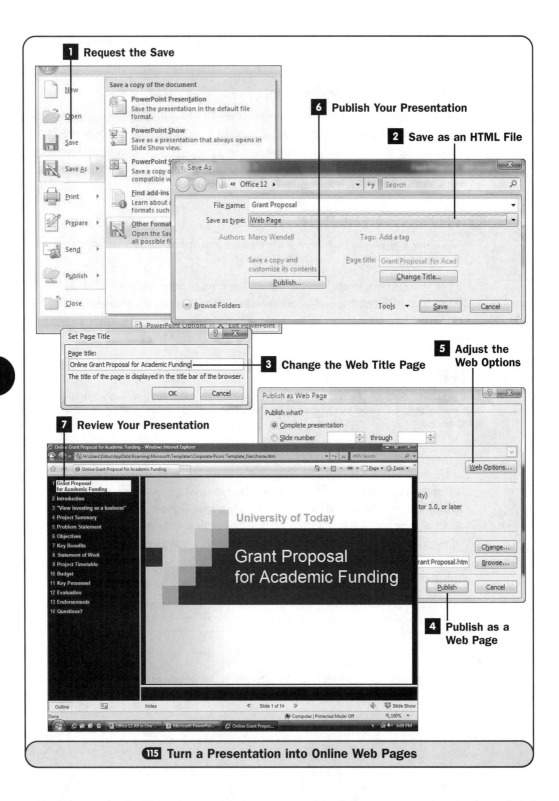

1 Request the Save

6 Publish Your Presentation

2 Save as an HTML File

3 Change the Web Title Page

5 Adjust the Web Options

7 Review Your Presentation

4 Publish as a Web Page

115 Turn a Presentation into Online Web Pages

5 Adjust the Web Options

Click the **Web Options** button to adjust several of your presentation's web settings, such as the color scheme used, the specific browsers supported, embedded graphics image sizes, and other web features. Generally, the defaults will work well unless your presentation is extremely large and heavy with graphics and special effects. Also, you may want to adjust some of the **Web Options** dialog box settings downward if most of your web audience will be viewing your presentation from a dial-up connection.

6 Publish Your Presentation

Click the **Publish** button to convert your presentation to HTML format, which is viewable from web browsers.

7 Review Your Presentation

Internet Explorer (or your computer's default web browser) opens and displays your presentation. A list of slides appears in the left pane, and each selected slide appears in the right pane.

Click the slide list item to see that slide. Your presentation is now a complete web page that you can send to your web hosting service with an *FTP* or a similar program.

116

▶ **NEW TERM**

FTP—Stands for *File Transfer Protocol*, which is the most common method of transferring web pages from one computer to a web hosting service's disk space for viewing over the Internet.

116 **About Giving Presentations**	
✔ **BEFORE YOU BEGIN** **95** About Presentation Creation in PowerPoint **98** Give a Presentation **112** Make an Automatic Presentation	

Giving presentations seems to be as much an art as a skill. Some extremely enjoyable, attention-getting speakers use absolutely no presentation handouts, notes, or overhead materials like those PowerPoint can produce. On the other hand, many professional speakers wouldn't enter a room without PowerPoint.

You must decide what is best for you, given your comfort level, your ability to capture an audience, your material, and the environment in which you plan to present your material. One thing is for sure: Tools such as PowerPoint are so powerful that it's easy to get caught up in special effects, color, and sound so much that your presentation's details take away from your message. You must keep in the forefront that your message should take priority over the presentation in every way.

▶ **NOTE**

A simple speech that you plan to give may be better presented without any overhead slides shown to your audience. However, you can still use PowerPoint to develop your content and thoughts and to arrange the topics you want to speak on.

Don't add a special effect unless that effect accents the message you're trying to convey on that slide. Don't add sound or video to the beginning of your presentation if you want to speak at the beginning. In other words, don't compete with your presentation's effects. When you create automatic presentations, you probably should rely more on sound and special effects to keep the audience's attention because you won't be there to direct things, but the message you want to convey is still paramount to the technical aspects of your presentation.

Although this may go against tradition, seriously consider *not* passing out handouts of your presentation, or even letting your audience know that you have them, until after your presentation ends. If you do provide handouts earlier, you may lose the interest of some audience members because they will assume that all the information is in the handouts. Or they may think they can study the handouts later, and in doing so, they may miss connecting important points that you make in your speech but that may not be explicit in the handouts. Do what you can to keep your audience attentive to your message—this may mean that you buck the trend and not pass out handouts before you speak.

Don't print, word for word, your speaker notes, either on slides or on a printed piece of paper you keep with you at the podium. You need to know your presentation well enough to give it cold, without any notes other than (perhaps) a card with key words that remind you of your presentation's order.

▶ **TIP**

Know your presentation cold but don't memorize it. Instead of coming across knowing your material inside and out, if you recite a memorized speech you come off sounding stiff and boring no matter how well you know your topic and no matter how interesting your topic is.

Unless you're teaching technical material, I'd suggest that you save questions for the end of your presentation. If you do not, you may be sidetracked from your presentation, you may go over time (upsetting both your audience and, possibly, the host conference personnel if you're speaking at a conference), and your entire presentation runs the risk of being derailed.

Finally, even though it should go without saying, how many times have you seen a speaker get up before the audience and not know how to work the equipment? You need to arrive before your audience and prepare your hardware, get your handouts ready to pass out after the talk, and test your entire presentation and hardware. When problems occur at the start of a presentation, you lose control of the situation in your audience's eyes, and you must fight to regain your audience.

▶ **NOTE**

As you can see, giving a presentation requires far more important considerations than using PowerPoint to create slides. Make PowerPoint an important part of your presentation but not the center of your presentation. PowerPoint should serve your presentation and not the other way around.

116

PART V

Organizing with Outlook

IN THIS PART:

14

Introducing Outlook

IN THIS CHAPTER:

Microsoft Outlook contains a huge assortment of features because of the number of jobs it performs. Word is a word processor that is perhaps the most powerful ever created, yet it does just one thing: word processing. Outlook, on the other hand, handles many diverse tasks. Outlook lets you manage the details of your life. Not only is Outlook a truly interactive contact, mail, planning, and scheduling program, but it's also fun to use.

---

117   About Outlook's Capabilities

✔ BEFORE YOU BEGIN	→ SEE ALSO
76 Attach a Comment to a Cell	**118** Master the Outlook Screen
	135 Use RSS Feeds

117

Here is a list that includes just a few of the tasks you can do using Outlook:

- Send and receive email

- Record business and personal contacts

- Organize your calendar

- Schedule meetings

- Manage appointments

- Track prioritized to-do task lists

- Write notes to yourself that act as yellow sticky notes when you view them (similar to Excel's comment feature)

In spite of their similar names, Outlook is not the same as Outlook Express. Outlook Express is a program that comes with Windows. Outlook Express is a slimmed-down version of Outlook but does not contain the scheduling and advanced group of other features that Outlook provides.

▶ NOTE

Windows Vista changed the name of Outlook Express to Windows Mail. This will help distinguish the two programs and reduce confusion.

▶ TIP

Outlook Express (and Windows Mail) does support a feature that Microsoft Outlook does not have. You can work with *newsgroups*. Microsoft Outlook does not support a newsgroup reader.

▶ **NEW TERM**

Newsgroups—Online electronic bulletin boards organized by topic. With them you can share files and messages with users from all over the world who are interested in the same topics you are.

Surprisingly, Microsoft didn't give Outlook 2007 a universal ribbon bar. Outlook is probably the least-changed interface of all the Microsoft Office 2007 products, and you'll continue to use a menu to access many of Outlook's features. Microsoft did, however, greatly improve upon a feature that has plagued Outlook users since the very first version: the search capability.

▶ **NOTE**

A ribbon does appear in some parts of Outlook, such as when you create a new email message.

Searching for data inside Outlook 2007 is quick and efficient. You can search by keyword through all your Outlook records. You can even search throughout your email attachments. A new **Search** pane appears throughout all of Outlook's windows, giving you a quick way to find exactly what you're looking for.

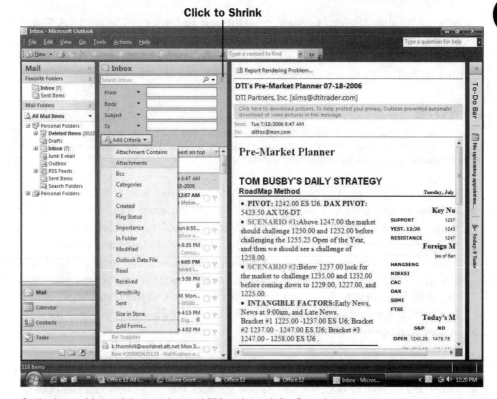

Outlook provides quick search capabilities through its Search pane.

117

In addition to the improved search capabilities, Outlook includes an **RSS** reader so that you can keep up with the latest news from the websites and other RSS feeds you subscribe to. (See **135** **Use RSS Feeds**.)

▶ NEW TERM

RSS—Stands for **Really Simple Syndication**, which is the process of subscribing to websites that support RSS. After you subscribe and tell Outlook that you've done so, updates on that site will appear inside your RSS window.

118	**Master the Outlook Screen**	
✔ **BEFORE YOU BEGIN**		→ **SEE ALSO**
117 About Outlook's Capabilities		**119** Set Outlook Options

Outlook's opening screen can vary considerably depending on how your version is currently set up. If you installed Outlook on a new system, your Outlook screen will differ from an Outlook screen that appears if you upgraded from a previous version of Outlook. When upgrading, Outlook retains most of the screen arrangement you previously used.

118

Most of the time Outlook opens in the **Outlook Today** view. The **Outlook Today** view is defined by a folder inside Outlook called the **Outlook Today** folder. It shows an overview of messages, to-do tasks, and appointments for the time period.

▶ NOTE

If today's a holiday, the **Outlook Today** view will tell you that. Most major as well as minor holidays appear, and you can adjust, add, and remove other days you want to be reminded of, such as birthdays and anniversaries.

Outlook stores email and other kinds of data in a series of folders. These folders work much the same way as they do in Windows Explorer; that is, you can move things into the folders, create new folders, rename folders, and delete folders. You can create folders that file Outlook email and other data into compartments where you can easily locate your data later. Outlook folders appear on the left side of your Outlook screen in most of Outlook's views. For example, if you click the **Mail** button in the lower-left corner of your screen, Outlook displays your **Inbox** and lists the other mail-related folders in a window pane against the left side of your screen.

▶ NOTE

To find the location of Outlook's files so you can back them up, select File, Data File Management, and click Data Files. You must close Outlook before backing up the files.

▶ **TIP**

The **Favorite Folders** area holds a special group of folders you can add or remove. You'll place folders here that you access most often. Right-click on any folder to send it to your **Favorite Folders** so that it's always available. To see folders not in your **Favorite Folders** area, you may have to click the plus sign to expand **Inbox**.

Being able to traverse Outlook is an important skill. This task gives you an overview of Outlook 2007's screens and how to navigate them.

1 Check Outlook Today

Select **Microsoft Outlook** from your Windows menu. Outlook will probably open in the **Outlook Today** view. Click to cross off any tasks you've completed for today. As you continue to complete tasks, you can click to cross them off, too.

The **Outlook Today** view displays all your appointments for the current period. Click on any item on the **Outlook Today** view to see the details for that item. For example, clicking on an appointment opens a window with that appointment's details.

▶ **NOTE**

If your Outlook doesn't open in the **Outlook Today** view but you want it to, select **Tools**, **Options**, click the **Other** tab, and then click the **Advanced Options** button. Click **Browse** and select **Personal Folders** to begin in the **Outlook Today** view. Outlook groups data in folders. You can select from several folders you want to see when you first start Outlook before closing this **Options** window.

118

2 Display Your Inbox

Click the **Inbox** link in your **Messages** section to display your email. If you have to-do notes, Outlook displays those in the **To-Do Bar** pane to the right of your screen. Not every Outlook user manages to-do tasks inside Outlook. You can hide your **To-Do Bar** by clicking its **Close** button to give your email more room.

▶ **TIP**

You can drag the edge of any window pane in Outlook to widen or shrink the columns of information.

You can always display your **Inbox** from any Outlook screen by clicking **Mail** in the lower-left screen's feature button list.

Navigation Pane

1 Check Outlook Today   To-do List

Click to Close Pane

Email Summary

Click to See Graphics

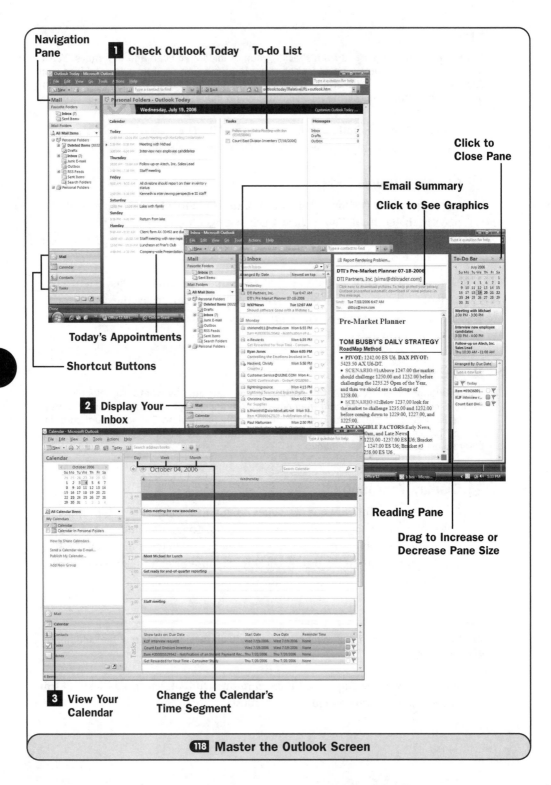

Today's Appointments

Shortcut Buttons

2 Display Your Inbox

Reading Pane

Drag to Increase or Decrease Pane Size

3 View Your Calendar

Change the Calendar's Time Segment

118

118 Master the Outlook Screen

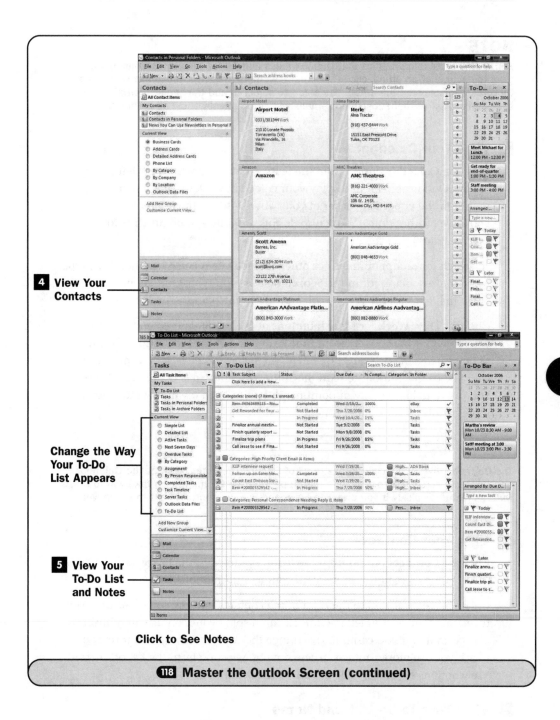

4 View Your Contacts

Change the Way Your To-Do List Appears

5 View Your To-Do List and Notes

Click to See Notes

118

▶ **NOTE**

Some emails contain graphics that Outlook hides initially for security reasons. If you trust the source of an email, click that email's warning message and select **Download Pictures** to display the full email. You can also select to add the sender's email to your safe senders list so that subsequent emails will automatically show all graphics.

3 View Your Calendar

Click the **Calendar** button from the feature buttons in the lower-left portion of your Outlook screen to display your calendar. Click on any date in the month in the upper-left corner of your window to see the appointments you have for that date. (You'll also do this to set new appointments for specific dates.)

To search for an appointment or other calendar item (such as a holiday), type what you're looking for in the **Search** box. As you type, Outlook narrows down the items found in your calendar that match your search term.

Click the **Day**, **Week**, or **Month** buttons at the top of your calendar to view your calendar in those different time segments. Outlook will still show any appointments in each day, but when you're viewing a week or a month, there won't be as much room to read the entire appointment's text, in most cases. You can double-click any appointment's text to open a window that shows more details for that appointment.

▶ **TIP**

The **Go** menu gives you quick access to all of Outlook's features, such as the **Calendar** and **Contacts** screens. Shortcut keys that appear on the **Go** menu also take you to these Outlook features quickly if you prefer to learn and use the shortcut keys to maneuver.

4 View Your Contacts

Click the **Contacts** button from the feature buttons in the lower-left portion of your Outlook screen to display your contact information.

Click any letter button to the right of the contacts that display to jump to contacts stored under that letter. Outlook can display your contacts in a business card format, but you can quickly change the contact display to a format in which you see more contacts at one time by selecting from the list of **Current View** options on the left side of your Outlook window.

5 View Your To-Do List and Notes

Click the **Tasks** button from the feature buttons in the lower-left portion of your Outlook screen to display your to-do list.

118

Drag any column dividers left or right to adjust the width of the columns. You can change the way your to-do tasks appear on your screen by choosing from the list of items on the left of your screen with the heading **Current View**.

Outlook also acts as a repository of notes that you write and manage. These notes look like the yellow sticky notes you write on and like the comments that appear in Excel cells (see **76 Attach a Comment to a Cell**). To see or manage Outlook notes, click the **Notes** button in the lower-left portion of your Outlook screen.

▶ **NOTE**

Outlook supports a journaling feature that records every activity you perform in Outlook on a timeline. You can view the journal by selecting **Go, Journal** (or pressing Ctrl+8). By default, the journal feature is turned off due to the large amount of computer resources it consumes.

---

119 **Set Outlook Options**

✔ BEFORE YOU BEGIN	→ SEE ALSO
117 About Outlook's Capabilities	**121** Create an Email Message
118 Master the Outlook Screen	**133** Navigate Times and Dates

119

Outlook is unique among the other Office 2007 programs in many ways (see **117 About Outlook's Capabilities**). You'll probably find yourself displaying Outlook's option details frequently when you first install Outlook. Then, after you get Outlook to behave the way you want it to, you'll probably navigate to the options far less frequently than you do in the other Office products.

One of the ways that Microsoft did *not* improve Outlook in Outlook 2007 was to group Outlook's options in a more intuitive format. For example, changing the way Outlook manages email often requires that you search several dialog boxes to locate an option you want to change; there is no single location for all of Outlook's email options.

This task gives you an overview of Outlook's options, but almost assuredly you'll have to wade through the options many times throughout your use of Outlook to locate what you're looking for. If you upgraded from a previous version of Outlook, as the majority of Outlook 2007 users will do, you will find that you may not need to adjust many—if any—options because the upgrade to Outlook 2007 is fairly accurate at preserving your option settings from your previous versions.

▶ **NOTE**

Given that the Outlook options are not viewed much after Outlook is customized for use, many Outlook users forget what is available. If you're an Outlook expert, review Outlook's options every once in a while (here's a great way to do that) because you might see an option that now will be helpful that you hadn't predicted would be when you first began customizing Outlook for your situation.

1 Request Options

Select **Tools**, **Options** from Outlook's menu bar. The **Preferences** dialog box page displays with several options available to you for the various Outlook features.

2 Adjust the Email Options

Click the **Junk E-mail** button to adjust the way Outlook handles junk mail sent to you. The **E-mail Options** button to the right of that allows you to control what happens after you read and optionally reply to or forward an email message.

119

3 Adjust the Calendar Options

The **Calendar** section of the **Preferences** page controls the time increment shown in your calendar's daily planner. The default is 15 minutes, but you can select a different interval if you routinely work with longer appointments or perhaps require a smaller increment between appointments.

Click the **Calendar Options** button to adjust the days in your workweek (required if weekend days routinely are part of your work schedule), adjust the start and stop time related to your typical workday (the default is 8 to 5), adjust the colors used in the calendar, and set your Outlook time zone, among other various calendar-related adjustments.

▶ **TIP**

If you use Outlook on your laptop and travel frequently, you can change Outlook's time zone to match your destination time zone without modifying your Windows time zone. When you're working at your destination, Outlook will schedule correctly for you, but your computer retains your home time zone, which can be critical for accounting-related programs you might work with.

4 Adjust the Task Options

Click the **Task Options** button to display task color options as well as task-related notification options so that you'll be appropriately informed of due tasks.

5 Adjust the Contact Options

Click the **Contact Options** button to display a list of options that relate to your **Contacts** folder. By default, Outlook displays your contact names in first-name order (although the contacts are sorted alphabetically by last name), but you can change the way Outlook displays and sorts your contacts. In addition, you can request that Outlook let you know if you attempt to add a contact twice, or, by unchecking the option labeled **Check for Duplicate Contacts**, Outlook can let you add duplicate contact entries. Outlook checks duplicates based on name only, and you may have two or more contacts that happen to have the same names (especially true of some family members).

6 Adjust the Search and Mobile Settings

Click the **Search Options** button to change the way Outlook indexes your information. To speed up the searches, Outlook constantly monitors your activity and indexes any new data that you type or that arrives in Outlook's folders through email or by moving and copying from other sources. You can limit the folders that Outlook indexes to reduce overhead.

▶ **NOTE**

Given today's fast computers and huge disk drives, the need to reduce indexing to make the computer run more efficiently isn't as vital as it used to be.

In addition, you can adjust the way Outlook performs a search by requiring that Outlook wait until you click the **Search** button before locating any matches instead of looking *as* you type the search term.

By default, Outlook does not search the **Deleted Items** folder (although you can click to display your **Deleted Items** folder and perform a search there if you want) when performing general Outlook searches. However, you can specify that Outlook index and search your **Deleted Items** folder if you routinely require that.

You can set up Outlook to send messages to your mobile phone. The **Notification** and **Mobile Options** buttons control how Outlook handles the synchronization between your computer and your mobile phone.

▶ **NOTE**

To use Outlook's mobile phone features, you must set up an account for mobile messaging. Doing so is beyond the scope of this book, but it's simple to do. Go to your Outlook Account Manager (you'll get there from **Tools, Account Settings**) and set up a new mobile phone account after clicking the **E-mail** tab.

119

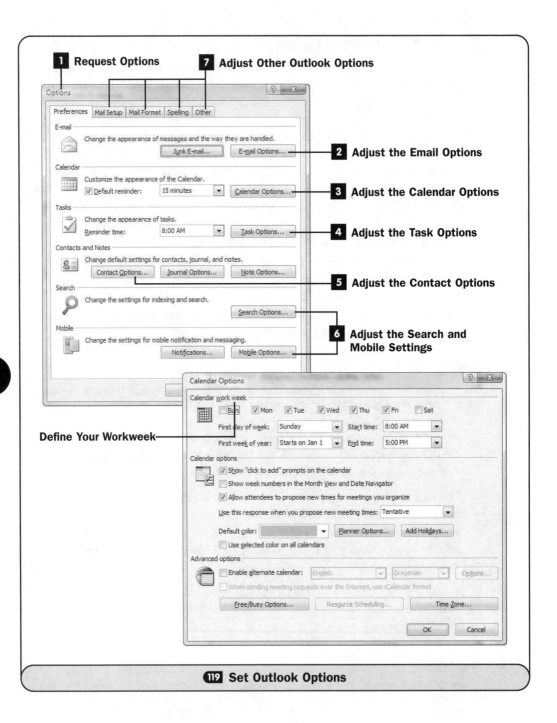

1 Request Options   **7** Adjust Other Outlook Options

2 Adjust the Email Options

3 Adjust the Calendar Options

4 Adjust the Task Options

5 Adjust the Contact Options

6 Adjust the Search and Mobile Settings

Define Your Workweek

119 Set Outlook Options

119

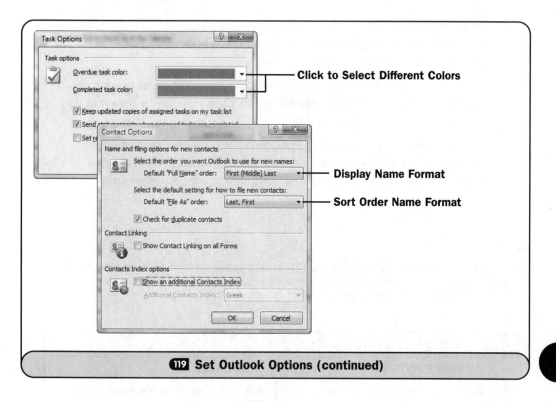

Click to Select Different Colors

Display Name Format

Sort Order Name Format

119 Set Outlook Options (continued)

119

7 Adjust Other Outlook Options

The rest of the tabs across Outlook's **Options** dialog box control additional email options as well as Outlook's spell-checker and miscellaneous items.

The **Mail Format** tab enables you to adjust the target format of your email messages. Outlook can create well-formatted, colorful emails, but to send such an email, Outlook sends the email in the HTML file format (the same format web pages use). Not all email systems are set up to receive email in HTML format. If you routinely send email that you want formatted properly no matter who receives the email, you'll need to change your Outlook message format to the **Plain Text** option. An in-between format called **Rich Text** is available and offers a few more formatting features than plain-text emails, but to ensure complete compatibility, select **Plain Text**.

▶ NOTE

More and more systems allow HTML-formatted emails, so sending in that format is less risky than it used to be. Due to heightened security concerns, some users require plain-text emails because in some circumstances a problem can come through an HTML email (typically antivirus programs catch these with ease); so even today, your HTML-formatted email might not arrive intact.

You can add a background texture or picture and specify a default font for your emails by clicking the **Stationary and Fonts** button and selecting the stationary you want to use for your emails.

Email signatures enable you to attach a message to the bottom of your emails (see **126 Create an Email Signature**). To specify, change, or create an email signature, click the **Signatures** button.

The remaining tabs, **Spelling** and **Other**, enable you to control whether Outlook checks the spelling of all emails before sending them, as well as how you want Outlook to display its **Navigation** pane, **Reading** pane, and **To-Do Bar**.

▶ **TIP**

If you're brand-new to Outlook, you probably should accept all its default option settings and use the program for a while before making any adjustments. You'll be better accustomed to what works well for you and what options need tweaking.

120

120	**Set Up an Email Account**
✔ **BEFORE YOU BEGIN**	→ **SEE ALSO**
118 Master the Outlook Screen	**121** Create an Email Message
	122 Check for New Mail

When you first install Outlook onto a computer that hasn't had a previous version used for email, or when you sign up for a new email account, you need to tell Outlook about that email account so that Outlook can send and retrieve messages. Setting up an email account can, in some instances, be difficult to describe and perform because of the differences among the email services.

Fortunately, most current email providers are following email account standards, and email account setup is fairly uniform. In addition, many *ISPs* automatically supply CD-ROMs or downloadable setup routines that prepare your Outlook email account when you set up your computer to access the Internet through that service. Nevertheless, when you must install your own email account, you can expect some fairly uniform steps as described in this task.

▶ **NEW TERM**

ISP—Stands for *Internet Service Provider*, which is a company that provides end-user Internet service. Examples include MSN and AOL, as well as local cable and DSL Internet services you might locate.

▶ **TIP**

You can set up multiple email accounts in Outlook and route all the messages to one **Inbox** folder or to different folders depending on the rules you set up. The **Tools, Rules and Alerts** menu option opens a dialog box you can use to tell Outlook which folders Outlook is to place email in when you receive email from each email account.

1 Prepare for a New Email Account

Select **Tools, Account Settings**. Click the **E-mail** tab and click **New** to begin a new email account setup.

2 Determine the Email Account Type

Modern email systems fall into one of three categories: POP3 (the majority of non-web-based email is POP3), IMAP, or HTTP (such as Hotmail). Outlook supports all three categories, and you'll click **Next** if you're setting up such an email system. You will select the **Outlook Add-in Connector** option only when setting up a specialized Outlook service such as an Outlook-to-mobile phone connection.

3 Enter Your Name, Email Address, and Password

In the **Add New E-mail Account** dialog box, you'll enter your name, email address, and password. Outlook requests your password twice to ensure that you enter it properly. The password doesn't show on your screen for security purposes.

▶ **NOTE**

The **Your Name** field contains the name that will appear in the **From** entry of an email recipient's email.

Click **Next** to move to the next screen.

4 Wait for Server Verification

Outlook now attempts to verify your email address and password settings. If Outlook fails to set up the email, there is one more thing it will try, so click **Next** if you get this message: An encrypted connection to your server is not available. Click Next to attempt using an unencrypted connection.

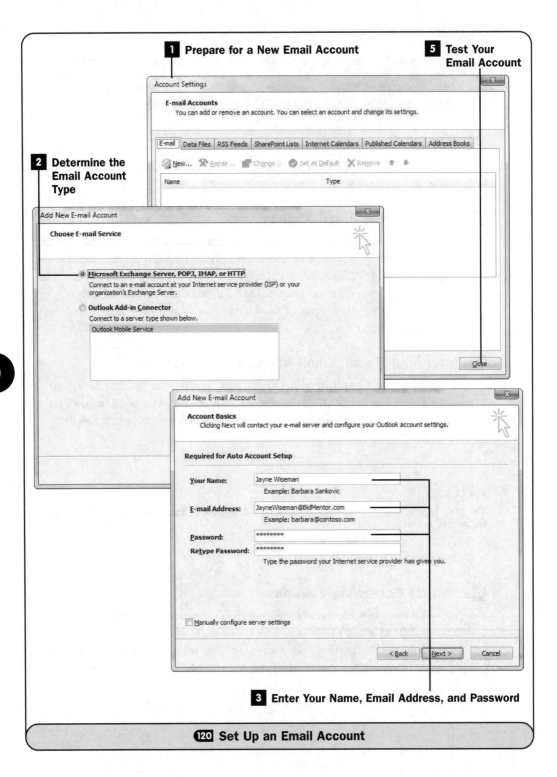

1 Prepare for a New Email Account

5 Test Your Email Account

2 Determine the Email Account Type

3 Enter Your Name, Email Address, and Password

120

120 Set Up an Email Account

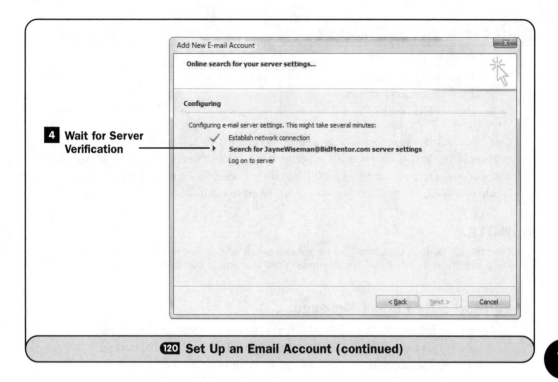

4 Wait for Server Verification

120 Set Up an Email Account (continued)

120

If Outlook is still unsuccessful, you probably need to contact your ISP to obtain Outlook setup instructions. Outlook will walk you through a series of dialog boxes that request specific POP3 and SMTP settings, technical nuances that are almost impossible to know without having documentation or phone support from the ISP you have the email account with.

If Outlook is successful, three check marks will appear to the left of the **Add New E-mail Account** procedures, and when you click **Finish**, your new email account will be set up in Outlook.

5 Test Your Email Account

Click **Close** to close the **Account Settings** dialog box and test your email. Perhaps the easiest way to test your email account is to send yourself an email. See **121** **Create an Email Message** and **122** **Check for New Mail**. The email you send should arrive in your Inbox in a matter of minutes and typically faster than that.

121 **Create an Email Message**

✔ BEFORE YOU BEGIN	→ SEE ALSO
118 Master the Outlook Screen	**122** Check for New Mail
120 Set Up an Email Account	

One of the most common tasks for Microsoft Outlook users is sending and receiving email. Outlook includes what is perhaps the most powerful email editor available because Outlook uses Microsoft Word as the basis for its editor! When you create a new email message, you are using Word to create that email.

▶ **NOTE**

Even though Outlook uses Word for its email-creation engine, you won't see a separate Word window open when you create email. You'll stay within Outlook's screens.

1 **Start a New Email Message**

From the **Inbox** folder, click **New**. From anywhere within Outlook, you can create a new email message by selecting **File**, **New**, **Mail Message**. The **Message** dialog box opens, where you can write your email.

▶ **TIP**

Ctrl+N is the shortcut key to create a new email when viewing your **Inbox** folder.

If you want to send an email to one of your contacts in your **Contacts** folder, you can first display your **Contacts** folder, locate the contact, select **Create**, and then select **New Message to Contact** to open the **New Message** dialog box with that recipient's email prefilled in the **To** field.

2 **Type the Recipient**

In the **To** field, type your email recipient's email address. If you want to send your email to multiple email addresses, separate each one with a semicolon (;). Instead of typing an email address, you can click your **To** button to display a list of your **Contact** folder's email addresses from which you can choose.

▶ **TIP**

If you send an email to a recipient inside your Contacts folder, type the recipient name's first few letters and press Ctrl+K. Outlook fills in the name and email for you, or if several matches occur, Outlook offers you a choice from which to choose.

3 Enter an Optional Carbon Copy Recipient

If you enter an email address in the **Cc** field, Outlook will send a copy of your email to the email address (or addresses, if you separate them with a semicolon) you specify. Instead of typing an email address, you can click your **Cc** button to display a list of your **Contact** folder's email addresses from which you can choose.

4 Enter an Optional Blind Carbon Copy Recipient

A carbon copy recipient, if you specify one in the **Cc** field, is seen by your primary recipient. In other words, if you send an email to Joe White and type Jane White's email address in the email's **Cc** field, Joe will see that you've sent a copy to Jane.

Outlook also supports a blind carbon copy field that you can add to any email. Click to select the email editor's **Options** ribbon and click **Show Bcc**. Outlook adds a **Bcc** field to your email. You can type one or more email addresses in the **Bcc** field (or click **Bcc** and select addresses from your **Contacts** folder), and the original recipient will not know that you've sent a copy of the email to the recipient in the **Bcc** field. A **Bcc** field works like a secret **Cc** field that only you and the **Bcc** recipient know about.

121

5 Type a Subject

Type the subject for your message. Your recipient sees the subject in the list of messages that he receives. The **Subject** field is important for organizing email messages in programs such as Outlook, so be sure to include a subject.

▶ TIP

Using a succinct subject helps you as well as your email's recipient. You'll be able to locate messages more easily in your **Sent** folder when you want to review an email you sent previously.

6 Type Your Message

Type your email body in the large message area at the bottom of the new message dialog box. Try to put yourself in the mind of your recipient. Short, succinct email messages are read more thoroughly and usually appreciated more than long, windy ones. It's the nature of an email message to get to the point.

On the other hand, some people overdo abbreviations and terseness in emails. Don't forsake grammar and spelling, and don't use abbreviations that may or may not be common to your audience. For example, IMHO is an

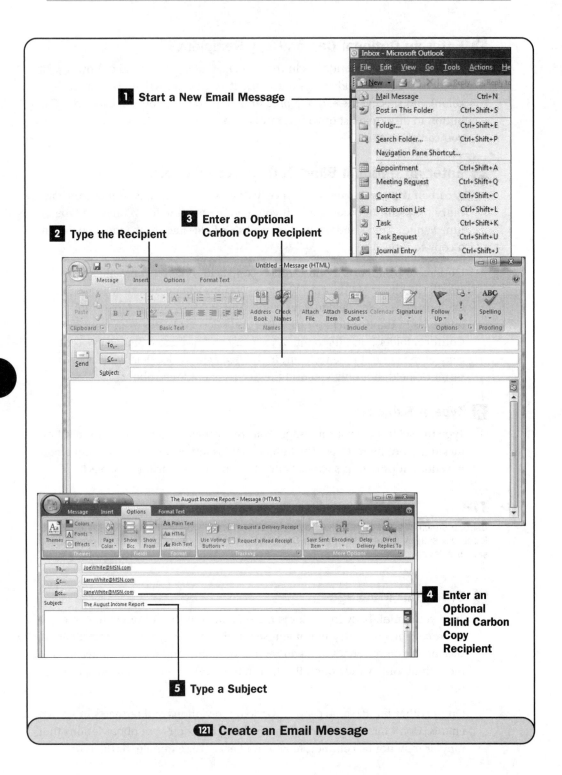

1 Start a New Email Message

2 Type the Recipient

3 Enter an Optional Carbon Copy Recipient

4 Enter an Optional Blind Carbon Copy Recipient

5 Type a Subject

121 Create an Email Message

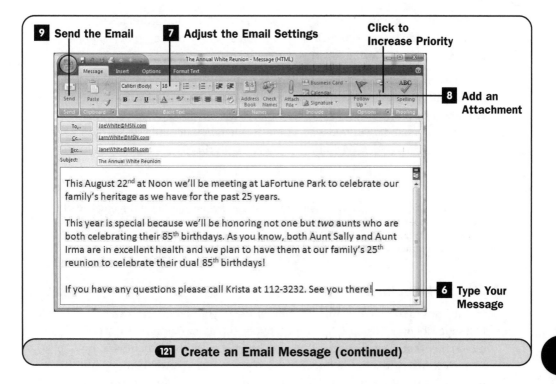

9 Send the Email   **7** Adjust the Email Settings   **Click to Increase Priority**

8 Add an Attachment

6 Type Your Message

121 Create an Email Message (continued)

121

abbreviation often used by bloggers, emailers, and chat rooms to mean "in my humble opinion." There's nothing wrong with using such an abbreviation in an email as long as you're sure that your recipient will understand the meaning. If you don't know your recipient's computer habits well, you probably should not assume that your recipient will understand such computer-savvy abbreviations.

7 Adjust the Email Settings

The **Message** and **Format Text** ribbons contain formatting operations you can apply to your email message. You can use a special font; add boldface, colors, and italic to your text; center and justify the text; and even check your email's spelling and grammar.

▶ TIP

All translation and dictionary functions available in Word are available to you as an Outlook email sender. You can access the spelling, grammar, research, thesaurus, and translation dictionaries by clicking the down arrow at the bottom of the **Message** ribbon's **Spelling** button.

As with other computerized messages, don't overdo the fonts and special effects. You don't want a bunch of colors, fonts, and text sizes to overshadow the message you're trying to convey in your email.

If you want to increase an email's importance, click the **Message** ribbon's exclamation point. If the recipient's email system supports priorities, your email will be flagged as one of high importance. Obviously, if you overuse this feature, nobody will take you seriously when you actually do send a high-priority message, so combine prudence with this feature.

▶ **TIP**

If you're in the middle of typing an email and must quit before you finish the email, click your Quick Access toolbar's **Save** button to save the email to your **Drafts** folder. When you return to Outlook, click to display the contents of your **Drafts** folder, double-click the message, and continue working on it.

8 Add an Attachment

If you want to attach a picture or another file to your email, click the **Message** ribbon's **Attach File** button's paper clip icon. From the **Insert File** dialog box that appears, locate the attachment, select the attachment, and then click **Insert** to add the attachment to your message. You can add multiple attachments to your message by holding down your Ctrl key while you click to select multiple items from the list that appears.

▶ **NOTE**

Don't send huge files as attachments unless you are certain that your recipient has a high-speed broadband Internet connection. Otherwise, you will tie up your recipient's email system for a long while during the download of the attachment the next time that recipient checks her email.

▶ **TIP**

Most graphics programs can compress a digital picture so that you can safely send it as an email attachment.

9 Send the Email

Click the **Send** button to send your email to all its intended recipients.

---

122 **Check for New Mail**

✔ **BEFORE YOU BEGIN**	→ **SEE ALSO**
121 Create an Email Message	**123** Reply To and Forward Email
	124 Organize Email

You need to check your **Inbox** folder regularly to see what email items await you. You can set Outlook to check for new, incoming email messages at any interval you prefer, and you can trigger the check for new messages anytime by clicking a button.

▶ **NOTE**

If you see a number to the right of one of your **Inbox** folders, that number represents the number of unread email messages awaiting you.

Pay attention to Outlook's icons. For example, as you read an email message, the message icon changes to show that the message has been read. Revert the Read message flag back to Unread by right-clicking the message and selecting **Mark as Unread** from the pop-up menu if you want to reverse the read status. You might do this when you don't have time to properly consider someone's message and you want to be sure that you'll read the message later. By marking it as unread, you make it less likely to get lost in the batch of read messages below it when you return to Outlook. A paper clip icon appears next to each message that contains an attachment file. When you open a message with an attached file, Outlook shows the attachment as an icon that you can right-click to save or open.

122

▶ **NOTE**

Never open email attachments from senders you don't recognize or have reason to distrust. Your antivirus program will be able to catch most problems; however, new attacks are created all the time, and the most common way to spread a computer virus is through the opening of attachments that contain malicious computer program code.

1 **Request Incoming Email**

Click the **Mail** button in Outlook's lower-left set of feature buttons. Click Outlook's **Send/Receive** button to receive any incoming email that is waiting for you. The email arrives in your **Inbox** folder unless you created rules to send it elsewhere based on the sender or some other attribute.

The column named **Inbox** shows the subject and recipient of each email in your **Inbox** folder. Also, the subject line appears. If you see a paper clip icon to the right of the subject, that email has an attachment.

2 Read Your Email

Click over any email in your **Inbox** folder to display that email's body in your Outlook **Reading** pane. Your **Reading** pane includes a scrollbar so that you can scroll the message up and down to read it.

▶ TIP

Double-click an email message in your **Inbox** folder to open that email in its own window that you can maximize. You'll find it easier to focus on the email without the rest of Outlook cluttering your reading area.

If you want to reply or forward the email, you can do so (see **123 Reply To and Forward Email**). You can also categorize and flag the email for follow-up if you want to do so (see **124 Organize Email**).

▶ NOTE

To delete an email from your **Inbox** folder, click to select it and press Delete. You can also drag the email to your **Deleted Items** folder in the **Navigation** pane at the left of your Outlook window.

122

3 View an Attachment

If an email has an attachment and you recognize and trust the sender, right-click the attachment in the **Reading** pane and select what you want to do with the attachment from the pop-up menu that appears. Most often you'll open the attachment in its own window or save the attachment to your disk drive in a location you specify.

▶ TIP

If you select **Preview** instead of **Open**, Word displays the first several lines of the attachment inside your **Reading** pane. This takes place if Outlook can display the attachment's contents. Outlook won't be able to preview some attachments depending on their type.

4 Adjust the Receive Frequency

Select **Tools**, **Options** and then click the **Mail Setup** tab. Click the **Send/ Receive** button to display the **Send/Receive Groups** dialog box. Adjust the **All Accounts** minute setting toward the bottom of the dialog box to check for new messages more frequently than Outlook's default 30-minute interval. As long as you have an *always-on Internet connection*, you can check for new messages every minute, if you want, without noticing denigration in computer performance.

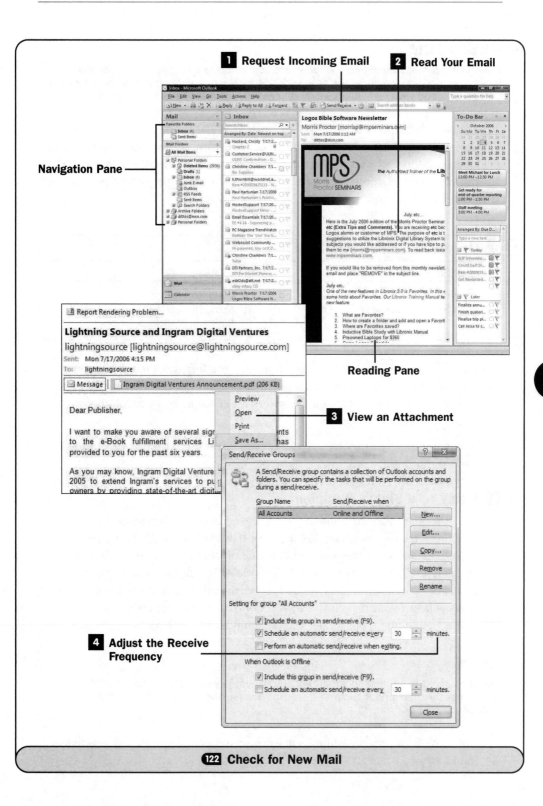

1 Request Incoming Email   **2** Read Your Email

Navigation Pane

Reading Pane

122

3 View an Attachment

4 Adjust the Receive Frequency

▶ **NEW TERM**

Always-on Internet connection—When you're connected to a high-speed broadband Internet service—as would be the case with DSL, cable, or a company networked Internet connection—and your computer's Internet connection is always live and available.

The minute setting under the **When Outlook is Offline** section applies to dial-up Internet connections that are not always on. If this applies to you, you won't want to check for new email more often than you want Outlook accessing your Internet connection and dialing into your Internet service provider (ISP) to get your email.

123   Reply To and Forward Email

✔ BEFORE YOU BEGIN	→ SEE ALSO
121 Create an Email Message	**124** Organize Email
122 Check for New Mail	**125** About Protecting Yourself Against Junk and Malicious Emails

123

Reading email is only part of your email process. You'll reply to many messages you receive, and Outlook makes it simple to do just that. In addition to replying to the sender, you might also want to forward an email message to another recipient or to multiple recipients.

Outlook maintains a history for each email you've sent, replied to, or forwarded. You can see that history anytime.

1 Reply to a Single Recipient

With the email you want to reply to selected, either in your **Inbox** folder or open in its own window (see **122** **Check for New Mail**), click the **Reply** button. Outlook opens a new message window and places the original email that you're replying to in the new window. Outlook fills in the **To** field with the sender of your original message and copies the original email in the message window below your text cursor. By repeating the original message at the bottom of your email, your sender will be reminded of what you're replying to.

▶ **NOTE**

Any attachment in the original email will not be sent in your reply. It's assumed that the sender has the attachment because it was the sender who sent you the attachment originally.

Type a reply. Your reply will appear above the copied email that you're replying to.

▶ **TIP**

Select **Tools, Options** and click the **E-mail Options** button to change the way Outlook generates replies. You can include the original message; you can indent the original message so that it's offset from your reply's left margin, making it easier to see where your message ends and the sender's begins; and you can prefix the sender's original message with a character, like >, to make it easier to distinguish your message from your sender's.

Click **Send** to send your reply.

2 **Reply to Multiple Recipients**

If the email's original sender sent the message to you and other recipients—which you can determine is true if you see names or email messages in the message's **Cc** field—you can send your reply to everybody who received the original email as well as the sender. Click the **Reply to All** button, and Outlook generates a new email message with the sender's email in the **To** field and all the carbon copy users in the **Cc** field.

▶ **NOTE**

If the message's original sender sent the email to blind carbon copy recipients, they will not receive your reply.

123

Being able to reply to multiple recipients is useful when you're in the middle of an email discussion. The sender blanketed several email addresses with the message, and you can add your response to all those recipients.

Don't overuse the capability to reply to multiple recipients, though, because when several people in an email discussion begin doing so, **Inbox** folders fill up quickly, and keeping track of who said what becomes difficult.

3 **Forward an Email**

Sending an email you receive to someone other than the sender is almost as simple as replying to the recipient. With the email message selected in your **Inbox** folder, or with the email open in its open window, click the **Forward** button. Outlook places the sender's email in a new message window. You must fill in the **To** and optionally the **Cc** and **Bcc** fields. Outlook automatically fills in the **Subject** field with the original message's subject, prefixed with "FW:."

▶ **NOTE**

If the original message has an attachment, the forwarded email will also include that attachment. You can right-click the attachment in the forwarded message window's **Attach** field and choose **Remove** to keep the attachment from being sent with the message.

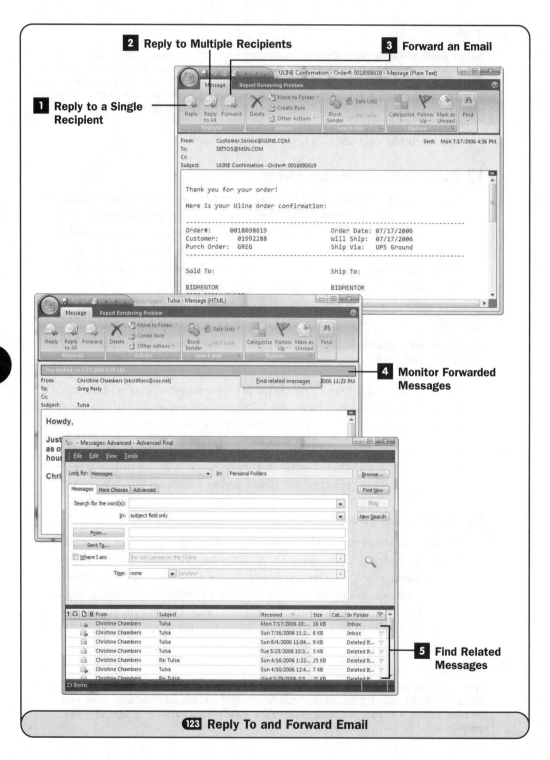

123 Reply To and Forward Email

After adding your own message to the top of the original message that appears at the bottom of your email message's window, click **Send** to forward the email to the recipient.

4 Monitor Forwarded Messages

If you reply to or forward a message, Outlook keeps track of the fact that you've done so. The next time you open that email message, Outlook places a banner across the top of the email letting you know the date and time you forwarded or replied to the email.

5 Find Related Messages

Outlook can show far more email history than simply telling you that you replied to or forwarded a message. If you click the email's **You replied...** or **You forwarded...** message and select the **Find Related Messages** option that appears, Outlook performs a search of all email communication between you and that recipient and displays the found emails in an **Advanced Find** window.

There you can search the history of emails between you and the recipient. Double-click any message appearing in the lower window pane to open that message in a new window.

124

▶ NOTE

Even if you deleted one or more of the messages displayed in the message history, you can still access the deleted message. Outlook includes a **Deleted Items** folder where emails and other Outlook data resides for three months or so. If the history window shows the message, it's still available even if it resides in the **Deleted Items** folder.

---

124 **Organize Email**

✔ BEFORE YOU BEGIN	→ SEE ALSO
122 Check for New Mail	**125** About Protecting Yourself Against Junk and Malicious Emails
123 Reply To and Forward Email	**136** Create and Share Electronic Business Cards

---

Email can flood an **Inbox** folder quickly. Keeping email organized is a requirement these days, given the number of emails that arrive. What messages do you keep? What messages do you file away? What messages do you want to follow up with now? What messages do you want to follow up with later?

Deleting and following up with messages received at the time you read the message isn't a problem. As **123 Reply To and Forward Email** shows, Outlook's reply and forwarding tools are simple to use. To delete a message, you only need to click to select the message and press Delete, or drag the message from your **Inbox** folder to your **Deleted Items** folder in the **Navigation** pane to the left of your Outlook window.

The messages you don't or can't respond to now but that you need to handle at a later time are the problem. Perhaps you're checking email quickly before leaving for the day in hopes of getting an answer to something, but three more messages arrive that you'll need to respond to or handle in some way over the next day or two. If you don't do something with those in-limbo messages, there's a chance you'll forget to handle them later. The next time you check email, another batch of emails will come in, and it is too easy to forget about the ones that filled your **Inbox** folder previously.

Fortunately, Outlook 2007 makes organizing your email less of a chore. You can flag emails, color-code emails into categories, and organize email into appropriate folders to ensure that your messages get the response you intend.

124

① Drag a Message to a Contact or an Appointment

If an email contains contact information you'll later need, don't keep the email in your **Inbox** or another folder. Instead, drag the email from your **Inbox** folder to your **Contacts** folder to create a contact you can more easily use later for mail merging or perhaps for creating an electronic business card (see **136 Create and Share Electronic Business Cards**).

Outlook creates a new contact with the sender's name in the **Full Name** field. If the sender included contact information, you can copy and paste that information into Outlook's appropriate fields.

② Drag a Message to Make an Appointment

If an email contains an appointment that you need to schedule, you're more likely to forget the appointment if you leave the email in your **Inbox** or another email folder. Instead of letting the message sit, drag the email from your **Inbox** folder to any date on your **To-Do Bar's Date Navigator** pane. Outlook opens an **Appointment** window with the date filled in for the appointment. Enter a start and end time for the appointment. The body of the appointment holds the email message to remind you of the appointment's details.

▶ **TIP**

If you work with several others on a project and you routinely schedule the meetings, teach other members in your group about this drag-to-appointment feature. Send your meeting's agenda to each of your recipients, and they only need to drag the agenda email to Outlook's **Calendar** folder and set the meeting time and date. Before the meeting, they can quickly print the agenda.

▶ **NOTE**

If the message doesn't require an appointment but does include a task you'll need to perform in the future, drag the message to your **Navigation** pane's **Tasks** button instead of to your **Calendar** button to create a new to-do item.

3 Flag a Message

Outlook enables you to flag a message for a follow-up later. Click a message's flag to display several flag options. The flag will remain with the email message and appear in your **Inbox** folder or elsewhere, depending on where you later move the message. The flag reminds you that you need to follow up somehow to this message.

Flagging a message does more than attach a flagged icon to it. Outlook also sends a copy of the message to your **To-Do Bar**, as well as your calendar and task list, so that you have ample reminders of a message you wanted to follow up with. If you flag a message to be followed up one week later, in a week you'll get an Outlook calendar reminder to handle that email.

124

4 Create Category Names and Colors

Outlook 2007 introduced organizing colors for your messages. The colors enable you to quickly spot messages from certain key people about key topics.

▶ **TIP**

Mark all related messages with the same color to quickly locate all emails in that group. You can assign multiple colors to the same message if a message falls in multiple categories.

Create category names and colors. Don't overdo the number of categories, or all the colors and categories will clutter Outlook and nothing will stand out the way you need certain colorized messages to do.

When you first install or upgrade to Outlook 2007, no category names are assigned to the colors. When you first assign a category color to an email, Outlook asks you for that category name. Subsequently, Outlook uses that name for that color's category when you assign the color to messages in the

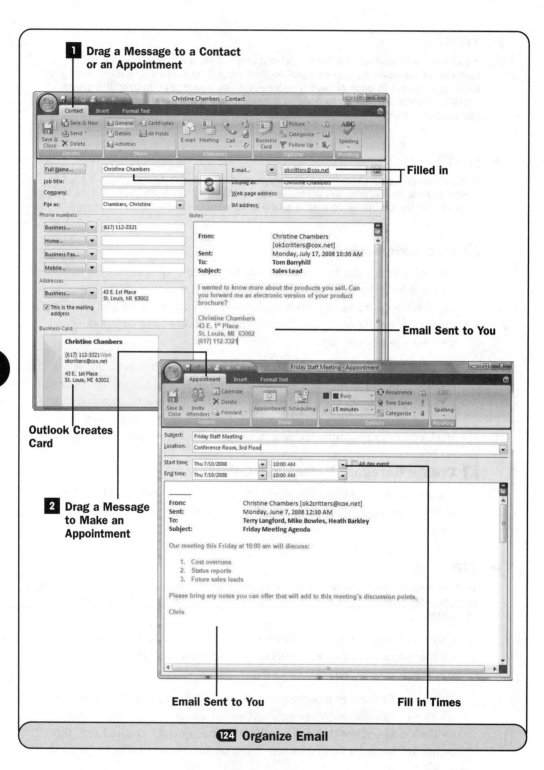

1 Drag a Message to a Contact or an Appointment

Filled in

Email Sent to You

Outlook Creates Card

2 Drag a Message to Make an Appointment

Email Sent to You

Fill in Times

124 Organize Email

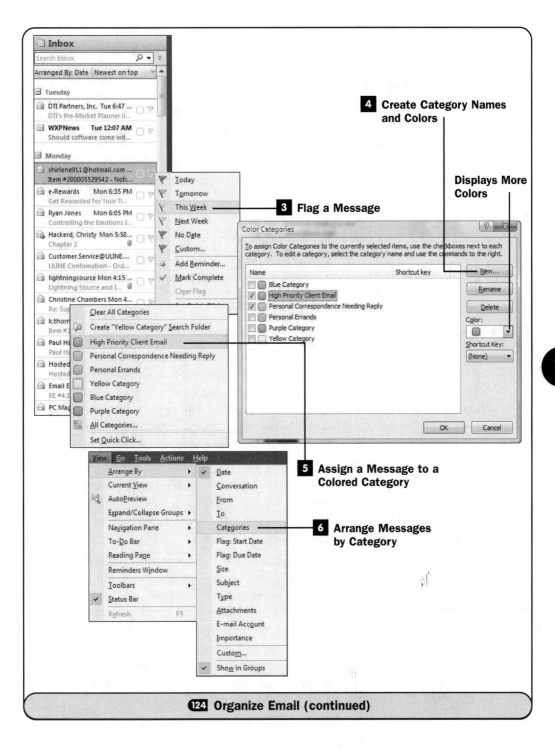

4 Create Category Names and Colors

Displays More Colors

3 Flag a Message

5 Assign a Message to a Colored Category

6 Arrange Messages by Category

124

future. It's probably best, however, to take some time now to assign categories to colors. At first, consider high-level categories that you'll utilize later, such as high-priority client emails or, perhaps, personal correspondence that requires follow-up later.

Click the **Categorize** button on Outlook's toolbar to display the category list. Select **All Categories** to display the **Color Categories** dialog box. Click to select a category color and then click **Rename** to assign a category name to that color. Complete more categories if you know more categories that you want to assign to set up your categories. Click **OK** to close the dialog box.

▶ TIP

Selecting **Set Quick Click** from Outlook's **Categorize** toolbar button opens the **Set Quick Click** dialog box. Select your most frequent category from the drop-down list and click **OK**. Subsequently, when you click an email's category icon to the right of the message in your **Inbox** folder, Outlook instantly assigns that category to the message so that you don't have to select from your category list.

124

5 Assign a Message to a Colored Category

Right-click the category icon to the right of an email to display a pop-up list of categories. You'll see both categories you've assigned new names to and category colors you haven't assigned names to (but those will have a default name such as **Blue Category**). Click to select the category that goes with the message. If you select an unsigned category, Outlook displays the **Rename Category** dialog box so that you can assign a more appropriate name to the category color you select.

Feel free to assign additional category colors to the same message if the message falls into multiple categories.

6 Arrange Messages by Category

Having all emails from the same category can be useful at times. Instead of keeping your email arranged in date order, you can select **View, Arrange By, Categories** to sort your **Inbox** folder (or whatever email folder you're viewing) in category order. All emails of the same color sort together. You then can address your messages by category topic. As you deal with each email, you'll probably reply to, forward, delete, and move emails from your **Inbox** folder because an organized Outlook user typically keeps the **Inbox** folder fairly clean. That way, new incoming messages and old messages are put where they belong and don't fall through the cracks and get ignored.

After you finish processing your categorized email folder, select **View, Arrange By, Date** to restore the email folder to a date-sorted view.

▶ **NOTE**

Keeping your **Inbox** folder sorted by date is important so that you'll see new email messages at the top of your **Inbox**, where they have the most prominence.

125 About Protecting Yourself Against Junk and Malicious Emails

✔ **BEFORE YOU BEGIN**

117 About Outlook's Capabilities
122 Check for New Mail

In today's world, you must address the problem of junk email (often called *spam*) and security threats that can arrive in your **Inbox** folder. No matter how careful you are, your **Inbox** folder will get some email that can cause problems, or at the very least, that fills your **Inbox** with junk that wastes your time to delete.

▶ **TIP**

The first step to stem the tide is to install and maintain antivirus software such as Norton AntiVirus. Keep such software up-to-date by installing any updates that the program requests to install.

Here are the rules of thumb for protecting yourself against junk email and email-based security threats:

1. Don't open attachments from senders you don't know or trust.

2. Even when you're sent an email from someone you know and trust, use caution. Look at the email's subject and text within its body to get a sense as to whether it truly was sent by your friend. Some email threats take over a user's Inbox and send malicious emails to everyone in the user's Inbox without the user's knowledge.

3. It's worth repeating: Install antivirus software and keep it up-to-date.

4. Use Outlook's Junk Email filters.

5. Don't click links inside suspicious emails.

Don't be fooled by *phishing* scams. Emailers of such scams are getting wiser and sending more official-looking emails. Fortunately, many of them still give themselves away with bad grammar and spelling, but that will change. An email from a company you do business with will almost always address you by name to show that it's real and will never ask for your password. If you are unsure whether an email is actually from your bank or some website you do business with, don't click the email's link. Instead, open your Internet browser and log in to the site by first typing the real web address yourself.

125

► **NEW TERM**

Phishing—Creating an email that appears to be from a known source, such as eBay, PayPal, or a major bank, that contains links to phony websites that try to sell you something or, worse, attempt to fool you into entering your username and password into a web page that looks to be from the original company but is not.

Some email problems can arrive embedded in graphics images inside an email message body. By default, Outlook does not display graphics images in your email **Reading** pane. Instead, Outlook displays an icon; you can right-click the icon and select **Download Pictures** from the pop-up menu to see the image. Also, a message appears toward the top of the email that you can click to download the images.

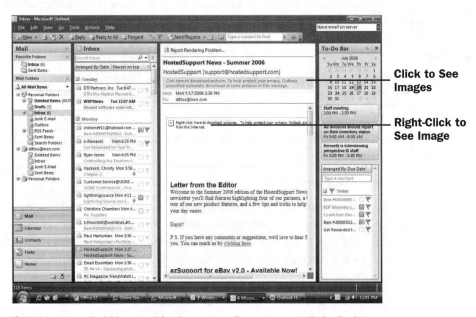

125

Click to See Images

Right-Click to See Image

Outlook generally hides graphics images until you request their display.

If you right-click an email message in your **Inbox**, select **Junk E-mail**, and select either **Add Sender to Safe Senders List** or **Add Sender's Domain (@sample.com) to Safe Senders List**, Outlook will not block subsequent messages you receive from that sender or from that sender's *domain*. Never request that Outlook allow email from a generic domain such as AOL.com to come through your system. For emails from friends, family, and associates who have email addresses with the large firms such as AOL.com, add the sender's email but not the domain to your safe senders list.

▶ NEW TERM

Domain—A web address such as SamsPublishing.com or BidMentor.com. A domain always appears inside a web address but also follows the @ in an email address.

You can use the right-click menu's **Junk E-mail** option to inform Outlook of a sender whose emails you no longer want to receive. By selecting the **Add Sender to Blocked Senders List**, you request that Outlook send that email to your **Junk E-mail** folder if the sender ever sends you another email.

▶ NOTE

Unless you're certain of the source, don't click email links that state you can unsubscribe to an email by following that link. Many spammers send email to millions of made-up, unverified, random email addresses. Those who click the **Unsubscribe** link indirectly tell the spammer that the email address is valid and should be saved for future use. Don't reply to any spam message for the same reason.

Review Outlook's junk email options regularly. Select **Actions**, **Junk E-mail**, **Junk E-mail Options** to display the **Junk E-mail Options** dialog box. Adjust your settings to suit your particular situation. For example, you can request that Outlook perform no automatic filtering of junk email, but if you do, Outlook will not monitor your email for known junk mail and your **Inbox** folder will fill with everything. If you select **Low**, Outlook moves only what it is certain is junk email to your **Junk E-mail** folder. A **High** setting catches most junk email but will also send some valid email that Outlook incorrectly identifies as junk to your **Junk E-mail** folder.

Anytime you set Outlook's junk email filter to a setting more severe than **No Automatic Filtering**, you should check your **Junk E-mail** folder every day or two to make sure that no valid email ends up there. If you find a valid email in your **Junk E-mail** folder, right-click that message and add the sender to your safe senders list.

The **Junk E-mail Options** dialog box also includes other settings that help you control the amount of junk email you receive.

▶ NOTE

If you accidentally add an email sender's address to your safe senders list or accidentally add a valid email to your blocked senders list, you can edit either list from within the **Junk E-mail Options** dialog box.

Click to Edit Lists

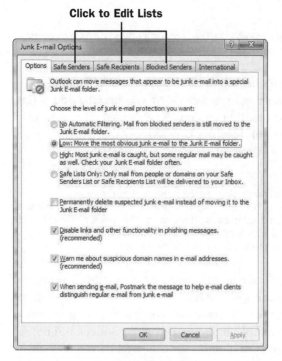

Control the amount of junk mail you receive from within your Junk E-mail Options dialog box.

► **TIP**

You can tell Outlook to regard all email addresses in your **Contacts** folder as safe by selecting **Tools, Options, Safe Senders** and clicking to set the **Also Trust E-mail from my Contacts** option.

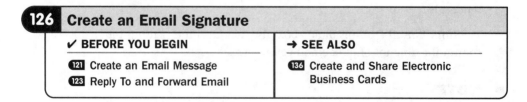

126   Create an Email Signature

✔ BEFORE YOU BEGIN	→ SEE ALSO
121 Create an Email Message	136 Create and Share Electronic
123 Reply To and Forward Email	Business Cards

You can add a message to the bottom of every email you send by creating an *email signature*. For example, if you routinely sell on eBay, you might want to create an email signature that directs all readers of your email to a list of your current auctions. A company might require that all emails sent from the company's domain include a privacy clause or perhaps an equal-opportunity employment clause.

▶ **NEW TERM**

Email signature—Text (which can have a hyperlink to a web page) that automatically appears at the bottom of every email you send.

Every time you create an email, Outlook automatically adds your signature to the bottom of the email. You don't need to do anything, except when you do not want to send the signature along with the email, in which case you can easily delete it from individual emails. To really catch the reader's eye, you can highlight your email signature in color or format the signature to look the way you want it to look.

▶ **TIP**

Outlook enables you to include an electronic business card in your outgoing message signatures. See **136 Create and Share Electronic Business Cards**.

1 Request a Signature

When composing an email message, click to display your **Message** ribbon if it's not already active. Click **Signature** and then select **Signatures** to open the **Signatures and Stationary** dialog box. (If the names of signatures appear when you first click **Signature**, you can select any of them to apply that specific signature to your email instead of the default signature Outlook may have added automatically when you first created the email.)

2 Create a Signature

Click the **New** button to create a new signature. Give your signature a name so that you'll be able to select the signature from a list of additional signatures you might add in the future.

▶ **TIP**

If you create two signatures, you can request that Outlook send one of them at the bottom of only email replies and forwarded email and the other at the bottom of any new email message you send. You can also select from a list of signatures at the time you compose a new email message.

3 Type the Signature Body

Type the text for the body of your email signature. Stay to the point and try to write compelling text that grabs the reader, especially if your signature is trying to sell the reader, get the reader to check a website, or perform some other action.

126

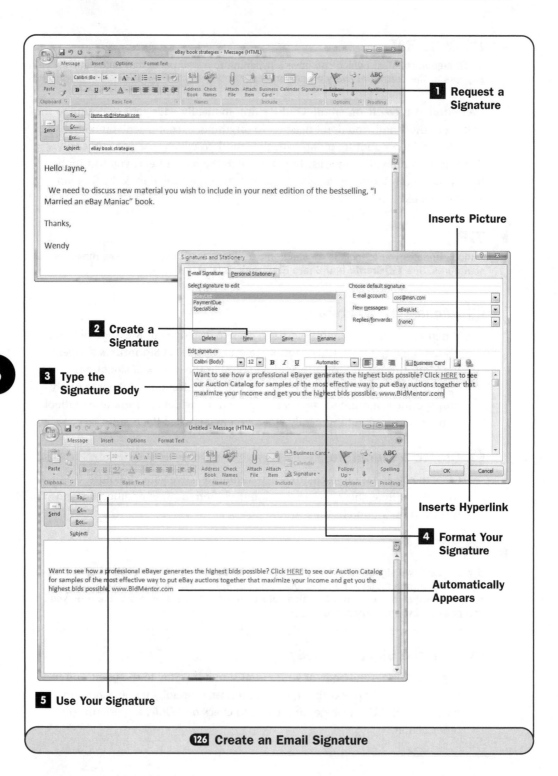

1 Request a Signature

Inserts Picture

2 Create a Signature

3 Type the Signature Body

Inserts Hyperlink

4 Format Your Signature

Automatically Appears

5 Use Your Signature

126 Create an Email Signature

4 Format Your Signature

After your signature reads the way you want it to, you can begin to format it to your liking. You can apply a specific text color or font to the signature's text. Also, you can insert a picture or hyperlink by clicking where you want to place the picture or selecting text to be used for the hyperlink and then clicking the appropriate buttons.

▶ TIP

If your goal for your signature is to get the email's recipient to click a link, some find that formatting the entire signature's text as a hyperlink is more likely to grab that click than an embedded hyperlink. You'll need to test this to see which works best in your situation.

Click the **Business Card** button to select an electronic business card to use for the signature, or possibly in addition to the signature's text you've created.

After you finish the signature, click **OK** to save it.

5 Use Your Signature

The next time you create a new email message, Outlook places your default signature at the bottom of the message. The first time you view your signature in an email message, look over the font and formatting to be sure that it won't clash too much (or fit in too much) with the body of the email. If it does, go back to the **Signatures and Stationary** dialog box and format the signature more appropriately.

▶ TIP

Adding a few blank spaces above a signature or using a smaller signature font size helps to distinguish a signature from your email message.

---

127 Create a To-Do List

✔ BEFORE YOU BEGIN	→ SEE ALSO
121 Create an Email Message	**133** Navigate Times and Dates
124 Organize Email	**137** Write Yourself a Note
	138 About OneNote

Outlook's strength is in its organization. One way you can accomplish all you need to get done is to make lists of tasks and cross them off as you do them. Outlook helps you automate just that. The **To-Do Bar** is new in Outlook 2007 and further strengthens Outlook's to-do capabilities.

The **To-Do Bar** integrates several Outlook functions, including tasks, appointments, emails flagged for follow-ups, and even OneNote elements (see **138 About OneNote**).

■ Review Your To-Do Bar

Look at your **To-Do Bar** to see everything that Outlook offers in a one-stop location. The **To-Do bar** includes your Date Navigator, near appointments, and tasks you've set up to do.

▶ TIP

Drag the line that separates your **To-Do Bar** from your **Reading** pane to increase or shrink the amount of space devoted to the **To-Do Bar**.

② Change the To-Do Bar's Subject

Suppose that you store a message or task that doesn't have a descriptive title. You can change a **To-Do Bar**'s title without actually changing the underlying email's subject or the task's title.

Click the task whose title you want to change, and type a new title. Often you'll shorten the title so that it fits well on the **To-Do Bar**.

127

③ Adjust Your To-Do Bar's Appearance

If your **To-Do Bar** doesn't exactly appear the way you prefer, you can change it. Select **View**, **To-Do Bar**, and click to select or uncheck the **Date Navigator**, **Appointments**, or **Task List** options to hide or display those elements on your **To-Do Bar**. The menu's **Options** choice opens your **To-Do Bar Options** dialog box. (The **To-Do Bar** view menu is also available if you right-click over a blank area of your **To-Do Bar**.)

④ Specify To-Do Bar Options

The **To-Do Bar Options** dialog box enables you to specify the maximum number of months and appointments you want to display at any one time on your **To-Do Bar**. You can click to uncheck the **To-Do Bar**'s task list if you prefer not to see your tasks on the **To-Do Bar**.

▶ TIP

If you use multiple monitors on your Windows desktop, you can expand Outlook so that its window expands past the first monitor. You can keep Outlook in one window and adjust Outlook's window so that your **To-Do Bar** fills the edge of the second monitor.

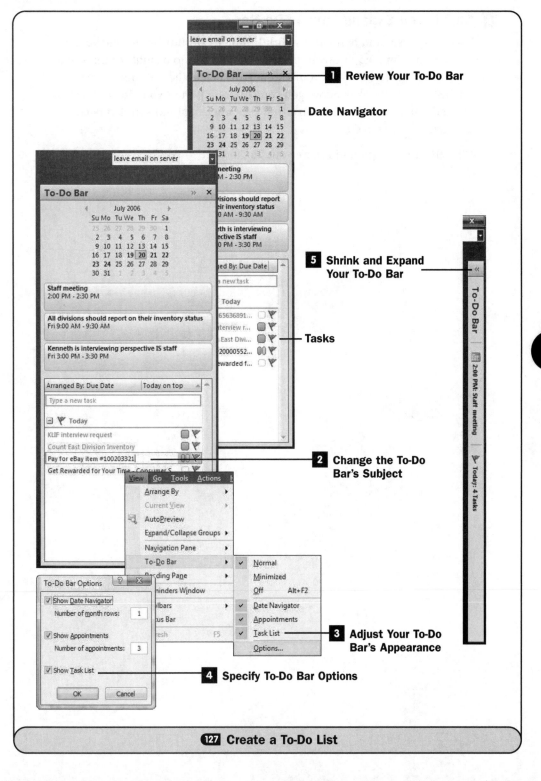

1 Review Your To-Do Bar

— Date Navigator

5 Shrink and Expand Your To-Do Bar

— Tasks

2 Change the To-Do Bar's Subject

3 Adjust Your To-Do Bar's Appearance

4 Specify To-Do Bar Options

127

5 Shrink and Expand Your To-Do Bar

You can quickly and temporarily shrink your **To-Do Bar** by clicking your **To-Do Bar**'s minimizing arrow. Your **To-Do Bar** shrinks to a single column that aligns with the right side of your Outlook window. When it's minimized against your Outlook window, you can click any part of your **To-Do Bar** to expand it back to its original size, and click once again to shrink it back to the edge of your screen.

Click the arrows again to restore your **To-Do Bar**.

127

15

Making Contact

IN THIS CHAPTER:

Your **Contacts** folder comprises a vital piece of Outlook. In the folder are your contacts for friends, family, clients, businesses, and others you associate with. After you store contact information, Outlook provides several ways to retrieve the data depending on how you want to see it.

Your **Contacts** folder provides a uniform repository of information to use when you send email, hold meetings, and make phone calls. You can add new contacts, delete the old ones you no longer need, and change information for a contact from your **Contacts** folder. Outlook 2007 includes a new electronic business card feature for each contact that you can easily share with others or use as your email's signature (see **126 Create an Email Signature**).

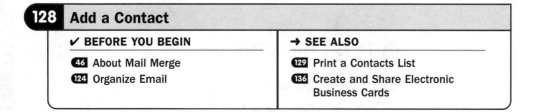

128	**Add a Contact**

✔ BEFORE YOU BEGIN	→ SEE ALSO
46 About Mail Merge	**129** Print a Contacts List
124 Organize Email	**136** Create and Share Electronic Business Cards

128

One way to add a new contact to your **Contacts** folder is to create a new contact entry and fill in the details. Actually, the first time you set up Outlook, this is probably what you'll do the most unless you've been storing your contact data in another program that you can import from. If you upgrade to Outlook 2007 from a previous version, all your contacts should appear the first time you start Outlook 2007, and generally you'll work your **Contacts** folder the same way you're used to.

▶ **NOTE**

Outlook 2007 automatically creates an electronic business card and displays that card at the bottom of any new contact you enter.

One quick way to create a contact, as you can see in **124 Organize Email**, is to drag an email message to your **Contacts** folder. You can also right-click the name of the sender of an email and select **Add to Contacts** to create a contact. Outlook creates a new **Contacts** dialog box and uses the email's message body to fill in the contact's comments. Creating a new contact from an email saves a step or two because Outlook can prefill the email address and often the name for you, but you'll still have to go through most of the motions to complete the rest of the contact's details such as the address and phone number, assuming that you know that information. If you don't know all a contact's information when you first create a contact, you can fill in details later.

1 View Your Contacts Folder

Click your **Contacts** button to display your contacts.

2 Request a New Contact

Click the **New** button to open a new **Contact** dialog box.

3 Complete the Name Information

Type your contact's name and optional title and company. The **File As** drop-down list box provides several combinations of title, name, and company from which you can choose to determine how your new contact will be sorted among your list of other contacts.

▶ **TIP**

If you click the **Full Name** button, Outlook displays the **Check Full Name** dialog box, which maintains separate fields for each part of a name (such as title, first name, and last name). The time you take to separate the parts of a name can pay off if you use your contact information in form letters (see **46 About Mail Merge**).

4 Complete the Phone and Address Information

Enter the contact's phone and address information. Click the down arrow to the left of the address area to select a different type of address to enter, such as the home address. You can store both a home address and a business address if you want, although only the selected type of address shows at any one time in the **Contact** dialog box.

▶ **NOTE**

Not every contact will have every kind of phone number available. If your contact doesn't have a business fax but does have an alternative phone number at work, click the down arrow next to **Business Fax** and select **Business 2** to enter and display that number. It's fine to leave such fields blank also.

Whatever type of address you elect to display in the **Contact** dialog box, if you click the **Address** button (which reads **Business** or perhaps **Home** depending on the address you chose to display), Outlook displays the **Check Address** dialog box, in which you can be sure to separate the various parts of the address. Outlook might display the **Check Address** dialog box on its own if you enter an address for your new contact that doesn't seem to follow a standard address format, although you can override the format and click **OK** to accept what you typed.

128

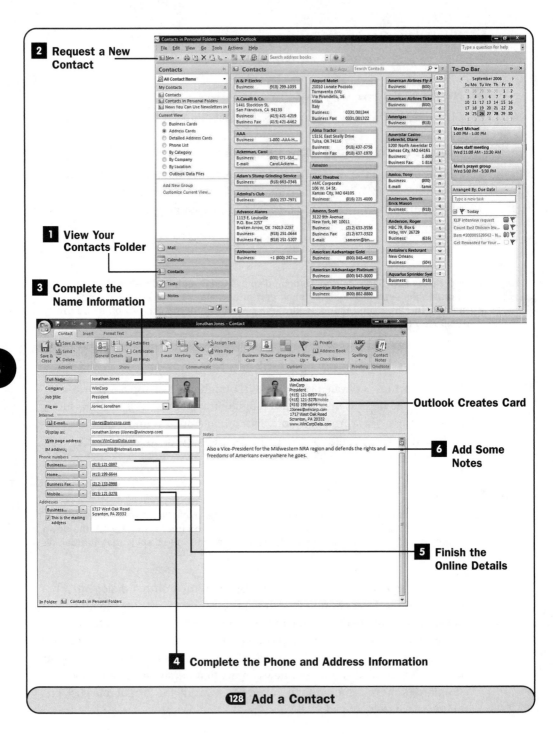

2 Request a New Contact

1 View Your Contacts Folder

3 Complete the Name Information

Outlook Creates Card

6 Add Some Notes

5 Finish the Online Details

4 Complete the Phone and Address Information

128

128 Add a Contact

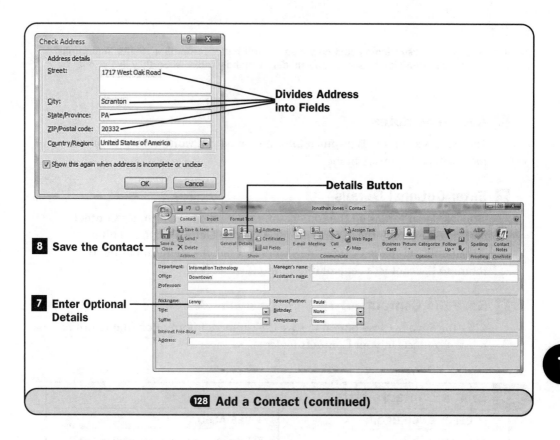

128 Add a Contact (continued)

5 Finish the Online Details

Enter the email, web page, and instant message (in the **IM address** field) address if you know any or all of those details. You can also select a picture from a photograph stored on your computer (perhaps that you took with a digital camera or scanned from a photograph). Click the picture icon and select the graphic image from the **Add Contact Picture** dialog box that Outlook opens. You'll notice that as you add details, including the optional picture, Outlook builds the electronic business card in the upper-right part of the **Contact** dialog box.

▶ **TIP**

A picture for business clients could help a sales staff better remember clients. And family head shots are often nice to see as a reminder of friendly faces when they live a long way from you.

6 Add Some Notes

The **Notes** section holds as much information as you want to keep for a contact, such as a spouse's name.

7 Enter Optional Details

Outlook doesn't show all the contact's information on the primary **Contact** dialog box but only the general details. Click the **Details** button to fill in additional data related to your new contact. Click the **General** button to return to the contact's general information.

8 Save the Contact

Click the **Save & Close** button to save the contact's information and return to a list of contacts in your **Contacts** folder.

129

---

129 | **Print a Contacts List**

✔ BEFORE YOU BEGIN	→ SEE ALSO
128 Add a Contact	**130** Create an Email Distribution List
	132 Search for Contacts and Other Outlook Data

Outlook can print a list of your contacts. That isn't too surprising. The surprise comes when you see how many forms such printed contacts can take. Outlook supports most of the popular time-organizing systems on the market and will format your contacts list to look exactly the way you want it to look. In addition, you can specify that only certain contacts be included in the list so that you can print both a business and a personal record to stay in touch when you need a paper-based list to refer to.

1 View the Contacts Folder

Click to display your contacts.

2 Display the Address Cards

Click to select **Address Cards** in your **Navigation** pane's **Current View** section. You can minimize your **To-Do Bar** to make more room for your contacts.

▶ **NOTE**

If your **Current View** section doesn't show a list of display views, click the arrow to expand your **Current View** section.

3 Select the Fields to Print

Perhaps you don't want to print every detail of every contact. Select **View**, **Current View**, **Customize Current View**, click the **Fields** button, and determine which fields you want to print. Scroll down the right-hand list and click on any field you want to remove; then click the **Remove** button. To add a field not on the right, scroll down the left list and click any field you want to add; then click the **Add** button. Use the **Move Up** and **Move Down** buttons to adjust the order. Click **OK** to close the **Show Fields** dialog box.

▶ **NOTE**

Removing and adding fields adjusts only the data you see, and subsequently print. It does not remove or add any information to your actual contact records stored in Outlook.

129

4 Select a Print Style

Select **File**, **Print**. Outlook enables you to select the output style you want to use. Several formats are available, including a phone-directory style that minimizes space and prints name, address, and phone only, not unlike a phone book.

5 Print Your Contacts

Click **OK** to print your contacts.

6 Set Up Special Page Details

Depending on how you want to print and the type of paper or card stock you want to print onto, you may need to click the **Print** dialog box's **Page Setup** button to adjust the target page. You can also access the **Page Setup** dialog box from the **File**, **Page Setup**, **Define Print Styles** menu option. The **Page Setup** dialog provides all the margin and page sizing measurements needed to ensure that you print your data exactly the way you intend.

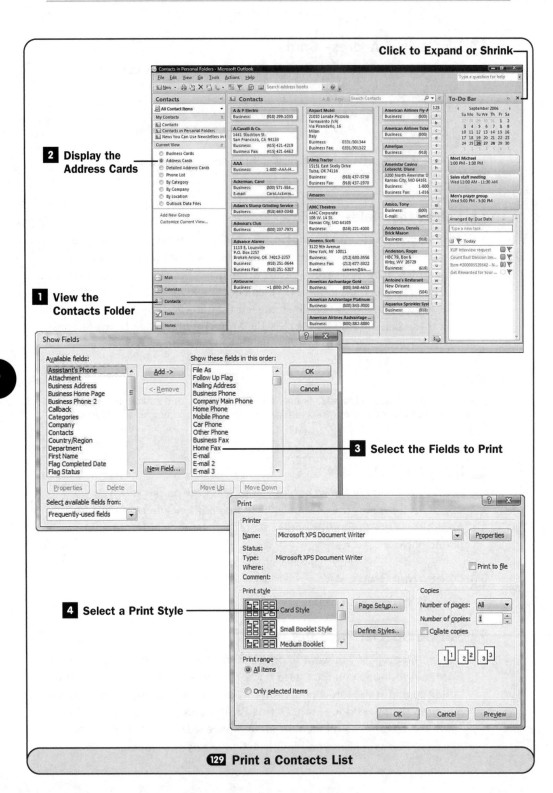

Click to Expand or Shrink

2 Display the Address Cards

1 View the Contacts Folder

3 Select the Fields to Print

4 Select a Print Style

129

129 Print a Contacts List

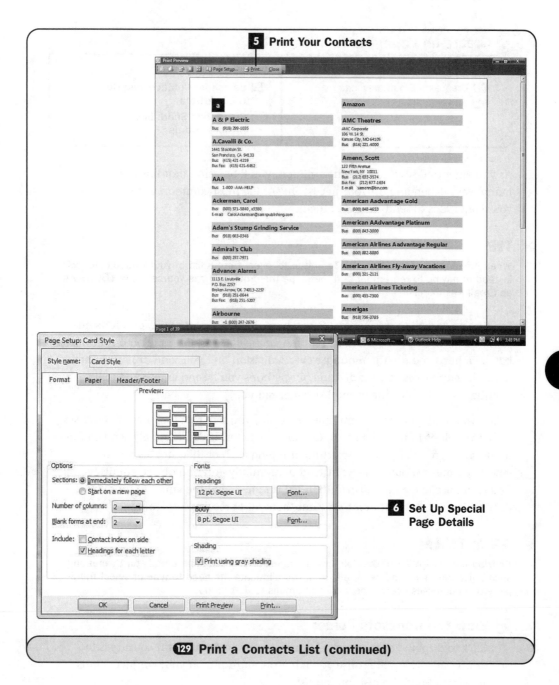

5 Print Your Contacts

6 Set Up Special Page Details

129 Print a Contacts List (continued)

130 Create an Email Distribution List

✔ BEFORE YOU BEGIN	→ SEE ALSO
121 Create an Email Message	132 Search for Contacts and Other Outlook Data
128 Add a Contact	136 Create and Share Electronic Business Cards

As you enter and save contact information, you'll be using that information in many ways depending on your needs. One of the most common ways you'll use your contacts is to send emails to them.

▶ TIP

When creating an email, click the **To** button to select from a list of your Outlook contacts instead of having to remember and then type the email address yourself. See 121 **Create an Email Message.**

Sending one email to one contact is common. But once in a while, and for some it will be far more often, you'll be sending emails to several people on a routine basis. Perhaps you are the manager over a division and you send announcements to all the employees in your division. Or perhaps you'll send emails to family members to tell about the annual summer reunion.

When you send an email to multiple recipients, you separate their email addresses with semicolons in the email's **To**, **Cc**, and **Bcc** fields. If you routinely send emails to the same group of people, selecting or typing each of their names for each email becomes tedious quickly. Instead of manually entering all the emails, you'll find it simpler to create a *distribution list* and just send the email to those on the distribution list the next time you want them all to receive something.

▶ NEW TERM

Distribution list—A list of multiple email addresses you can send emails to. By creating such a list and then sending emails to it, you eliminate the need to type or select multiple email addresses every time you send emails to that group.

1 View the Contacts Folder

Click to display your contacts. Minimize your **To-Do Bar** if it consumes too much screen space, because you'll be concentrating on your contact details while you build the distribution list.

2 Request the Distribution List

Select **File, New, Distribution List**. (Ctrl+Shift+L is the shortcut key for this; just remember *L* for *List*.) Outlook opens the **Distribution List** dialog box.

3 Add Contacts to the List

Click the **Select Members** button on your **Distribution List** ribbon. Outlook opens the **Select Members** dialog box. Scroll down the list and click individual contacts to add them to the distribution list you're building. Hold down your Ctrl key as you click to select multiple names. If you select a name you don't want to add, click it once more to deselect it.

▶ **NOTE**

Don't select a contact for which no email address appears in the **E-mail Address** field inside the **Select Members** dialog box.

You can type a name in the **Type Name or Select from List** box to start a search for contacts that begin with the letters you enter if you want to locate a contact more quickly than scrolling through the list below.

4 Finish the List

Click the **Members** button to add your selected names to your distribution list. After you do, all the names appear to the right of the button along with their email addresses. You can click inside this text box and delete any entry by backspacing over it. In addition, you can add more names to those already present.

Click **OK** to close the dialog box.

5 Name and Save the List

Type a name in the **Distribution List** dialog box's **Name** field to name this distribution list. Click the **Distribution List** dialog box's **Save & Close** button to return to your **Contacts** folder.

6 Locate Your Distribution List

Your new distribution list will appear as an entry inside your **Contacts** folder. A distribution icon will appear to designate it as a list, although the name you assigned to it will also be a good reminder of the entry's purpose.

To see the distribution list, double-click its entry in your **Contacts** folder. The **Distribution List** again opens to show all that list's entries. You can manage your contacts there as needed by adding new ones and removing ones that no longer are to be part of your list.

7 Send an Email to the Distribution List

Click **Mail** and then click **File, New, Mail Message** (Ctrl+N is the shortcut key) to open a new email message dialog box. Instead of typing an email or

130

130

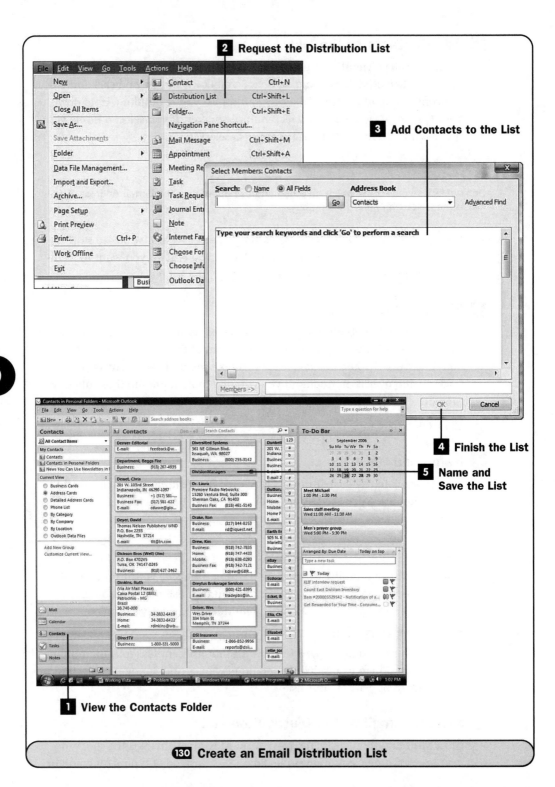

2 Request the Distribution List

3 Add Contacts to the List

4 Finish the List

5 Name and Save the List

1 View the Contacts Folder

130 Create an Email Distribution List

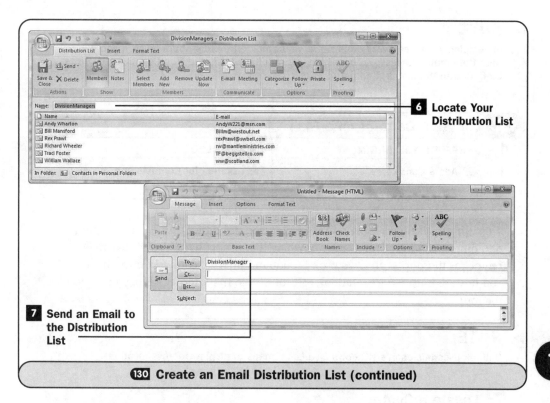

6 Locate Your Distribution List

7 Send an Email to the Distribution List

130 Create an Email Distribution List (continued)

clicking **To** to select a list of names, type the first few letters of your distribution list's name and press Ctrl+K. Outlook opens the **Check Names** dialog box, from which you can select the distribution list. Outlook places the full name of your distribution list in the **To** box but puts a plus sign next to the name.

If you click the name, Outlook expands the list to show every name in the list, inside the **To** field, separated by semicolons. You cannot shrink this list back to your distribution list name, so don't expand the list unless you need to. You might need to if you're sending a special email to everyone on a regular distribution list except one perhaps, such as a birthday candidate whom you don't want to know about the party you've inviting everyone to. Expanding the list and removing the one name is far easier than creating yet another distribution list without the one name.

When you click **Send**, Outlook sends your email to everyone on your distribution list.

▶ **NOTE**

All recipients will see every other name and email on the distribution list. If you don't want the email addresses to be visible, you will have to fill the **Bcc** field instead of the **Cc** field with the distribution list.

---

131   Locate a Contact on a Map

✔ **BEFORE YOU BEGIN**	→ **SEE ALSO**
128 Add a Contact	132 Search for Contacts and Other Outlook Data

---

This is a surprisingly simple and yet enjoyable and useful task: Locate a contact and almost instantly view a map of where the contact lives! You'll have to be online, as those with an always-on broadband Internet connection will be. If you have dial-up service, Outlook will connect to the Internet when you request the map.

131

▶ **NOTE**

Outlook uses Microsoft's *Windows Live Local* maps to display address locations.

1 Locate a Contact

Open your **Contacts** folder and scroll to the contact you want to map. You can click the scrollbars, click a letter button to get to the contact's alphabetized name, or search for the contact.

2 Open the Contact Window

Double-click to open the contact's window. There isn't a way to display a map of a contact except from the contact's specific window.

3 Locate the Address to Map

Click the down arrow next to the address to display the address type you want to locate on a map. Some contacts will have multiple address types, such as home and business. If you have only one address stored for your contact and have selected that address as the mailing address, you won't need to open the address drop-down list box to select a different address.

▶ **TIP**

To designate one of the multiple addresses as the mailing address and the default address that Outlook displays when you view the contact, select the address and click to check the option labeled **This Is the Mailing Address**.

4 Request the Map

Click the **Contact** ribbon's **Map** button. Outlook browses the web to locate the map. Outlook opens your operating system's Internet web browser and displays the map.

5 View the Map

Outlook places an icon of a pushpin at the address on the map. When you're at the map, you can point to the pushpin and zoom in to the map for more detail or zoom out from the map for less detail but to see more area, get driving directions, delete the pushpin (to clear clutter from the map), or send the map as an email attachment, depending on which selection you choose from the options that pop up when you point to the pushpin.

▶ **NOTE**

As you add new addresses to the map, the **Scratch Pad** window updates to show the multiple addresses. Click over any to see details of that particular address.

Select **Collections, Add Pushpin** to add another address to the map if you want to mark several locations that appear on the same map.

131

6 Get Driving Directions

To get driving directions, click **Driving Directions** and enter a starting address and an ending address in the **Start** and **End** boxes. If the pushpin's location is your destination or starting point for the directions you want to receive, select **Drive From** or **Drive To** from the pop-up menu that appears when you point to the pushpin, and type the address of the destination or origin; Outlook fills in the other box with the pushpin's address. Click **Get Directions** to see the driving directions you can print for the trip. Scroll the direction's text box to see all the directions on the screen.

▶ **TIP**

Before requesting directions, click to select the **Quickest** or **Shortest** option below the direction entry area depending on your trip's priority. (Often, but not always, depending on highway conditions and available roads, these will produce the same results.)

If you want to check on traffic before you leave, click the map's **Traffic** option to get real-time traffic data around the address. This information isn't available for all towns and locations, but you will often get the data, especially if you're viewing a populated area.

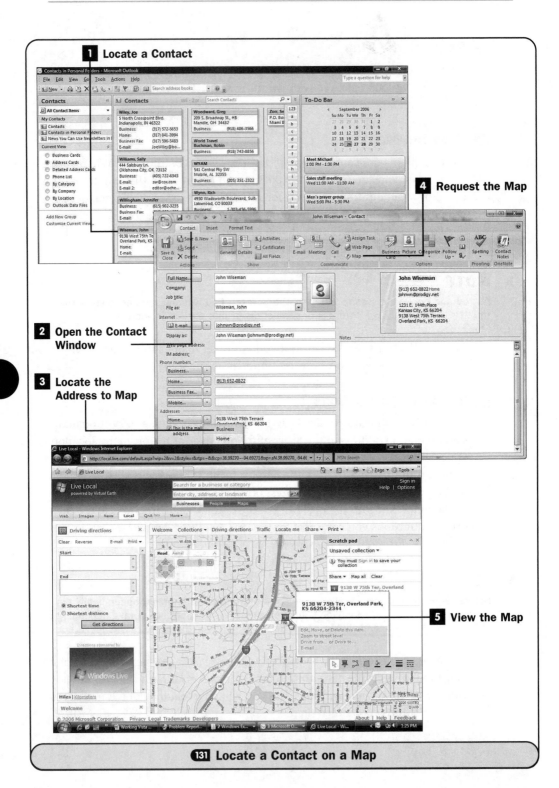

131

1 Locate a Contact

2 Open the Contact Window

3 Locate the Address to Map

4 Request the Map

5 View the Map

131 Locate a Contact on a Map

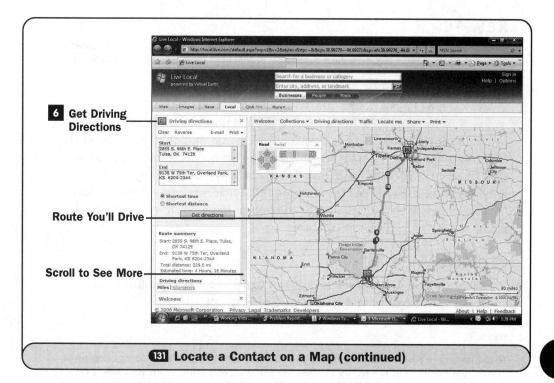

6 Get Driving Directions

Route You'll Drive

Scroll to See More

131 Locate a Contact on a Map (continued)

132

▶ **NOTE**

Outlook provides several printing options while you view the map. From the map's **Print** option, you can print the map and customize how you want it to appear on paper.

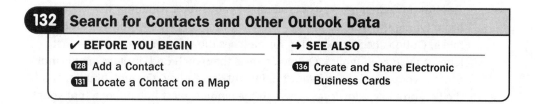

132 **Search for Contacts and Other Outlook Data**

✔ **BEFORE YOU BEGIN**	→ **SEE ALSO**
128 Add a Contact	**136** Create and Share Electronic
131 Locate a Contact on a Map	Business Cards

Outlook 2007 greatly improved on the search capabilities in previous versions of Outlook. Many users regard the search capabilities of earlier versions with disdain, and for good reason: The search typically was slow, was bloated, and produced mediocre results.

Finding what you want to find with Outlook 2007 is a breeze. You'll be able to locate contacts easily and locate email fast. Although all of Outlook 2007's search features are quick, Outlook's new ***Instant Search*** feature is the quickest way to locate what you want to find.

▶ NEW TERM

Instant Search—Available in a search box at the top of your Outlook screen, this search produces quick results because data is indexed in a search table as you enter and edit Outlook data.

Unless you run Outlook 2007 in the Windows Vista environment, Outlook will request that you install the Instant Search the first time you use it. When you request the installation, Outlook downloads some information from the Internet and installs the needed Instant Search tools. The Instant Search box appears in Outlook whether or not it's been installed to run. If you haven't upgraded to Windows Vista yet or haven't installed Instant Search, you can still search from the Instant Search box, but the results will appear more slowly, especially if you maintain a lot of Outlook data and emails.

■ Locate Your Email

Click to display your **Inbox** folder, **Sent Items** folder, or any other email folder you've created and stored email messages in.

132

▶ TIP

To create a new email folder, right-click your **Inbox** folder entry on your **Navigation** pane, select **New Folder**, and name your folder. You can drag any email from your **Inbox** or other email-related folder to the new folder. By creating a series of folders, you can organize your email into categories such as **Business** and **Personal**. Get as detailed as you want with as many folders as you want to create.

② Search for Text

The Instant Search box rests at the top of your **Inbox** window. Click there and begin typing the word or phrase you're wanting to locate within your **Inbox** folder. Outlook begins searching for matches the moment you type the first letter. As you keep typing, Outlook refines the search and displays emails that contain your search term below the Instant Search box. Outlook highlights the background yellow everywhere in the email subject line or body that your search term is found.

▶ NOTE

If no match is found in your **Inbox** folder, Outlook displays the message No Matches Found. You can click the link labeled **Try Searching Again in All Mail Items** to search all your email folders for the text you're looking for.

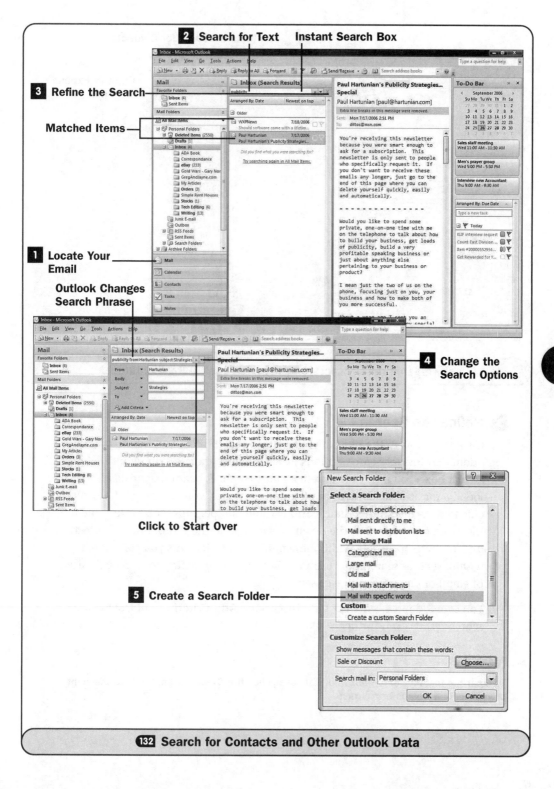

2 Search for Text   Instant Search Box

3 Refine the Search

Matched Items

1 Locate Your Email

Outlook Changes Search Phrase

4 Change the Search Options

Click to Start Over

5 Create a Search Folder

132

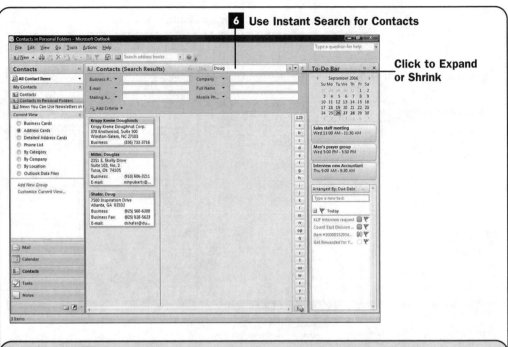

132

132 Search for Contacts and Other Outlook Data (continued)

3 Refine the Search

Click the arrow to the right of your Instant Search box's text box to open additional Instant Search options. (Clicking once more restores your Instant Search box.) You'll be able to refine your search. For example, instead of looking for one search term in all email messages, you can search for a specific term located in an email's **Subject** line and perhaps look for a name in the **From** text box. Click the down arrows next to the **From**, **Body**, **Subject**, and **To** boxes to specify additional email-related elements you can search within, such as searching within the **Bcc** field or searching for a specific size of email or date an email was sent to you.

You can add more search criteria by clicking **Add Criteria** to narrow your search results even further.

▶ NOTE

To clear the Instant Search box and start over, click the **Clear** button, the **X** to the right of your Instant Search box phrase.

❹ Change the Search Options

Click the down arrow to the right of your Instant Search box phrase and select **Search Options** to change the Instant Search box's behavior. The **Search Options** dialog box appears, where you can limit the folders searched, change the highlighting color of located text, and modify other behavior related to your Instant Search box.

▶ TIP

Outlook remembers recent searches. Click to display the Instant Search box's drop-down list box to see recent searches that you can request again just by selecting them.

❺ Create a Search Folder

A Search Folder is an email folder that contains shortcuts to emails. These are shortcuts because Outlook doesn't actually move or copy messages to a Search Folder. A Search Folder is virtual in that it only appears as though it holds email. That email matches the criteria you've requested for that Search Folder.

Seeing a Search Folder in action helps one understand its purpose and content. To create a Search Folder, select **File**, **New**, **Search Folder**. Outlook displays the **New Search Folder** dialog box.

Listed in the dialog box are several criteria you can designate for a new Search Folder you want to create. Scroll down to see more options. Suppose you want to create a Search Folder that holds only email that contains specific words, such as "Sale" or "Discount." Scroll to the **Mail with Specific Words** option, click the **Choose** button, and add **Sale** and **Discount** to the list. When you click **OK**, the **New Search Folder** dialog box displays **Sale or Discount** in its **Show Messages** text box to indicate the kind of mail that will be stored in this Search Folder. When you click **OK** to close the **New Search Folder** dialog box, Outlook adds a new folder to your **Navigation** pane inside the **Search Folders** folder. Outlook also begins searching through your emails for any that meets the criteria of the search.

If Outlook locates any email that qualifies for the Search Folder, it stores a shortcut to that email in your Search Folder. For all practical purposes, the email appears to reside in the folder, so the fact that it's only a shortcut isn't vital except that it means the original email is still safely tucked away in its original location. If you change the criteria of a Search Folder and a message no longer qualifies for that Search Folder, Outlook removes the message from the Search Folder, but it still resides in its original location in another email folder. Also, Outlook constantly monitors your Search Folder criteria, and every time you receive, send, or create new email messages, if any new

132

messages match your Search Folder's criteria, Outlook stores the message there.

▶ **NOTE**

If you delete a message from your Search Folder, Outlook *does* remove the message from its original location, as well as removing its entry from the Search Folder.

You can customize criteria for your Search Folder instead of selecting from the **New Search Folder** dialog box's provided actions by scrolling the dialog box down to **Create a Custom Search Folder**, clicking **Choose**, and entering your own criteria for the new folder. You can create as many Search Folders as you need; Outlook stores them all in your **Navigation** pane's **Search Folders** folder. Click the plus sign next to your **Navigation** pane's **Search Folders** folder to display the Search Folders you've created.

Anytime you want to perform a search that you'll most likely have to repeat in the future, create a Search Folder for that search. You'll never need to enter the search again, just display the contents of that Search Folder to see the current search results.

132

6 **Use Instant Search for Contacts**

Locating a contact in your **Contacts** folder is relatively simple when you begin to populate your **Contacts** folder. Often you'll scroll to the contact you want to see and then double-click the contact to see the details if you need more than the current **Contacts** folder view allows.

As with all Outlook folders, your **Contacts** folder sports an Instant Search box. Type the first few letters of whatever contact you want to find—and you don't have to limit your search to last names; type any text or numbers from any contact field—and Outlook immediately begins locating contacts that match your search.

▶ **TIP**

Click to expand the **Contacts** folder's Instant Search box to add more search criteria so that you can limit your search to first or last names, phone numbers, addresses, or any of the other Outlook contact fields available.

16

Living with Outlook

IN THIS CHAPTER:

Outlook becomes your electronic secretary, reminding you of appointments, taking notes, and even handing out your business cards (electronically!). Navigating Outlook's date and time calendars, managing your appointments, and jotting notes for later reference are often daily requirements, and Outlook won't let you down.

Until Outlook 2007, another feature was missing from Outlook that now has become commonplace for many users through add-on programs, and it's nice to see Outlook 2007 support this feature, which is called RSS feeds. Outlook now provides you with a real-time look at changing web data. So in addition to scheduled appointments, Outlook lets you know about breaking news available on your favorite website.

---

133 Navigate Times and Dates

✔ BEFORE YOU BEGIN	→ SEE ALSO
117 About Outlook's Capabilities	**134** Set Up an Appointment
118 Master the Outlook Screen	

133

You can change Outlook's calendar to work the way you prefer. Look at a day, week, or month at a glance. Print calendars for your reference offline or to give your schedule to others.

Click Outlook's **Calendar** button in the lower-left corner to view your calendar. The calendar appears in these major sections:

- **Date Navigator**—Appears as a monthly calendar pane with one month displayed by default and enables you to move quickly through the calendar year.

- **Daily Scheduler**—Enables you to enter and edit appointments for today or other days.

When you first open Calendar, the Date Navigator always highlights the current date (getting its information from your computer's internal clock and calendar) by placing a square outline around the day. The current date's daily scheduler appears on your screen showing your current day's appointments, if any exist, plus a current list of tasks.

1 View Your Calendar

Click the **Calendar** button in the lower-left hand corner of your Outlook screen.

2 Change the Day Viewed

Click a specific date inside your **Date Navigator** panel, or click anywhere and press your left- and right-arrow keys to move the date selector across the dates. As you do, the daily scheduler changes to show your appointments for each day you select.

3 Change to a Month View

Click the **Month** button atop the daily schedule to see your whole month at a glance. Click the **Week** button to see a week, and **Day** once again to view the day's appointments you selected in the **Date Navigator** pane.

▶ **TIP**

When you're viewing a week or month of dates, additional options appear at the top of your calendar. You can elect to show only your work weekdays or the entire week in your weekly view. In your monthly view, you control the level of details showing by selecting **Low**, **Medium**, or **High**.

▶ **NOTE**

Notice that Outlook automatically selects all **Date Navigator** pane days for the month when you click the **Month** button to view a month's calendar. By dragging your mouse to select a range of days yourself, you can see a calendar for those selected days instead of being limited only by a day, week, or full month. Hold Ctrl and click dates to see a high-level view of those dates even if they aren't contiguous.

4 Change the Month Viewed

Change months by clicking to the left or right of your Date Navigator's month name or by clicking the calendar's month and selecting from the pop-up month list that appears.

5 Email a Calendar

Click the **Send a Calendar via E-mail** link to send a calendar to one or more email recipients. Outlook displays the **Send a Calendar via E-mail** dialog box, where you can select a date range and the detail of that range. You can select the amount of detail you want the email to include and specify whether you want to show working hours only (which you'd probably elect to do if you're sending your calendar to a business associate).

After setting the options, click the **OK** button, and Outlook attaches the calendar to the email. Fill in the recipient and subject details and click **Send** to send the email.

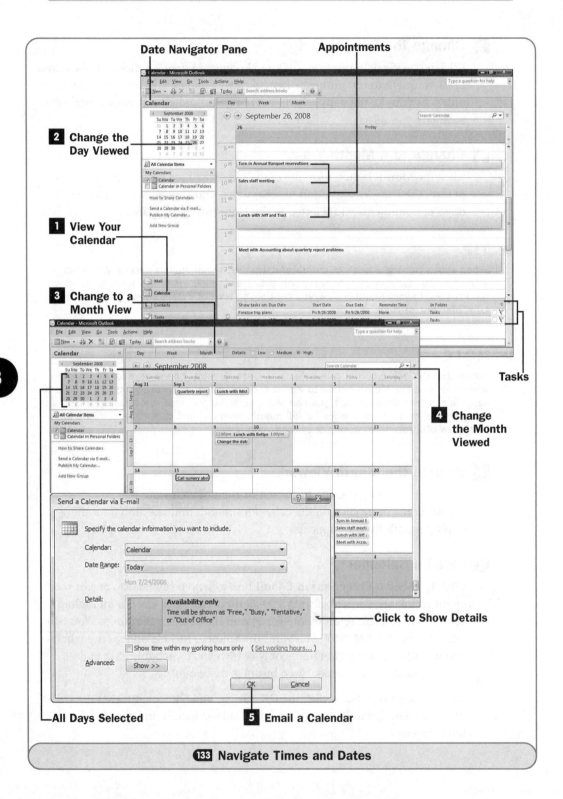

Date Navigator Pane

Appointments

2 Change the Day Viewed

1 View Your Calendar

3 Change to a Month View

133

Tasks

4 Change the Month Viewed

Click to Show Details

—All Days Selected

5 Email a Calendar

133 Navigate Times and Dates

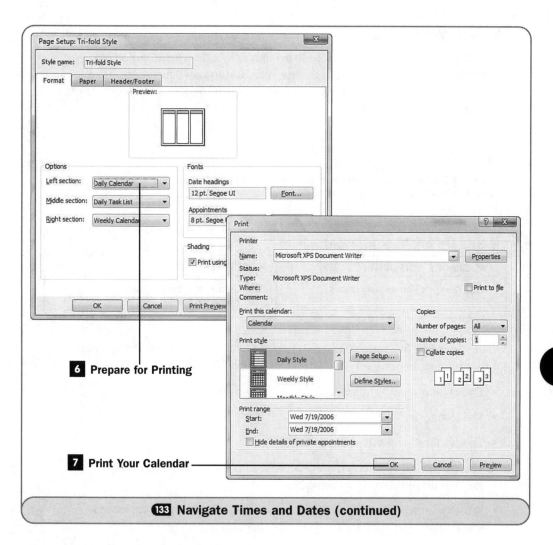

6 Prepare for Printing

7 Print Your Calendar

6 Prepare for Printing

Select **File**, **Page Setup** to display the **Page Setup** dialog box. Select the calendar format you want to print. Outlook supports just about every type of calendar format and day-planner book format possible. You can change the amount of detail that will appear on the printed page, specify the type of paper, and enter a header or footer to include on the printed calendar pages.

▶ **TIP**

Click the **Print Preview** button as you change various **Page Setup** dialog box options to see how the final printed calendar will look.

Click the **OK** button to close your **Page Setup** dialog box.

7 **Print Your Calendar**

Select **File**, **Print** to display your **Print** dialog box. The **Print** dialog box includes a **Page Setup** button in case you want to make further changes to your calendar's format, as well as options for start and end dates to limit the printing to specific days.

▶ **TIP**

The **Define Styles** button quickly formats your printed calendar to one of several industry-wide day-planning calendar book formats.

134	**Set Up an Appointment**

✔ **BEFORE YOU BEGIN**	→ **SEE ALSO**
133 Navigate Times and Dates	**136** Create and Share Electronic Business Cards

134

When you create an Outlook appointment, you enter as few or as many details for that appointment as you want. You can control the following details:

- The appointment's subject

- The location

- The start and end times and dates

- The amount of lead time Outlook gives before reminding you of the appointment in an alarm type of dialog box

- Which contacts should attend the appointment (great for letting attendees know of an upcoming meeting you're scheduling)

- The *appointment recurrence*

- The appointment's priority

▶ **NEW TERM**

Appointment recurrence—An appointment is said to recur if it comes up more than one time. A recurring appointment could be a weekly staff meeting or a regular payment due date.

1 **Select the Day View**

Display your calendar and click the **Day** button to display a single day view. Click to select the day you want to schedule an appointment for in your **Date Navigator** pane.

▶ **NOTE**

If your selected day has appointments already, you'll see them. If surrounding days have appointments, Outlook includes buttons you can click to see the most recent or the next appointment on surrounding days.

❷ Locate the Appointment Time

Double-click the time you want to make the appointment for. The **Appointment** dialog box opens, where you can enter the appointment's details.

▶ **NOTE**

Sometimes you'll want to make an appointment for the entire day, such as a vacation day. Go ahead and select the date and start time as described here. When you enter the appointment details, click the **All Day Event** option to change the appointment to an all-day event without a start or stop time.

❸ Enter the Appointment Details

Enter the appointment's subject and location. Outlook keeps track of your locations as you add them so that you don't have to retype them for subsequent appointments. (You need only to select them from the drop-down list that Outlook adds to as you enter new locations.)

Set the start and end times or click the **All Day Event** option if you want to schedule an all-day appointment.

Type any notes related to the appointment in the large text area beneath the appointment details.

▶ **TIP**

Click your **Format Text** ribbon to display formatting buttons for the appointment body's text.

❹ Set a Reminder Time

Click the arrow next to the reminder time (in the **Options** group of your **Appointment** ribbon) to select a different reminder time if you don't like the default reminder time.

❺ Determine the Recurrence

Click the **Recurrence** button to open the **Appointment Recurrence** dialog box if this appointment will occur more than once. Outlook fills in the start and stop times and includes a default duration, all of which you can change.

134

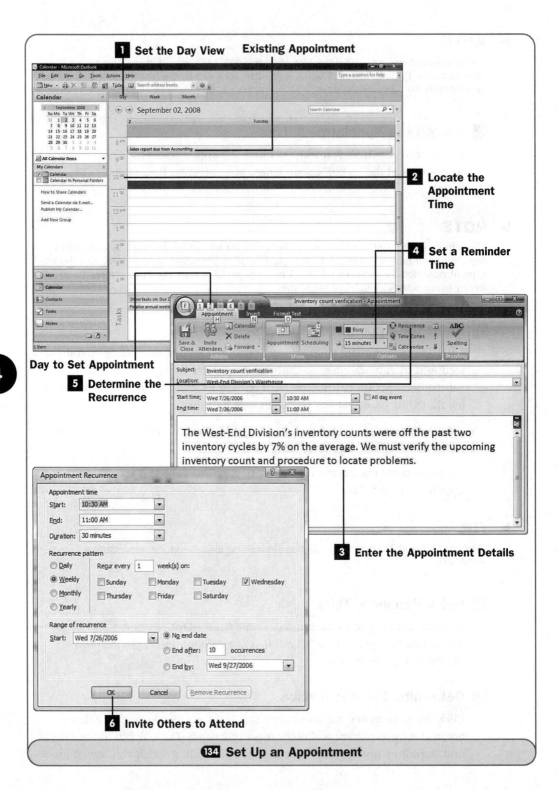

1 Set the Day View   Existing Appointment

2 Locate the Appointment Time

4 Set a Reminder Time

Day to Set Appointment

5 Determine the Recurrence

The West-End Division's inventory counts were off the past two inventory cycles by 7% on the average. We must verify the upcoming inventory count and procedure to locate problems.

3 Enter the Appointment Details

6 Invite Others to Attend

134 Set Up an Appointment

134

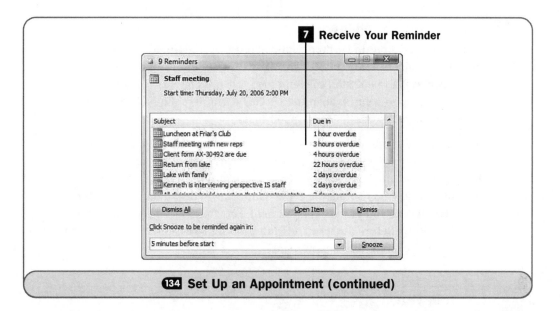

7 **Receive Your Reminder**

134 **Set Up an Appointment (continued)**

Select the recurrence details. Perhaps you want the appointment to recur every week, every month, or every year. You can select the day of week and determine how many times the appointment is to recur (or leave the **No End Date** option selected to keep the recurring appointment going forever).

▶ **NOTE**

If a recurring appointment ever terminates, you only have to click the appointment in your Calendar's **Day** view window and press Delete. You'll then let Outlook know whether you want to delete the single appointment or the whole series of recurring appointments.

6 **Invite Others to Attend**

Click the **Appointment** ribbon's **Invite Attendees** button to turn the appointment into a meeting. Click the **Address Book** button to open your Outlook **Contacts** address book to select members of the meeting to invite. Outlook sends those members a meeting reminder email to let them know about the appointment.

▶ **TIP**

Outlook's meeting scheduler can get as complex as you need. Click the **Scheduling** button to open Outlook's **Meeting** scheduler, which acts somewhat like a meeting worksheet with a list of attendees. There you can color-code different attendee names and meeting times. The ribbon includes a **Meeting Workspace** web page creator where you can store a list of meeting agenda notes and attendees who have RSVP'd.

7 Receive Your Reminder

At the designated reminder time, Outlook displays a reminder (along with previous reminders if you didn't clear them) in the **Reminder** dialog box. Click **Dismiss All** to erase all the reminders, **Dismiss** to erase only the selected reminder, or **Open Item** to open the selected reminder's dialog box, where you can read your notes for that appointment.

The **Snooze** button and time options to the left of the **Snooze** button enable you to select a time to be reminded again in the future of the appointment that just popped up. For example, if you set a 24-hour reminder for an appointment, the day before the event, Outlook will display the **Reminder** dialog box telling you of that appointment. You can select a reminder time (such as **1 Hour Before Start** or **5 Minutes Before Start**) and click **Snooze** to be reminded again of the appointment.

---

135 Use RSS Feeds

135

→ **BEFORE YOU BEGIN**

117 About Outlook's Capabilities

118 Master the Outlook Screen

119 Set Outlook Options

RSS (Really Simple Syndication) feeds bring web data to your desktop. Instead of going to a website to view new information on the site, and instead of requesting an email of the website's changes, you can set up an RSS feed for the site, and Outlook lets you know when new items appear on the site.

▶ **NOTE**

The website must be set up to offer RSS feeds before you can request them. Most major websites now offer RSS feed capabilities. News sites and blogs routinely offer RSS feeds due to their frequent updates.

Before RSS feeds, you would need to visit a website regularly to see any new postings. If no new postings had been made, you wasted the time it took to surf there. Sites then began offering emailed updates; however, you'd receive the emails every day or week or month depending on their setup, and such emails wouldn't offer any reliable way to learn immediately about new items on the site. RSS feeds are automatic and feed directly to your desktop the moment the feed has a new bit of website information, so you get virtually instant updates to the websites you want to monitor.

▶ **TIP**

You don't have to provide your email address to receive an RSS feed. Websites don't have to collect any such data for you to receive their feeds, and you can remove a feed anytime you want.

▶ **NOTE**

You must be logged in to the Internet to receive RSS feeds. Dial-up users will receive the feeds only when they dial into the Internet.

When a new RSS feed is available, a clickable summary comes to your Outlook RSS reader. You can click this headline to see the details on the site without leaving Outlook to do so.

1 Locate a Site with an RSS Feed

Locate a site with an RSS Feed that you want to subscribe to. Most such sites have an orange **RSS** button. (Sometimes this orange button says XML instead of RSS.)

If you use Internet Explorer 7.0 or later, IE's toolbar includes an **RSS** button that turns orange if the site you're currently viewing offers an RSS feed. Click IE's **RSS** button, or the site's **RSS** button, to subscribe to that site's RSS feeds.

135

2 Verify Your RSS Subscription

The site will ask you to verify your subscription to its RSS feed. A dialog box appears that enables you to change the name on your feed as well as direct the feed to an Outlook folder. By default, Outlook creates a **Feeds** folder when you subscribe to your first RSS feed, and your feeds will reside in that folder. You can elect to download any feed event's attached file if one is available so that you can read the entire feed offline. Click **Subscribe** to add the site to your Outlook feeds.

▶ **NOTE**

Attachments can fill your available disk space quickly because feeds can get numerous. For most sites, you'll probably prefer to subscribe to the feed but not its attachment. Clicking any feed summary you're interested in will download the attachment at that time.

3 View Your Feeds

Your **Navigation** pane holds your **Feeds** folder. Inside the **Feeds** folder will be your feeds, each listed by name in its own folder.

In the background, Outlook quietly updates your feeds. Click the plus sign next to your **Feeds** folder to expand the folder contents to see what resides there at any time.

135

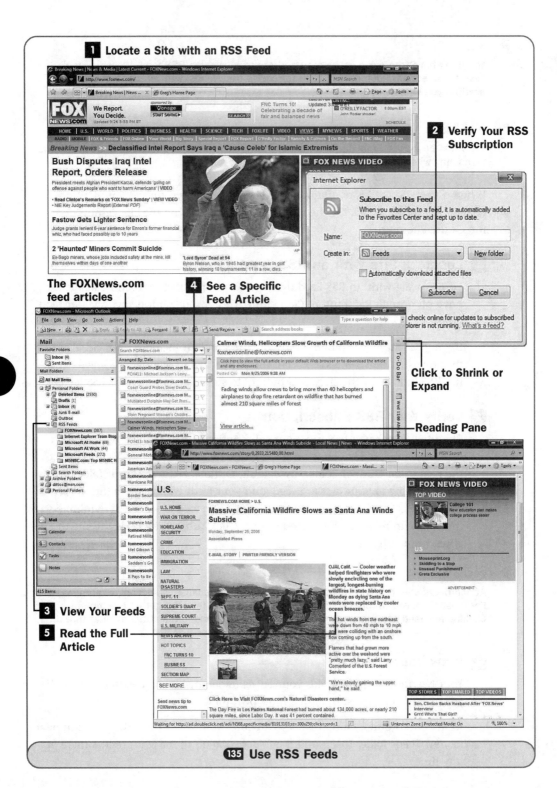

1 Locate a Site with an RSS Feed

2 Verify Your RSS Subscription

The FOXNews.com feed articles

4 See a Specific Feed Article

Click to Shrink or Expand

Reading Pane

3 View Your Feeds

5 Read the Full Article

135 Use RSS Feeds

▶ **NOTE**

Outlook uses your **Send/Receive** frequency option setting (see **119** **Set Outlook Options**) to determine how often to check your RSS-subscribed sites for new feeds to place in your **Feeds** folder.

4 See a Specific Feed Article

After you click to see a specific feed folder, its contents appear in the center of your Outlook screen in a window pane with the title of that feed at the top. Click an article you're interested in to see a summary of that article in your **Reading** pane to the right of your Outlook screen.

▶ **TIP**

Click to shrink your **To-Do Bar** to give yourself more room to read the feed summary.

5 Read the Full Article

Assuming that you didn't elect to download attachments, click the **View Article** link to open your web browser to the feed's original details.

By using RSS feeds, you take control of when you want to view content without running the risk of missing content. The summaries are sent to your **Feeds** folder regularly and await your attention there. You don't have to browse through all the websites you normally peruse to see new updates to those sites.

136

---

136 Create and Share Electronic Business Cards

✔ BEFORE YOU BEGIN	→ SEE ALSO
128 Add a Contact	**150** Use Drag and Drop to Move Data
132 Search for Contacts and Other Outlook Data	

New with Outlook 2007 are *electronic business cards*. You have complete control over the look of your electronic business card. You can add a logo and customize the art and decide whether you want to use a photo. You control all information displayed. All contacts in your **Contacts** folder have an electronic business card that Outlook creates when you add that contact's details. Also, when you receive an electronic business card from others, you can add that person to your **Contacts** folder simply by dropping the person's electronic business card onto your **Contacts** folder.

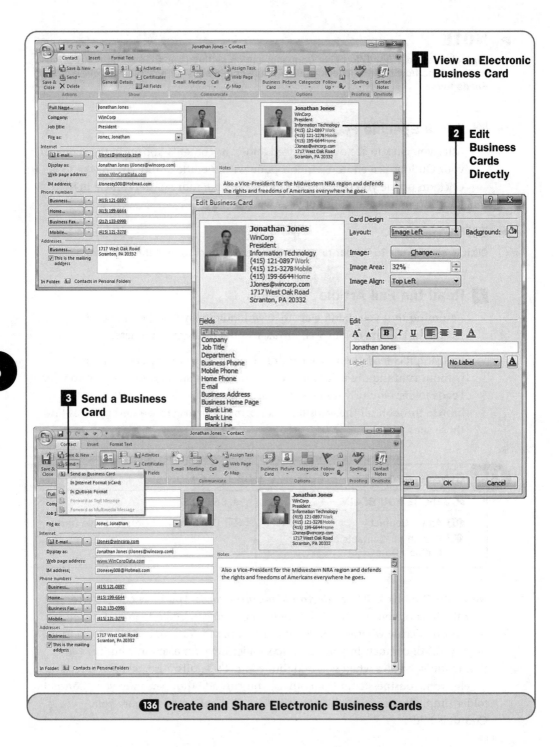

1 View an Electronic Business Card

2 Edit Business Cards Directly

3 Send a Business Card

136

136 Create and Share Electronic Business Cards

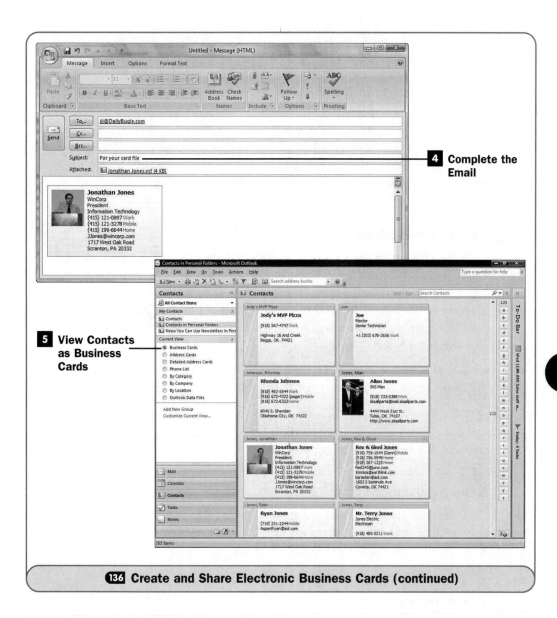

4 Complete the Email

5 View Contacts as Business Cards

136

136 Create and Share Electronic Business Cards (continued)

▶ NEW TERM

Electronic business cards—Outlook-based, graphics business card images that you can share with others through email.

In reality, you can think of an electronic business card as being a different way to view your contact information. The electronic business card takes on the business card format that has been used successfully for years and is instantly recognizable. In addition, when you print your **Contacts** folder, you can choose to print only the business card view and print onto business card printer stock paper to produce a business card file of all your contacts.

1 View an Electronic Business Card

Locate and double-click any contact in your **Contacts** folder to view its **Contact** dialog box. At the bottom of the dialog box is that contact's electronic business card. If you change information on the card, that information changes elsewhere in the **Contact** dialog box. If you change information in the **Contact** dialog box (such as the phone number), Outlook updates the electronic business card information.

2 Edit Business Cards Directly

Click the **Contact** ribbon's **Business Card** button to edit the contact's business card. The **Edit Business Card** dialog box opens. Here you can change the look of the business card, move the image's location, and remove details from the business card that you may not want to share with others if you ever attach the card to an email or use the card in an email signature (see **126 Create an Email Signature**).

136

Click the **OK** button to save the electronic business card format changes you made, or click **Reset Card** to revert the card to its previous state.

▶ NOTE

Surprisingly, there isn't a way to add a unique background image to a specific electronic business card without using the contact's picture for the background.

3 Send a Business Card

Click the arrow to the right of the **Send** button to display a list of options for the contact. Select **Send as Business Card** to send the electronic business card to an email recipient. Outlook opens an email containing the electronic business card.

4 Complete the Email

Fill in the recipient and the subject, add an optional message at the top of the email, and click **Send** to send the email to your recipient.

When your recipient receives and opens the email, he will see the business card at the bottom of any message you included in the email. Your recipient can drag the business card to his Outlook **Contacts** folder to create a new contact for that business card. You can, of course, do the same. When you receive an email with an electronic business card, just drag the card to your **Contacts** folder (or to your **Contacts** button in Outlook's lower-left corner) to create a new contact that includes that card's details.

▶ **NOTE**

If the recipient has an Outlook version that predates Outlook 2007, he will be able to see the business card in the email's body if he has HTML-based email. If not, the business card rides along as an email attachment. Your recipient will also be able to drag the business card (or attachment) to his **Contacts** folder to create a new contact.

5 **View Contacts as Business Cards**

When viewing your **Contacts** folder, click **Business Cards** in your **Navigation** pane's **Current View** group to view all your contacts' business cards only.

---

137 **Write Yourself a Note**

✔ BEFORE YOU BEGIN	→ SEE ALSO
117 About Outlook's Capabilities	**138** About OneNote
	140 Create a New Notebook, Section, and Pages

137

Outlook notes are the equivalent to the sticky yellow-paper notes you've seen and used. You can post a note inside Outlook and retrieve, edit, or delete the note later. To see your notes, you'll click the **Notes** button in the lower-left corner of your Outlook screen.

Some say that Outlook's notes are unnecessary if one uses OneNote (see **138** **About OneNote**). That's not true, because Outlook's notes and OneNote's data are different items used for different purposes. It's true that the notes inside Outlook are perhaps its most underutilized feature (outside of the resource-heavy journal), but that doesn't change the fact that Outlook's notes are quick to create and come in handy when you need to jot something down quickly for later reference.

1 **Request a Note**

To create a new note, click the **New Note** toolbar button that appears when you click Outlook's **Notes** button to display a yellow-note window.

2 **Type the Note**

The yellow note works like a miniature word processor inside Outlook. Just start typing, and the note's details appear. Depending on how much information your note is to hold, you can drag the note's lower-right corner to increase or shrink the note size.

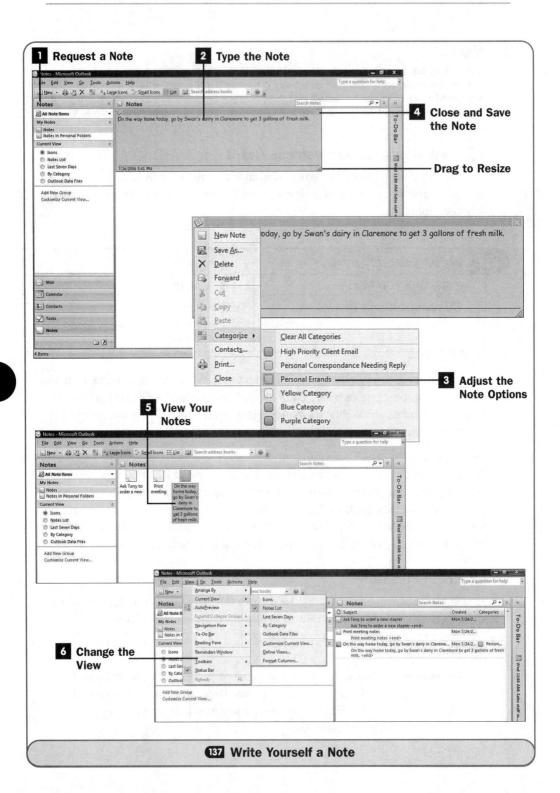

1 Request a Note

2 Type the Note

4 Close and Save the Note

Drag to Resize

3 Adjust the Note Options

5 View Your Notes

6 Change the View

137

137 Write Yourself a Note

▶ **NOTE**

Surprisingly, Outlook offers no way to format the note's text. You cannot boldface, italicize, or even change the font size of a note's text.

❸ Adjust the Note Options

Click the note window's icon in its upper-left corner to display a list of options available. You can categorize the note using your email's color-coding system (see **124 Organize Email**). After you change the organizing color for the note, the note's background changes to that color.

The options also allow you to save the note and create a new one, save the note in a file on your disk, forward the note as an email, copy and paste to and from the note's body, create a new contact from the note, print the note, or close the note.

▶ **NOTE**

When you first create a note, these options seem like overkill. After all, you just want to jot yourself a note. After you've typed several notes, however, being able to organize them by a color category and print them will become more helpful.

❹ Close and Save the Note

When you finish typing the note's text, click the **Close** button (the **X** in the note window's upper-right corner) to save the note in Outlook's **Notes** folder.

❺ View Your Notes

When you view your **Notes** folder, you will see your notes as a series of icons in your **Notes** window. If all a note's contents will display below the note, Outlook shows you the entire message; otherwise, you must point to a note before Outlook displays what the note says.

Double-click any note to open the note; you can then edit the note, change its category, print the note, or perform the other note options available from the menu that appears when you click the icon in the note window's upper-left corner.

▶ **TIP**

When you double-click a note, Outlook opens that note in its own window. You can leave the window open to be sure that you handle the note later, perhaps before leaving for the day.

137

6 Change the View

Click to select a new view of your notes by clicking the appropriate button in the **Current View** of your **Navigation** pane. Depending on what your notes say and the number of them you've created, you might find that a different view, such as the **Notes List** view, is more helpful for managing your notes than the default icon-based note view.

137

PART VI

Enhancing Your Work with Other Office Features

IN THIS PART:

17

Making Notes with OneNote

IN THIS CHAPTER:

OneNote is Microsoft Office's note-taking application that not only collects notes you enter but gives you ways to organize the notes that match just about any filing system that works for you.

There is an overused phrase for products being marketed: "It works the way you do." Despite the triteness of this phrase for most products, OneNote truly works the way you do and adapts to whatever note-taking format you need.

OneNote first appeared in Office XP. OneNote was originally thought to be a solution looking for a problem. Then people began using OneNote. Those people couldn't imagine *not* having OneNote. OneNote stores your thoughts, your notes, and your data.

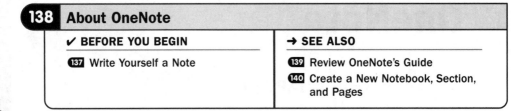

138 **About OneNote**

✔ BEFORE YOU BEGIN	→ SEE ALSO
137 Write Yourself a Note	**139** Review OneNote's Guide
	140 Create a New Notebook, Section, and Pages

138

OneNote manages your notes. It's true that Outlook also manages notes for you (see **137 Write Yourself a Note**), but Outlook requires that you take text-only notes and provides minimal organization of those typed notes for you.

OneNote is far more versatile than Outlook for note-taking. If you want to type a quick note on your keyboard, OneNote accepts your typing and files the note according to your wishes. If you have a tablet PC or laptop and write notes using the handwriting stylus, OneNote saves your handwriting. If you want to record a conversation and store it as a note, perhaps as an addition to meeting notes you were typing and writing by hand, OneNote keeps them all together. If you want to copy web page content into a page of notes that you've been typing, that's fine. Copy pictures and videos from your disk to your notes. Capture a screen from any program and put the screen's image in your notes.

The capability of OneNote to capture data—and, more important, to manage that data together in one document you call your *notes*—truly is powerful.

OneNote uses a note-organization system based on the real-world concept of notebooks filled with sections. You distinguish the notebook sections by section dividers with colored tabs that label each section. Each section holds one or more pages.

Where OneNote distinguishes itself from its real-world notebook counterparts is in its capability to store not only text, typing, and pictures on its notebook pages but sound, video, web pages, and links as well. And the truly powerful thing about this eclectic repository is that OneNote can store all those kinds of data on a single page in its notebook! You put data where you want it, in the format you want it to be in.

Why have notes in a file cabinet, emails, word processing documents, database files, videos of presentations, and sticky notes on your monitor when they can all reside in one OneNote notebook? Obviously, much of your data should remain where it is (such as in the database, which is much better equipped to manage huge amounts of data), but with OneNote, you can organize all that data into one spot and provide links to any data that isn't stored directly in a OneNote notebook.

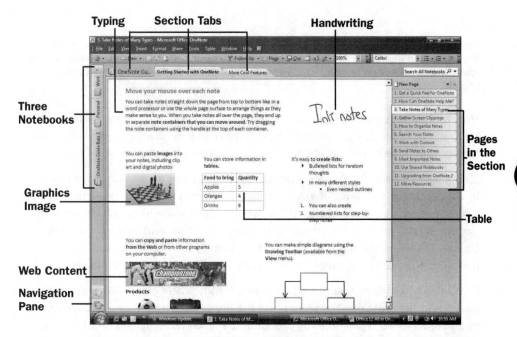

OneNote stores any kind of computer data on pages in sections in notebooks.

OneNote initially comes with three notebooks already created for you:

- **Work** notebook
- **Personal** notebook
- **OneNote Guide** notebook

The **Work** notebook includes sections for your meetings, projects, planning, and other business you might need to track notes for. Obviously, you may not need all these, and you can rename or remove the sections and add your own. The **Personal** notebook includes sections for travel notes, recipes, to-do items, and account information such as frequent-flier numbers and other kinds of data you'll run across and need to access. The **OneNote Guide** notebook is an introduction to OneNote. What makes the OneNote Guide so effective is that the guide uses OneNote to teach you OneNote (see **139** **Review OneNote's Guide**).

You differentiate each notebook by a named, colored tab down the left side of your OneNote window. When you click a notebook tab, that notebook's section dividers appear across the top of your screen, and the pages within the selected section are named down the right side of the screen. All notebooks have at least one section, and all sections have at least one page. It's up to you to add more sections and pages as you need them.

▶ **TIP**

When adding new pages to a section, you can number them sequentially if you want, like numbered pages in a book, but naming the pages with their contents enables you to know what's on a page by glancing down the page names to the right of the OneNote window.

You can create as many notebooks as you want, but you don't have to make them all available and open. Only those notebooks you have open appear on the **Navigation** pane to the left of your OneNote window.

138

The power comes in the freedom that OneNote gives you to organize your notes in whatever way you want. If you want to start writing or typing in the middle of a new notebook page, go ahead. If you want to draw something anywhere on the page or stick a web link anywhere on the page, just click and stick. In addition, OneNote searches through almost any data looking for something you want to find. (OneNote can sometimes locate text that appears in graphics images.)

If you don't like where you put a table, drag it somewhere else. Don't worry about margins or the order of what you put on the page. Make room for handwritten notes between two typed notes by dragging the typed notes apart to make room for your handwriting.

▶ **NOTE**

Sometimes a note just doesn't fit your nice, organized notebook system. After you set up work and personal folders, if you need to jot a quick note that doesn't fit anywhere, just put the note in OneNote's **Unfiled Notes** notebook. You can leave any unorganized notes there as long as you want, or later organize some or all of them into notebooks, sections, and pages.

139 Review OneNote's Guide

✔ BEFORE YOU BEGIN	→ SEE ALSO
138 About OneNote	140 Create a New Notebook, Section, and Pages
	142 Add Drawings to Notes

If you're new to OneNote, the best place to begin is to look at the **OneNote Guide** notebook that installs with your **Work** and **Personal** notebooks. Even if you've used OneNote in the past but are new to OneNote 2007, you should review the OneNote Guide to see what new features OneNote 2007 provides.

One of the most important new features is OneNote 2007's **Navigation** pane, which shows you which notebooks are currently open. The **Navigation** pane opens to show section divider tabs in each notebook, or you can shrink the **Navigation** pane to show only the currently selected notebook's section tabs across the top of your screen.

1 Display the OneNote Guide

Click the **OneNote Guide** notebook tab to display the sections and pages of the OneNote Guide. You'll see that the OneNote Guide has two sections: **Getting Started with OneNote** and **More Cool Features**.

Before working through the OneNote Guide, click the arrow at the top of your **Navigation** pane to expand the pane. By expanding the pane in this way, you can see all the sections in each notebook currently open inside OneNote. Click again to shrink the **Navigation** pane back to its one-column state to give more screen room to the **OneNote Guide** notebook.

▶ TIP

The pages in the OneNote Guide appear on the right side of your screen. You won't be able to read the entire page names unless you drag the pane dividing line to make more room for the page names but less room for the contents in the center of your screen.

2 Move and Manipulate Notes

Read through the first page or two of the OneNote Guide. It asks you to type your name at the arrow on the first page. Click anywhere near the arrow and begin typing. If you're working from a tablet PC, you can write your name there.

139

Scroll down through the pages. The oval atop each page is that page's name that appears in the page list to the right. You can change a name if you want, and the name's tab on the left changes.

As you go through the pages, click anywhere on the page to see OneNote's *note containers*. Drag a container to a different location. If the container holds text, click inside the container to edit or add more text. As you do, the note container grows to include your new text. Note containers can overlap if you move one over another. If a container includes graphics, click any image inside the note container to display sizing handles you can drag to resize the image.

▶ NEW TERM

Note container—A box that OneNote adds to each element on a page. When you type, write, or add any other kind of OneNote data to a page, OneNote encloses that item in a note container that appears when you click that item. You can drag or resize a note container to position it anywhere on the page you want.

■3 Open More Cool Features

The OneNote Guide has two sections: the **Getting Started with OneNote** section and the **More Cool Features** section. As expected, OneNote distinguishes these **OneNote Guide** notebook sections with colored, named tabs across the top of your screen.

Click the **More Cool Features** tab to display that section in the **OneNote Guide** notebook. You'll see a page full of links. These links are not links to web pages; they are links to other pages within that notebook section. So if you click the **Drawing Tools** link, the page named **Drawing Tools** appears. You could have also paged down to that page or clicked to select it from the list of pages to the right (see **142 Add Drawings to Notes**).

■4 View the Drawing Tools

Click to display the **Drawing Tools** page if you haven't already. You'll see a page that describes OneNote's drawing tools. You don't have to have a separate drawing program to create graphical notes in OneNote. OneNote's **Drawing** toolbar is just a menu selection away when you select **View, Drawing Toolbar**.

You'll use OneNote's **Drawing** toolbar more often than you might think at first. The tools aren't just for making pictures. OneNote's drawing tools are useful for highlighting important items in your notes. Suppose that you save a web page as a note and want to highlight specific information on the page. You can use the drawing tools to circle text, add stars to show importance, and then use your tablet PC to accent the web page so that you'll later be able to refer to the most critical parts of the page when needed.

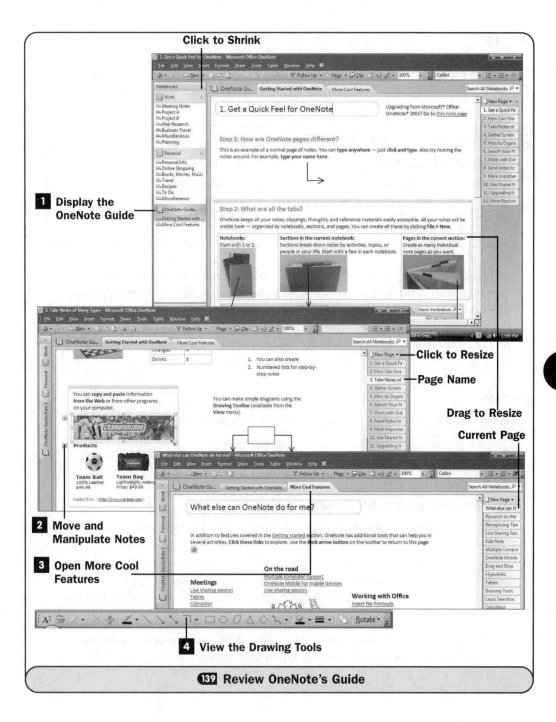

Click to Shrink

1 Display the
OneNote Guide

2 Move and
Manipulate Notes

3 Open More Cool
Features

4 View the Drawing Tools

Click to Resize

Page Name

Drag to Resize

Current Page

139

▶ **TIP**

You don't need a tablet PC to draw or add handwritten notes to documents. Companies such as Watcom provide PC-based drawing pads you can easily connect to your desktop computer.

---

140 **Create a New Notebook, Section, and Pages**

✔ BEFORE YOU BEGIN	→ SEE ALSO
16 About Styles, Themes, and Templates	**141** Add Text Notes
138 About OneNote	**142** Add Drawings to Notes
139 Review OneNote's Guide	

Although many may use OneNote's **Work** and **Personal** folders that OneNote comes installed with, you're never limited to those two folders, of course. If they don't apply to your needs, close them to move them out of your way, along with the **OneNote Guide** notebook if you want. Don't feel as though you must close any open notebooks, however, unless they are cluttering your OneNote screen too much.

140

▶ **TIP**

Right-click over a notebook's tab and select **Close This Notebook** to close it.

Being able to create a new notebook, sections, and pages is the cornerstone of OneNote.

1 **Request a New Notebook**

Select **View**, **Task Pane** to display the **New** pane at the right of OneNote. OneNote offers several ways to create new notebooks, sections, and pages. You can leave the **New** pane open while you set up a new notebook if you want. Clicking on **New Page**, **Subpage**, **Section**, **Section Group**, or **Notebook** from the **New** pane is a quick way to create any of those. The drawback is that the **New** pane consumes screen real estate.

Without using the **New** pane, you can select **File**, **New Notebook** from the menu to open the **New Notebook Wizard** dialog box.

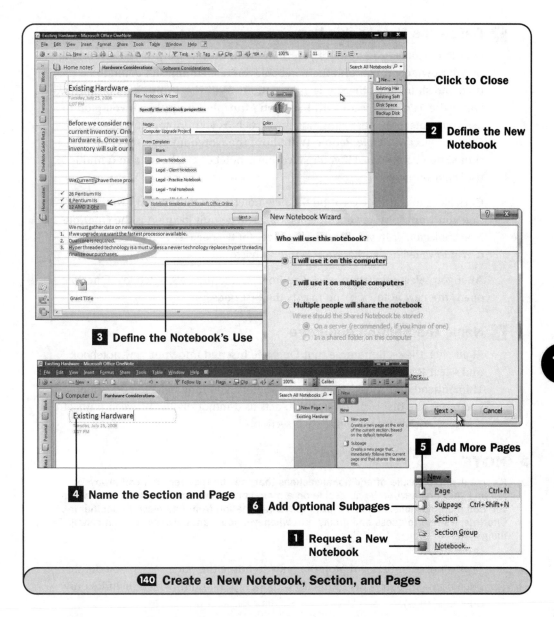

140 Create a New Notebook, Section, and Pages

2 Define the New Notebook

Enter a name for your new notebook in the **New Notebook Wizard** dialog box, select a notebook color, and optionally choose a template for your new notebook. (For this task you don't need a template, because you're creating a blank notebook from scratch.) For a review of templates, see **16 About Styles, Themes, and Templates**.

Click the **Next** button.

3 Define the Notebook's Use

OneNote enables you to share your notes with others easily. If you're working on your own computer and the notebook you're creating isn't going to be used and shared by others, select the option **I Will Use It on This Computer**. Otherwise, click to select **I Will Use It on Multiple Computers** if you plan to use your notebook on several machines, such as your laptop and desktop. Click to select **Multiple People Will Share the Notebook** and select the shared notebook source if you're creating a notebook to be used in a multi-user environment.

Click Next to continue creating the new notebook. OneNote asks which location you want to store your notebook in. The default location is the OneNote Notebooks folder in your Documents folder (or My Documents if you're running a Windows release earlier than Windows Vista).

After you select a location, click **Create** to create the new notebook. OneNote opens the new notebook and inserts the first page.

4 Name the Section and Page

140

Right-click the section name that OneNote inserted into your new notebook and select **Rename**. Type a name that matches the contents of your section. Think ahead and consider additional sections you may need to add before you name the first section. A section acts as a major divider between parts of a notebook. The pages divide each section.

▶ **NOTE**

It's fine if you're unsure of additional sections that may be required. You can always rename your first section if you decide on a more consistent naming scheme later when you add more sections. You can always move information from one place to another in OneNote; it's fine to guess and brainstorm whenever you want because you can change things later.

Type a name in the oval atop the page to name the page. When you do, the page name also appears in the list of pages to the right (which includes only one page now).

Finish the page contents.

5 Add More Pages

To add additional pages, click the **New Page** link if the **New** pane is still open, or click the **New Page** button atop your page names in the right pane. (Ctrl+N is the shortcut key to create a new page.)

▶ **NOTE**

To delete a page, click its page name in your right pane and press Delete. Selecting **Edit, Undo** restores the deleted page to your notebook. (**Ctrl+Z** is the shortcut key for the **Undo** command.)

6 **Add Optional Subpages**

You can add a *subpage* by clicking to open the **New Page** menu above your list of pages in the right window pane. Although you should name subpages, you don't have to, because they are linked to the most recent page, and the subpages are all treated as a group of pages.

▶ **NEW TERM**

Subpage—A page that's linked to the most recent page. Subpages can have names but are considered extensions of whatever page they're linked to. A document might have an overview page and several detailed subpages to describe an event or item.

141 Add Text Notes	
✔ **BEFORE YOU BEGIN**	→ **SEE ALSO**
138 About OneNote	**142** Add Drawings to Notes
140 Create a New Notebook, Section, and Pages	**143** Add Any Data to Notes

141

Although OneNote handles pictures, links, videos, and sound data as easily as text, your OneNote notebooks will certainly include more text data than any other kind of data, in most cases. Your keyboard is still the primary means for getting new data into your computer. Even tablet PC users use their keyboards to enter data when they must enter a lot at one time.

OneNote handles text as easily as a word processor. Actually, when you think of how you can just click and start typing text anywhere you want it on a notebook page, no matter what else appears around that text, you'll realize that OneNote handles text *better* than word processors in its capability to give you the freedom to place text where you want it to go.

1 **Type the Text on a Page**

To type text on a page, click where you want the text to begin and start typing. A note container will appear the moment you begin typing.

▶ **NOTE**

OneNote uses Word's spelling dictionary to underline misspelled words. As with Word, you can right-click any word flagged as a misspelled word to request a correction or to add it to your Office 2007 spelling dictionary. OneNote doesn't include a grammar checker.

▶ **TIP**

Does your text require a quick calculation? Great, just type a formula in your text, such as **$359656*110=**, press your spacebar, and OneNote inserts the answer after the equal sign.

2 Move and Add to the Text

You can move the note container to another location during your typing or after you've typed the text. As you type, the note container expands to hold the text. Resize the note container, and your text's margins adjust accordingly.

3 Format the Text

The toolbar includes several formatting options. Select text and then choose a font or font size. Select **Format, Font** to display an **Apply a Font** pane to the right of your screen to apply common text format changes and to apply a color to text you select.

141

▶ **NOTE**

If all your text won't fit on the screen when you open the **Apply a Font** pane, OneNote displays a scrollbar at the bottom of your screen so that you can shift the page left and right as needed. Close the **Apply a Font** pane to give your page more room.

Because OneNote is a note-taking tool that uses notebooks, you can apply a notebook-paper background to your text notes by selecting **Format, Rule Lines** and choosing the style of lines you want to appear in the background.

4 Create a Bulleted List

Anytime you want a bulleted list, you can create one. Whether you're inside a note container or creating a new one, when you're ready for the list, click the **Bullets** toolbar button, and the first bullet appears. Type the list, and OneNote keeps adding bullets as you press Enter. To stop the list and return to a regular line of text, press Backspace at the extra bullet or click the **Bullets** button once again.

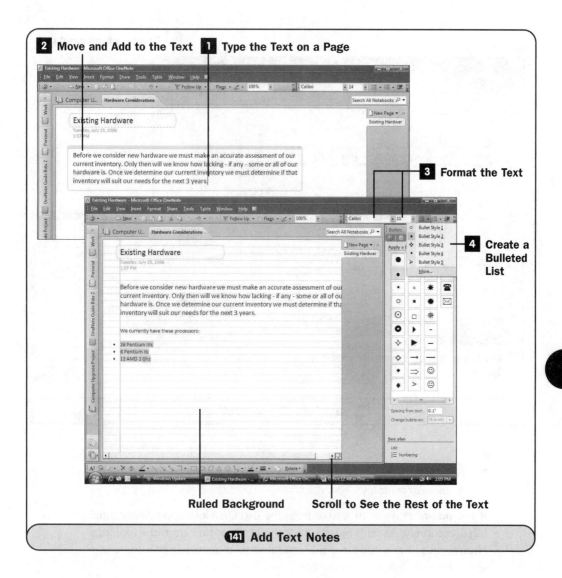

2 **Move and Add to the Text**   1 **Type the Text on a Page**

3 **Format the Text**

4 **Create a Bulleted List**

Ruled Background   **Scroll to See the Rest of the Text**

141 Add Text Notes

▶ **TIP**

Click the arrow to the right of the toolbar's **Bullets** button to display a list of bullet styles you can select from. Click **More** from the list, and OneNote opens an **Apply a Bullet** pane with numerous bullet styles you can choose from.

Word supports several bullet styles, such as check marks and arrows.

5 Create a Numbered List

Anytime you want a numbered list, you can create one even more easily than a bulleted list. Just type the number **1** followed by a period and space.

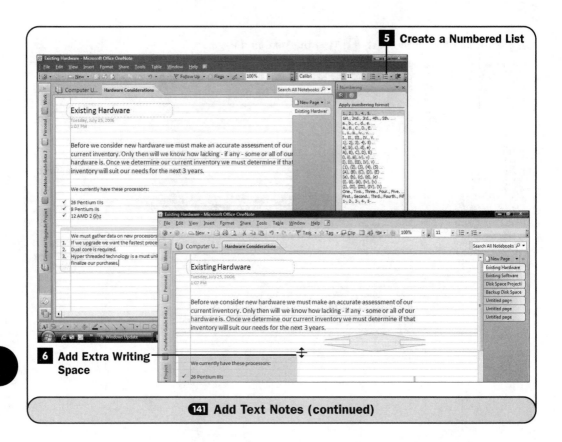

5 Create a Numbered List

6 Add Extra Writing Space

141 Add Text Notes (continued)

OneNote instantly recognizes that you're starting a list and numbers subsequent lines accordingly.

If you add or remove lines to or from the list, OneNote updates the numbering accordingly. As with bullets, click the **More** option from the toolbar's **Numbering** button drop-down list to select from a variety of numbering styles, including Roman numerals.

6 Add Extra Writing Space

If you want to insert text (or any other kind of data) between two note containers in a page that already holds a lot, you can move note containers individually to make room for the new text, but it's simpler to select the **Insert, Extra Writing Space** option, point to where you want more space, and drag the line that appears down until you've made enough room for the item you want to insert. When you use the **Extra Writing Space** option to insert space, all items below the extra writing space move down, and you don't have to select individual note containers to move when you want more room.

142 Add Drawings to Notes

✔ BEFORE YOU BEGIN	→ SEE ALSO
140 Create a New Notebook, Section, and Pages **141** Add Text Notes	**143** Add Any Data to Notes

Certainly, drawings are the second-most-popular data item (after text) that you will add to your OneNote notes. It's not that you will necessarily add a bunch of graphics images and drawings; often, you'll just use the drawing tools to mark up text and items that already appear on your pages. For example, you might circle important dates in a calendar that's on a OneNote page.

OneNote includes drawing tools that are powerful enough to create organizational charts and flow diagrams, as well as simple graphics images. You don't have to be an artist to use OneNote's drawing tools. OneNote uses *digital ink* to place all artwork on your notes, so editing is simple. Learn how to use these tools now so that you can customize your notes as you need to.

▶ NEW TERM

142

Digital ink—As you draw parts of any graphics image, OneNote keeps track of each stroke separately so that you can select parts of a drawing and erase, resize, duplicate, and color parts of your drawing.

1 Display the Drawing Toolbar

Select **View, Drawing Toolbar** from the menu to display the **Drawing** toolbar at the bottom of your screen.

2 Select the Line Color and Thickness

Lines you draw can vary in thickness and color. Before drawing, you should make sure that the thickness and color are set to your preferences. Click the **Drawing** toolbar's **Color** button to select a color, and click the **Thickness** button to select a thickness (in points).

▶ TIP

Of course, if you draw a line or circle and see that it's the wrong color or thickness, you can undo the stroke, change the color and thickness, and draw it again.

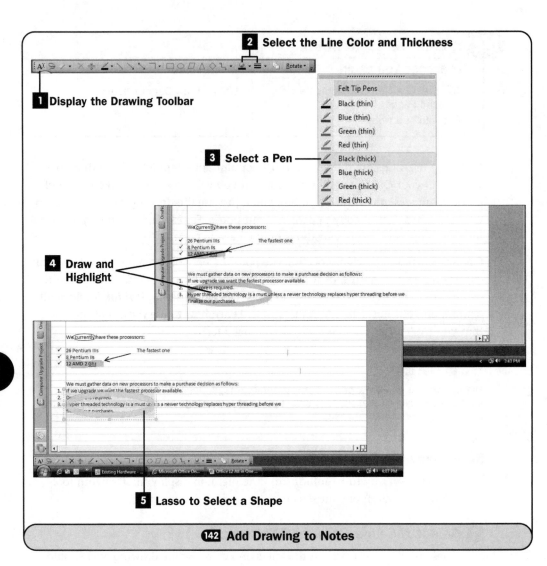

142

3 Select a Pen

You might find that OneNote's selection of pens from the **Pen** drawing tool works for just about everything you want to draw, so instead of setting the color and thickness first, you might go straight to the **Pen** tool.

Notice that the list of pens includes color highlighters (the lower half of the pop-up pen selection list).

4 **Draw and Highlight**

After you've selected a pen or line thickness, click to select the tool shape you want to draw. You can draw a line, an arrow, a rectangle, an oval, a triangle, and other shapes. Click a shape to select it, and then drag your mouse where you want to put that shape onto your note. The shape appears on your drawing using the pen or color and thickness you selected.

▶ **NOTE**

The drawing tools are especially useful if you have a drawing pen or use a tablet PC. You can perform any and all drawing necessary with your mouse or trackball, but a digital pen gives you much more control over what you produce.

5 **Lasso to Select a Shape**

After you've placed a shape, you can resize or move it. At first, selecting a shape is difficult if the shape shares the same space in your notes as text. The **Drawing** toolbar's **Lasso** tool is best for selecting shapes that appear on the page. Click to select the **Lasso** tool, and then drag to circle whatever shape you want to select. OneNote selects that shape and adds sizing handles around it. You now can resize and move the shape or press Delete to delete it altogether.

143

▶ **NOTE**

The **Drawing** toolbar's **Rotate** button enables you to rotate the selected shape.

▶ **TIP**

You can also use the **Drawing** toolbar's **Lasso** tool to select text and pictures as well as graphics you draw.

143 **Add Any Data to Notes**

✔ BEFORE YOU BEGIN	→ SEE ALSO
141 Add Text Notes	**154** Use OneNote to Enhance Other Office Programs
142 Add Drawings to Notes	

Given that OneNote works with virtually any data means that you need to understand how to add nontext data to your notebook pages. As you may have already come to expect if you've followed the OneNote tasks that came before this one, OneNote makes it simple to add just about anything to your pages.

Whether it's web page data, video, or sound, your OneNote page includes the data. Not only does the page include it, but you can organize all those kinds of data so that everything appears in the order and the folder you want it to appear in.

▶ **TIP**

OneNote supports several ways to put data onto a OneNote notebook page. Always remember that the Windows copy and paste commands are one of the simplest ways to put data onto a page. Copy and paste an Excel worksheet, for example, and the worksheet data goes right on your notebook page in a cell container.

1 Grab the Web Page Data

Surf to the Internet web page that contains text or pictures (or both) that you want to put in your OneNote notebook. Select the parts of the web page you want to send to OneNote.

▶ **NOTE**

OneNote works well with Internet Explorer. When you install OneNote, OneNote creates a connection to IE through the Internet Explorer toolbar. Other web browsers may or may not contain the connection described here.

143

Click Internet Explorer's arrow to the right of the **Tools** button and select **Send to OneNote**. The information, in the same format as it appears on the web page, arrives on a new OneNote page stored in your **Unfiled Notes** section, from where you can move the note container to another notebook page.

2 Format the Web Data

Although the web data comes into OneNote with the same font and colors as the web page, the information may or may not align the same. If, for example, you copied text but not pictures from the web page, the text that wrapped around the picture on the original web page won't wrap the same inside OneNote's note container.

Therefore, you may want to use OneNote's formatting tools to format the data.

▶ **NOTE**

At the bottom of the web data, OneNote inserts a cross-reference that tells which web page the data in the note container came from. This includes a link to the page that is active. If you click it, you'll arrive once more at the website. You can erase the cross-reference if you want.

⑧ **Cross-Reference with a Hyperlink**

OneNote uses hyperlinks to cross-reference other OneNote data. The data can be anywhere in OneNote: another notebook, another section, or another page. Your link will even send you straight to a specific paragraph if you want it to.

Right-click the note container you want to cross-reference elsewhere in OneNote. Select **Copy Hyperlink to This Paragraph**, and OneNote creates a link to that note container. The note container can hold pictures, text, video, or sound.

④ **Plant the Link**

Change to the page where you want the link to that note container to appear. Press Ctrl+V (or select **Edit, Paste**) to paste the link to the current page at the current location. By default, OneNote uses the first few letters of your link's note container text for the text that appears on the link. To change the text, highlight the link and press Ctrl+K to display the **Hyperlink** dialog box. Change the **Text to Display** field to contain the text you want displayed for the link, and click **OK**. The link's text changes. Anytime you click that link, the cursor jumps to the page with the note container for that link. Click the toolbar's **Back** button to return to the note you were reading that contains the link when you're ready to do so.

▶ **TIP**

At any point you can press Ctrl+K and type a complete web page address in the **Hyperlink** dialog box to point to that web page. You don't first have to browse to the page to insert a link to it as long as you know the web address (such as http://www.microsoft.com).

⑤ **Capture the Screenshots**

At any point, you can capture a screen (or any portion of a screen) in any Windows program and send that screen to a notebook page.

To capture the current screen, press Windows+S. The screen highlights, and a pop-up box appears in your Windows Notification area requesting that you drag to select a rectangular portion of the current screen for OneNote. As soon as you finish dragging to select the rectangular area, OneNote sends a graphics image of that selected screen to a new page in your **Unfiled Notes** section. You then can move, annotate, or format the captured image any way you want.

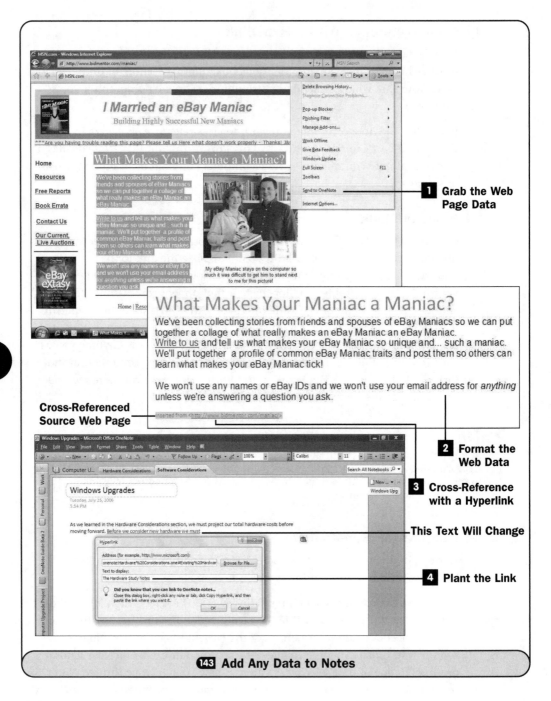

1 Grab the Web Page Data

2 Format the Web Data

Cross-Referenced Source Web Page

3 Cross-Reference with a Hyperlink

This Text Will Change

4 Plant the Link

143 Add Any Data to Notes

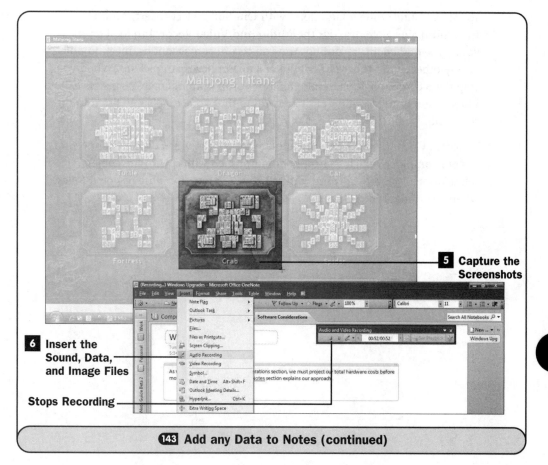

5 Capture the Screenshots

6 Insert the Sound, Data, and Image Files

Stops Recording

143 Add any Data to Notes (continued)

▶ **NOTE**

Instead of going to your **Unfiled Notes** section, you can click any notebook page where you want to insert the screenshot and select **Insert, Screen Clipping** to insert the screenshot there.

6 Insert the Sound, Data, and Image Files

To insert pictures, video, or sound data, use OneNote's **Insert** menu. Select **Insert, Pictures, From Files** or **Insert, Pictures, From Scanner or Camera** to insert a digital image from a file or captured from your scanner or digital camera.

You can insert just about any file by selecting **Insert, Files** and selecting the file. OneNote inserts an icon representing that file that, when clicked, opens the file's original program and displays the data in that file.

To record sound while taking notes with OneNote, select **Insert, Audio Recording**. OneNote displays the **Audio and Video Recording** toolbar on your page and begins recording. You can record conversations, meeting notes, or any other sound that your computer's microphone can pick up. When you stop the recording by clicking the toolbar's **Stop** button, OneNote inserts a **Play** button at the location of the recording that you can click to listen to the recording.

To record video (assuming that you have the proper video camera connection to your computer, which is usually accomplished with a FireWire cable), select **Insert, Video Recording** and follow the same procedure as you'd follow when recording sound.

143

18

Automatic Office

IN THIS CHAPTER:

In this chapter, you'll get a taste of some of Office's more advanced features, such as the automation of certain Office tasks. If you find yourself repeating the same series of keystrokes or menu selections over and over, you can automate those steps to speed the work in the future.

Microsoft Office has been around so long now that other programs can often directly read Office files. Of course, Office 2007 added a new file format that takes advantage of XML-based file formats. At first that might seem to limit which other programs can handle Office data directly, but the XML format is a universal format that more and more programs are starting to support. By taking the lead, Microsoft has helped to ensure that your Office documents will be usable in other programs as well as over the Internet without modification.

---

144 **About Office Macros**

→ **SEE ALSO**

145 Create a Macro
146 About Visual Basic for Applications

144

The purpose of a *macro* is to automate any repetitious task that would normally require you to follow a long sequence of commands. At its most fundamental level, a macro does nothing more than imitate keystrokes and mouse clicks the user might make. Office perceives menu clicks, ribbon button clicks, and typing as *instructions* that it is to follow. When you request that Office record a macro, what you're asking Office to do is watch you perform a series of instructions and then remember that series so that you can repeat them later at your discretion.

▶ **NEW TERM**

Macro—A sequence of recorded actions that can be played back at any time, for any number of times, to perform an oft-used, repetitive, or tedious task.

Why would you want the same series of instructions repeated? Suppose that you found yourself saving a backup of a Word document to a USB-based flash drive that is referred to as drive D: on your computer. For safety, you'll want to save to your flash drive D: every few minutes. The original document appears on C:, and the shortcut Ctrl+S keystroke (and the **Quick Access** toolbar's **Save** command) saves the document to C:; but just for safety, you want to save the file to your drive D: once in a while so that a second copy is available.

The following lists the steps you must perform to save the backup to the D: flash drive:

1. Click your **Office** button to display the **Office** menu.

2. Select the **Save As** command to override Word's default C: drive location that it would store to if you selected Save.

3. Press your keyboard's Home key to move the text cursor to the beginning of the filename. The file normally saves the document in the current folder and disk, although you are going to override that location.

4. Type **D:** so that Word saves the file on your D: flash drive.

5. Click **Yes** to overwrite your previous backup file on D:. (This assumes that you've saved the file at least once before in the D: default folder.)

6. Click the **OK** button to save the document. The default disk drive and folder will now be on D:, so you must restore the default to its original location.

7. Click your **Office** button to display your **Office** menu once more.

8. Select **Close** to close the document from Word's work area.

9. Click your **Office** button again to display the **Office** menu.

10. Select **2**. The **2** on the recent documents area of your **Office** menu will be the second-to-last file you edited, which was the file in its original C: drive location before you saved it to D:. You are now working, once again, with the original file on drive C:, and you've placed a copy of it on D:.

▶ **NOTE**

The final four steps had to close the document and reload it from drive C:. Otherwise, your edits would all go to D: after you'd saved the file to D:, and you would not have two copies being saved.

Whew! That's a lot of steps just to save a copy onto drive D:. If you create a macro to do all that, you only need to press a keystroke or select from a menu or button to accomplish all those steps, because the macro will do the work for you. You'll just sit back and watch. Watch quickly, though, because the macro will step through the process much faster than you can.

▶ **NOTE**

Office's macro-recording process is sensitive to three things: the keys you press, the buttons you click, and the entries you make in dialog boxes. Macros do not record mouse movements such as "up and to the right." Specifically, the macro recorder isn't concerned with where your mouse pointer is located as much as with what it's pointing to when you click.

Creating macros is simple. Office watches you and learns by your example to create macros. As **145 Create a Macro** shows, when you're ready to create a macro, you only need to tell the program to begin recording your next interactions with the program, either from the keyboard or from mouse clicks. When you tell the application to stop recording your actions, you name the macro and store it. To run the macro without calling it up as a file (for instance, from some kind of **Open** menu command), you can assign a trigger for the macro's execution, such as a dedicated keystroke.

▶ **TIP**

One of the under-appreciated qualities of a macro is not just how it saves time but how it reduces errors. When you perform the same sequence of commands repeatedly, it's possible you'll lose track in what you're doing, slip up, and then find yourself selecting **Undo**—maybe several times—until you reset things to the point before the error occurred. With a macro, you eliminate most chances for errors to crop up because of improper typing.

The macro-related commands appear on your Office application's **Developer** ribbon. By default, your ribbon doesn't show the **Developer** tab, so one of the first things you'll do when creating your first macro is display the **Developer** ribbon.

145

You'll use the Developer ribbon to create and manage macros.

As a macro is recorded, the commands and text you enter are reinterpreted as textual instructions, written in the Visual Basic programming language (see **146** **About Visual Basic for Applications**). You don't have to know anything about Visual Basic, or any other programming language, to record and use macros. However, you do need to know that after macros are converted to Visual Basic, they are stored in Office using a compartmentalized structure that's meant to help those who actually do use Visual Basic. A Visual Basic programmer can use his or her Visual Basic knowledge to modify macros and add more power to them.

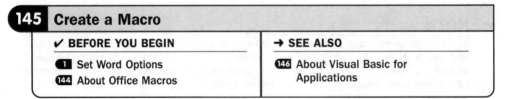

145   Create a Macro

✔ **BEFORE YOU BEGIN**	→ **SEE ALSO**
1 Set Word Options	**146** About Visual Basic for
144 About Office Macros	Applications

When you find yourself performing the same series of keystrokes over and over, perhaps in a series of menu selections or dialog box selections, you should store those keystrokes in a macro. After the keystrokes are recorded in a macro, you can easily repeat them simply by requesting the macro.

The process of recording a macro (a recorded sequence of commands, remember) mainly consists of performing the commands as you normally would, but with the macro recorder turned on. The trick to making a proper recording, however, is setting up your document beforehand so that the commands you're recording can apply to *any* document you may be editing in the future, not just the exact one you're looking at now.

▶ **NOTE**

You can create a macro by writing Visual Basic commands (see **146** About Visual Basic for Applications), but doing so requires extensive programming knowledge. It's much simpler to record a macro so that it imitates your keystrokes for a particular task.

1 Show the Developer Tab

Open your **Word Options** dialog box (see **1** Set Word Options), click to select the **Popular** group, and then click to select the option labeled **Show Developer Tab in the Ribbon**. By default, this option is unchecked, and you'll need to select it to record a macro. Click **OK** to close the **Word Options** dialog box.

2 Prepare Your Document

Set up your document to appear exactly as it should before you would normally execute the first action you'll record in the macro. For example, if your macro is to change the formatting of a selected paragraph in Word, select a paragraph now and let that be the "guinea pig" selection for your macro recording.

3 Request a Macro

Click to display your **Developer** ribbon. To begin recording, click **Record Macro**. Word opens the **Record Macro** dialog box.

▶ **TIP**

If you ever need to make certain that *no text or data in the document* is selected before a macro begins, press your Esc key before performing any of the macro's intended keystrokes. This ensures that you don't overwrite existing text that might happen to be selected when you later run the macro.

4 Name the Macro

In the **Record Macro** dialog box, enter a name for the macro. Make the name meaningful so that you'll know what the macro does if you later view a list of macros. Add a description, if you prefer, in the **Description** field.

145

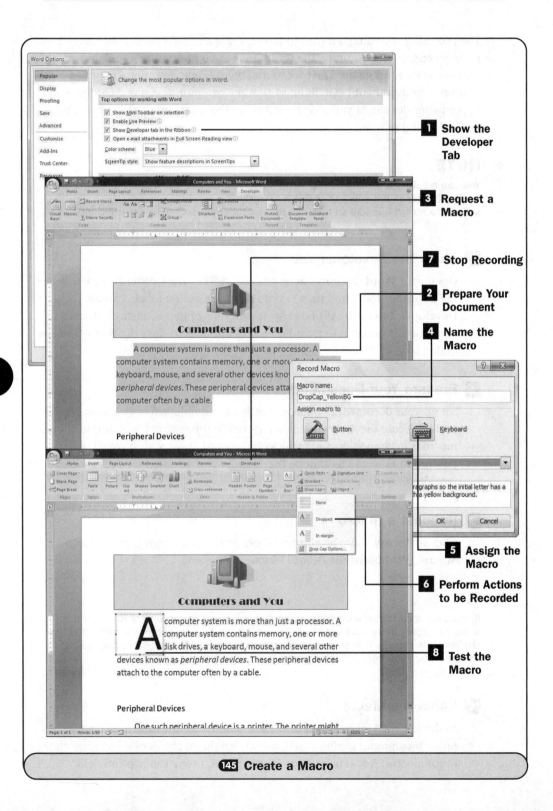

1 Show the Developer Tab

3 Request a Macro

7 Stop Recording

2 Prepare Your Document

4 Name the Macro

5 Assign the Macro

6 Perform Actions to be Recorded

8 Test the Macro

145 Create a Macro

▶ **NOTE**

Do not use spaces in the macro name. If you want to separate words, you can use the underscore (_) to do so.

If the macro will be used only in the current document and no other, click the **Store Macro In** drop-down list box and select the name of your current document. Otherwise, leave the option set to **All Documents** so that all documents you create will be able to run the macro when you request it.

⑤ Assign the Macro

You can set up your macro to execute on a keystroke or a button click. Depending on which you want, click either the **Button** or the **Keyboard** button in the **Record Macro** dialog box.

If you assign the macro to a button, the **Word Options** dialog box opens to allow you to select a button to assign the macro to. The button will appear in your Office **Quick Access** toolbar, which can fill quickly with macro buttons if you're not careful.

Most users click the **Record Macro** dialog box's **Keyboard** button and assign their macro to a keyboard shortcut. The **Customize Keyboard** dialog box opens. Press the keystroke you want to assign to the macro, such as Alt+Shift+Y. If the keystroke is already assigned to a command or macro, you'll see what it's assigned to in the **Currently Assigned To** field. If the keystroke you press is unassigned, **Unassigned** appears in the **Currently Assigned To** field. Office supports a huge number of keyboard shortcuts. You'll almost certainly try several before you find one that's unassigned. Most of the Alt+Shift keystrokes will be unassigned, but most others will be assigned to other commands. After you assign a keystroke, click **Close**, and the macro recorder will begin recording your actions.

145

⑥ Perform Actions to be Recorded

Carefully reproduce all the actions you want the macro to repeat for you. The record takes note of every action you do through the menu, ribbon, or keyboard. If you use your mouse, the macro will not record your mouse movements, but it will record any buttons you click with your mouse.

▶ **TIP**

Do as much as you can from your keyboard even if you have a mouse equivalent. For example, if you want the macro to select the current paragraph, select the paragraph with your keyboard by holding Shift and pressing the arrow keys instead of dragging to select the paragraph with your mouse.

7 Stop Recording

When you're satisfied that your sequence of commands has been completely demonstrated for the recorder, click Stop Recording on the Developer ribbon.

8 Test the Macro

This is a good time to make certain the macro works the way you expect it to. Open a document to which you can apply your new macro commands.

For example, if your macro assumes that you've first highlighted a paragraph, highlight a paragraph in a document and press the keystroke to trigger the macro.

The commands recorded in the macro are executed.

▶ **NOTE**

You often will not notice each step of the execution; you will see only the *results* of the macro, instantaneously. This is because Office stops updating its own windows when executing a macro, which speeds things up tremendously.

146

Examine the results closely. If something appears amiss, repeat the test. If you don't get the results you intend after a second test, you can record the macro again. Repeat this procedure from step 1, but in step 5, instead of entering a new name, choose the bad macro's name from the **Macro Name** field so that you can replace it. A dialog box will ask you to confirm overwriting the original macro.

---

146 About Visual Basic for Applications

✔ BEFORE YOU BEGIN	→ SEE ALSO
144 About Office Macros **145** Create a Macro	**147** Customize the Quick Access Toolbar

---

Not all macros are keyboard based. In addition to the keyboard-recorded macros, many macros provide additional commands that go beyond the simple selection of menu options. Microsoft standardized the Visual Basic for Application (VBA) *programming language* several years ago to form the foundation behind macros.

▶ **NOTE**

Microsoft often uses the shortened name *Visual Basic* instead of *Visual Basic for Applications.* Microsoft offers a standalone programming language named Visual Basic that is identical to VBA. When used in the context of an Office application such as Excel, however, VBA and Visual Basic for Applications are both accepted.

When you record a macro, your Office application isn't actually recording your keystrokes and mouse clicks, although that is the practical upshot of what it's doing. In reality, every time you press a key, select from a menu, type text, or click a button, the application adds a new VBA command to that macro's *program*.

▶ NEW TERMS

Programming language—A set of commands that you can put together to control a computer or another application such as Microsoft PowerPoint.

Program—A set of instructions written in a programming language such as VBA. The program makes your computer do something.

Until you learn a programming language, its programs can be cryptic indeed. For example, a macro you record that colors a selected paragraph's background yellow and converts the paragraph's first letter to a drop cap letter is actually a VBA program that looks like this:

```
Sub DropCap_YellowBN()

'

' DropCap_YellowBG Macro

' Follows company standards for lead-in paragraphs so the initial
  letter

' has a drop cap and the paragraph is colored with a yellow background.

'

    Selection.Shading.Texture = wdTextureNone

    Selection.Shading.ForegroundPatternColor = wdColorAutomatic

    Selection.Shading.BackgroundPatternColor = wdColorYellow

    Selection.MoveLeft Unit:=wdCharacter, Count:=1

    Selection.MoveRight Unit:=wdCharacter, Count:=1, Extend:=wdExtend

    With Selection.Paragraphs(1).DropCap

        .Position = wdDropNormal

        .FontName = "+Body"

        .LinesToDrop = 3

        .DistanceFromtext = InchesToPoints(0)

    End With

    Windows("Computers and You").Activate

End Sub
```

146

You've got to admit, recording your keystrokes and mouse clicks is a lot easier than writing all those VBA programming language statements! Nevertheless, if you knew VBA, you could have written this code instead of recording the macro and achieved the same results.

▶ **NOTE**

Not everything in a macro's program is cryptic. Programming languages use common words and phrases for commands and program elements. Although you may not be able to write VBA programs from scratch, you can look through this program and tell what much of it is doing, such as shading the background yellow, and adding the drop cap.

In Office 2007, you get a complete Visual Basic environment from which you can write VBA programs that control virtually every aspect of your document work. From the **Developer** ribbon, you can click the **Visual Basic** button to see a programming environment open on your screen.

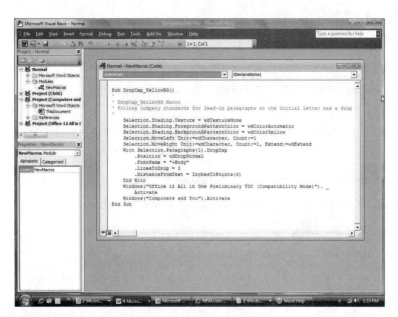

When you write a Visual Basic program to control an Office application, you'll use Visual Basic's own environment.

You might wonder how Visual Basic can supplement and add functionality to an Office application other than automating simple, routine tasks. After all, Excel supports VBA, but with all the worksheet power and commands that Excel already provides, how could a VBA program controlling Excel's environment and worksheet add any benefit to the Excel user?

146

If all VBA did was automate simple, routine tasks in recorded macros, VBA would be a welcome addition to Office. Simple recorded macros, though, must run in the same environment and with the same set of worksheets and columns each time. The keyboard macro has no room for ambiguity. For example, what if one of your company divisions was to shut down for remodeling one month? The keyboard macro that you may have recorded to consolidate all your company's four divisions would consolidate either a blank worksheet or an old one for the missing division's new data, producing an error.

Because Visual Basic is a complete programming language, the employee who needs such a consolidated report, for instance, can write a series of commands that handle unexpected conditions more gracefully than keyboard-recorded macros can. Perhaps the VBA program could read each worksheet and, if data other than zeros appears for the month totals, add that worksheet to the summary but ignore any other worksheet in which the division had no activity for the period. Such a macro—a Visual Basic program written in the VBA language—would work when a recorded macro would not.

▶ **NOTE**

If you want to learn more about Visual Basic, check out *Sams Teach Yourself Visual Basic 2005 in 24 Hours, Complete Starter Kit*, 0-672-32739-2 (Sams Publishing, 2006).

147

---

147 **Customize the Quick Access Toolbar**

✔ **BEFORE YOU BEGIN**

1 Set Word Options
145 Create a Macro

Your **Quick Access** toolbar is always there when you need it, sitting atop your Office 2007 application offering buttons for performing the following actions:

- Saving the current document

- Undoing recent edits

- Repeating your most recent edit

As you saw in **145 Create a Macro**, when you record a macro and assign a button to it, the button appears as a new button on your **Quick Access** toolbar. Although it's true that new **Quick Access** toolbar buttons can flood your **Quick Access** toolbar rather quickly, for common macros, the **Quick Access** toolbar is as good a place as any to stick a macro button.

In this task, you'll learn how to customize your **Quick Access** toolbar.

1 Move Your Quick Access Toolbar

Your **Quick Access** toolbar doesn't have to sit above your Office 2007 ribbon. Click the down arrow to the right of your **Quick Access** toolbar and select **Show Below the Ribbon**. When you do, Office 2007 moves your **Quick Access** toolbar to a row under your application's ribbon.

2 Modify Your Quick Access Toolbar

You can modify the buttons that appear on your **Quick Access** toolbar. For example, click to select Quick Print to add a print button to your Quick Access Toolbar. Click More Commands and the **Options** dialog box opens, where you can further customize your **Quick Access** toolbar.

147

3 Remove Quick Access Toolbar Buttons

Whenever you want to remove a button from your **Quick Access** toolbar, click the button's entry in the right pane of the **Options** dialog box and click **Remove**. The button goes away from your **Quick Access** toolbar when you click **OK**.

4 Add Features to Your Quick Access Toolbar

To add a new button to your **Quick Access** toolbar, scroll and locate the feature you want to add in the left pane of the **Options** dialog box. You can add several if you want.

▶ NOTE

You aren't limited to file-related commands. Click the drop-down list box labeled **Choose Commands From** to select another set of buttons you can choose from. You can add as many buttons from as many sets as you want.

To change the buttons' order, click the button (in the right **Options** dialog box pane) and click the up-arrow or down-arrow button to move that button up or down the list. This actually moves the button left or right on your **Quick Access** toolbar because the **Quick Access** toolbar resides horizontally across

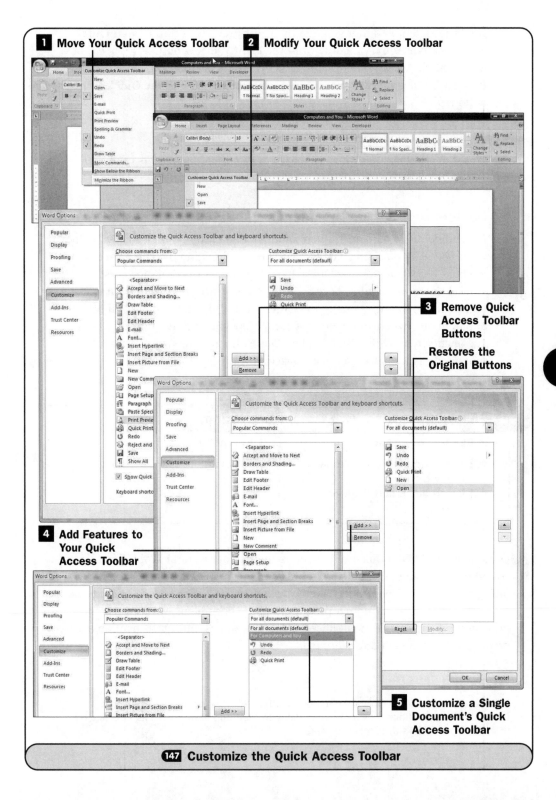

1 Move Your Quick Access Toolbar   **2** Modify Your Quick Access Toolbar

3 Remove Quick Access Toolbar Buttons

Restores the Original Buttons

147

4 Add Features to Your Quick Access Toolbar

5 Customize a Single Document's Quick Access Toolbar

147 Customize the Quick Access Toolbar

your screen. Suppose that you add the **Print Preview** button to your **Quick Access** toolbar. You'll probably want the **Print Preview** button to appear next to the **Quick Access** toolbar's **Quick Print** button, so after adding the **Print Preview** button, you will move it up so that it rests next to the **Quick Print** button.

▶ **TIP**

Click **Reset** to revert the **Quick Access** toolbar to its original state before you began customizing it in this session.

5 Customize a Single Document's Quick Access Toolbar

Depending on the document, you might want a custom **Quick Access** toolbar while you work on a single document without changing the **Quick Access** toolbar everywhere you use Office 2007. If you click the drop-down list box labeled **Customize Quick Access Toolbar** and select the current document's name before making changes, the **Quick Access** toolbar changes will be apparent only when you open that specific document in the future. All other documents in all Office 2007 applications will retain the **Quick Access** toolbar that was in place before you customized the one.

148

148	**Share Office Files with Other Applications**
✔ **BEFORE YOU BEGIN**	→ **SEE ALSO**
45 Save a Document in a Different Format	**149** About Office's XML File Format
87 Import and Export Worksheet Data	

Office plays well with others! When you're saving your work in Word, Excel, or PowerPoint, the **Save As** dialog box always provides you with both Office-based file types and other file formats. Obviously, macros you create for an Office application may not work in another program, but the documents, worksheets, and presentations you save in non-Office formats will almost always be available to programs that can read those formats.

▶ **NOTE**

Until others with whom you work upgrade to Office 2007, you can appreciate that all Office 2007 applications provide the capability to read and save data files in Office 97 through Office 2003's document formats.

The long-term impact that Office 2007's new XML-based file format will have isn't fully apparent yet (see **149 About Office's XML File Format**). Nevertheless, Microsoft is counting on the new file format causing a shift away from purely application-specific file formats to a more generalized file format that is universally compatible. It's ironic that Microsoft Office is one of the reasons so many applications use proprietary file formats because Microsoft kept the Office formats (pre-2007) proprietary.

An additional improvement in Office 2007's capability to save files readable by non-Office programs is the inclusion of the Adobe *PDF* file format. The PDF format, founded by Adobe Systems, is a universal file format readable by web browsers, many programs, and multiplatform computers. You don't have to use a PC-compatible computer to read PDF files.

▶ **NOTE**

Due to some legal wrangling, Microsoft doesn't provide direct saving to a PDF. After you download an add-in program, as explained in this task, you can save your files to the PDF format.

▶ **NEW TERM**

148

PDF—Stands for *portable document format*, which provides a fixed-layout file format that maintains the same document look whether the document is viewed online or printed.

1 Save in a Previous Office Format

When you save an Office 2007 document (including Word documents, worksheets, OneNote notes, and presentations), the **Save** command saves your work in Office 2007's native format. You can select **Save As** from the **Office** menu that appears when you click the **Office** button, and select the application's **97–2003 Document** format to save the document as a backward-compatible document that you and others can read in previous versions of Office.

▶ **TIP**

You don't have to select any special option or file format when opening Office documents from pre-Office 2007 programs. For example, you can run PowerPoint 2007 and open a PowerPoint 97 presentation just by selecting the **Open** command and selecting the presentation.

2 Save in Other Formats

Instead of saving in another Office format, you can select a different file format to save your Office 2007 data in. For example, if you save an Excel file and use the **Text (tab delimited)** or one of the **CSV** (for *comma-separated values*) formats, most accounting and database programs can read the

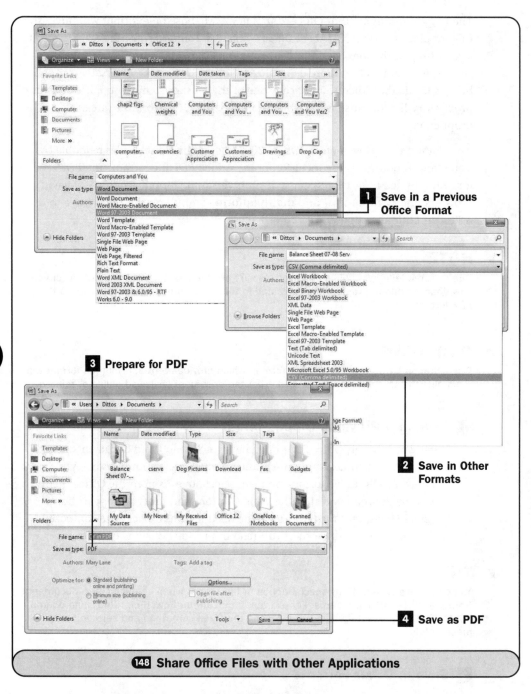

1 Save in a Previous Office Format

3 Prepare for PDF

2 Save in Other Formats

4 Save as PDF

148 Share Office Files with Other Applications

worksheet data. The formatting of the worksheet will almost surely be lost, but most programs that read tab-delimited and comma-separated files provide a way you can tell the program what each tab-separated or column-separated column of data represents.

3 Prepare for PDF

Office 2007 doesn't allow you to save data in the PDF file format immediately upon installing Office 2007, but it's fairly simple to install the proper upgrade to do so. Go to the following web address:

http://office.microsoft.com/en-us/officeupdate/cd101950461033.aspx

Download the Microsoft Save as PDF or XPS Add-in for 2007 Microsoft office programs add-in routine. The instructions will guide you through the installation. (If you live outside the United States, you need to search Microsoft.com for your country's PDF installation package.)

▶ **NOTE**

Microsoft also supports the XPS file format (see **149** **About Office's XML File Format**). You'll install that add-in at the same time you install the PDF file-saving add-in program.

4 Save as PDF

After you've installed the PDF file-saving add-in program, a new PDF file-saving option will appear on your **Save As** list. Select **PDF** from the **Save as Type** list. When you do, a new option appears on the **Save As** dialog box. If you click to select **Open File After Publishing** and you have Acrobat installed, Office will open your Adobe Acrobat Reader program immediately after saving the file so that you can review the file in its PDF format. If you haven't installed Adobe's Acrobat Reader, the option will be unavailable.

After you save to the PDF format, you cannot use any Office program to change the PDF file directly. You can always make changes to the original Office 2007 data file and then resave the file in the PDF format.

▶ **TIP**

To read a PDF file, you can use Word 2007. Adobe Systems also offers a free PDF reader at www.Adobe.com called *Acrobat Reader*.

149 About Office's XML File Format	
✔ **BEFORE YOU BEGIN**	→ **SEE ALSO**
148 Share Office Files with Other Applications	**152** Create an Office Data Shortcut

Only time will tell whether the *XML* file format will be as popular as Microsoft and others think it will. Microsoft introduced the XML format to Office data in Office XP, but the format wasn't the default file-saving format then. Office 2007 changes that format slightly, and all files you save with Office 2007 conform to an XML-based format.

▶ **NEW TERM**

XML—Stands for *Extensible Markup Language*, which provides a way for websites and applications to share data seamlessly.

XML is based on HTML, the website language that is still in widespread use today and that appears on virtually every website in existence. HTML describes the format of a page. HTML tells where data should go, what color and font it should appear in when the user uses a web browser to view the file, what sites hyperlinks should link to, and so on. Whereas HTML describes the format of a web page, XML describes the content of a web page.

Here is a possible XML section from a web page:

```
<CARMAKE>Swifty</CARMAKE>

<CARMODEL>Dove</CARMODEL>

<ENGINEPARTNO>546-32XS</ENGINEPARTNO>

<WHOLESALE>$21,039</WHOLESALE>

<SUGGESTEDRETAIL>$38,765</SUGGESTEDRETAIL>
```

The items inside angled brackets are *tags* that describe data. Over time, industries will begin to standardize on descriptors. Therefore, <CARMAKE> (and its corresponding ending tag of </CARMAKE>), over time, might begin to be used by automobile companies. The more people who use the tag, the more systems will understand its meaning. Before XML, if a unique tag appeared in a file, a web browser—and the corresponding database that might process web data behind the web browser—would have to ignore the data.

▶ **NEW TERM**

Tag—A term, inside angled brackets, that defines what is coming next. In a web browser, HTML tags tell the browser what to boldface, for instance. If a web browser sees <B>Office 2007</B>, the browser knows to boldface "Office 2007." </B> is called the ending tag.

All web browsers and applications that read HTML understand HTML tags. There are only so many HTML tags. If an HTML file has the <COLOR> tag, any HTML program understands what to do with it. The problem comes in when companies and applications want to share data. Until XML came along, they had to convert the data to text in a comma-delimited or tab-separated file format. The other company or program could then read the data, but what would the data represent? The sending company would have to define each field. So a car company that shares data with one of its suppliers might have to send a file format description that says, "The first field in the

149

text file is the car's make, the second field is the model, the third field is the engine part number," and so on. The receiving company would have to reprogram its computers to read data in the order it was sent to them.

▶ **NOTE**

Yes, all this is background—and not background you'll directly use in Office 2007! Nevertheless, you need a small history of XML to get a glimpse into why Microsoft shifted its data files to an XML-based format.

Two files are often associated with XML data: a *Document Type Definition* (*DTD*) and the XML file itself. The DTD tells the receiving company all the descriptor tags, such as <CARMAKE>, that reside in the corresponding XML file and what each tag represents. It's hoped that as more and more companies use XML, DTD files will become standardized across industries. Suppose that the <CARMAKE> tag *is* standardized in the car industry. If you ever become a supplier for a car manufacturer, you will instantly be able to interact with that company's data, sending the company your specifications and data, because you will adopt the same DTD used by the car company.

▶ **NEW TERM**

149

Document Type Descriptor—Also called the *DTD* and sometimes referred to as the *Document Type Definition*, the Document Type Descriptor is a dictionary that describes each XML tag in an XML file and what it represents.

Don't discount XML's importance even though the definition of XML may seem fuzzy. It seems fuzzy because it *is*. XML is a concept that's certainly difficult to describe in one task and difficult even in one complete book. In spite of its initial ambiguity, most major companies have converted, or will convert, their web pages and information connections from a straight HTML and proprietary format to XML code. In the year 2000, Cisco, Incorporated, claims to have processed 95% of its business over the Internet. When Cisco converted to XML in late 2000, it began saving $175 million annually over traditional HTML-based technology. That's quite a savings, and Cisco did this long before many other companies made the shift.

The bottom line is that if you process, manage, create, or read data that interacts with others, you stand a much better chance of interacting with few troubles if you use XML-based data.

▶ **NOTE**

Office 2007, by using an XML-based data format, enables you to work with the very same data in multiple Office programs, such as Access, Word, and Excel. No more converting is necessary on your part.

Microsoft has made it clear that it believes XML is the file format of today and tomorrow. The Office 2007 file format is XML based. Among the advantages Microsoft offers are the following:

- Smaller file sizes than earlier Office versions—Office 2007 uses several compression algorithms to squeeze file sizes.

- Easier and more reliable recovery—If an Office 2007 file gets damaged, as might occur if power goes out during a file save, for instance, the Office 2007 XML-based file format is easier and more accurately recovered.

- Greater compatibility—As the preceding paragraphs explained, XML files are more compatible with other computers and programs than previous Office files were.

▶ **NOTE**

OneNote does not support data in the XML format at the time of this writing.

When you save a file in Word, Excel, or PowerPoint, you're saving in an XML format. Office 2007 uses the same file extensions as previous versions of Office but adds the letter *x* to designate the XML format. For example, Word documents no longer use the .doc filename extension but instead use .docx. The files are somewhat compressed to save space. If you want to save a file in a pure, generic XML format, you can do so as long as you select the **XML** file type option when you save the file.

The following figure shows a Word document as it appears on the screen.

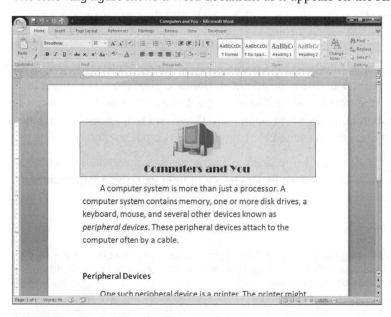

A Word document's native file format is XML based.

If, when saving that .docx file, you used the **Save As** option and saved the file in a pure XML format, you could actually read the Word document in Windows' Notepad program, or any other program that loads text-based files. The next figure shows how the Word document looks when viewed in Notepad.

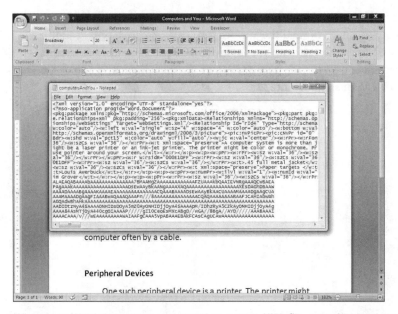

When your Word documents are saved as a pure XML file, even Notepad can read them.

It's certainly true that even though you can open the XML document in Notepad, it doesn't *look* like it does in Word! However, the idea of XML files is not that people can read them; it's that other computers, other operating systems, and other programs can read them. Look through the XML code, though, and you'll begin to spot some tags inside angled brackets. The tags are complex because the DTD for Office is complex. As long as the DTD for Office is stored on the machine that is to read the document, that machine can interpret the tags and should be able to (in theory) produce a document that looks just like your Word document without having Word.

In summary, Office 2007 supports XML, both in a compressed native file format and in a pure XML file format. To confuse matters further, Office 2007 programs can save files in the XML-based **XPS** format, which is somewhat akin to (and a competitor with) Adobe's PDF file format. If you ever need to save a document in XPS format, you'll first need to download the PDF and XPS add-in program (see **148 Share Office Files with Other Applications**). As with the PDF format, you must have a separate program to read any XPS file you save. Microsoft makes an XPS reader available here:

http://office.microsoft.com/en-us/officeupdate/cd101950461033.aspx

▶ NEW TERM

XPS—Stands for *XML Paper Specification*, which is designed to ensure that XPS files look the same printed or viewed onscreen. In addition, XPS can prevent edits to an XPS file and adds security when needed for sensitive files.

This task has certainly provided far more theory than the other tasks. And it's true that you've only skimmed the surface and perhaps have only a hint of what XML is all about. If you want a more in-depth look at XML and its benefits, check out *Sams Teach Yourself XML in 24 Hours, Complete Starter Kit*, 0-672-32797-X (Sams Publishing, 2006).

149

19

Sharing Data Among Office Applications

IN THIS CHAPTER:

Sharing data among the Office applications is a necessity. You'll create tables of data in Excel that you may want to include in your Word documents. In addition, you may need the table in a PowerPoint presentation, and perhaps you'll also want to embed the table in one of your OneNote notebooks. No problem.

You can drag and drop data between two Office programs, create links in one program to the data of another, and use OneNote to enhance the data integration of all your notes. In this chapter, you'll see several of the more common ways you can share data among your applications.

---

150 Use Drag and Drop to Move Data

✔ BEFORE YOU BEGIN	→ SEE ALSO
148 Share Office Files with Other Applications	**151** Link to Office Data
	152 Create an Office Data Shortcut

150

Suppose that you want to use part of an Excel worksheet inside a Word document. Word cannot open Excel worksheets directly, but you can easily place Excel data inside a Word document. Actually, you can use just about any kind of Office 2007 application's data inside a different Office 2007 application.

To do so, you'll use the Windows Clipboard to hold the data. To do that, you'll use the following:

- Drag and drop operations with your mouse
- Copy and paste

Dragging and dropping is probably the easiest method, given that you can look at where you want to insert the data you drag in its target document. It's not obvious that Office is using the Windows Clipboard to perform the drag operation, but it is.

Sometimes, screen room isn't ample, so to simulate a drag operation you can use copy and paste. The data, however, doesn't always enter the target document and look and behave exactly as it did in its original document. After all, PowerPoint has no spreadsheet calculation capabilities, so you shouldn't expect to apply all of Excel's power to a worksheet you place in a PowerPoint presentation, but you'll often have some ability to edit and manipulate the data you place there, as this task demonstrates.

1 Resize Program Windows

To move from Excel to Word, resize your Excel and Word windows so that you can see both the source Excel worksheet and the destination Word document.

▶ **NOTE**

Depending on your screen size and resolution, seeing both Word and Excel isn't always the most straightforward thing to do. Dragging and dropping between two programs is made far easier if you run dual monitors on your computer. You then can open a separate program window on each monitor and drag from one to the other.

② Select Cells to Drag

In your Excel worksheet, select the cells you want to drag to the Word document.

▶ **TIP**

Feel free to adjust your two open program windows to match what you're trying to accomplish. You may want to shrink the Word window some and give more room to the Excel window to see better what you're selecting.

③ Drag and Drop the Selection

To drag the selected Excel data to your Word document, you must point to the edge of the selected data in Excel. Your mouse pointer will change from the cell-pointing thick white cross to a four-headed arrow to let you know that's where you can drag from.

Drag the data to Word. As you drag, you'll notice that the mouse pointer changes to a box shape as it moves from Excel to Word. Drag the mouse until it rests at the position in your Word document where you want the Excel data to go, and release your mouse button.

▶ **NOTE**

If your screen size simply doesn't allow for reliable drag-and-drop operations, copy the selected Excel data to your Windows Clipboard and click your **Home** ribbon's **Copy** button. Switch to your Word document, click where you want the Excel data to go, and click the Word **Home** ribbon's **Paste** button.

④ Adjust the Received Data

Maximize your Word window to see the Excel data. Generally, the data arrives in nice shape, but you'll probably have to change the format some to conform to the surrounding document you were writing before copying Excel's data.

The Excel worksheet might show up as a Word table depending on the complexity of the worksheet. If you're unable to format the worksheet, double-click the worksheet data in your Word document, and you should be able to edit it as a Word table.

150

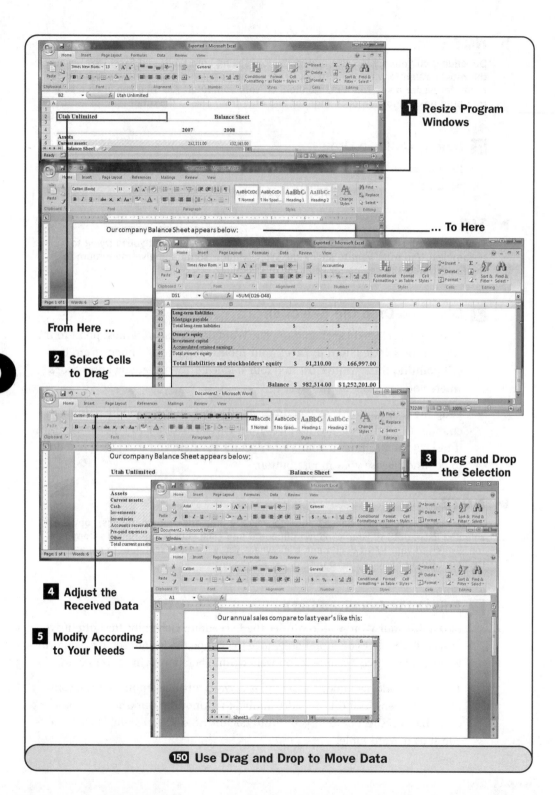

1 Resize Program Windows

... To Here

From Here ...

2 Select Cells to Drag

3 Drag and Drop the Selection

4 Adjust the Received Data

5 Modify According to Your Needs

150

150 Use Drag and Drop to Move Data

5 **Modify According to Your Needs**

You won't always be dragging data from Excel to Word, of course. You can move data between numerous combinations of Office 2007 data in the same way that you saw here. In the same way, you might drag a Word document to a worksheet to introduce the worksheet, or perhaps send an Excel table to a PowerPoint presentation.

Although dragging and dropping is the most intuitive method for a Windows user, as you work with Office 2007, you'll discover new ways to share data. For example, you can create a new Excel worksheet from within a Word document without ever starting Excel! Click to display Word's **Insert** ribbon. Click the **Table** button, and select **Excel Spreadsheet**. An Excel worksheet opens inside your Word document, and Word's ribbon changes to offer buttons identical to those on Excel's ribbon. You can now perform all Excel operations possible on the worksheet that's embedded inside your Word document.

▶ **NOTE**

Click on any part of the Word document outside the embedded Excel worksheet to return to Word's ribbon buttons. Double-click the Excel worksheet, and Excel's ribbon buttons appear.

151

---

151 **Link to Office Data**

✔ **BEFORE YOU BEGIN**	→ **SEE ALSO**
148 Share Office Files with Other Applications	**152** Create an Office Data Shortcut
150 Use Drag and Drop to Move Data	

Suppose that you create a monthly sales report using the same Word document and the same Excel worksheet every time. Although the data within the Excel worksheet changes to reflect each month's figures, the structure and formulas remain the same. You don't have to drag the updated Excel table to your Word document (see **150** **Use Drag and Drop to Move Data**) before printing the Word document each month. Instead of copying the data to Word and *embedding* the data, you can create a *link* to the Excel data.

▶ **NEW TERMS**

Embedding—Inserting a copy of data from a source into a destination document. If the data at the source changes, the document holding the embedded data doesn't update to reflect those changes.

Link—A pointer to data elsewhere. If the data at the source changes, the data document holding a link to that data updates to reflect the new changes.

As long as you've inserted a link to an Excel worksheet in your monthly sales report's document or document template, you need only change the Excel worksheet each month. You won't have to copy the actual Excel data into the report because the link points to the Excel data and displays the information there.

1 Resize Your Program Windows

To link from an Excel worksheet to Word, resize your Excel and Word windows so that you can see both the source Excel worksheet and the destination Word document.

▶ NOTE

Depending on your screen size and resolution, seeing both Word and Excel isn't always the most straightforward thing to do. Creating a link between programs is made far easier if you run dual monitors on your computer. You then can open a separate program window on each monitor to more easily view both programs.

2 Select the Cells to Link To

Select the cells in the Excel worksheet that you want to link and transfer to the Word document.

3 Drag and Drop the Link

With your right mouse button (make sure that you're clicking and dragging with the *right* button or a link won't be possible), drag the edge of the highlighted cells to the location in your Word document where you want to place the link.

▶ NOTE

You might have to practice doing this a while if you're not used to dragging using your right mouse button.

4 Anchor the Link

When you release your right mouse button, Word opens a menu that includes these options: **Move Here, Copy Here, Link Excel Object Here, Create Shortcut Here, Create Hyperlink Here,** and **Cancel**.

Select **Link Excel Object Here** to indicate to Word that you want to create an object link to the cells (as opposed to moving or copying the data, which embeds the data in the Word document instead of inserting a link). Although the cells appear as though Office copied them into the Word document, the cells represent only the link that you created between the Excel source file and Word's destination document.

151

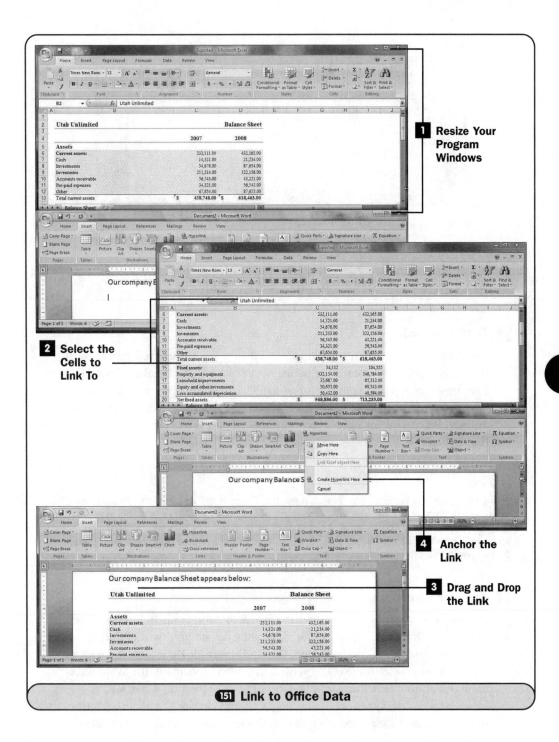

1 Resize Your Program Windows

2 Select the Cells to Link To

4 Anchor the Link

3 Drag and Drop the Link

151

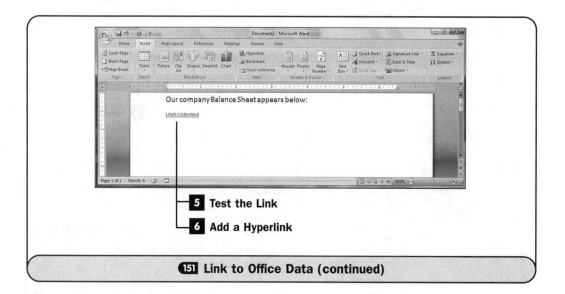

5 Test the Link

6 Add a Hyperlink

151 Link to Office Data (continued)

151

5 Test the Link

The destination file (in this case the Word document) always reflects the most recent changes to the source file (which in this case is the Excel worksheet). Save the Word document and change the Excel worksheet's data. Save the worksheet and start Word once more. When you open the document with the linked data, your most recent Excel changes to that worksheet will appear in the document.

▶ NOTE

When you open a document with linked data, the Office 2007 application always asks whether you want to update the links, meaning update the links to reflect the most recent changes to the source data. Asking you this is a security measure in case you open a document that contains a link to an unreliable data source, as might be the case if you open a file attached to an email.

6 Add a Hyperlink

Instead of embedding data or inserting a link to data, you can insert a hyperlink to any Office 2007 data on your computer. When you right-click data from one program to another, select **Create Hyperlink Here** from the pop-up menu. In the case of an Excel hyperlink in a Word document, the Word document will show a link that looks like a web page hyperlink. When you're viewing the Word document, if you hold Ctrl and click the hyperlink, Word's ribbon changes to show Excel's buttons, and the worksheet appears in the editing area.

▶ **NOTE**

You must press Ctrl before clicking the hyperlink for Word to trigger the link. By not linking on a simple mouse click, Word allows you to highlight the link with your mouse (which might otherwise trigger the link if a click was all that was required) and format or move the link. The Ctrl with the click informs Word that you're ready to trigger the link.

152   **Create an Office Data Shortcut**

✔ **BEFORE YOU BEGIN**

148 Share Office Files with Other Applications
150 Use Drag and Drop to Move Data
151 Link to Office Data

Instead of inserting a copy or a link, you can insert a shortcut in the destination document. When you insert a link, the Office 2007 document you use as the destination shows an icon instead of actual data. When the user of that document double-clicks the icon, the data appears.

▶ **NOTE**

You'll probably use shortcuts less often than links and embedded data when producing reports because you'll want reports to show actual data and not a placeholder icon.

152

If you often work with data from one program while working inside another Office 2007 program, the shortcut icon is nice because the source data doesn't get in your way until you're ready to see it. In addition, the icon loads more quickly than the underlying data would load, and speed can become an issue if your data set is large.

1 **Resize Your Program Windows**

To insert a shortcut from an Excel worksheet to a Word document, resize your Excel and Word windows so that you can see both the source Excel worksheet and the destination Word document.

▶ **NOTE**

Depending on your screen size and resolution, seeing both Word and Excel isn't always the most straightforward thing to do. Creating a link between programs is made far easier if you run dual monitors on your computer. You then can open a separate program window on each monitor to more easily view both programs.

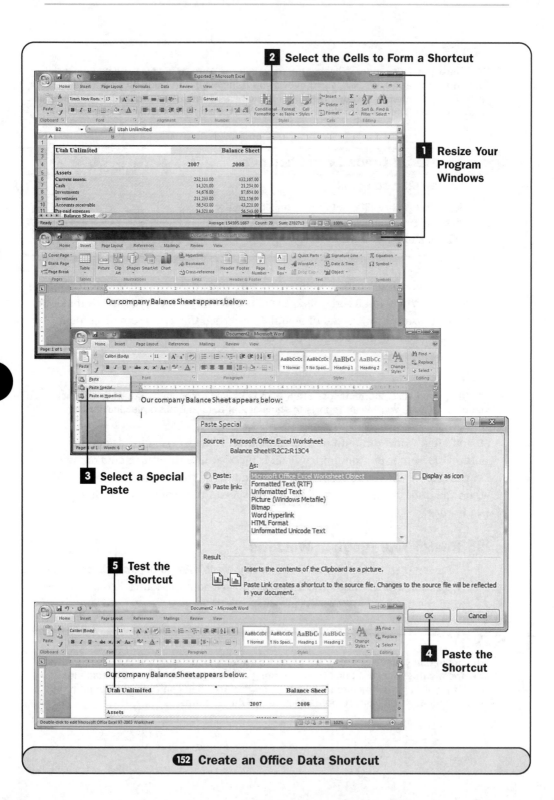

152 Create an Office Data Shortcut

2 **Select the Cells to Form a Shortcut**

Select the cells in the Excel worksheet that you want to link and transfer to the Word document. Press Ctrl-C to copy the cells to your Clipboard.

3 **Select a Special Paste**

Click the Word document location where you wish to place the shortcut. Click Word's Home ribbon's Paste button arrow and select Paste Special. The Paste Special dialog box opens.

4 **Paste the Shortcut**

Click the Paste link option and select Microsoft Office Excel Worksheet object.

Click OK to create a shortcut that represents the data.

5 **Test the Shortcut**

Double-click the icon. Excel will start, and the shortcut's data will appear in Excel. The data never combines with the actual Word document's data. The shortcut acts more like a trigger to display the Excel data in Excel.

153

153	**Convert a Word Document to a PowerPoint Presentation**
✔ BEFORE YOU BEGIN	**→ SEE ALSO**
16 About Styles, Themes, and Templates **17** Use a Style	**160** Create a Web Page with PowerPoint

Word and PowerPoint share a special link that enables you to turn a set of notes into a presentation. As you create a document in Word that you might want to use as a presentation, you'll use the Heading styles to format your notes. For example, you might use the Heading 1 style for slide titles and Heading 2 through Heading 5 for each slide's subsequently indented text.

When you read the document in PowerPoint, PowerPoint understands the Heading styles in Word and automatically generates a presentation. PowerPoint uses the Heading 1 style for slide title, and so on. If your Word document includes styles other than the Heading styles, PowerPoint ignores that text.

▶ NOTE

Not only can you create a Word document that you want to become a PowerPoint presentation as well as remain a Word document, but you also can modify an existing Word document and make it serve as a PowerPoint presentation by modifying the styles of the text you want to send to slides.

1 Prepare a Word Document

You can create a Word document that will also become the basis for your PowerPoint presentation. This is useful if you're planning a presentation but want to organize your own speaker notes first. You can develop the presentation and write what you want to say in Word. All text that is to appear on the presentation's slides should be formatted with one of the Heading styles.

Before you do this with a real project, it's probably best to start with a new Word document and see how PowerPoint interprets a Word document in this manner. You'll then be better able to judge how to format the Word styles.

2 Format the Slide Titles

Apply the Heading 1 style to all text that is to stand alone on its own slide. This will probably include the presentation's title.

At this point you're not worried about the presentation's coloring and background. You're starting with the presentation's content. PowerPoint 2007 makes formatting a presentation so simple that the formatting is not a critical part of the presentation's creation at this point. The message is more important than the medium, they say.

153

▶ **TIP**

To apply a style quickly, select the line or paragraph you want to apply a style to. Press Ctrl+Shift+S, and Word displays the **Apply Styles** dialog box. Select or type the style, such as Heading 1, that you want to apply to the selected text.

3 Format the Section Titles

Apply the Heading 2 style to all text that is to form individual section titles over bulleted text.

4 Format the Slide Details

Apply the Heading 3 style to all text that is to make up the detailed text on each slide. Often this will be bulleted or numbered text that forms talking points in your presentation.

▶ **NOTE**

You may need to reapply bullets and numbers to text after you apply the Heading 3 style. Therefore, it might be best not to format text with bullets and numbers until you've applied all the Heading 3 styles to your presentation.

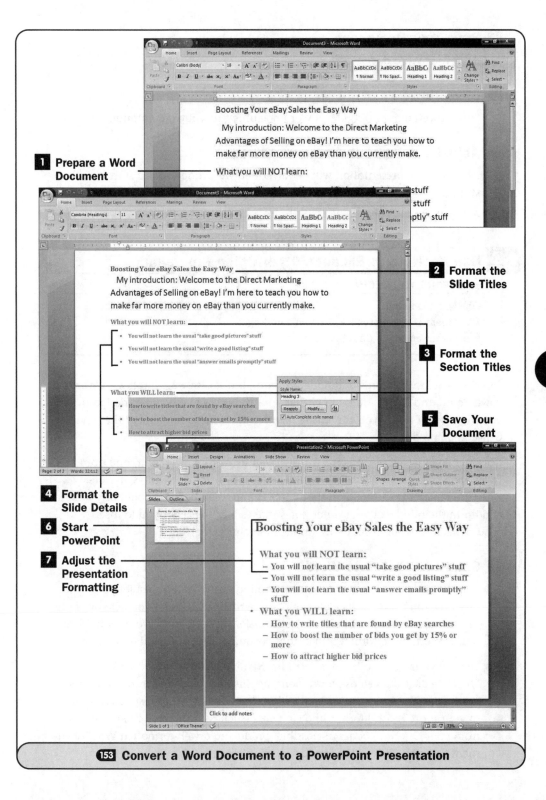

1 Prepare a Word Document

2 Format the Slide Titles

3 Format the Section Titles

5 Save Your Document

4 Format the Slide Details

6 Start PowerPoint

7 Adjust the Presentation Formatting

153

153 Convert a Word Document to a PowerPoint Presentation

5   Save Your Document

Save your Word document.

6   Start PowerPoint

Start PowerPoint and load the Word document as your presentation.

7   Adjust the Presentation Formatting

Although the presentation will be formatted well enough for a start, you'll still have to adjust the text size and apply colors and background images to your slides to finalize the presentation.

---

154   Use OneNote to Enhance Other Office Programs

✔ **BEFORE YOU BEGIN**

138 About OneNote

140 Create a New Notebook, Section, and Pages

152 Create an Office Data Shortcut

154

OneNote works well as a standalone program, but it also works well with Word, PowerPoint, and Excel. After you gather your thoughts and begin to design an organized set of notes, you can easily transfer those notes into one of the other Office 2007 programs.

Not only do OneNote documents transfer well to Word, PowerPoint, and even Excel, but your other Office documents also can transfer right into OneNote. OneNote's freeform editing area that enables you to embed just about any kind of data in the middle of your other notes makes it a breeze for you to insert documents from your other Office applications into OneNote.

1   Send Your Notes to Word

OneNote is better designed for brainstorming than Word is. Just jot your notes any way you want in OneNote's freeform writing area. After you get your notes in some order, you might be ready to transfer those notes to Word for publication, or perhaps to format into a final document that you send to others.

To send your notes to Word, select **File**, **Send To**, **Microsoft Office Word**. OneNote doesn't even ask for a filename. Instead, OneNote starts Word and loads your notes directly into a new Word document. Word respects as many of your margins and formatting elements (such as numbered lists) that come from your OneNote pages as possible, producing a well-formatted Word document that you can further format and publish.

2 Annotate PowerPoint Slides

Although PowerPoint provides drawing tools, nothing beats OneNote at being able to annotate exactly what you want to annotate. Make notes, circle important slide details, and store them in your OneNote documents for later retrieval.

▶ **NOTE**

You cannot put annotated slides back into a PowerPoint presentation.

Although you cannot directly load a PowerPoint presentation into OneNote, you can select **Insert, Files As Printouts**. OneNote does a little background trick to load the PowerPoint slides. OneNote forces a print of the slides from PowerPoint, but it captures the printout and inserts that printed file into your OneNote editing area. Once the slides are there, you treat them as though they were normal OneNote data.

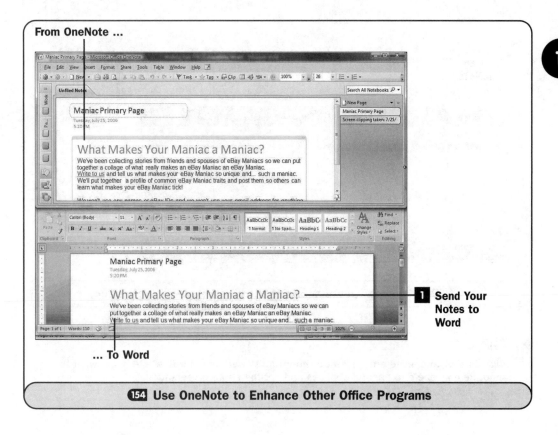

From OneNote ...

154

1 Send Your Notes to Word

... To Word

154 Use OneNote to Enhance Other Office Programs

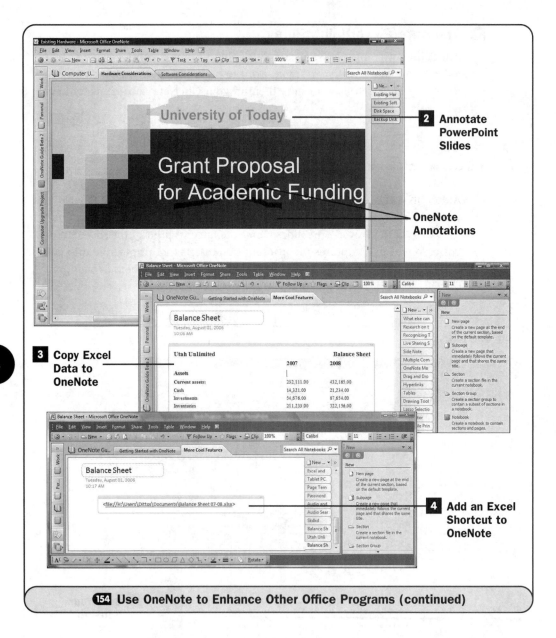

154

2 Annotate PowerPoint Slides

OneNote Annotations

3 Copy Excel Data to OneNote

4 Add an Excel Shortcut to OneNote

154 Use OneNote to Enhance Other Office Programs (continued)

▶ **TIP**

You can copy and paste one slide at a time from PowerPoint into OneNote if you want to annotate only one or a handful of slides and not the entire presentation.

3 Copy Excel Data to OneNote

If you want to transfer Excel data to OneNote, use copy and paste. Select a portion of the worksheet you want to place into a OneNote notebook for annotation or review, click Excel's **Copy** button, and paste the worksheet data into OneNote.

The data comes into a OneNote note container as text you can edit. All of OneNote's annotation drawing tools operate as you'd expect, so you can draw lines, draw circles, and add other highlighting elements to the data after it's in OneNote. As with PowerPoint slides that you annotate into OneNote, you cannot send the annotated data back to an Excel worksheet.

4 Add an Excel Shortcut to OneNote

The Excel data you copy to OneNote exists in OneNote as embedded data. There is no link to the original Excel worksheet, so any changes you make to the Excel worksheet from inside Excel are not propagated to your OneNote data.

If you send an Excel worksheet as a link to OneNote, your OneNote document will display a link to the worksheet instead of actual data. You can click the link to view the worksheet, and any recent changes to the worksheet will appear.

154

▶ **TIP**

If you insert an Excel or Word document into your OneNote page using the **Insert, Files** menu, OneNote places an icon in your OneNote notebook to represent the file as opposed to showing a link to the document. Double-click the icon to open Excel or Word and view the data.

20

Combining Office and the Internet

IN THIS CHAPTER:

Microsoft ensured that all Office 2007 programs integrate well in an Internet-connected world. The Internet is so much a part of computer users' lives, and Office needs to help users access and use Internet information. In addition, computers are connected to each other thanks to the Internet, so Office uses the Internet to display and retrieve information but also as a transport mechanism for up-to-date online help, file transfer, updates, and more.

This chapter reveals ways to combine the Internet and your use of the Office programs.

155 About Office and Online Access

✔ BEFORE YOU BEGIN	→ SEE ALSO
148 Share Office Files with Other Applications	**158** Create a Web Page with Word
	159 Create a Web Page with Excel
	160 Create a Web Page with PowerPoint

155

The programs in Office 2007 offer a complete set of tools that integrate the Office products and the Internet. From any Office product, you can access files and web pages on the Internet.

▶ NOTE

Obviously, an always-on, high-speed Internet connection through a DSL, cable modem, T1, or T3 line makes your Office-Internet connection far handier than if you're limited to a dial-up service. If you use dial-up, your computer must dial and connect every time you access any Office-related Internet service.

Sometimes combining Office and the Internet requires that you locate data on the Internet that you want to access. It's not always easy to locate data on your own computer, let alone on the vast Internet! If, for instance, you know of a Word document that you want to open in Word, you can do so, but you must know the Internet location of the document. As long as you know its location, you can feel free to open that document directly from Word.

For example, suppose that your company's website has a list of sales documents that you want to download sometime when you're on the road. Start Word on your laptop, click your **Office** button, and type the Internet web address of the document before your document's filename. Typically, the web address will begin http://www. Therefore, you might type `http://www.MyCompany.com/SalesDocs/NewProduct23a1.doc` for the filename when you see Word's **Open** dialog box. As long as you have Internet access, Word will go to the Internet and open the file as though it resided on your own computer and you'd selected one of your own disk drives.

▶ **NOTE**

You must have permission to access any files you want to access from the Internet. Also, you must know where they are located. Generally, a company's website's internal pages (those pages not available through links on public web pages) are great places to store documents and files that employees may need to access while on the road.

Microsoft makes good use of the Internet to keep your Office up-to-date. Depending on your computer update settings, Office 2007 can automatically update itself with bug fixes and security updates while you use your computer. If you've updated to the latest version of Windows and turned on the automatic updates, you probably will get your Office programs updated regularly also. Not everyone runs the latest version of Windows, however, and not everyone prefers to turn on automatic updates.

If you want to make sure that you have the latest Office 2007 updates, one of the easiest ways is to start OneNote and select **Help, Microsoft Office Online**. OneNote will open your web browser, go to the Office 2007 website, and click to select the **Check for Updates** link. The website will analyze your Office 2007 installation. If you don't have the latest updates, Office will download and install any updates you might need.

155

Click to Update ———

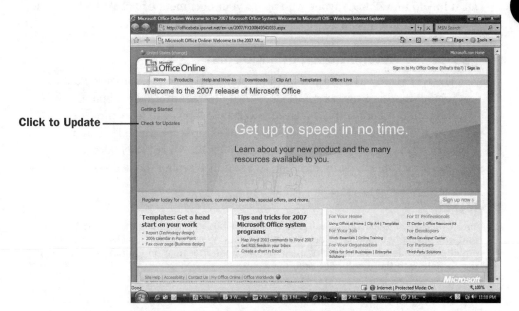

The Office 2007 website includes updates you can install and a wealth of helpful advice, templates, and online tutorials.

▶ **TIP**

In today's online world with security being such a problem, keeping Office 2007 up-to-date is one of the best ways to ensure that you have the latest security patches to keep your system running at its best.

---

156   Insert a Web Hyperlink into a Document

✔ BEFORE YOU BEGIN	→ SEE ALSO
155 About Office and Online Access	**157** Insert Live Stock Prices into an Excel Worksheet

---

Not only do you perhaps use the Internet a lot, but your clients, friends, family, and business associates do, too. These days it seems as though it's the rare individual who doesn't spend a few minutes and often more each week working online. It's reasonable, therefore, to expect that those who view and work with the Office 2007 documents you create and distribute have Internet access.

When you want to link to something online, whether it be in an Excel worksheet or a Word document or a PowerPoint presentation or an email, go ahead and create a link to that data. Anyone who opens your document can click the link, if he wants to go straight to the online source documentation you reference.

1 Set the Automatic Hyperlink Option

The easiest way to insert a hyperlink in a Word document or PowerPoint presentation or Excel worksheet is to turn on the **AutoCorrect** option that will automatically convert any website address you type into a hyperlink. You have to do nothing special except type the link, such as http://www.SamsPublishing.com, and Office 2007 turns the address into a clickable hyperlink as soon as you finish typing the address.

▶ **NOTE**

Your Office 2007 applications will also turn email-based references that follow the format mailto:Person@domain.com into a hyperlink. When a person clicks such a link, his email program (such as Outlook) opens a new email message and automatically fills in the **To** field with the email address.

To turn on the automatic conversion of a typed web address to a clickable hyperlink, click your **Office** button and select **Word Options**. Click the **Proofing** tab and click the **AutoCorrect Options** button. Click to select the **AutoFormat As You Type** page, and click to select the option labeled **Internet and Network Paths with Hyperlinks**. Click **OK** twice.

☑ Test the Automatic Hyperlink

After you've ensured that the automatic link-creation option is checked, type a web address in a document. After you type the address, press your spacebar or type any punctuation character such as a period, and the Office 2007 program will change the text to a hyperlink. You'll see the underline indicating the hyperlink.

After the hyperlink appears, you may find that you cannot click to surf to the hyperlink's location. This is because if, for example, Word allowed you to click a hyperlink to jump to that location, you wouldn't then be able to click and drag selected text that is a hyperlink to a different part of your document. You also wouldn't be able to click to select a hyperlink to format it. Therefore, if you want to test a hyperlink in one of your Word documents, you must hold down your Ctrl key and click the hyperlink. You'll then see the target web page when your Internet browser appears. Excel requires that you click and hold your mouse button down over a hyperlink before Excel will take you to that hyperlink's web page.

▶ NOTE

156

Repeat these steps and click to uncheck the option if you don't want Word, Excel, and PowerPoint to convert your web addresses to hyperlinks automatically. For example, some publishers don't allow hyperlinks in manuscripts. If you write an article for a magazine whose editorial guidelines don't allow embedded hyperlinks, for example, you would want to turn off Word's automatic hyperlink formatting feature.

☑ Manually Insert a Hyperlink

You won't always type an actual hyperlink, but you may want to insert a hyperlink where a word or phrase appears in your data. For example, suppose that you type the phrase `Click here to see our results` and you want that phrase to be clickable as a hyperlink to a web page where the results are posted. Type the phrase and then select it.

Click to display your **Insert** ribbon and click the **Hyperlink** button (or press the shortcut key, Ctrl+K) to display the **Insert Hyperlink** dialog box. In the **Address** field, type the full web link, such as `http://www.MaxCorpTies.com/Results`, and your Office 2007 program will convert your text to a hyperlink. This way you can convert any text (or even a selected graphic image) to a clickable hyperlink.

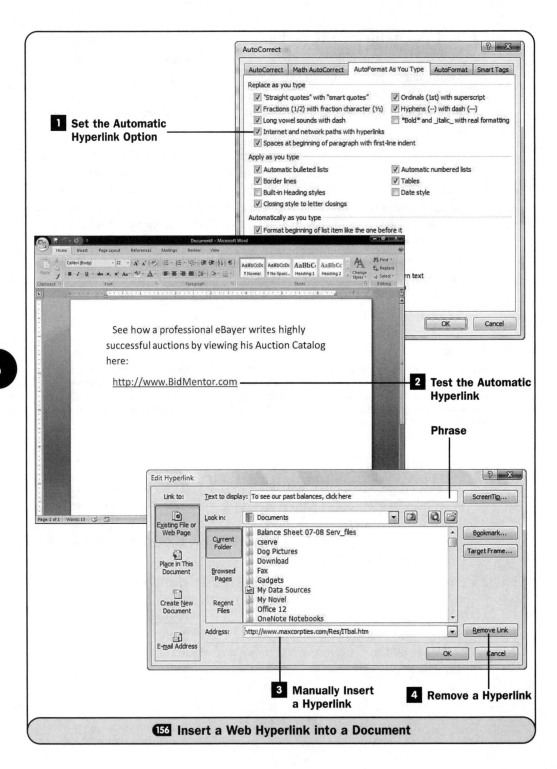

1 Set the Automatic Hyperlink Option

2 Test the Automatic Hyperlink

Phrase

3 Manually Insert a Hyperlink

4 Remove a Hyperlink

156

156 Insert a Web Hyperlink into a Document

▶ **TIP**

Your hyperlink doesn't have to be Internet based. You can add a hyperlink to your own disk drive or to a file on your network from the **Insert Hyperlink** dialog box by typing the target file's full disk or network path before the filename in the **Address** field.

4 Remove a Hyperlink

If you type a web address and your program converts it to a hyperlink, if you immediately click your **Quick Access** toolbar's **Undo** button (Ctrl+Z is the shortcut key), Word, Excel, or PowerPoint will remove the hyperlink and keep the address formatted the same way that surrounding text is formatted.

If you fail to undo the automatic hyperlink immediately after the program converts it, you can select the hyperlink and display the **Insert** ribbon's **Insert Hyperlink** dialog box again. Click the **Remove Link** button to remove the hyperlink from whatever text it applies to. When you click **OK**, the text that was a hyperlink is now just text and not clickable.

---

157 | **Insert Live Stock Prices into an Excel Worksheet**

✔ BEFORE YOU BEGIN	→ SEE ALSO
155 About Office and Online Access	**158** Create a Web Page with Word
156 Insert a Web Hyperlink into a Document	**159** Create a Web Page with Excel
	160 Create a Web Page with PowerPoint

157

Many investors and traders use Excel to analyze stock prices. As long as you have an Internet connection, you can work with live stock price data; Excel can go to the web and retrieve current stock prices. With this capability, you can make real-time investment decisions.

This task shows you how to use *smart tags* to insert live quotes into your worksheets. Although using smart tags requires a little arrangement, given how much data the smart tag brings into Excel, it's exactly because so much data is available that the smart tag feature is so beneficial. Although you can use the **Research** task pane (available from the **Review** ribbon's **Research** button) to type a stock symbol and get a quote, that quote is fixed and won't update as you refresh your worksheet.

▶ **NEW TERM**

Smart tags—Data that Office recognizes and can sometimes provide additional information about. If you type a stock symbol, a smart tag icon might appear, meaning that you
can click the icon to get additional information about that stock. Type a contact name,
and a smart tag can appear, offering Outlook data about that person, if the person is
stored in your **Contacts** folder.

❶ Turn On Smart Tags

Before Excel can watch for smart tags, you must make sure that the proper
AutoCorrect option is turned on. Click your **Office** button to display the
Office menu. Click the **Proofing** tab and then click the **AutoCorrect Options**
button. Click the **Smart Tags** tab, and make sure that the option labeled
Label Text with Smart Tags is checked. If not, click to check it.

You must also make sure that the **Financial Symbol (Smart Tags Lists)**
option is checked so that smart tags for stock symbols will activate.

Click **OK**.

❷ View the Smart Tag Menu

In an Excel worksheet, type the stock symbol name, in uppercase letters,
whose price you want to view, and move to the next cell. Immediately, a
small, dark arrow appears in the stock symbol cell's lower-right corner. This
arrow indicates that a smart tag is present for the cell's contents.

Point to the arrow, and a smart tag icon appears. This is the small letter *i* (for
information) enclosed in a circle. Click the icon, and the stock symbol's smart
tag menu appears. You are presented with a list of several options related to
that stock's company, including options to access a refreshable stock price, to
display a page on MSN MoneyCentral's website about the stock price, or to go
to the web to view a company report or recent news about the company, as
well as some additional options related to your response when that smart tag
appears.

▶ **NOTE**

You don't have to honor a smart tag's offer. In other words, you might want to type a
stock symbol's name in one place and ignore the smart tag icon. In another place, you
can insert the stock symbol's price by accepting the smart tag's stock price. This way
you label stock prices.

❸ Insert Live Stock Data

One problem that some investors find with the financial smart tag isn't that
it doesn't insert a stock price; it's that it inserts *too much* information related

157

to the stock price. When you select the option **Insert Refreshable Stock Price** from the smart tag's menu, an **Insert Stock Price** dialog box opens that offers to insert the stock price information on a new worksheet or *starting* at whatever cell you want the price information to go to. This is due to the fact that more than just a stock price appears.

▶ **NOTE**

It makes sense that more than one price is available. Do you want a closing price, an opening price, or a current price? After market hours, you might need any one of those. If the market is open, you might want the current price, but many strategies work with the most recent closing price, and if Excel returned only the current price, you couldn't analyze the data the way you need to.

Therefore, expect a lot of data to come into the worksheet where you place it when you select a stock price. Many investors elect to insert the price information in a separate worksheet, or at least many cells away from the primary analysis area of the worksheet. After the information arrives for that stock, they then can choose which price they're interested in: the last (current) price, the previous day's close, the high, the low, and even other information about the stock, such as volume and percent change from the previous close.

You need to note where the price data is that you want to view and then use that cell back in your worksheet's analysis section.

4 Use the Price Information

After you've placed the live stock data out of the way on the current worksheet or a different worksheet, and after you've noted which cell the price you want to work with is stored in, return to your worksheet's analysis or reporting area and type an equal sign followed by the stock price cell address, such as =E31. The price from that cell will appear in your worksheet without all the extra data that arrived from the smart tag.

5 Modify a Smart Tag's Display

Sometimes you'll use data, such as a stock symbol, but you don't want the smart tag to be available. Perhaps the smart tag's icon keeps popping up where you don't need it and you want it out of the way. Consider a company whose common name is the same as its stock symbol, such as IBM. You might want **IBM** to appear in a cell without a smart tag being available in that cell. Or perhaps you want a list of stock symbols to appear next to their prices, but you don't want smart tags to appear in that column of symbols.

157

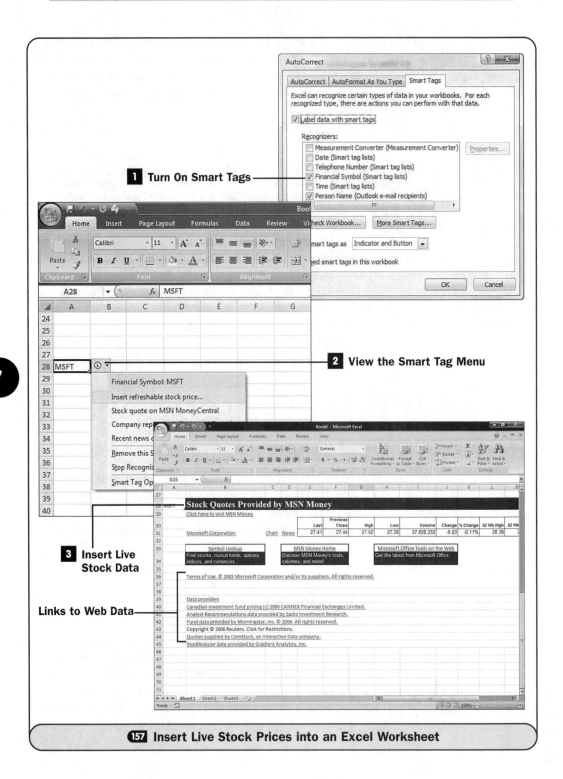

1 Turn On Smart Tags

2 View the Smart Tag Menu

3 Insert Live Stock Data

Links to Web Data

157 Insert Live Stock Prices into an Excel Worksheet

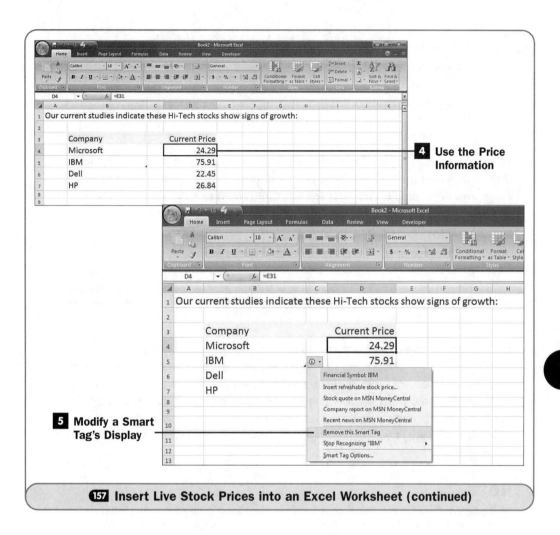

4 **Use the Price Information**

5 **Modify a Smart Tag's Display**

157 Insert Live Stock Prices into an Excel Worksheet (continued)

When the inappropriate smart tag arrow appears, click the smart tag icon and choose **Remove This Smart Tag** from the menu. The smart tag can pop up later if you type the symbol elsewhere, but this option keeps the smart tag from appearing in the current cell. You then can have a clean list of company names or stock symbols where you want them without smart tags getting in the way.

158   Create a Web Page with Word

✔ BEFORE YOU BEGIN	→ SEE ALSO
155 About Office and Online Access	**159** Create a Web Page with Excel
156 Insert a Web Hyperlink into a Document	**160** Create a Web Page with PowerPoint

Word is versatile. You can create web pages in Word that are HTML-based and that display over the Internet the way they appear in Word (with a few minor exceptions depending on the web browser that is used to view the Word-based web pages). Not only can you create your own web pages in Word, but Word also allows you to create blog posts directly from the documents you create.

▶ **TIP**

Word is a great source tool for creating blog posts. You get the advantage of Word's powerful writing tools and spelling and grammar correction features that keep your posts as accurate as possible.

158

It's true that Word was not designed to be used as a web page designer. If you need to create an extensive website, Word will perhaps slow you down more than help. Nevertheless, for quick and simple web pages, Word does just fine. Also, by being able to store Word documents in a web-compatible format, you can quickly publish Word documents you've created in the past without having to run them through some kind of web page program's conversion process before posting them to the web.

▶ **NOTE**

Web pages you create with Word might have some display problems in non-Internet Explorer browsers such as Firefox. You should test all web pages in both browsers to ensure they load and look as expected in both.

1   Save as a Web Page

One of the easiest ways to create a web page from a Word document is to save the document as a web page using the standard HTML extension. The extension informs Word that you want others to be able to view the document on the Web.

Click your **Office** button and select **Save As**. The **Save As** dialog box opens. Type a filename, and before clicking **Save**, select **Web Page Filtered** for the **Save as Type** drop-down list box option. Other options appear, such as **Web Page Single** and **Web Page**; however, those are for multipage websites, and you probably want to save your Word document as a single page. Word is poorly equipped to manage and edit multipage websites.

▶ **NOTE**

If your Word document contains graphics, Word will create a new folder to hold those graphics. The HTML file that is created will look in that folder for graphics when displaying the document as a web page.

Click the **Change Title** button to enter a web page title, one that will appear in the browser's title bar when a user views the web page. Click **Save** to save the document. Save the document on your own computer's disk storage. Click **Yes** if prompted to save the document in the default web page format. After you proof the web page from within a web browser, you can send the web page to a *web server*.

▶ **NOTE**

As soon as you save the document as a web page, Word hides the ruler and expands the margins to your full screen. Given that the document is no longer a Word file, the concept of printed margins no longer applies. A web page can be as long and wide as the web designer wants it to be.

▶ **NEW TERM**

Web server—A computer that's always available to send pages to anyone who wants to view them over the Internet.

158

If you use Windows Vista, save your web page to your SharePoint Drafts folder. This is where Internet Explorer expects to find web pages among your local documents.

2 **View the Web Page**

Start your web browser. Select **File, Open,** and click the **Browse** button to locate the web page you just stored. Click to display the web page in your web browser.

▶ **TIP**

Internet Explorer's newest versions don't show the menu bar by default, but they contain the typical menu that includes the **File** option. Press Alt+F to display the **File** menu if you use Internet Explorer and don't see a menu.

3 **Proof the Web Page**

Inside your web browser, your web page should appear and look like a web page. Scroll through the document to ensure that everything made it to the web page just fine.

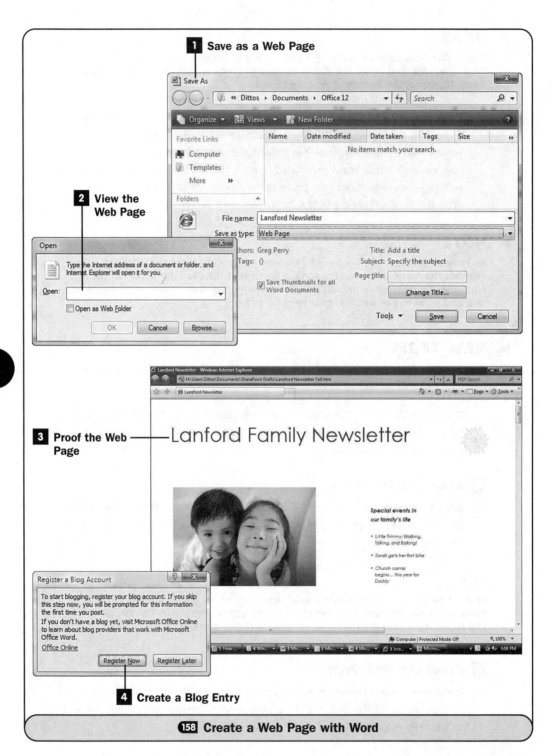

1 Save as a Web Page

2 View the Web Page

3 Proof the Web Page

4 Create a Blog Entry

158 Create a Web Page with Word

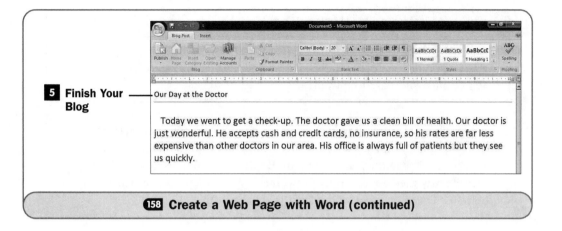

5 Finish Your Blog

Our Day at the Doctor

Today we went to get a check-up. The doctor gave us a clean bill of health. Our doctor is just wonderful. He accepts cash and credit cards, no insurance, so his rates are far less expensive than other doctors in our area. His office is always full of patients but they see us quickly.

158 Create a Web Page with Word (continued)

▶ **NOTE**

After you've ensured that your new web page appears correctly in the web browser, you or someone who knows how will need to upload your web page source file (and folder if your page has multiple images) to a web server for others to access your document on the Internet.

158

4 Create a Blog Entry

One of the advantages of a blog over a traditional web page is that a blog is simple to update. Often, adding new content to a blog requires only an email to be sent, or a text post to be added to the web page using a standard interface.

Word will publish your document to a blog. Type your new blog posting, and click your **Office** button to display the **Office** menu. Select **Publish, Blog.** Word displays a blog registration dialog box, and you can register your blog information with Word so that Word knows where the post will go.

▶ **NOTE**

You must have access to the blog to add posts, and you must inform Word of that registration when prompted to do so.

5 Finish Your Blog

After you register your blog, Word adds a placeholder to the top of your blog where you can type a blog posting title. This is like the subject line in an email; your blog entry will be titled and referenced by the title you type there. Click the placeholder text and type a title.

Click **Publish,** and select a blog to send the post to from the list of blogs you've registered with Word. In a few seconds, your post will appear on the blog site.

159   Create a Web Page with Excel

✔ BEFORE YOU BEGIN	→ SEE ALSO
155 About Office and Online Access 158 Create a Web Page with Word	160 Create a Web Page with PowerPoint

You can easily save an Excel worksheet as a web page. If your worksheet has embedded graphics, they are saved as well in a folder that the web page will access. The Excel-generated web pages are HTML-based and display over the Internet the way they appear in Excel (with a few minor exceptions depending on the web browser that is used to view the web pages).

▶ **TIP**

Excel is actually easier than Word for generating web pages. Excel's **Publish** feature generates web pages and enables you to view those pages in your web browser without having to locate and open the pages to proofread them as you do for Word-generated web pages.

Obviously, Excel was never meant to be used as a web page designer. Excel's **Publish** feature is a great way to put worksheets on the web. Excel doesn't have an inherent web page designer, however, so treat Excel as a tool for generated web-based worksheet pages but not to create web pages. Word is better, and a dedicated web page designing program is better still.

▶ **NOTE**

After your worksheet is stored as a web page, users who view the web page over the Internet will be able to view your worksheet data but not interact with the worksheet's cells as would be possible using Excel. The web-based worksheet is strictly for viewing.

1 Determine the Scope of the Web Page

First load or create the worksheet you want to save as a web page. Normally, Excel saves the entire workbook as a web page. If your workbook contains only one worksheet, that worksheet will make up the web page. Even for one-worksheet workbooks, you don't have to save the entire worksheet to the web. Select the cells you want to save as a web page if you don't want to save the entire worksheet to a web page.

2 Save the Web Page

The easiest way to create a web page from an Excel worksheet is to save the worksheet as a web page from the **Save As** dialog box. Excel will save the current worksheet in a web-based file format.

Click your **Office** button and select **Save As**. The **Save As** dialog box opens. Type a filename, and before clicking **Save**, select **Web Page** for the **Save as Type** drop-down list box option.

▶ **NOTE**

If your Excel worksheet contains graphics, Excel creates a new folder to hold those graphics. The web page that results will go to that folder for graphics when displaying the worksheet as a web page.

Click the **Change Title** button to enter a web page title, one that will appear in the browser's title bar when a user views the web page. If you selected only part of the worksheet to be sent to the web page before opening the **Save As** dialog box, click **Selection**; otherwise, leave the **Entire Workbook** option selected.

If you clicked **Save** now, your worksheet (or the selected cells) would save as a web page, and you could open Internet Explorer and proofread the web page. The **Publish** button, unavailable on Word's **Save As** dialog box (see **158 Create a Web Page with Word**), simplifies your proofing, so don't click **Save** just yet.

3 Publish the Page

Click **Publish** on the **Save As** dialog box to open the **Publish as Web Page** dialog box. The **Choose** drop-down list box includes several options, such as **Entire Workbook** and **Range of Cells**. Although the **Save As** dialog box lets you select the entire workbook or a selected range to go to the web page, the **Publish as Web Page** dialog box gives you these same choices. With it, you can set up the current worksheet's web page from this dialog box. Anytime you subsequently save the worksheet, the web page will update according to the options to set here and not those you set in the **Save As** dialog box. Therefore, select whether you want to save the entire workbook or only a selected range of cells, and you won't have to make this decision in the future as you'd have to do if you used the **Save As** dialog box alone.

Type a name for your web page filename. If you want to re-create the web page every time you make changes to the worksheet and save it subsequently, click to check the option labeled **AutoRepublish Every Time This Workbook Is Saved**.

Leave the option labeled **Open Published Web Page in Browser** checked so that Excel will open your browser and display your worksheet-based web page the moment you click **Publish**.

Note the location where you're saving the web page in the **File Name** field so that later you or a webmaster can send the files to a web server for viewing over the Internet.

Click **Publish** to send the worksheet to a web page.

159

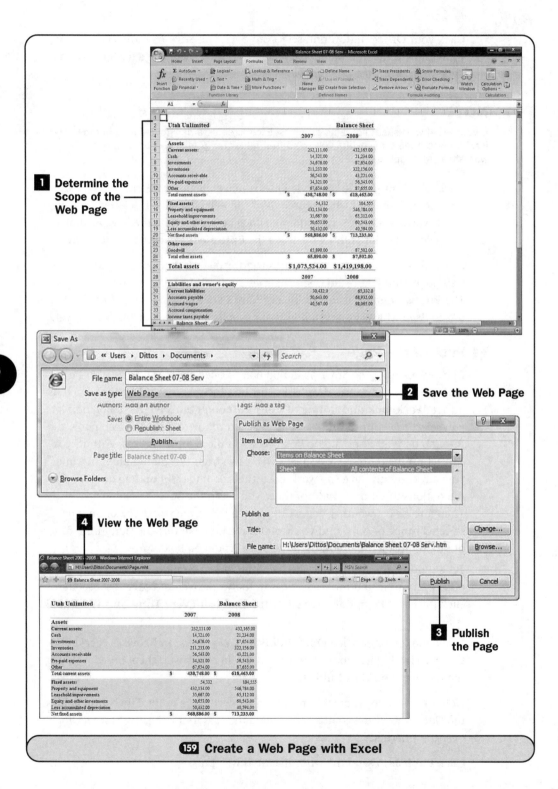

1 Determine the Scope of the Web Page

2 Save the Web Page

4 View the Web Page

3 Publish the Page

159

159 Create a Web Page with Excel

4 **View the Web Page**

As soon as you click **Publish**, Excel opens your web browser and displays your worksheet. You can scroll down and across the page if needed to view the entire web page. The web page title bar should reflect the title you added to the worksheet.

You won't be able to edit the worksheet or traverse it cell-by-cell, but the worksheet should take on an identical appearance to the worksheet in Excel, assuming that your browser is fairly recent.

---

160 **Create a Web Page with PowerPoint**

✔ BEFORE YOU BEGIN	→ SEE ALSO
158 Create a Web Page with Word	**161** Send Email from Word, Excel,
159 Create a Web Page with Excel	PowerPoint, and OneNote

You can easily save a PowerPoint presentation as a web page. The presentation will look to those who view it over the Internet just as it looks in a presentation, with each slide appearing as the user moves through the presentation.

The PowerPoint-generated web pages are web-browser friendly, so any modern web browser can view them. PowerPoint makes a powerful presentation program, but it also makes a surprisingly good web-based trainer. If you need to train others over the web, doing so in a web-based PowerPoint presentation makes sense. Your "students" who view the PowerPoint presentation over the web can move at their own pace—dictated by their individual learning speeds—to master whatever content you want to offer them.

160

▶ **TIP**

PowerPoint is easier than Word for generating web pages. Like Excel, PowerPoint includes a **Publish** feature that generates the web pages more automatically than Word's simple **Save As** dialog box. In addition, you can select specific slides to go to the web pages or choose to send the entire presentation.

Obviously, PowerPoint was never meant to be used as a web page designer. PowerPoint's **Publish** feature is a great way to put presentations on the web, but PowerPoint doesn't have inherent web page design tools. Word is better, and a dedicated web page designing program is better still at creating websites from scratch.

1 Prepare for the Web Page

The easiest way to create a web page from a PowerPoint presentation is to save the presentation as a web page from the **Save As** dialog box. PowerPoint will save the current presentation—or any portion of the presentation—to a file that uses a web-based file format.

Click your **Office** button and select **Save As**. The **Save As** dialog box opens. Type a filename, and before clicking **Save**, select **Web Page** for the **Save as Type** drop-down list box option.

▶ NOTE

If your PowerPoint presentation contains graphics, as most will, PowerPoint creates a new folder to hold those graphics. The web page that results will go to that folder for graphics when displaying the presentation as a web page.

Click the **Change Title** button to enter a web page title, one that will appear in the browser's title bar when a user views the web page.

If you clicked **Save** now, your presentation would save as a web page, and you could open Internet Explorer and proofread the resulting web page. The **Publish** button, unavailable on Word's **Save As** dialog box (see **158 Create a Web Page with Word**), simplifies your proofing, so don't click **Save** just yet.

2 Publish the Presentation

Click **Publish** on the **Save As** dialog box to open the **Publish as Web Page** dialog box. The **Publish What?** options determine exactly which slides you want to send to a set of web pages. Of course, leave the **Complete Presentation** option selected if you want every slide to go to the set of pages.

You can click to include the speaker notes or uncheck the option to omit them.

▶ TIP

Presenters often include their speaker's notes in online presentations because they are not there to walk the viewers through the presentation.

Unless you know that your primary audience will use older web browsers, leave the **Browser Support** option set to **Microsoft Internet Explorer 4.0 or Later** to achieve the highest quality presentation. Select where you want to save the presentation web pages in the **File Name** text box, and make a note of that location so that you or a webmaster can later send the files to a web server so that others can access your presentation over the Internet.

160

If you leave the **Open Published Web Page in Browser** option selected, PowerPoint will open your web browser and display the web-based presentation as soon as you publish the presentation.

3 Set the Web Options

Click the **Web Options** button to modify the web-based options specific to PowerPoint presentations. You can determine the presentation's navigation control colors, determine browser options, and even set the target viewing screen's default resolution (by clicking the **Pictures** tab and adjusting the **Screen Size** option).

Click **OK** after you finish setting any web options.

4 Accept the Web-Based Presentation

As soon as you click **Publish**, PowerPoint opens your web browser and displays your presentation. Depending on your browser and security settings, you might have to click to accept the display of the presentation. Your presentation contains controls that are valid and won't cause security problems, but many browsers guard against automatically displaying presentations in case a security threat is somehow programmed into the presentation.

To view your presentation inside your web browser, therefore, you might have to close an information dialog box and click your browser's information bar and choose **Allow Blocked Content** to see your presentation.

160

▶ NOTE

Anyone who views your Internet presentation might also have to override security settings to view your presentation, as you are doing. That's the nature of computing today. If you create a web page that introduces your web audience to the presentation before they click a link to view it, you could tell them there to expect the security warnings and that they can safely override them.

5 View the Presentation

After the presentation starts, you will see your slides in your web-based browser. To the left are slide titles (called the Outline), assuming that every slide has a title (highly recommended). Your web audience can hide the Outline and give more screen space to each slide by clicking the **Outline** button at the bottom of the screen. The **Expand Outline** button shows second-level details of each slide in the **Outline** pane (such as each slide's bullet points).

160

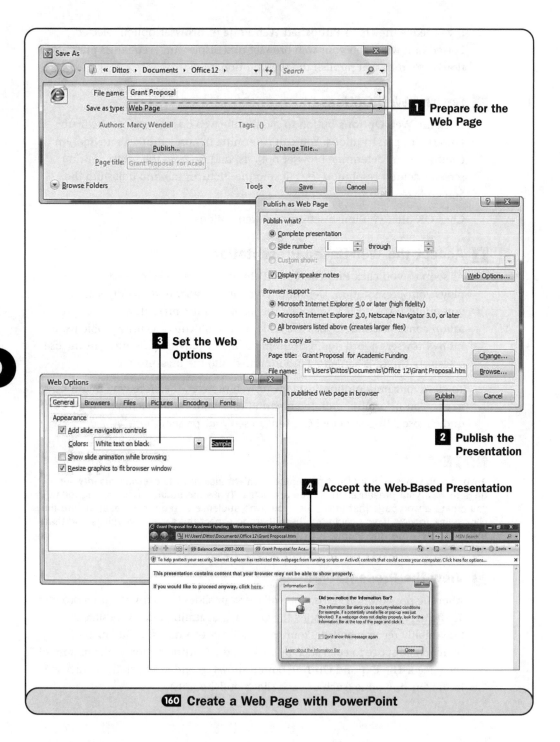

1 **Prepare for the Web Page**

3 **Set the Web Options**

2 **Publish the Presentation**

4 **Accept the Web-Based Presentation**

160 Create a Web Page with PowerPoint

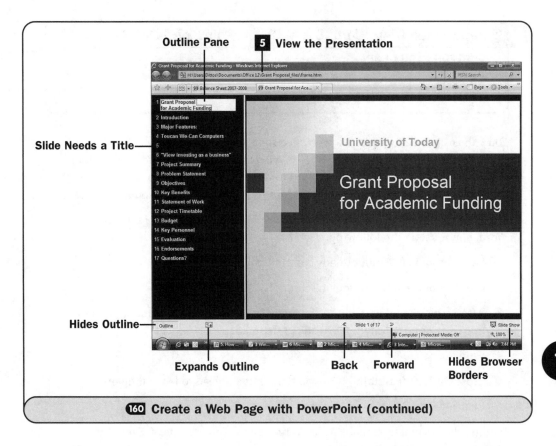

160 Create a Web Page with PowerPoint (continued)

To view a presentation over the web, you must navigate using slightly different controls from those you use when PowerPoint is displaying the slide show. For example, the Page Up and Page Down keys don't move forward or backward through a web-based presentation.

Click any title in the Outline to jump to that slide. The **Back** and **Forward** buttons along the bottom of the screen move the presentation back or ahead one slide at a time. Click the **Slide Show** button in the lower-right corner to view the presentation in a full-screen mode, moving forward by clicking your left mouse button and moving back through the slides by clicking the right mouse button and selecting **Back** from the pop-up menu.

161   Send Email from Word, Excel, PowerPoint, and OneNote

✔ **BEFORE YOU BEGIN**

117 About Outlook's Capabilities
155 About Office and Online Access

161

You can easily send documents, worksheets, presentations, and OneNote note pages in emails. Of course, with Outlook, you can send emails and add another Office 2007 data file to that email, but Word, Excel, PowerPoint, and OneNote all make it simpler to send emails of your data rather than going through Outlook.

When you send a Word document, for example, to an email recipient using Word, you must do the following:

1. Start Outlook if it's not already running.

2. Create a new email message in Outlook.

3. Attach the Word document to the email by locating the document on your hard drive and specifying it as the attachment.

4. Send the message.

5. Close Outlook (assuming that you don't have a need to leave it open).

6. Return to Word.

Sending the document straight from Word saves a couple of steps. Even if you already have Outlook running, it's simpler to send an email straight from Word, Excel, PowerPoint, or OneNote.

1   Prepare to Send a Document from Word, Excel, or PowerPoint

From Word, Excel, or PowerPoint, click your **Office** button to open the **Office** menu. Select **Send** and then select **Email**.

Your Office 2007 program opens a new email message. Fill in the **Subject** field with the document's filename, and attach the Word document, Excel worksheet, or PowerPoint presentation to the email.

2   Finish the Email

Fill in the **To** recipient field or click **To** and select from your Outlook **Contacts** list. Type a message in the email's body so that your recipient will know what the attachment is all about.

▶ **TIP**

All of Outlook's ribbon commands appear atop the email. Feel free to set the priority and change the body's formatting just as you would if you created the message in Outlook and attached the file there.

3 Send the Email

Click the **Send** button to send the email to your recipient. Obviously, your recipient must have Office 2007 to read your email's attachment.

▶ **NOTE**

If you know that the recipient has an older version of Office, save your Office 2007 file to an older version, such as Excel 2003, before requesting the **Send** option. The attachment will then be saved in that older version, and your recipient will be able to open your document.

4 Open OneNote's Email

You can send a OneNote page to an email recipient, but the method differs slightly from what you saw in the previous steps. Click OneNote's **File** menu and select the option labeled **E-mail**. OneNote opens an email and embeds the current OneNote page in the email's editing area.

161

▶ **NOTE**

OneNote not only sends its emails as attachments but also puts the page directly in the body of the email. You can send only single OneNote pages in emails this way, not sections or complete notebooks.

5 Finish OneNote's Email

Fill in the **To** recipient field or click **To** and select from your Outlook **Contacts** list. Your message body is your OneNote page, so there's no traditional way to add text to the body. Instead, OneNote includes a new email field labeled **Introduction**. Type a short note to your recipient that describes what you're sending and why.

▶ **TIP**

Although this isn't a traditional email in which you can add text to the body as you'd normally do, you are still working inside OneNote! So you can add a OneNote element such as handwriting to the page before you send it. The element will appear as a Note Container in OneNote just as it would appear if you'd added the message inside OneNote's editing area.

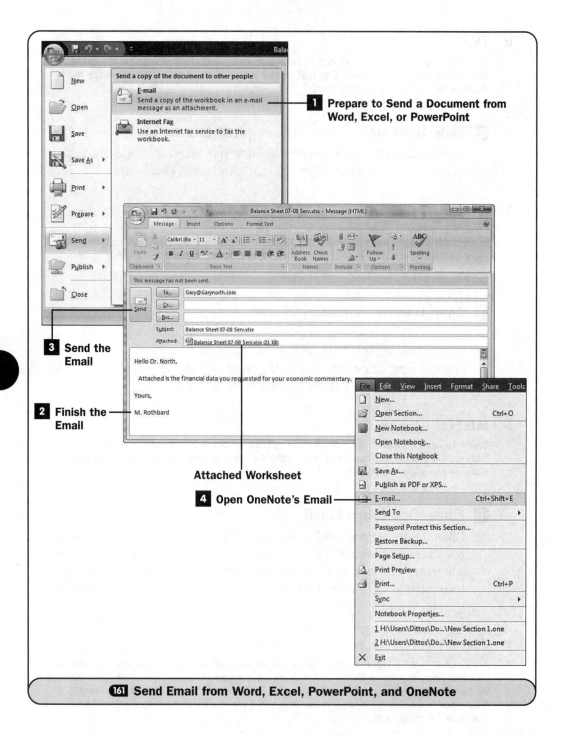

161

1 Prepare to Send a Document from Word, Excel, or PowerPoint

3 Send the Email

2 Finish the Email

Attached Worksheet

4 Open OneNote's Email

161 Send Email from Word, Excel, PowerPoint, and OneNote

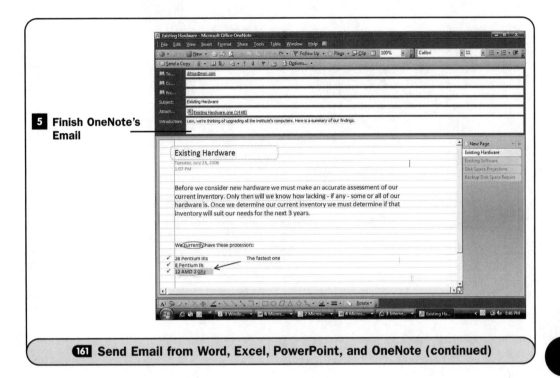

5 **Finish OneNote's Email**

161

Click **Send a Copy**, and your email will be on its way.

If your recipient has OneNote, he or she will be able to open the attachment. Otherwise, the email's body will show your OneNote page when the recipient opens the email. Your recipient won't be able to edit or annotate the page because most of the graphical elements will arrive in the received email as a single graphics image. If your recipient does have OneNote installed, he or she can open the email's attachment from within OneNote and make more extensive edits if desired.

Symbols

A

B

C

F

G

M

O

P

Q-R

S

T

U

V

W

X-Y-Z

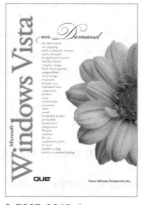